The London Group: a history
1913-2013

David Redfern

To Keith.
With best
wishes from
Dave,

January, 2020

Published on the 100th anniversary of The London Group's formation
with the help of a generous bequest by Anne Cloudsley, a member 2002–2012

The Author

David Redfern was born in 1947 in Staffordshire and studied at Reading University and The Slade School of Fine Art. From 1971 to 1983 he was Head Gallery Assistant at the Serpentine Gallery, and managed and taught on art and design courses at Croydon College from 1984 to 2011. He was elected to The London Group in 2000, and in 2003 was invited to take on the rôle of Group Archivist. As a practising artist David Redfern has a studio in Deptford, South East London, and has shown at the Hayward Gallery, Whitechapel Gallery, Serpentine Gallery and many open submission exhibitions. More information at davidredfernartist.com.

Cover images

Front cover

Top: Catalogue cover, The London Group Retrospective Exhibition 1914–1928
Bottom: Catalogue cover, London Group 1914–64 Jubilee Exhibition, Tate Gallery
Images courtesy of The London Group Archive 2013

Back cover
Names of all members of The London Group 1913–2013

Contents

Introduction

The London Group came into existence in 1913 and this is the first complete history of the Group's first hundred years. As a member of The London Group I write this history with insight and purpose. Insight in that as a member of the Group there have been many illuminating conversations with both long term and newly elected artists, and purpose because the Group's history needed to be recorded before vital details fade and disappear.

This history is unashamedly chronological since it is the simplest and clearest way to describe The London Group's survival from decade to decade, year to year. The reader will find a very, very simplified introduction to what was happening in the visual arts at the beginning of each decade, and I apologise for any omissions which the reader considers should have been included. Similarly, each individual year has an historical introduction briefly outlining what major events occurred in that year, as a background against which the Group was operating.

The exhibition catalogue has been the primary source for this history. The Group has always sought to publish a catalogue to its annual exhibitions, firstly to inform the visitor to the exhibition but also to record the who, what and when. Tate Britain's Tate Archive holds a large section of London Group catalogues, particularly from the early period. More recent catalogues are being archived for inclusion in the Tate holding in due course.

There are no images of works produced by the members of the Group. Some would see this as a missed opportunity, but it would be an impossible task to select work from over 400 members, given the limited budget of this publication. The London Group has always sought to treat individuals fairly and equally and, as a member, I would not promote one member above another. Neither is there any critical analysis of the Group. That is for others who are more distanced and less involved. This history seeks to lay down an accurate and inclusive description of the Group's activities to help researchers form their critical responses.

Some of the images found in this publication are photographs of venues where The London Group has organised exhibitions. The Group has no permanent headquarters or exhibition facilities. Since 1913, annual exhibitions have taken place largely as a result of members' connections and personal initiatives, in commercial galleries in the Group's early days and, more recently, in London Art Schools and Colleges. The London Group was set up as an exhibiting society "to bring contemporary visual arts to the general public" and it has continued to do this for one hundred years. The photographs of exhibition venues are a micro-history in their own right, chronicling the changing face of London as a commercial and dynamic organism.

Not only has the Group as a whole had difficulty in finding a suitable venue to hold the annual exhibition, artists themselves had difficulty in getting their work to the venues! In a letter to Claude Rogers dated August 10th (year unknown), Ethelbert White recounted this amusing incident: "He (a young David Bomberg) had climbed the stairs of the Goupil Gallery under a canvas of vast proportions and was met by Nevinson at the top who informed him, partly in joke, that no works could be hung if the member's subscription had not been paid. Bomberg with a good-tempered grin hauled his enormous canvas back down into Regent Street, and although members of the hanging committee ran down to recall him, all they saw was a great sail tacking across Piccadilly." (From "The Affectionate Eye, the life of Claude Rogers" by Jenny Pery).

An introduction to the text

The text is sliced up into decades. At the beginning of each decade there is a very brief 'potted' history of the important movements and artists operating in that decade.

Each decade is then broken down into an individual year. At the beginning of each year there will be a short description of notable historical and cultural events, against which The London Group activity can be set. Each year will record the President at that time, the election of new mebers and any exhibitions. Where archive documents were available there will also be press reviews of exhibitions, minutes of Annual General Meetings, financial statements and any other significant and relevant events.

Linked to the text will be photographs and images, both black & white and coloured, illustrating parts of London where The London Group organised exhibitions. Most of the photographs were taken in 2013 and, literally, give a snapshot of the city at the beginning of the twenty-first century and the changes which have occurred since The London Group was formed 100 years ago in 1913.

What is The London Group?

The London Group was notionally set up as a group to challenge the aesthetic restrictions of the Royal Academy, the New English Art Club (NEAC) and the traditional art establishment holding sway at the beginning of the 1910s. There is a written constitution first formulated in 1913 and little changed since.

Under the terms of the written constitution, "the association shall be called 'The London Group' and will consist of visual artists of any nationality" and a "roll of members shall be kept". The object of the Group "shall be to advance public awareness of contemporary visual art by holding exhibitions annually". From amongst the Group members shall elect four 'Officers', a President, Vice President, Honorary Secretary and Treasurer. Officers are elected at the A.G.M. (Annual General Meeting) and will hold office for one year when they will be eligible for re-election. The President will "represent the Group on all private and public occasions". Then, "a Working

Committee consisting of the Officers together with eight elected members shall conduct the business of the Group, including the organisation, selection and hanging of exhibitions." This makes a requirement for twelve active members to serve for two years from a total membership of between eighty to one hundred members and, "shall if possible reflect the range of interests in the Group". Following this election, "a Membership Committee consisting of the Working Committee and five other members elected at an A.G.M. shall elect new members to the Group". Therefore, seventeen members form the Selection Committee and nine votes are required from this body to be elected a full member of the Group. In order to pay for exhibiting annually, hiring galleries, advertising, promotions etc. each member pays an Annual Subscription fixed at the AGM. Stories of mythological proportion abound as to who and who didn't pay their annual subscription, but it would appear that at least two 'Tate exhibiting Sculptors' and one RA exhibited as members but never paid. Equally, one internationally respected member resigned from the Group but forgot to cancel his annual bankers order. Members have responsibilities to the Group. "Members are expected to attend meetings, an apology for absence shall be forwarded to the Honorary Secretary if a member is unable to attend, (members are expected) to further the object of the Group and to exhibit as regularly as possible at the Group's exhibitions".

"The Group shall normally hold an Annual General Meeting within the first three months of any year." The London Group has a tradition of free speech and robust discussion at these AGMs and are not normally stuffy but can be quite entertaining. Refreshments are often served! An agenda needs to be sent out and a quorum of 20% of total membership is required. The agenda is more or less stipulated by the constitution. It begins with minutes and there then follows a President's Report, the Treasurer's audited report, nomination and election of the Officers, Working Committee and Membership Committee. Dates are set for forthcoming annual exhibitions and for the election of new members and there then follows, "Discussion on any other business" which is where the dogs are let loose.

Within the constitution, Article 15 deals with Exhibitions. "There shall be not less than one exhibition annually, containing whenever possible non-members' work. All members work will be shown". This non-censorious aspect of the Group's policy has always been its strength and appeal to artists. Neither is there a mention of commission charged on sales, although this has been agreed by AGMs in the past to help the Group's finances. Selection of non-members' work in Open Submission exhibitions "shall be by the Working Committee" (the four Officers and eight elected members). Eight of the twelve Committee members' votes are required for accepting a work for exhibition. However, a submission fee, fixed at the AGM, is charged to help with expenses and a commission on sales is also required.

The London Group "may be dissolved by a resolution duly passed by not less than two thirds of the members present at an Extraordinary or General Meeting, including proxy and postal votes" with twenty-two days advance notice. "The quorum at the meeting must be not less than one third of the total membership of the Group." Is this one (tortuously complicated) reason for the continued existence of the Group?

The Constitution ends with Article 19, dealing with changes to the Constitution itself. Changes can only be made following similar AGM procedures as indicated above.

There are usually about ninety members, most of whom are active in that they exhibit work with The London Group in the annual exhibitions. Very roughly speaking, about three new members are elected each year. The Committee is always looking for ways to engage more members to become more fully involved with the operation of the Group and its exhibitions, aware that an organisation is only effective when as many as possible pull their weight.

46 Gordon Square
Bloomsbury, London WC1

46 Gordon Square was the address at which the painter Vanessa Bell and her sister the writer Virginia Wolf were living when Bell organised her 'Friday Club' meetings, from 1905 onwards. These informal discussion/conversational meetings later evolved into the Bloomsbury circle. In the 1900s forming groups was "all the rage", The London Group being only one of a large number of artist groupings. Vanessa Bell and Duncan Grant were to be active, influential and supportive members of The London Group for many years. Roger Fry, the influential writer, critic and painter member of The London Group, was also connected with the Bloomsbury set and formed the Grafton

Group, his own offshoot of the Friday Club. The Grafton Group was formed in 1913, exhibited at the Alpine Gallery and ended in 1914. As well as exhibiting Bloomsbury Post-Impressionists the Grafton Group also supported Henri Gaudier-Brzeska, Frederick Etchells, Wyndham Lewis, William Roberts and Edward Wadsworth, all of whom were early members of The London Group. Later, Fry and Wyndham Lewis had a spectacular falling out over the awarding of a lucrative interior design contract and it was not until Lewis had departed The London Group that Fry was elected to the Group in 1917.

In 1907, Sickert brought together a group of artists for "at homes", effectively discussion and exhibition of work, in rented rooms in Fitzroy Sreet, North London close to his studio in the same street. The Fitzroy Street Group began with Spencer Gore, Harold Gilman, Nan Hudson, Lucien Pissarro, Ethel Sands, the brothers William and Albert Rothenstein and Walter Russell. Robert Bevan, Malcolm Drummond, Jacob Epstein, Augustus John, Henry Lamb, J.B. Manson and William Ratcliffe joined their informal meetings in later years. As will be seen later in this book, these names will become very familiar in the formation of The London Group. Some Fitzroy Street members were to form the core of the Camden Town Group in 1911.

The 1910s

In May 2006, Tate Modern painted a Time Line along its walls indicating who it considered were the most important (international) artists in each decade. Groups, schools, isms, movements and individuals were all sketched out (some rather difficult to read or to understand their groupings). In this publication, at the end of each decade's introduction, there will be found a Tate Modern Time Line which gives the artists recorded on the Tate Modern wall beginning with the 1900s, as a lead in to the 1910s, below.

Tate Modern Time Line for 1900–1910 The Photo-Secession including Alfred Stieglitz, Paul Strand, Edward Steichen and Gertrude Kasebier. Fauvism with Henri Matisse, André Derain and Maurice de Vlaminck. Cubism including Pablo Picasso, Georges Braque, Juan Gris, Fernand Léger, Albert Gleizes and Jacques Lipchitz. Expressionism linking Oskar Kokoschka, Egon Schiele, Emil Nolde, Georges Rouault and Ernst Barlach. Die Brücke with Ernst Ludwig Kirchner and Karl Schmidt-Rottluff. Futurism involving Filippo Marinetti, Umberto Boccioni, Giacomo Balla and Gino Severini. Individuals Henri Rousseau and Eugène Atget.

In terms of considering the need for a new exhibiting society like The London Group, the 1908 Allied Artists' Association exhibition at the Royal Albert Hall was a significant forerunner. The exhibition was organised by the art critic Frank Rutter who took on the mammoth task of hanging every work submitted without going through any jury selection process. Evidently Rutter used a bicycle to supervise the hang of the exhibition! It was at this exhibition that Gilman and Spencer Gore noticed Bevan's brightly coloured canvases (Bevan had worked in Pont Aven) and invited him to attend Sickert's 'at homes' in Fitzroy Street.

Tate Modern Timeline for 1910–1920 Continuing from the 1900s, Expressionism with Ernst Barlach, Emil Nolde and Georges Rouault. Cubism around Pablo Picasso, Georges Braque, Jacques Lipchitz and Fernand Léger. In the 1910s, The School of Paris, including Amedeo Modigliani, Chaim Soutine, Marc Chagall, Natalya Goncharova, Michael Larionov, Constantin Brancusi and Foujita Tsugouhara. Orphism with Sonia Delaunay, Robert Delaunay and Frantisek Kupka. Vorticism uniting Wyndham Lewis, C.R.W. Nevinson, David Bomberg, Henri Gaudier-Brzeska and Jacob Epstein. Suprematism and Kasimir Malevich. Constructivism with Vladimir Tatlin, Alexander Rodchenko, El Lissitzky and Naum Gabo. De Stijl including Piet Mondrian, Theo van Doesburg and Georges Vantongerloo. Individual Georgio de Chirico. Blaue Reiter group Wassily Kandinsky, Franz Marc and Paul Klee. Dada including Tristan Tzara, Man Ray, Marcel Duchamp, Francis Picabia, Hannah Höch, Sophie Taeuber, Kurt Schwitters, John Heartfield and Hugo Ball. Bauhaus with Walter Gropius, Josef Albers, László Moholy Nagy and Oskar Schlemmer.

In the early 1900s there existed a small community of artists who lived and worked in Cumberland Market in Camden, North London. William Roberts wrote that Sickert and 'his Camden Town crowd' met other artists in John Flanagan's 'balconied rooms' across the Cumberland Market. There were balconies in Robert Bevan's painting "Cumberland Market, North Side" (1912) owned by Southampton City Art Gallery. Could it be that these rooms were where The London Group was first mooted? Robert Bevan was a member of the Camden Town Group and a Founder Member of The London Group in 1913. He was elected Treasurer to the new London Group and served from 1913 to 1919. Bevan was also a member of the informal trio of artists taking the name of the Cumberland Market Group, Gilman and Ginner being the other two members of this alliance.

Cumberland Market
Camden, London NW1

The photograph above shows Cumberland Market North Side as it was in 2006. The square has become a childrens' play area and Community Centre whilst new council housing surrounds the square. Cumberland Market used to be a hay market, selling feed for the horses which pulled London horse-drawn cabs. The hay was brought in on carts which were parked on the cobbles of the square. Robert Bevan had a studio on the west side and painted many pictures of the horses and carts lined up there.

"The London Group, perhaps the most stimulating and exciting of the many societies which go to form the art life of London, dates directly from 1908 when the pioneer Frank Rutter started the Allied Artists' Association in a mood of dissatisfaction with prevailing conditions. The outcome of many meetings at the Café Royal was the formation in 1911 of the Camden Town Group which had as its first President the late Spencer Gore, and as its secretary J.B. Manson, now Director of the Tate Gallery. This Group absorbed other small societies such as the 'Cumberland Market Group' and 'Nineteen Fitzroy Street' and in its turn developed into the London Group under the Presidency of the late Harold Gilman." (From a catalogue introduction to The London Group's 1937 Open Exhibition).

The Café Royal
Regent Street, London W1

The Café Royal photographed here in January 2009 shortly after closing for 'redevelopment'. It was here that the Camden Town Group met to thrash out the group's identity and where The London Group venture was first floated.
The Café Royal was a novel venue and, famously, contained a boxing ring to entertain guests. The huge, golden brass doors subtly reflect pedestrians and traffic passing by.

1910

This is a summary of what happened politically, socially and culturally in the year, a pattern to be continued throughout the book.

On May 6th King Edward VII died and King George V succeeded. In June Captain Scott set sail for Antarctica in an attempt to be the first to reach the South Pole. In a general election the Liberals led by Asquith win but do not gain a majority resulting in a hung parliament. The Conservatives were led by Balfour and the recently formed Labour Party (1900) by Henderson. Meanwhile there is a Welsh coal-miner's strike. "Black Friday" (18th November) sees the Suffragette movement in violent protests outside parliament. There is fear of a German invasion. The Girl Guide movement is formed. The Daily Mail sponsors a London to Manchester air race. Protons and electrons in the atomic structure are first discovered.

Ralph Vaughan Williams composes "Fantasia on a Theme by Thomas Tallis". Stravinsky composes "The Firebird" and Gustav Mahler completes his last symphony "Symphony No 9".
Kandinsky writes, "Concerning the Spiritual in Art" (published 1911). East European artists Archipenko, Exter, Malevich, Meller, Shterenberg and Sonia Delaunay were all represented in the Salon des Indépendants in Paris. In Moscow the 'Jack of Diamonds' exhibition was organised by Larionov. In St. Petersburg the 'Union of Youth' holds its first exhibition.
Roger Fry organised 'Manet and the Post-Impressionists' at the **Grafton Galleries**, Grafton Street, London showing from 8th November to 15th January 1911. The exhibition included Gauguin, Van Gogh and Cézanne. Their work was a revelation to young English painters with an emphasis on strong, clear colour. Clive and Vanessa Bell meet Roger Fry at this time. Through the Bloomsbury circle Fry meets E.M. Forster, Duncan Grant, Lytton Strachey and Virginia Wolf. **Walter Sickert** becomes art critic for the periodicals "Art News" and "New Age", moves to Hampstead and establishes a private art school. **Marinetti**, the Italian Futurist, visits London. He delivers "Une Discours futuriste aux Anglais" at the Lyceum Theatre. The Women's International Art Club holds another exhibition.
In June and August Brighton City Art Gallery showed "Modern French Artists" consisting of French Post-impressionist paintings.

1911

In December Amundsen reached the South Pole ahead of Scott. The Russian Prime Minister is assassinated. "The Siege of Sidney Street" breaks out in the East End of London between anarchists and the Metropolitan Police. The Coronation of George V takes place. A Government formed by the Liberals introduces unemployment and national health insurance. The population of London reaches 7 million.

Sibelius writes Symphony No 4. Diaghilev produces 'Petrushka' with the Ballets Russe in Paris and visits Covent Garden for the first time.

The Cubists show together for the first time at the Salon des Indépendants in Paris. Exhibitors were Léger, Robert Delaunay, Le Fauconnier, Metzinger and Gleizes. Braque and Picasso did not show. Marc Chagall arrives in Paris. Marc and Kandinsky present the first 'Blue Rider' exhibition in Munich (German Expressionism). In December Kandinsky publishes "Concerning the Spiritual in Art". Between 1911 and 1912 Mondrian moves from figuration into abstraction by means of his "Flowering Apple Tree" series. Matisse visits Moscow for a major commission.

19 Fitzroy Street
London W1

Number 19 Fitzroy Street was the 'headquarters' of the Fitzroy Street Group.
It was from the Fitzroy Street Group that the Camden Town Group evolved in 1911 and number 19 was also used as the new group's showroom and meeting place. It was here that discussions took place on the formation of The London Group in October/ November 1913. Number 19 was still intact when Malcom Easton of The University of Hull Art Department visited it in the late 1960s. Opposite is a photograph of the undeveloped north western end of Fitzroy Street as the whole of Fitzroy Street probably looked at the beginning of the twentieth century (without the parked cars!).

Fitzroy Street
North western end

In January Henri Gaudier-Brzeska arrived in **London** and later in the year meets Epstein back in Paris. Students at the Slade this year included Bomberg, Kramer, Paul Nash, Nevinson, Roberts and Wadsworth. The **Camden Town Group** evolved from the Fitzroy Street Group. To circumvent the New English Art Club's censorship, the Camden Town Group organised their own public art exhibitions in a commercial gallery, just as The London Group were to do. The name came from the location of Sickert's studio in Golden Square, Camden Town where initial formative meetings took place. Camden Town Group subject matter focused on workaday situations and street-life around North London. There were sixteen original members: Walter Bayes (1913), Robert Bevan (1913), Malcolm Drummond (1913), Harold Gilman (1913), Charles Ginner (1913), Spencer Gore (1913), J.D.Innes, Augustus John (1940/43), Henry Lamb, (1913), Wyndham Lewis (1913), Maxwell Gordon Lightfoot, James Bolivar Manson (1913), Lucien Pissarro (1913), William Ratcliffe, Walter Sickert (1916) and Doman Turner. (The dates in brackets are the dates when this individual was elected to The London Group and this format will be continued throughout the book. It also highlights the involvement of London Group members in other groups and throughout British art history in general). In June the first Camden Town Group exhibition was opened followed by the second in December. Between 1911 and 1912 three Camden Town Group exhibitions were held in the Carfax Gallery, 24 Bury Street. However, Arthur Clifton of the Carfax Gallery ended the agreement with the Camden Town Group on the grounds that they were "a financial liability". The three exhibitions were not financially successful which ultimately led to the Group looking to broaden its artistic and financial horizons by linking with other contemporary artists' groupings, hence the origins of The London Group. Gauguin and Cézanne were exhibited at the **Stafford Gallery** and Gauguin, Matisse and Picasso were shown at the **Grafton Galleries**. At the **New English Art Club** Sickert presented his Camden Town Murder series.

The Carfax Gallery
24 Bury Street, London SW1

On the left is the shirt manufacturer Turnbull & Asser Ltd who now occupy 24 Bury Street where the Carfax Gallery was situated at the time of the three Camden Town Group Exhibitions between 1911 and 1912. At its northern junction Bury Street joins Jermyn Street (Wiltons Restaurant can be seen on the right of the photograph) which runs parallel to Piccadilly, home of the Royal Academy.

1912

On 17th January Captain Scott and his party arrive at the South Pole to find that Amundsen had beaten them by only a few days. Scott and his group were all to perish on their return journey. Start of the First Balkan War when Bulgaria besieged the Turks at Adrianople (October 1912 to May 1913). The unsinkable Titanic sinks after hitting an iceberg in the North Atlantic on its maiden voyage. Unrest continues at home with strikes organised by Trade Unions. Sylvia Pankhurst forms the East London Federation of Suffragettes.

First performance of Arnold Schoenberg's explosive cabaret, "Pierrot Lunaire", famous for its 'sprechgesang' (speech–song). Frederick Delius composes, "On Hearing the First Cuckoo in Spring". Les Ballets Russes perform Debussy's "L'après-midi d'un faune" in Paris. Les Ballets Russes also perform Stravinsky's "The Firebird" at London's Covent Garden and is the first public performance of Stravinsky in the UK.

In May at the Galerie Barbazanges, Paris, Roger Fry organises "Exposition de Quelques Artistes Indépendants Anglais" including Bloomsbury painters and those who were to form the Vorticists. Epstein meets Brancusi, Modigliani and Picasso in the same city. Picasso, Braque and Gris make the first collages ('coller' is 'to glue' in French), papier-collés and assemblages. The first publication of Cubist theory, "Du Cubisme", is published in August by Gleizes and Metzinger. There is extensive Futurist activity in Italy. Boccioni sculpts "Development of a Bottle in Space". In Russia the Russian Futurists declare their manifesto, "A Slap in the Face of Public Taste" written by David Burliuk, Kruchenykh, Khlebnikov and Mayakovsky (the original text was bound with sackcloth). Many new groups hold exhibitions including "Jack of Diamonds" (second), "Donkey's Tail" and "The Union of Youth". A large number of magazines and artists books are published at this time. Many Russian Futurists travel to Paris, France and Germany. 'Pravda', the Soviet Communist Party's newspaper, is first published. In New York, Marcel Duchamp paints "Nude Descending a Staircase". (Exhibited in the Salon de la Section d'Or).

In London, another hugely important exhibition takes place. Roger Fry organises the "Second Post-Impressionist Exhibition of English, French and Russian Artists" at the **Grafton Galleries** between October 5th and December 31st, 1912. Picasso, Matisse, Cézanne, Derain and Vlaminck were all shown. Fry organised an English section in this exhibition showing Frederick Etchells, Cuthbert Hamilton, Lewis and Wadsworth. "Futurist Painters" opened at the **Sackville Gallery**, 28 Sackville Street, London in March showing the work of Umberto Boccioni, Carlo Carrá, Luigi Russolo and Gino Severini. Bomberg in lar was hugely influenced by this exhibition.

Marinetti delivered three 'lectures' at the **Bechstein Hall** (now the Wigmore Hall). Gore, Ginner, Wyndham Lewis and Epstein provided decorative schemes for "The Cave of the Golden Calf" at the **Cabaret Theatre Club**, 9 Heddon Street off Regent Street. The Cave of the Golden Calf was opened in 1911 by Madame Strindberg. The third and final Camden Town Group Exhibition was held at the **Carfax Gallery** in December, paving the way for negotiations to begin on the formation of what was eventually to be called The London Group. **The Stafford Gallery** held an exhibition of Picasso drawings.

"The Cave of the Golden Calf"
9 Heddon Street, London W1

Heddon Street is a small street just west of Regent Street close to the back of the Royal Academy. In the early 1910s this was the spot where the artists' community hung out. Number 9 was situated right up in the corner and is now part of "The Living Room" restaurant.

1913

The suffragette Emily Wilding Davison throws herself beneath the King's horse at the Epsom Derby and dies four days later. In October 810 miners are killed in Britain's worst pit disaster at Senghenydd, Wales. In London a peace treaty is signed ending the first Balkan war. The House of Lords rejects the Third Irish Home Rule Bill. Freud publishes "Totem and Taboo". D.H. Lawrence writes "Sons and Lovers".

There are many iconic events in contemporary music. May 29th sees the first performance of Stravinsky's "The Rite of Spring" in the newly completed Theatre des Champs-Elysees, Paris with choreography by Nijinsky. 'Sensational premiere' of Sergei Prokofiev's "Piano Concerto No.2", Op. 16. Gustav Holst composes "St. Paul's Suite" for his pupils at St. Paul's School, London. December 3rd saw the first performance of the Russian Futurists performance "Victory over the Sun" at the Luna Park Theatre, St. Petersburg with a prologue by Khlebnikov, libretto by Kruchenykh, music by Matiushin and design by Malevich.

In New York the Armory Show opens in February introducing modern European Art to America and is, predictably, not well received. Marcel Duchamp creates "Bicycle Wheel" one of the first 'ready-made' sculptures. In Russia Malevich is working towards Suprematism. The "Donkey's Tail" group forms around Natalia Goncharova and Mikhail Larionov.

Marinetti's performances and readings in **London** cause quite a stir. "The Futurist Painter Severini Exhibits his Latest Works" solo show at the **Marlborough Gallery** in April. Nevinson meets Severini. Whilst travelling with Epstein Bomberg meets Derain, Max Jacob, Modigliani and Picasso in Paris during the summer. In July Ezra Pound famously meets Henri Gaudier-Brzeska at the Allied Artists' Association exhibition in the Albert Hall. Kandinsky was also an exhibitor at this exhibition. At the Carfax Gallery, Gore and Gilman show together in January Sickert in March, Bevan in April, Lucien Pissarro in May and Bayes in October. Frank Rutter organised the "Post-Impressionist and Futurist Exhibition" at the **Doré Galleries** in October, just when discussions were beginning on the formation of The London Group. London Group members-to-be Epstein, Frederick Etchells, Hamilton, Lewis, Nevinson and Wadsworth exhibited together. (The Daily Sketch in its 18th October edition ran an article, "You wouldn't think these were paintings would you" about the Futurist painters and sculptors. Most of the illustrations were deliberately upside down or on their side! November, **"The Albert Hall Picture Ball"**, a high society event with costumes designed by Lewis and Nevinson, 'The Very Latest School of Painting: Futurist Figures'. Other fancy-dress costumes were based on Post-Impressionist paintings à la Diaghilev and Apache Indians! Marinetti gave 'a performance'. In December Epstein held his first one-man show at the **Adelphi Gallery** including drawings of "The Rock Drill" which he was working on at the time. Epstein rented rooms above Harold Monro's Poetry Bookshop, an important centre for artists and poets at this time. Harold Gilman and Charles Ginner exhibited together at the **Allied Artists' Association** under a new aesthetic philosophy, "Neo-Realism". Neo-Realism was defined as "the plastic interpretation of life through the intimate research into Nature".

In July 1913 the art critic and painter Roger Fry opened the Omega Workshops at 33 Fitzroy Square, London. Omega brought avant-garde design to Edwardian Britain as had been the case in Europe, particularly Paris. Artists were encouraged to design interiors, fabrics, ceramics, furniture and clothing which were on sale at the workshop/retail outlet in Fitzroy Square. Omega designs used bold colour and largely abstract pattern. The general public's shopping experience was changing at this time with large, attractive emporia selling standardised, mass-produced goods. Fry and the Omega desired "the directly expressive quality of the artist's handling" rather than the "deadness of mechanical reproduction". Vanessa Bell, Duncan Grant, Wyndham Lewis, Frederick Etchells and Henri Gaudier-Brzeska were all involved in Omega, the Grafton Group and also in The London Group at the same time. However, Fry insisted that working for Omega, no one individual was to sign their work, everything produced there carried the Greek letter Ω (omega). Many Omega employees were struggling artists or conscientious objectors during the First World War and were given employment by Fry who was a Quaker and pacifist. Clients of Omega included Maud Cunard, E.M. Forster, Lady Ottoline Morrell, George Bernard Shaw, Gertrude Stein, H.G. Wells, Virginia Woolf and W.B. Yeats. Following a huge argument over alleged improprieties in the awarding of an Ideal Homes Exhibition contract, Wyndham Lewis, Cuthbert Hamilton, Edward Wadsworth and Frederick Etchells wrote a "Round Robin" letter on 10th October 1913 saying, "We the undersigned have given up our work there (Omega)". The Omega Workshops survived the war due to the indefatigable efforts of Roger Fry, finally closing their doors in 1919. Fry was elected to The London Group in 1917.

The retail outlet and workshop for the Omega Workshops were housed at 33 Fitzroy Square. Artists and designers worked on the upper floors, but no one actually lived in the building. Fitzroy Street runs north into Fitzroy Square. 1913 would appear to have been an extremely busy year for this area of London. G.B. Shaw and Virginia Woolf were also resident in the square at one time. The Post Office Tower now looms over this pleasant square of greenery in central London.

The Omega Workshop 1913-19
33 Fitzroy Square, London W1

Our attention must now turn to the formation of The London Group. This version of the founding of The London Group was written by Alfred Thornton (1924) as a catalogue foreword to the "London Group, Retrospective Exhibition, 1914 – 28" held in the Burlington Galleries, Burlington Gardens, London W1 between April and May 1928.

"The London Group owes its origin to the amalgamation of several small groups of painters who were dissatisfied with the conditions prevailing towards the end of the first decade of the present century.

In 1908 Frank Rutter, to whom we are indebted to much that follows, started the Allied Artists' Association on the lines of the 'Société des Artistes Independants' with the help of Walter Sickert, as well as Spencer Gore, Harold Gilman and others. At that period a group of artists, who for the most part met each other for the first time in connection with the Allied Artists' Association, formed a habit of meeting frequently at the Café Royal. A constant subject of conversation was the condition of the New English Art Club. The question was, should they attempt to reform that society, which from being a pioneer had grown to be conservative and in its peculiar way academic, or should they secede and form a new society? At length the formation of a new society was decided on, and this was named the 'Camden Town Group'. There were already other small societies in existence, such as the 'Cumberland Market Group' and 'Nineteen

Fitzroy Street', – the latter consisting of a studio at which members pictures were shown weekly during certain months of the year.

The London Group owes its origins to these various groups and the following notes are based on the minutes of meetings held by the Camden Town Group and kept by its Honorary Secretary, J.B. Manson. The Camden Town Group was formed in May 1911, and the late Spencer Gore was elected its first President. Its membership consisted originally of fifteen artists, the majority of whom were to be included in the membership of The London Group. The first Camden Town Group Exhibition was held in June 1911 at The Carfax Gallery, no longer in existence. A second and a third exhibition were held respectively in December 1911 and December 1912 at the same gallery. At a meeting of the Camden Town Group held on December 2nd 1911, amongst other rules, one was created which provided for each member's work being grouped by itself at exhibitions, and another forbade the election of women.

But as soon as October 25th 1913 there appear in the minutes the names of women members. These voted when it was decided to increase the numbers of the society, and it was this decision which changed the society into the London Group. Moreover it was then resolved that the Camden Town Group and the Fitzroy Street should amalgamate."

Here's a personal description of the social life of the artists at that time, as recollected by William Roberts (elected to The London Group in 1914) in his 1957 article, 'William Roberts and Vorticism's Year':

"Among others I had as neighbours Bernard Meninsky, John Flanagan, Colin Gill and Geoffrey Nelson. It was in John Flanagan's rooms across the (Cumberland) Market that Sickert and his Camden Town crowd met a number of other artists to make arrangements for promoting a larger organisation, The London Group. In Flanagan's balconied rooms were held many an all–nightly revel to the Jazz-music of a gramophone; our full-throated singing of 'Way down on the Levee' and 'Hold your hand out, you naughty boy', if too long sustained in the still small hours, brought visits from constables disturbed on their beats. But Flanagan, by the judicious use of a little blarney, knew how to quieten the apprehensions of these uniformed intruders solicitous for the peace of the neighbourhood".

More formal records of the evolution of The London Group are contained in archived minutes of meetings. Facsimiles of the minutes of the first nine meetings before the first London Group exhibition in March 1914 can be found on the internet as part of Tate's Camden Town Project. The citation is 'Group records', in Helena Bonett, Ysanne Holt, Jennifer Mundy (eds.), The Camden Town Group in Context, May 2012, http://www.tate.org.uk/art/research-publications/camden-town-group/group-records-g2020536.

Camden Town Group minutes for a meeting held at 19 Fitzroy Street on the

2nd December 1911, during their second exhibition at the Carfax Gallery, record a discussion about enlarging the Group in the near future. Bevan, Ginner, Gore, Lamb, Lewis, Pissarro and Ratcliffe all spoke in favour of this idea and nearly two years later the enlargement finally got underway.

Original minutes appear to be a blue typescript copy dated 25th October 1913 and produced by James Bolivar Manson (soon to be The London Group's Honorary Secretary). Those present at this meeting were, in exact order and title, Drummond, D. Grant, W. Bayes, Bevan, Gilman, Epstein, Lewis, Gore, Manson, Sickert (who chaired the meeting) and Misses Hudson & Sands. Gilman was also acting as proxy for Ginner, twelve plus one proxy. The new faces in this meeting were the sculptor Jacob Epstein and painters Duncan Grant and Percy Wyndham Lewis, all of the others belonged to the Camden Town Group or their circle. Six members of the Camden Town Group, including J. D. Innes, Augustus John, Maxwell Gordon Lightfoot and J. Doman Turner, did not attend this meeting for various reasons and only William Ratcliffe was to have a lengthy association with the new group. The first minute records, "Resolved that C.T.G. and Fitzroy Street be amalgamated". The meeting then moved on to decide how to elect new members into the as yet unamed new society. "Mr. Bayes proposed that 1 black ball in 6 of the total number of members should exclude". This was seconded by Mr. Gore and was carried. Other motions accepted were that voting should be by post, names of candidates should be posted three weeks in advance and that only artists resident in the UK were elligible.

The second meeting took place at 19 Fitzroy Street on November 15th, 1913. Sickert also chaired this meeting of twenty artists including ten who were not at the first meeting. The ten were W. Ratcliffe, H. Sund, Renee Finch, C.R.W. Nevinson, W.B. Adeney, C. Hamilton, H. Lamb, H. Squire, E.A. Wadsworth and F. Etchells (all as typed in the minutes). Lewis seems to have been very active in recruiting the majority of these ten from his circle. Grant and Hudson, present at the first meeting, did not attend. It was 'Resolved that the Society be called "THE LONDON GROUP"'. Charles Ginner recalled that, "a large meeting eventually took place at No. 19, Fitzroy Street. Here, unless my memory has played truant, I have a vision of Jacob Epstein, during a discussion on the naming of this new society, leaning against the mantelpiece and saying to the assembled company, amidst general approbation, "Let us call it 'The London Group'"". (Charles Ginner, 'The Camden Town Group', Studio, November 1945, pp.129–36). Other matters resolved were that the Executive structure was to be President, Treasurer and Secretary, Gilman was elected President and Bevan the Treasurer, the Presidency was only for one year, new members were to be elected at a special meeting and that an exhibition was to be arranged for the spring, 1914 where pictures by each artist were to be hung in individual groups.

The newly titled London Group met a week later on 22nd November at 19 Fitzroy

Street with Sickert again in the chair and J.B. Manson recorded as Honorary Secretary. Nineteen members met together and resolved, "That members of THE LONDON GROUP become ipso facto members of Fitzroy Street." Other resolutions at this third meeting were that The London Group should exhibit twice a year, the President should ask Mr. Marchant (of the Goupil Gallery) if he would be willing to put on these exhibitions, the Group should meet every Saturday until further notice, the yearly subscription should be £2 and that candidates show actual work for inspection.

The fourth meeting a week later was attended by nineteen members with Sickert as chairman and was primarily devoted to the process of electing new members. Unfortunately the system decided upon proved unworkable as at the next meeting on December 6th no new members were elected at all! Dates of the first exhibition at the Goupil Gallery were to be March 1914 and March 1915, "an Autumn Exhibition at the same gallery was discarded". The agreement with Mr. Marchant was to be scrutinized by Sickert's solicitor.

On Saturday, December 6th The London Group held its first membership elections. Sickert was again in charge of proceedings at 19 Fitzroy Street with eighteen other members present. The list of proxies makes interesting reading in that it was recognition of how important these elections were to the make-up of this new group. Lamb nominated Gore, Hamilton nominated Wadsworth, Ginner likewise Drummond and Pissarro (whose relationship with The London Group ended here) asked Manson to cast his vote for him. Fourteen candidates were put up for election, Therese Lessore (sic), Hamilton Hay, W. Rothenstein, Fanny Eveleigh, S. de Karlowska, Darcie Japp, A. Rothenstein, Walter Taylor, Fox-Pitt, Mark Gertler, Miss Gosse, Miss J. Etchells, D. Bomberg and C. Winzer. As has been said previously, an overcomplicated voting system failed to elect any of them!

The next meeting of The London Group was almost a month later. By that time the exhibition "The Camden Town Group and Others" had opened at Brighton Art Gallery on 16th December 1913 (see below). Spencer Gore was the organising force behind this exhibition which was testing out the ideas discussed in previous meetings, notably hanging work not only as individual groups but also in stylistic groupings.

Wendy Baron, writing in "The Painters of Camden Town 1905-1920" (Christies catalogue, 4th to 24th January 1988) in an essay entitled "Camden Town to London via Fitzroy Sreet" makes the following points, "The Camden Town Group had been an exclusive society of sixteen elected members. Membership of Fitzroy Street was also by election, but there was no discrimination against women and the number of members was not finite. It was, in short, possible to storm the bastions of Fitzroy Street, before the rules for election to the new society were formulated, and thus become ipso facto a member of the new London Group. An influx of new members into the Fitzroy Street Group between October and November 1913 significantly altered the balance of the society and marks the moment when the two original leaders of the Group, Pissarro and Sickert, lost control of the enterprise. Both resigned from the Fitzroy Street and London Groups before the first exhibition of the latter in March 1914... The existence of the new society and the factions it stimulated represented the culmination of his (Sickert's) ambition, first expressed in Fitzroy Street in 1907, to create an ambience in London wherein young painters could encourage each other towards independence and professional self-confidence".

Writing in the catalogue to the exhibition "A Countryman in Town: Robert Bevan and the Cumberland Market Group" (Southampton City Art Gallery, 2008) Frances Stenlake offers the following explanation for the formation of The London Group, "Meanwhile the Camden Town Group took up an offer of space at the Goupil Gallery in Regent Street and decided to expand the size of its membership, resulting in the formation of the London Group in the autumn of 1913, with Bevan appointed Treasurer. The ban on women now lifted, Karlowska (Bevan's wife) was elected a member in January 1914." In the same catalogue John Yeates has a slightly different view, "At the end of 1912, Fitzroy was all but a spent force; but help, of sorts, came from William Marchant, of the Goupil Gallery, who proposed an alliance of various groupings and individuals (excluding the Bloomsbury Group) which was effected in November 1913, with an exhibition in the Brighton Art Gallery arranged by Spencer Gore, comprising both Neo Realist and Vorticist works."

Robert Upstone writes in the catalogue to "Modern Painters: the Camden Town Group" (Tate Britain, 2008) that J. B. Manson had said of the enlargement of the Camden Town Group to form the new London Group that it was a move to "extend the means of free expression thus won to other artists who were experimenting with new methods, who were seeking or who had found means of expression... Cubism meets Impressionism, Futurism and Sickertism join hands and are not ashamed, the motto of the Group being that sincerity of conviction has a right of expression."

The art critic for the Manchester Daily Guardian wrote on the 20th January 1914, under the heading 'The Revolutionaries', "Everyone will be pleased that such a society has come into existence, the frivolous because it will tend to keep the older societies free of eccentricities, and the serious because they know that if art is a real thing every generation must have its fling and dance to its own piping. If its members find the New English (Art Club) and the International Society are not sympathetic, the London Group is almost overdue."

An invitation from Brighton Art Gallery to mount an exhibition was one of the last acts of the 'dissolving' Camden Town Group. The "Exhibition by the Camden Town Group and Others" was held between December 16th 1913 and January 14th 1914 in Brighton at the Public Art Galleries and was considered to be 'a dry run' for The London Group. There were thirty-six exhibitors in total, a quarter of them women.

The 'Index to Artists' from the catalogue reads as follows, Adeney W.B., Bayes Walter, Bevan Robert, Bomberg David, Drummond Malcolm, Duckett R., (this is most likely a misprint. Ruth Doggett was elected to The London Group in 1920) Epstein Jacob, Etchells Frederick, Etchells Jessie, Eveleigh Fanny, Finch Renée, Fox-Pitt Douglas, Gilman Harold, Ginner Charles, Gore Spencer F., Gosse Sylvia, Hamilton C.F., Hay J. Hamilton, Hudson Anna Hope, Karlowska S. de, Lawrence Mervyn, Lessore Thérèse, Lewis Percy Wyndham, Manson James B., Nash John, Nash Paul, Nevinson C.R.W., Ogilvie M., Pissarro Lucien, Ratcliffe William, Sands Ethel, Sickert Walter, Squire Harold, Sund Harold, Taylor Walter, Wadsworth E..

Henry D. Roberts (Director) wrote this Notice introducing the exhibition, "It has been somewhat difficult to find a title to this exhibition. That given to it – 'Work of English Post Impressionists and Cubists' – is hardly sufficiently explanatory, as there are many works exhibited which do not come under either of these titles. It is, however, sufficiently indicative of the general tendency of the exhibition.

The Fine Arts Committee have contented themselves with inviting the Camden Town Group to form the exhibition, and are not responsible for the selection or arrangement, which has been undertaken by the Camden Town Group, acting through Mr. Spencer F. Gore.

Mr. J.B. Manson and Mr. Percy Wyndham Lewis have been good enough to write an introduction to the catalogue, but the Fine Arts Committee obviously are not responsible for the opinions therein stated". When you read Lewis' introduction you will understand the reason for this disclaimer!

These two introductory forewords are well worth recording in full as they are the nearest thing to a London Group (and Futurist) 'manifesto' as can be anticipated. The following is from the catalogue to "The Camden Town Group and Others", Brighton & Hove Art Gallery archive.

"INTRODUCTION. ROOMS I – II by J.B. Manson
Mr. Walter Sickert can scarcely have imagined some eight years ago, when he instituted his Saturday 'At Homes' in the Studio at 19 Fitzroy Street, that he was thereby paving the way for the Camden Town Group.

However, finding himself in these days the innocent progenitor of so spirited a descendant, he assumes even this responsibility with his usual light-hearted grace. Mr. Sickert may not have foreseen the Camden Town Group as the outcome of his early experiment, but he did then realise the necessity of providing some scope for the free expression of newer artistic thought.

The right of free speech in art has been a peculiarly unsatisfied need in England, where art has meant for the public the sentimental anecdote produced according to the best recipes evolved to suit the taste of institutions eminently British.

Eight years ago the then revolutionaries, the New English Art Club, had already found its respectable level; it had reached a point of safety. It was too tired or too wise to venture further.

But self-complacency, whether new English or old, has never won the respect of tumultuous youth; nor have brain and brawn been bred on sponge cakes even when disguised in the pink and chocolate of the officially distinguished.

There is no limit to development or to new ideas. New modes of expression, whatever their value, must and will be heard. For this reason, the movement, small and imperceptible at first, became the vehicle for the expression of the new ideas, hot from the mint, which agitated the impressionable minds of these younger English artists who had escaped being cast in the Royal Academic mould. With Mr. Spencer Gore and Mr. Harold Gilman in league, there was no restraining the forward movement wherever it might lead; for the alert curiosity, the interest displayed by those artists in every new aspect of art which might be utilised for the more complete and more intimate realisation of emotion, made inevitably for advancement. So the movement kept alive and grew. With Mr. Lucien Pissarro as a leader, the link with traditional art through Camille Pissarro, Corot, and Claude, was complete. The influence of Mr. Pissarro made itself immediately felt. The 'At Homes' of the society became widely known. The younger generation found there work which kindled its curiosity, or stimulated its interest in life. Distinguished foreign visitors made the Studio in Fitzroy Street a meeting place, regarding it as an oasis in the desert of British Art. There they discovered the modern movement in art, whose very existence in this country was unsuspected, so had it been ignored or inadequately recognised by official art institutions.

The need to appeal to a wider public became at last a necessity. In 1911 the Camden Town group was formed and held its first exhibition in the Carfax Gallery. The Group at that time represented a coherent homogeneous school of expression; differing in degree as to the work of individual members, but with the unity of a common aim. The exhibition, small and select as it was, attracted considerable attention, and other exhibitions followed. It was then felt to be desirable to extend the means of free expression thus won to other artists who were experimenting with new methods, who were seeking or who had found means of expressing their ideas, their visions, their conceptions in their own way. For this reason the London Group is being formed. More eclectic in its constitution, it will no longer limit itself to the cultivation of one single school of thought, but will offer hospitality to all manner of artistic expression provided it has the quality of sincere personal conviction. The Group promises to become one of the most influential and most significant of art movements in England.

To conceive a limit to artistic development is an admission of one's own limitations. Nothing is finally right in art; the rightness is purely personal, and for the artists himself. So, in the London Group, which is to be the latest development of the original Fitzroy Street Group, all modern methods may find a home. Cubism meets Impressionism, Futurism and Sickertism join hands and are not ashamed, the motto of the Group being that sincerity of conviction has a right of expression.

A live society in which is room for manifold schools of thought, in which individuality and personal feeling have scope to develop is the object of the London Group. It is well, perhaps, that the vital qualities in modern art should be concentrated in one definite group, instead of being scattered in the medley of modern exhibitions.

ROOM III (THE CUBIST ROOM) by Percy Wyndham Lewis.

Futurism, one of the alternative terms for modern painting, was patented in Milan. It means the Present, with the Past rigidly excluded, and flavoured strongly with H.G. Wells' dreams of the dance of monstrous and arrogant machinery, to the frenzied clapping of men's hands. But futurism will never mean anything else, in painting, than the art practised by the five or six Italian painters grouped beneath Marinetti's influence. Gino Severini, the foremost of them, has for subject matter the night resorts of Paris. This, as subject matter, is obviously not the future. For we all foresee, in a century or so, everybody being put to bed at 7 o'clock in the evening by a state-nurse. Therefore the Pan Pan at the Monaco will be, for Ginos of the future, an archaistic experience.

Cubism means, chiefly, the art, superbly severe and so far morose, of those who have taken the genius of Cèzanne as a starting point, and organised the character of the works he threw up in his indiscriminate and grand labour. It is the reconstruction of a simpler earth, left as choked and muddy fragments by him. Cubism includes much more than this, but the 'cube' is implicit in that master's painting.

To be done with terms and tags, Post Impressionism is an insipid and pointless name invented by a journalist, which has been naturally ousted by the better word 'Futurism' in public debate on modern art.

This room is chiefly composed of works by a group of painters, consisting of Frederick Etchells, Cuthbert Hamilton, Edward Wadsworth, C.R.W. Nevinson, and the writer of this foreword. These painters are not accidentally associated here, but form a vertiginous, but not exotic, island in the placid and respectable archipelago of English art. This formation is undeniably of volcanic matter and even origin; for it appeared suddenly above the waves following certain seismic shakings beneath the surface. It is very closely knit and admirably adapted to withstand the imperturbable Britannic breakers which roll pleasantly against its sides.

Beneath the Past and the Future the most sanguine would hardly expect a more different skeleton to exist than that respectively of ape and man. Man with an aeroplane is still merely a bad bird. But a man who passes his days amid the rigid lines of houses, a plague of cheap ornamentation, noisy street locomotion, the Bedlam of the press, will evidently possess a different habit of vision to a man living amongst the lines of a landscape. As to turning the back, the most wise men, Egyptians, Chinese, or what not, have remained where they found themselves, their appetite for life sufficient to reconcile them, and allow them to create significant things. Suicide is the obvious course for the dreamer, who is a man without an anchor of sufficient weight.

The work of this group of artists for the most part underlines such geometric bases and structure of life, and they would spend their energies rather in showing a different skeleton and abstraction than formerly could exist, than a different degree of hairiness or dress. All revolutionary painting to-day has in common the rigid reflections of steel and stone in the spirit of the artist; that desire for stability as though a machine were being built to fly or kill with; an alienation from the traditional photographer's trade and realisation of the value of colour and form as such independently of what recognisable form it covers or encloses. People are invited, in short, to entirely change their idea of the painter's mission, and penetrate, deferentially, with him into a transposed universe, as abstracts, though different to, the musicians. ...

Hung in this room as well are three drawings by Jacob Epstein, the only great sculptor at present working in England. He finds in the machinery of procreation a dynamo to work the deep atavism of his spirit. Symbolically strident above his work, or in the midst of it, is, like the Pathè cock, a new born baby, with a mystic but puissant crow. His latest work opens up a region of great possibilities, and new creation. David Bomberg's painting of a platform announces a colourist's temperament, something between the cold blond of Severini's early paintings and Vallotton. The form and subject matter are academic, but the structure of the criss-cross pattern new and extremely interesting."

With a volcanic energy like Lewis's, who could doubt that he, and his group of compatriots, would not remain for long tied to a group that still espoused Post-Impressionism. The following artists showed in the Brighton exhibition but not in The London Group's first exhibition in the Goupil Gallery, London: Ruth Doggett (printed 'R. Duckett' in error in the Brighton catalogue), Fanny Eveleigh, James Hamilton Hay, Mervyn Lawrence, Paul Nash, M. Ogillvie and Walter Sickert. However, some of these would be elected into The London Group at a later date, Doggett in 1920, James Hamilton Hay in late 1914, Paul Nash in late 1914 and Walter Sickert, following his 1914 resignation, in 1916. Could Sickert have been scared off by what he saw and read at Brighton?

**The Public Art Galleries
Brighton**

The richly decorated entrance to the Public Art Galleries in Brighton is close to
the Royal Pavilion. Both buildings were influenced by Indian architecture which
was 'in vogue' at the time of the Royal Pavilion's construction between 1803 and
1822. There were obviously links between artists in London and the seaside town
of Brighton. Archive material held in the Brighton History Centre records London
Group member Walter Taylor, for example, as having residencies in both London and
Brighton.

1914

Shakleton's expedition to the South Pole. Outbreak of the First World War. In July, Austria declares war on Serbia following the assassination by a Serbian terrorist of Archduke Franz Ferdinand and his wife in Sarajevo on June 28th. On the 4th August Britain declares war on Germany. Germany then declares war on Russia. Lenin and Trotsky had emigrated to Switzerland. It would be the first major war to be fought in the air and with war machines (tanks).

Ralph Vaughan Williams writes "A London Symphony: The Lark Ascending". James Joyce writes "The Dubliners". May 21st, Diaghilev's production of "Le Coq d'Or" opens at the Paris Opera with design by Natalia Goncharova.

"Blue Rider Group" members Klee and Macke visit Tunisia in search of bold, bright colour. Kandinsky paints his final 'Improvisation'. In January F.T. Marinetti visits Moscow to meet the Russian 'Futurists' (some were unimpressed). In April Tatlin visits Braque in Paris and sees 'corner sculptures'. Tatlin is already making assemblages with found objects from 1913. Malevich was working towards his iconic "Black Square" at the end of the year. There is a large display of Russian Art at this year's Salon des Indépendants.

In January or February Gaudier-Brzeska begins work on the "Hieratic Head of Ezra Pound". Roger Fry shows photographs of Picasso's 'constructed sculptures' in the Grafton Group exhibition at the **Alpine Club Gallery**. March 11th, newspapers report the slashing of Velasquez's "Venus and Cupid" (the Rokeby Venus) in the **National Gallery** by Suffragette Miss Richardson. She said "I have tried to destroy the picture of the most beautiful woman in mythological history as a protest against the Government for destroying Mrs. Pankhurst, who is the most beautiful character in modern history". In April a large exhibition of Futurism opens at the Doré Galleries and received extensive press coverage. Later in the year Marinetti lectures in London. An article entitled "Vital English Art", signed by F.T. Marinetti and C.R.W. Nevinson is printed in The Observer on the 7th June and on the 12th June Marinetti and Nevinson deliver a lecture at the **Doré Galleries**. Marinetti had claimed that the **Rebel Art Centre** was "Futurist HQ". Lewis was furious over this "impertinence". Nevinson was the only British artist to sign up to the Futurist manifesto and to align himself with Marinetti. Lewis and Wadsworth were against what they called 'Marinettism' and worked towards a more angular abstraction under the 'Vorticist' banner. Nevinson soon broke with the Futurists (who glorified war) following his experiences in an ambulance unit at the Front. Russian and Italian Futurists experiment with language and sound. Through May and June the **Whitechapel Art Gallery** presented "Twentieth Century Art: a Review of Modern Movements", a review of contemporary art. The Introduction to the catalogue divides the exhibition into four sections, the first, artists influenced by Sickert and Lucien Pissarro, the second from Puvis de Chavannes, Legros and Augustus John, the third from Cézanne and the fourth a loose grouping of 'abstract' painters including the Rebel Art Centre and 'Mr. Bomberg'. Richard Cork writes, "Working with his friend Jacob Epstein, as well as the gallery's founding Director Charles Aitken, Bomberg brought together some world-class painters and sculptors for this ambitious show. In the same year, Vorticism erupted as London's uninhibited response to Cubism, Expressionism and Futurism. The Whitechapel Boys were keenly aware of the innovative vitality galvanising this pre-war period and they contributed to its energy. Their prowess seems still more admirable in view of the grim poverty from which they emerged." (RA Magazine, Spring 2009). The Whitechapel Boys all lived in the area and gathered in the Whitechapel Library (known locally as the "University of the Ghetto"). It must be remembered that Bomberg and Epstein were Founder Members of The London Group in 1913 and must have been extremely active during this period. Apart from these two, other artists in The Whitechapel Boys were Mark Gertler (1915), Jacob Kramer (1914), Bernard Meninsky (1919), C. Winsten and Wolmark. The latter had been proposed for The London Group but had failed to attract enough votes. He was very disappointed. Whitechapel Boys writers were Joseph Leftwich, Rodker (who wrote "The Future of Futurism" in 1926), S. Winsten and the poet Isaac Rosenberg. In July David Bomberg holds his first one-man exhibition at the **Chenil Galleries**, Kensington. Amongst other works he shows "Vision of Ezekiel" (1912), "In the Hold" (1913) and "The Mud Bath" (1914). Hulme wrote the only review of Bomberg's exhibition, broadly supportive and observing that his work was "more individual and less derivative" than the English Cubists. Gilman and Ginner founded the Cumberland Market Group and exhibited together again as "The Neo-Realists" at the **Goupil Gallery**, even though they are heavily involved with The London Group. Sickert, writing in "The New Age" of 30th April, wrote an aggressive and negative review of their exhibition.

London Group President: Harold Gilman (1913)

At the sixth meeting of the new London Group membership on 3rd January 1914, David Bomberg, Stanislawa de Karlowska, Jessica Etchells, Douglas Fox-Pitt, Sylvia Gosse, Thérèse Lessore and Walter Taylor were elected. Seventeen members attended this meeting and there were five proxy votes, Frederick Etchells being given the proxy votes of three English Cubists, Hamilton, Wadsworth and Lewis. Twenty-six candidates had been put forward and amongst the unsuccessful artists were A. Rothenstein, W. Rothenstein, Mark Gertler (with 13 against and only 6 for), Paul Nash and Eric Gill who scored 15 for and 5 against, which meant he was selected but declined membership because he "desired to make work instead of to exhibit it".

Malcolm Easton from the University of Hull, who died in 1993, discovered the following interview. The citation is 'Malcolm Easton, The Camden Town Group into the London Group: Some Intimate Glimpses of the Transition 1911–14', in Helena Bonett, Ysanne Holt, Jennifer Mundy (eds.), The Camden Town Group in Context, May 2012, http://www.tate.org.uk/art/research-publications/camden-town-group/group-records-g2020536. "The interview with Gilman appeared in the Standard, 3 February 1914, and as it has not, I think, been quoted since and is of considerable interest, I give it here complete: 'The principles underlying the formation of this party of artists [London Group] were described to one of our representatives by Mr. Harold J.W. Gilman, the well-known "realist". "There are at present two well-defined sections in English art", he said, "which are known as realists and formulists. They both arise from the revolt against naturalism, and they support one another in the sense that one can learn from the other. These sections are combining in 'The London Group'. There are, of course, artists who cannot be classed wholly with either section, but who constitute a bridge between the two." He demonstrated with a small cactus in a pot on the table. If he was a formulist, he would simply paint a very obviously heartshaped object with a sort of elliptic circle underneath it to represent the top of the pot and it wouldn't matter what colour it was. "That is to say, I am rendering so much of it as consists of planes and curves… On the other hand, if I am a realist I want the object to remain a cactus after I have painted it".'

Sickert had chaired the sixth meeting in January but was absent for this meeting and so Spencer Gore took the chair for the seventh meeting on 7th February 1914. The Brighton exhibition had closed on January 14th and no doubt there was much evaluation of the positives and negatives of this exercise. Those present for this meeting were, "S.F. Gore (Chair), Etchells, Therese Lessore, J. Etchells, S. de Karlowska, P.W. Lewis, Hamilton, Wadsworth, Ratcliffe, Bayes, Adeney, Bevan, Epstein, Finch, Gilman, Nevinson, Ginner, Sund, Manson". Ten candidates were put forward for election but only Gaudier-Brzeska was successful, Paul Nash, again, just failing to win the required number of votes. The practicalities of the first London Group exhibition were then addressed. First of all, each member had to pay a half-year subscription (10/6) before their work was hung. The Hanging Committee was to be Epstein, Finch, Gilman, Gore, Lewis, Manson and Wadsworth. Each member was allowed to submit five works including two large ones to hang in the large gallery of the Goupil Galleries and the sending in day was 27th February. This date is extremely useful in that the date of the opening of the first London Group exhibition is unclear and is not printed in the exhibition catalogue. Marchant would not have wanted work hanging around not earning money and so it is likely that the exhibition opened in the first week of March.

The next meeting took place on the 7th March with Sickert again absent and this time Bayes in the chair. Those present copied exaclty from the minutes, "Bayes (chair), Gilman, Bomberg, Finch, Bevan, de Karlowska, Epstein, Adeney, Brzeska, Nash, Squire, Ratcliffe, Lewis, Ginner, Wadsworth, Gore, Manson". Stanley Spencer was elected to The London Group by 15 votes for and 2 against at this meeting but he resigned soon afterwards.

The ninth meeting a week later was also concerned about resignations. Hand written on the bottom of the typed minutes was, "Letter from Marchant. Resignation of Lamb Pissarro. To suggest that 5 resignations shall liberate Marchant from his agreement". It is ironic that the originator of these priceless minutes, James Bolivar Manson, should resign himself after only one showing with The London Group in March 1914. His good friend Lucien Pissarro resigned over the inclusion of Lewis and his growing number of associates in the Group. Pissarro never exhibited with The London Group and his resignation no doubt influenced Manson's decision. Both were shown, however, in the 1928 London Group Retrospective as they were both founder members. Edward Wadsworth replaced Manson as Honorary Secretary. Sickert also resigned from The London Group before the Group's first exhibition because he thought work by Frederick Etchells, Lewis and Epstein was 'pornographic' and did not wish to be associated with them, yet it was Epstein, "leaning on the mantelpiece in Sickert's studio", who coined the title 'The London Group'. Sickert was to resign and re-join The London Group a number of times in his life.

Four artists, Henri Gaudier-Brzeska, Duncan Grant, Henry Lamb and Lucien Pissarro were recorded as members in the catalogue to The London Group's first exhibition at the Goupil Gallery, although these four did not show in the "Camden Town Group and Others" exhibition at Brighton Public Art Galleries in December 1913.

"The First Exhibition of Works by Members of the London Group" was held at the Goupil Gallery, 5 Regent Street, London SW in March 1914. Harold Gilman was indicated as President of The London Group, followed by a list of members (with the number of works exhibited in brackets) as follows, W.B. Adeney (5), Walter Bayes (2), R.P. Bevan (5), D.Bomberg (5), Gaudier-Brzeska (5 sculptures), M.C. Drummond (3), Jacob Epstein (2+3 sculptures), F. Etchells (5), Jessie Etchells (4), Renée Finch (5), D. Fox-Pitt (0), Harold Gilman (5), Charles Ginner (5), Spencer F. Gore (4), Sylvia Gosse (5), Duncan Grant (0), C.F. Hamilton (2), A.H. Hudson (3), S. de Karlowska (4), H. Lamb (0), Thérèse Lessore (5), P. Wyndham Lewis (5), J.B. Manson (4), John Nash (4), C.R.W. Nevinson (5), Lucien Pissarro (0), W. Ratcliffe (5), Ethel Sands (2), Harold Squire (5), Harold Sund (4), Walter Taylor (0) and Edward Wadsworth (5). The Group would have wanted to have had a strong turnout for the first show, so could these numbers be indicative of the 'enthusiasm' of these Founder Members? D. (Douglas)

Fox-Pitt, Duncan Grant, H. (Henry) Lamb, Lucien Pissarro and Walter Taylor did not exhibit. There were seven women and twenty-five men in total, thirty-two members of whom only twenty-seven supported the fledgling group by submitting work. One hundred and eight paintings and seven sculptures were presented in three galleries, the Long Gallery, the Small Gallery and the Large Gallery. The Hanging Committee for this first showing was Jacob Epstein, Renée Finch, Harold Gilman, Spencer F. Gore, P. Wyndham Lewis, J.B. Manson and Edward Wadsworth. The paintings were not hung as an artist's block, as had been discussed and loosely agreed at earlier meetings; different artists were hung next to each other. Titles suggested a mixture of landscape, still life and portraiture. The Small Gallery appears rather exciting with Wyndham Lewis, Nevinson, Wadsworth, Epstein and Bomberg packed together. There were a large number of drawings in this gallery too, notably Wyndham-Lewis' "Enemy of the Stars", a drawing for a sculpture. Jacob Epstein and Gaudier-Brzeska were the only exhibitors of sculpture, Epstein showing "Group of Birds", "Bird pluming itself" and "Carving in Flenite" whilst Gaudier-Brzeska exhibited "Maternity (Stone)", "Alabaster Group", "Dancer (Red Stone)", "Boy with Coney (Alabaster)" and "Torso (Marble)". Prices for paintings in the whole exhibition averaged between £10 and £30, although you could have picked up Gaudier-Brzeska's "Alabaster Group" for £150 or Jacob Epstein's "Group of Birds" for £100. Similarly, David Bomberg's "In the Hold" was priced at £50 and Harold Gilman's "An Eating House" and "Miss Silvia Gosse" for £30 each. Other notable exhibits were R.P. Bevan's "Under the Hammer" (£40), Spencer F. Gore's "Croft Lane, Letchworth" (£30) and "The Wood" (£35), P. Wyndham Lewis' "Eisteddfod" (£40) and "Christopher Columbus" (£70), C.R.W. Nevinson's "The Non-Stop" (£30), Edward Wadsworth's "Radiation" (£40) and three of Charles Ginner's paintings with Dieppe in the title. For a first exhibition the catalogue is singularly uninformative, no sizes, no media, no illustrations, no addresses, no 'manifesto' statement or 'declaration of war' against the Royal Academy. The only mention of materials is for Gaudier-Brzeska who had used stone, red stone, alabaster, marble and flenite. Again, the only remotely interesting items in the catalogue, and more by insinuation than statement, were, "The Members of The London Group are solely responsible for the judgement, organisation and arrangement of this exhibition", (could this be the Goupil Gallery covering its back?) and, "By a delivered judgement in the Court of Chancery on the 8th of July 1907, and confirmed in the Court of Appeal on the 20th November 1907, Messrs. William Marchant & Co. were given the sole and exclusive right to the title: The Goupil Gallery". The slightly larger than A5 catalogue was bound in grey-green sugar paper with THE LONDON GROUP printed in black, very ordinary!

Valuable evidence for the date of the first London Group exhibition can be found in Tate's on-line Camden Town Project. The citation is 'Malcolm Easton, The Camden

Town Group into the London Group: Some Intimate Glimpses of the Transition 1911–14', in Helena Bonett, Ysanne Holt, Jennifer Mundy (eds.), The Camden Town Group in Context, May2012http://www.tate.org.uk/art/research-publications/camden-town-group/group-records-g2020536. "The first exhibition under the title 'London' was discussed at the meeting of 7 February. It took place on 5 March, under Marchant's aegis, at the Goupil Gallery. As far as press and public were concerned, vorticism swamped the show. To use Pissarro's terms, the 'drunkards' triumphed over the 'teetotallers'". A footnote entry enlarges on the event, "Here (issue of 6 March 1914) is the Daily News and Leader on the subject: 'The eccentric ladies and gentlemen who call themselves "the London Group" are holding their first exhibition in the Goupil Gallery, Regent Street. They are "cubists" sans peur et sans reproche, and they claim they are converting not only the world of art, but every man with brains and imagination to the belief that they are men and women of genius… The picture that will attract most attention is called "The Arrival", and is the creation of the ingenious young cubist known as C.R.W. Nevinson. Lovely ladies paused before it all yesterday afternoon murmuring "How sweet!" It resembles a Channel steamer after a violent collision with a pier. You detect funnels, smoke, gang-planks, distant hotels, numbers, posters all thrown into the melting-pot, so to speak. Mr. Nevinson acted as interpreter, explaining that it represented a "state of simultaneous mind". "Isn't it all just heavenly!" exclaimed the girls. "You see", said one, "the poor dears have all grown so tired of photography. Their work is in a transitional stage and is naturally rather opaque; but at any rate it's a welcome escape from impressionism." A brother cubist is P. Wyndham Lewis. His chef-d'oeuvre is entitled "Christopher Columbus" – which is precisely what you will exclaim when you see it. A crowd tried its best to find the explorer. Mr. Lewis, pointing rapidly to odd corners of the canvas, said: "There's his head, that's his leg. Don't you get me?" It seemed as clear as a London fog. "Our object is to bewilder", said he; "we want to shock the senses and get you into a condition of mind in which you'll grasp what our intentions are." The artists are as quaint as their pictures. They look a cross between the last word in "knuts" and the first word in the students of the Quartier Latin of a quarter of a century ago. They rejoice in being impossible, inconsequent and incoherent, but they say in effect: "We are the fad of the moment. The newspapers may ridicule us, but Society is falling at our feet, and is even paying us to decorate their drawing-rooms.'" " (Footnote 31).

Ezra Pound was a strong supporter of Lewis and his followers, Gaudier-Brzeska in particular. Further evidence for the first exhibition date comes from his review in 'The Egoist' dated 16th March 1914 in which he begins, "The exhibition of new art now showing at the Goupil Gallery deserves the attention of everyone interested in either painting or sculpture". Note that he separates painting and sculpture, Epstein and Gaudier-Brzeska both showed what were to become important examples of contemporary sculpture.

There had been sixteen original Camden Town Group members and no female members in the sixteen at Sickert's insistence. Twelve Founder Members of The London Group came from the Camden Town Group, as follows, Walter Bayes (O), Robert Bevan (the first London Group Treasurer 1913-19) (O), Malcom Drummond (O), Harold Gilman (the first London Group President) (O), Charles Ginner (O), Spencer F. Gore (President of the Camden Town Group in 1910 who unfortunately died during the first London Group exhibition in March 1914) (O), C.F. Hamilton (N), Percy Wyndham Lewis (as a Cubist) (O), James Bolivar Manson (the first London Group Secretary) (O), Lucien Pissarro (never exhibited, quickly resigned) (O), William Ratcliffe (N) and Walter Sickert (who resigned immediately over inclusion of 'Futurists') (O). Founder Members from the Camden Town Group circle were Renée Finch (N), Douglas Fox-Pitt, (did not exhibit in first show) (O), Sylvia Gosse (I), A.H. 'Nan' Hudson (O), Thérèse Lessore (married Sickert in 1926) (I) and Walter Taylor (I). The following Founder Members were considered Post-Impressionists and grouped around Roger Fry, Bernard Adeney (N), Frederick Etchells (N), Jessie Etchells (I), Duncan Grant (O), Ethel Sands (O) and Edward Wadsworth (N). Then came the English Cubists (before they became The Vorticists with Wyndham Lewis), David Bomberg (I), Jacob Epstein (O), Henri Gaudier-Brzeska (I) and C.R.W. Nevinson (N). And finally those considered to be 'independents', Henry Lamb (N), John Nash (I), Harold Squire (N) and Harold Sund (sometimes known as Harald, also in the Allied Artist's Association) (N).

As a key to the above, (O) indicates an October 1913 Founder Member, those who were involved in the first meeting, (N) indicates a November 1913 Founder Member, invited to further enlarge the embryonic group whilst (I) indicates 'independent involvement' but a full member by the first exhibition in March 1914.

In May 1914 Lewis took Frederick Etchells, Cuthbert Hamilton and Edward Wadsworth with him and founded the Rebel Arts Centre at 38 Great Ormond Street. Lewis had established the R.A.C. in March 1913 with monies supplied by the painter Kate Lechmere. Lewis wanted the R.A.C. to be in direct competition with Fry's Omega Workshops. Many years later William Roberts wrote of this conflict between Lewis and Fry; "This was not a dispute of two erudites over a subtle point of aesthetics, but a clash between rivals for the profits of the English interior-decorating market. There were lucrative commissions to be had by a skilled manifesto-ist at the head of his own group of abstract artist-decorators: and so we get the abortive Rebel Art Centre". (William Roberts and Vorticism's Year, 1956, published by the William Roberts Society). On June 20th, 1914 the Vorticist Manifesto appeared in the first issue of 'Blast' edited by Wyndham Lewis. Signators of the manifesto were R. Aldington, Arbuthnot, Lawrence Atkinson, Henri Gaudier-Brzeska, Jessica Dismorr, Cuthbert Hamilton, Ezra Pound,

William Roberts, Helen Saunders, Edward Wadsworth and Percy Wyndham Lewis. Gaudier-Brzeska, Hamilton, Wadsworth and Wyndham Lewis were all Founder Members of The London Group in 1913, Roberts was elected in 1914 and Dismorr was to be elected to the Group in 1926.

By the end of the year nine new members were recorded as becoming full members of the The London Group in 1914, Adrian Allinson, Horace Brodzky, Benjamin Coria (Mexican), Stanislawa de Karlowska (married to Robert Bevan and sometimes recorded as a Founder Member as she showed in the first London Group exhibition), Mary Godwin, James Hamilton Hay, Jacob Kramer, Paul Nash and William Roberts.

5 Regent Street
London W1

Number 5 Regent Street was the venue for the first London Group exhibition in March 1914. The Goupil Gallery was located here at that time. Today it is an office block named Charles House and probably not the original building if compared to the older style architecture on the left. The Goupil's exhibition galleries were situated on the first floor. Below is a view looking north up Regent Street towards Piccadilly, where The London Group's 'enemy', the Royal Academy, is located. 5 Regent Street is the first light toned building on the left of Regent Street just beyond the zebra crossing.

1915

The German submarine U20 sinks the Cunard liner Lusitania with the loss of 1,200 lives and the first German bombs fall on London. German and Austrian forces end the Russian occupation of Poland. Italy declares war on Austria. In the UK Prime Minister Asquith forms an all-party coalition. In cinema D.W. Griffith makes "The Birth of a Nation". Einstein formulates his "Theory of General Relativity".

In Russia Malevich and Tatlin show in the "Tramway V" exhibition. Malevich paints "The Red Square" and exhibits "The Black Square" in "The Last Exhibition of Futurist Painting: 0.10", Petrograd (St. Petersburg), 17.12.15 to 17.01.16, generally considered to be the beginnings of Suprematism. In December Malevich publishes "From Cubism to Suprematism: The New Painterly Realism". Gabo makes his first construction. De Chirico paints "Mystery and Melancholy of a Street". Duchamp paints "La Mariée mise à nu".

What was to become the Tate Gallery was "charged to collect historic British and modern foreign art" (Tate Britain time line). The first Vorticist exhibition was held at the **Doré Galleries**, 35 New Bond Street, London opening on the 10th June 1915. Tragically, Henri Gaudier-Brzeska had been killed at the age of 23 leading a charge in France five days earlier. Exhibitors were Jessica Dismorr, Frederick Etchells, Henri Gaudier-Brzeska, William Roberts, Helen Saunders, Edward Wadsworth and Percy Wyndham Lewis. Six additional artists were invited to exhibit; they were Bernard Adeney, Lawrence Atkinson, David Bomberg, Duncan Grant, Jacob Kramer and Christopher Nevinson. Adeney, Gaudier-Brzeska, Kramer, Nevinson, Roberts, Wadsworth and Wyndham Lewis (one of his exhibits was "The Crowd") had all exhibited in the March 1915 London Group exhibition. Frank Rutter organised "Post-Impressionist and Futurist" at the same gallery in October. The **Goupil Gallery** showed work by Cumberland Market Group artists (Gilman, Ginner and Bevan), but this was to be their one and only exhibition. In July, the second and last issue of 'Blast: War Number' edited by Wyndham Lewis was published. David Bomberg joined the Royal Engineers in November whilst Sickert joins the Royal Academy, returns to teaching at the Westminster School of Art and writes for the "Burlington Magazine". The Ben Uri Art Society was established by Lazar Berson in London's East End, "to provide support for the many Jewish artists and craftspeople who were flourishing there in the face of poverty, anti-semitism and isolation from mainstream culture".

London Group President: Harold Gilman (1913)

Two new members were elelcted to The London Group this year, Mark Gertler and

Randolph Schwabe.

"The Second Exhibition of Works by Members of The London Group", The Goupil Gallery, 5 Regent Street, London S.W. March 1915. Again, no specific dates were given. The catalogue to this exhibition achieves the miraculous in that it gives even less information than the first catalogue! "The Works are for sale, and prices may be obtained on application". Was William Marchant making his presence felt? The design and layout of the catalogue was identical to the first, except that the cover was plain white. Harold Gilman was confirmed as President whilst Edward Wadsworth joined him as Honorary Secretary. Spencer F. Gore had died from pneumonia in March 1914 during the Group's first exhibition, whilst Duncan Grant, C.F. Hamilton, H. Lamb, J.B. Manson and Lucien Pissarro resigned as they do not appear in this year's list of Members, thirty-five in total for 1915. The 1915 Hanging Committee was M.C. Drummond, Jacob Epstein, Harold Gilman, Charles Ginner, S. de Karlowska, C.R.W. Nevinson and Edward Wadsworth. There were only ninety oil paintings, drawings and watercolours plus five sculptures this year, hung in the same three galleries. Bomberg, Frederick and Jessie Etchells, Finch, Gertler, Squire and Sund did not exhibit, the remainder were limited to four works each this year. Landscape, still-life and portraiture were most evident in the exhibition but echoes of the War burst into the show with C.R.W. Nevinson's "My arrival at Dunkirk", "Ypres after the Second Bombardment" and "Returning to the Trenches". Gaudier-Brzeska exhibited "A Mitrailleuse in action", a drawing done in the trenches at Craonne, "One of our shells bursting" and two sculptures "Singer" and "Statuette in alabaster". Edward Wadsworth showed two woodcuts in the Small Gallery entitled "Typhoon" and "Harbour of Flushing". The women members of The London Group are well represented in this second exhibition, Mary Godwin showing four works, Sylvia Gosse four, 'Nan' Hudson three, S. de Karlowska four, Thérèse Lessore one and Ethel Sands one whilst Jessie Etchells and Renée Finch did not exhibit. Gilman, Ginner and Bevan exhibited "Miss Ruth Doggett", "Leeds Roofs" and "The Market2 respectively. It was in this exhibition that Wyndham Lewis showed "The Crowd" and "The Workshop" and it was to be the last time that he exhibited in an anuual exhibition with The London Group. It was in this exhibition too that the public were exposed for the first time to the shock of Jacob Epstein's "Rock Drill".

The Tate Archive has a press cutting headed "War as the Futurist sees it" from the March 5th edition of the Daily Graphic illustrating Nevinson's "Returning to the Trenches" and "My arrival at Dunkirk" and also Epstein's "Rock Drill". This fixes a date of around about the 5th March for the opening of the second exhibition, echoing the 5th March 1913 for the first.

Denys Wilcox in "The London Group 1913-39" provides two press reviews (p.8). The first from 'The Connoisseur', Vol. 40, May 1915, p.56, "the works of Mr

Epstein and others of the London Group revealed that the aesthetic tendencies of the most advanced school of modern art are leading us back to the primitive instincts of the savage . . .", and secondly, to quote Wilcox, "The Times review of the exhibition used the headline: 'Junkerism in Art', suggesting that the excesses of modernism were essentially Germanic in character". That review was dated 10th March. Lewis wrote a robust reply to this jingoistic article.

Rupert Lee recollected in 1957, "I remember that at the second exhibition held near the beginning of the war Nevinson was exhibiting because I also remember an awkward happening. Adrian Allinson was a conscientious objector and Marchand,(sic) proprietor of the Gallery in a patriotic rage instructed his doorman to look out for an artist in a big black hat and throw him into the gutter. Allinson stayed away but Nevinson turned up wearing a big black hat and escorting a General. He was thrown into the gutter."

"The Third Exhibition of Works by Members of the London Group", The Goupil Gallery, 5 Regent Street, London S.W., November to December 1915. Eight months later William Marchant and The London Group held their second exhibition of 1915. There were small but dramatic changes in membership since March. Gilman remained as President and Wadsworth as Honorary Secretary. Mark Gertler and Randolph Schwabe had joined the Group and Gaudier-Brzeska had been killed in the War. Only one sculpture was shown in this exhibition, C.R.W. Nevinson's "Une Americaine". Frustratingly there is very little information in this identically formatted catalogue. Only catalogue number, artist's name and title of the work were printed. Seventy-eight oil paintings, watercolours and drawings were exhibited in the three Goupil galleries and members were allowed to show five works each. The Hanging Committee was H. Brodzky, Jacob Epstein, Harold Gilman, Charles Ginner, M. Godwin and Edward Wadsworth. However, a large number of members did not show, Bomberg, Coria, Drummond, Epstein, both Etchells, Finch, Hay, Hudson, Kramer, Lewis, Roberts, Sands, Squire, Sund and Wadsworth all failed to submit for whatever reason but largely to do with involvement in the War. These sixteen non-exhibiting members formed approximately 50% of total membership which stood at thirty-four at this time. The eighteen remaining exhibitors showed seventy-eight paintings, watercolours and drawings in total, again mainly landscape, still-life and portraiture. The titles indicated even less reference to the one year old World War, only Nevinson (the only English Cubist exhibiting) appeared fully involved with "A Deserted Trench", "Bursting Shell" and "La Guerre de Trous". Mark Gertler exhibited "Swing Boats", "Fruit Stall" and "Creation of Eve". Robert Bevan showed "The Corner House" and "Tattersall's". Gilman and Ginner were still painting in Leeds, whilst the Nash brothers were working from nature with Paul showing "Moonrise over Orchard" and John, "Steam Ploughing". Four women exhibited in the third exhibition, Mary

Godwin (5), Sylvia Gosse (5), S. de Karlowska (5) and Thérèse Lessore (5), a healthy twenty works in total. The catalogue in the Tate Archive is heavily annotated in small writing in pencil; whoever was making these observations was obviously paying very close attention to colour and composition. If the placing of crosses next to exhibits indicated a mark of quality, then this particular observer picked out Adrian P. Allinson (2), W. Ratcliffe, Charles Ginner (2), Randolph Schwabe and Mark Gertler (2).

In the March 2009 edition of 'Galleries' Sarah Drury wrote a review of "Robert Bevan and The Cumberland Market Group", an exhibition shown at Southampton Art Gallery and Abbot Hall Art Gallery. She wrote, "Cumberland Market was London's centre for horse feed and building materials after the hay market at Piccadilly closed, and Bevan took rooms there in 1914. The market was already in decline but he found it an ideal spot to observe his favourite subject, the working horse. The only exhibition of the short-lived group consisting of Bevan, Gilman, Ginner and John Nash (later augmented by McKnight Kauffer and Nevinson), took place at the Goupil Gallery in April 1915." This is significant event in that Bevan, Gilman, Ginner, John Nash and Nevinson were all Founder Members of The London Group in 1913 and thus in more than one group. McKnight Kauffer was to be elected to The London Group in 1916 no doubt from the Cumberland Market Group connection. Furthermore, Gilman and Bevan were respectively President and Treasurer of The London Group in 1915. It should also be noted that the Cumberland Market Group exhibition in April followed on immediately after the March London Group exhibition at the Goupil Gallery.

1916

February 21st, the Battle of Verdun in France (Franz Marc lost his life in this battle). In excess of one million soldiers are killed in the Battle of the Somme. The first Zeppelin was shot down over England. In September tanks are used in warfare for the first time. Compulsory Conscription introduced in Britain for the first time. In March, Wyndham Lewis enlists. The Kingdom of Poland is restored by Germany. The 'Mad Monk' Rasputin was murdered by Prince Felix Yusupov. The Bolshevik Revolution began in Russia. In the Easter Rising rebellion in Dublin, Irish republican forces attempt to take power and are brutally put down. The Irish Republic is proclaimed. In the UK in December David Lloyd George (Liberal) becomes Prime Minister (succeeding Asquith) and holds office until 1922. Einstein publishes his General Theory of Relativity. (Special Theory of Relativity published in 1905).

"The Planets" by Gustav Holst is premiered. Nielsen's "inextinguishable" Symphony No 4. James Joyce writes "Portrait of the Artist as a Young Man" and Ezra Pound compiles and publishes "Gaudier-Brzeska: a memoir". Pound continues to support Vorticism in his writings and reviews despite Vorticism's demise. Charlie Chaplin makes "The Vagabond" and "The Pawnshop".

The first public showing of Picasso's "Les Demoiselles d'Avignon" at the Salon d'Antin in wartime **Paris**. It was finally sold to M.J. Doucet in 1923. In **Italy** Boccioni dies and Futurist painters meet Russians Larionov and Goncharova. In **Zurich** Hugo Ball and Tristan Tzara set up the Cabaret Voltaire as a protest against the war and was to evolve, eventually, into Dada. In **London** Wyndham Lewis decorates the "Restaurant de la Tour Eiffel" at 1, Percy Street. Lewis had lived in Paris from 1902 to 1909 when he was in his early twenties. C.R.W. Nevinson holds his first one-man show at the **Leicester Galleries** in September.

London Group President: Harold Gilman (1913)

"The Fourth Exhibition of Works by Members of The London Group", The Goupil Gallery, 5 Regent Street, London S.W., June 1916. The title to this show is slightly misleading in that for the first time non-members were exhibited. Marchant, of the Goupil Gallery, wanted to ensure that his galleries were well filled remembering that half of the Group did not exhibit in the last London Group exhibition. The ten non-member exhibitors were Laurence Atkinson (a signatory of the "Blast" manifesto in 1914), H.W. Bray, Nina Hamnett, E. McKnight Kauffer, T. R. Maynard, J. Moncur, Walter Sickert, C.W. Stock, Hubert Wellington and Ethelbert White. "By 1916 the work of non-members was shown in the annual exhibitions, and it is perhaps the admission of such work which has tended to obscure the basic aims of the London Group. From its beginnings the Society had a revolutionary and anti-academic character which it has been able to retain by the frequent addition of new members whose art has a virile and personal quality." (extract from a Leicester Galleries 1937 London Group catalogue). Phyllis Barron was the only artist elected to The London Group this year shortly before this exhibition. Harold Gilman continued as President whilst C.R.W. Nevinson, replacing Wadsworth, stepped in as Honorary Secretary. Activity within the Group seemed to be at a low ebb. The Hanging Committee for this show was Jacob Epstein, René Finch (sic), D. Fox-Pitt, Harold Gilman, Charles Ginner (conscripted this year), Sylvia Gosse and C.R.W. Nevinson. Ninety paintings, watercolours and drawings were displayed in the Long, Small and Large Galleries of the Goupil Gallery, but only one sculpture was shown, Jacob Epstein's "Torso in Metal from the 'Rock Drill'". Some believe that Epstein cut up his torso as a protest against the butchery and disfigurement of war. Members were allowed to exhibit four pieces and non-members two. Size, media and price were not printed in the catalogue, neither was there an indication of how non-members came to exhibit, be it by invitation, open submission, grape-vine or whatever. Apart from Nevinson the titles of the works did not make reference to World War 1, approaching its second anniversary. Indeed, there were such titles as "Cafe Royal at the hour of the Aperitif" (Allinson), "Petunias" (Godwin), "Le Chapeau Haute Forme" (Gosse), "Under the Pier" (Fox-Pitt), "Landscape with Nymph" (P. Nash) and "Picnic on Hampstead Heath" (Finch). There is definitely a feeling of denial leafing through this catalogue. The influence and participation of the Vorticists within The London Group had dissipated even though Wyndham Lewis is still recorded as a member. A new direction was signalled with the presence of Sickert and Gertler.

"The Fifth Exhibition of Works by Members of The London Group", 23rd November to 14th December 1916 (these were the first specific dates given in a catalogue), The Goupil Gallery, 5 Regent Street, London S.W. Seventeen non-members exhibited in this "Members of The London Group" exhibition, the second of 1916. Non-members exhibiting were Laurence Atkinson (2), Keith Baines (2), C. Billing (2), E.M. O'Rourke Dickey (2), R. Doggett (1), N. Hamnett (2), Gladys Hynes (2), R. McIntyre (2), Bernard Meninsky (2), Malcolm Milne (2), J. Moncur (1), C.E. Nelson (2), F.J. Porter (2), H. Saunders (2), Matthew Smith (2), C.W. Stock (2) and H. Wellington (1). The catalogue records Harold Gilman as President, C.R.W. Nevinson as Honorary Secretary and Walter Taylor as Honorary Treasurer. Members were as follows, W.B. Adeney (0), A.P. Allinson (0), Phyllis Baron (0 and newly elected), R.P. Bevan (5), D. Bomberg (0), H. Brodzky (0), B. Coria (5), M.C. Drummond (0), Jacob Epstein (0), Frederick Etchells (0), Jesie Etchells (0), Renee Finch (0), D. Fox-Pitt (2), Mark Gertler (0), Harold Gilman (5), Charles Ginner

(5), M. Godwin (4), Sylvia Gosse (4), Hamilton Hay (5, recently deceased), A.H. Hudson (2), S. de Karlowska (5), E. McKnight Kauffer (5, elected after the Fourth Exhibition), J. Kramer (1), Thérèse Lessore (5), Wyndham Lewis (0), John Nash (4), Paul Nash (5), C.R.W. Nevinson (5), W. Ratcliffe (4), W. Roberts (0), Ethel Sands (5), R. Schwabe (5), W. Sickert (4, re-elected this year), Harold Squire (0), Harold Sund (0), Walter Taylor (3), Edward Wadsworth (0) and Ethelbert White (0, elected after the Fourth Exhibition). The Hanging Committee was D. Fox-Pitt, Mark Gertler (did not exhibit), Harold Gilman, Charles Ginner, C.R.W. Nevinson, W. Sickert (always in the background but formally elected this year and immediately brought into 'officership') and Walter Taylor. Seventeen Members of The London Group did not submit work for exhibition. Seventeen exhibiting non-members were a direct replacement of seventeen non-exhibiting elected members. It would appear that with almost half of the elected members of The London Group not showing (seventeen out of thirty-eight), non-member exhibitors were keeping the Group going during the war period. One hundred and twenty-two oil paintings, watercolours and drawings were shown in the Goupil's three galleries, but this year for the first time in The London Group's short history, no sculpture was exhibited. No titles appear to make any reference to the ongoing war at all. Even Nevinson was now painting "A Music Hall", "From an Office Window" and "A Landscape in Provence". Bland titles like "Landscape", "Flowers", "Portrait" and "Study" abound although Sylvia Gosse's "Bachelor's Buttons" seems quite evocative.

This was to be the last of The London Group exhibitions at The Goupil Gallery. Next year the Group was to move north east to Tottenham Court Road. William Marchant, owner of the Goupil Gallery, held strong views against conscientious objectors and pacifists as feeling in the country as a whole began to harden following the bloody battles of the Somme. Both Allinson and Gertler were conscientious objectors and Marchant would not offer space in his gallery to any group which supported such ideals. The Group held a special meeting to discuss this crisis and voted to look for other premises rather than give in to Marchant's unacceptable demands. Ambrose Heal offered the Mansard Gallery, a new gallery at Heals in Tottenham Court Road, to The London Group and a sympathetic and functional space was available for the forseeable future.

1917

Between July and November the British Expeditionary Force loses 300,000 men, the Germans lose 200,000. Fronts in Flanders and at Passchendaele. László Moholy-Nagy is wounded at the front. In April the United States enters the First World War. In London 162 are killed in a German bombing raid. In February in Petrograd the Russian Revolution begins. In March, the Republic is established. In April and May Lenin, Trotsky and other Bolshevick leaders return. The Winter Palace is stormed in October. October 26th, the revolutionary Council of People's Commissars takes power in Petrograd. In November the new Russian government offers Germany an armistice which is concluded in December. In December the Russian Civil War begins with the revolt of the Don Cossacks and lasts for approximately four years.

In Paris Diaghilev stages Satie and Cocteau's "Parade" with designs by Picasso. Duchamp signs a urinal 'R. Mutt' and entitles it "Fountain". Picabia launches "391". Ezra Pound and the collector John Quinn organise an exhibition of the Vorticists at the Penguin Club, New York. In Italy De Chirico and Carrà introduce Metaphysical painting. In Leiden Mondrian and Theo van Doesburg found "De Stijl".

The remaining Vorticists in The London Group resign when Roger Fry is elected. Leonard and Virginia Wolf found the Hogarth Press. Lewis serves in a siege battery on the Western Front. Epstein enlists in the Royal Fusiliers. (He had had a one-man exhibition at the Leicester Galleries in February). The writer and critic T.E. Hulme is killed by a German shell. Bomberg and Lewis become war artists and transfer to a Canadian regiment. The Canadian Government appoint Charles Ginner as an official war artist. English warships are painted in dazzle camouflage under the supervision of Lieutenant Wadsworth of the Royal Navy Volunteer Reserve. Paul Nash shows works from the Ypres Salient at the **Goupil Gallery**.

London Group President: Harold Gilman (1913)

"Sixth Exhibition, London Group", The Mansard Gallery, Messrs. Heal & Son, 196 Tottenham Court Road, W., 26th April to 26th May 1917. This was the first exhibition at the Mansard Gallery in Heals, Tottenham Court Road. There is no indication of this new move in the catalogue to the exhibition which is a very minimal A6 publication in coarse yellow paper. Harold Gilman was recorded as President with E. McKnight Kauffer as the Honorary Secretary and Walter Taylor as the Honorary Treasurer. Edward McKnight Kauffer was an American émigré who came to London from Paris on the outbreak of the First World War. Today he is well known for his posters, especially those for the London Underground and Shell. Kauffer was elected as a figurative painter but his design skills were put to good use by the Group, designing posters and flyers for their exhibitions. He resigned from The London Group in 1919 over their policy to only exhibit "non-commissioned art". The Hanging Committee for this first exhibition of the year were Jacob Epstein (non-exhibitor), D. Fox-Pitt, Mark Gertler, Harold Gilman, Charles Ginner, E. McKnight Kauffer, C.R.W. Nevinson, R. Schwabe, W. Sickert (who only exhibited one work, "Suspense") and Walter Taylor. If the list at the front of the catalogue is a full list of members then there were thirty-seven of them at this time. There were also recorded five 'Lay Members' whose role was not recorded. They were The Hon. Evan Morgan, M.H. Sands, Herbert Fletcher, Miss R. Fagelund and Karl Knudsen. There were one hundred and fifteen works exhibited and members were allowed five works each whilst non-members, only two. Twenty-three members exhibited and twelve non-members including Jean Fautrier, Ruth Doggett, Roger Fry, Nina Hamnett, Bernard Meninsky, C.W. Stock, F.J. Porter and Keith Baynes. There appeared to be no sculpture exhibited in the three rooms, only titles are given in the catalogue, no sizes or media. In one of the two catalogues held in the Tate Archive there are tiny pencil notes in the margin. They appear to be prices and if so C.R.W Nevinson's "White Horses" could be bought for £30, Robert Bevan's "House at Hampstead" for £50 or Charles Ginner's "Oxted, Surrey" for £25. And then there was Mark Gertler's "Merry-go-round" for £200. Harold Gilman's "Portrait of Mrs Mounter" was also shown. The titles indicate mainly landscape, still-life and portraiture and the only title to hint at the country being at war was Sylvia Gosse's "A Hero and Heroine of England". The eight page catalogue certainly gives the air of austerity and lack of resources during the First World War.

There was extensive press coverage of this exhibition. The Tate Archive contains nineteen reviews of this show, most of them favourable, but the usual 'wild eccentrics' and 'children with paint boxes' descriptions still appear. The 'Sunday Times' wrote, "It is one of the most stimulating shows this progressive society has yet organized". Under the headline, "Colour gone mad", the 'Star' reviewer wrote, "There can be no finer tonic... no better pick-me-up than a walk round this collection. Your tired feeling will give place to a strong desire to man-handle some of the artists; the spots before your eyes will turn to whirling stars and prismatic parallelograms". Pride of place must go to the 'Evening News' whose review headline was "The man who has painted a noise". The man in question was Mark Gertler and his picture, "The Merry-Go-Round". "But the picture is not a picture; it is a shriek, a groan, a hoot, a blare, a tempest of wild rending and most discordant noise". Denys Wilcox writes, "The London Group was the only exhibiting society during the period that was prepared to show challenging and politically 'dangerous' work." (The London Group 1913-1939, p.12). Wilcox also discovered a letter from St John Hutchinson, a lawyer who acted for artists and writers, to Gertler expressing his "concerns about the public exhibition of the picture at such a sensitive time" and that its exhibition might "drive them (critics) to write all sorts of rubbish about German art and German artists in their papers and may raise the question acutely and publicly as to your position."

"Seventh Exhibition, London Group", The Mansard Gallery, Heal and Son,196 Tottenham Court Road. 2nd November to 29th November 1917. A very similar catalogue to the earlier exhibition in 1917 except blue paper has taken the place of yellow. Officers remain the same but Roger Fry and Nina Hamnett were elected as members this year. The Hanging Committee for this second exhibition of the year consisted of R.P. Bevan, Roger Fry (only recently elected), D. Fox-Pitt, Harold Gilman, S. de Karlowska, E. McKnight Kauffer, Thérèse Lessore, R. Schwabe and Walter Taylor, two out of the nine being women. Two new Lay Members join the others, Mrs F.E. Coburn and Mrs. H.W. Nevinson. In the exhibition itself there were six non-members exhibiting, Lawrence Atkinson, Clara Billing, Keith Baynes, Neville Lewis, Raymond Mc.Intyre and Bernard Meninsky. One hundred and five exhibits were listed, none, apparently, being sculptures. C.R.W. Nevinson's title caught the eye, "When Men were free" accompanying two paintings of France during his war service. Other works of note included Paul Nash's "Cherry Orchard" and Charles Ginner's "Hospital Ward". Six women had work shown in this exhibition, Clara Billing (2), Mary Godwin (5), Sylvia Gosse (5), Nina Hamnett(5), S. de Karlowska (2), Thérèse Lessore (4) and Ethel Sands (4). Again no sizes, prices or media were printed in the catalogue and titles were much the same, landscape, still life and portraiture, although there were a number of drawings hung in the Water Colour Room. On the first page of the catalogue membership of the group is recorded. Both Roger Fry and Wyndham-Lewis appear on the same page as members of The London Group, and were to be so recorded until the last time in the May 1919 catalogue.

Frank Rutter of the 'Sunday Times' was unimpressed by the seventh exhibition. On the 11th November he wrote, "To say that the seventh exhibition of the London Group... is not so good as most of the previous exhibitions of this society is to state a truth which can hardly be denied. Even making allowance for the fact that the Wyndham Lewis section and many other of the most talented of the younger men are now either in the Army or wholly absorbed in war work, the exhibition might have been very much better than it is.... For a progressive body, the London Group shows little progress this autumn." P.G. Konody of 'The Observer' wrote, "Compared with the artistic revolutionaries collected under Mr. Roger Fry's banner, the are (sic) rebels of the London Group... must strike one as being singularly normal and moderate. This is the most remarkable as the two groups overlap. Somehow the painters belonging to both groups seem to reserve their saner efforts for the London Group exhibition." The 'Times' of 10th November was of the same opinion. "In the present Exhibition of the London Group,... the high spirits and recklessness of the new movements in art seem to have died away: and instead there is a rather arid aesthetic Puritanism."

Heals
Tottenham Court Road
London W1

The Mansard Gallery was a smallish exhibition space made up of two rooms,
The Mansard Gallery and the Water Colour Gallery. The Group hung approximately
one hundred works in their exhibitions here with very little sculpture, perhaps
because the galleries were on the upper floors and had to be reached by stairs or
lift. Tottenham Court Road is on the eastern edges of Fitzrovia, close to the Omega
Workshops and Camden Town in the North. It is worth noting that Heal's was also a
furniture and furnishings store selling quality, well designed and colourful items.

1918

First World War hostilities come to an end at 11 a.m. on the 11th November, Armistice Day. A revolt in Germany, beginning in the Navy, forces Kaiser Wilhelm II to abdicate and he is harboured by the Dutch. Germany becomes a republic. Wilfred Owen, the War Poet, is killed one week before the end of the War. Propertied women over 30 voted for the first time in a UK General Election following the introduction of the Representation of the People Act. The election results in a coalition government of Conservatives led by Bonar Law and Liberals led by Lloyd George. The Labour Party led by Adamson receives the second highest number of votes but not enough seats to form a government. The Royal Air Force is established. In October the Spanish Flu outbreak began which killed 50 million people worldwide and was said to have begun on the French battlefields. Over 3,000 Londoners are killed each week by the 'flu.

In France Ozenfant and Le Corbusier issue the Purist manifesto, "Après le Cubisme". In Germany, Richard Huelsenbeck writes the "Dadaistsiches Manifest" supported by Dadaists in Berlin and Zurich. In Italy, Morandi begins his 'metaphysical period'. In Russia Tatlin heads the Visual Arts Section of the Commissariat of Enlightenment, Marc Chagall is appointed Vitebsk Region Commissar of Arts whilst Prokofiev emigrates to the USA. Lucien Pissarro and his brother form the Monarro Group to support the ideals of Impressionism, especially Monet and their father Camille Pissarro (MONet, pisARRO) against the onslaught of the Vorticists and Cubists. J. B. Manson was the secretary in England whilst Theo van Ryselburghe was the Paris agent. The Monarro group lasted three years.

A Henri Gaudier-Brzeska Memorial Exhibition is held at the **Leicester Galleries** between May and June, organised in the previous three years by his partner Sophie Brzeska. Ezra Pound wrote a preface to the catalogue. Frederick Etchells, Nevinson, Roberts and Wadsworth receive painting commissions from the Canadian War Memorials Fund.

London Group: President: Harold Gilman (1913)

In the catalogue introductions Edward McKnight Kauffer was recorded as being Honorary Secretary and Walter Taylor as the Treasurer. Emil Davies Esq. joined the continuing Lay Members. No new full members were recorded as being elected to the Group this year.

"Eighth Exhibition, London Group", Mansard Gallery, Heal and Son, 196 Tottenham Court Road, W.C., 2nd May to 1st June 1918. A flyer for the exhibition designed by McKnight Kauffer gives the dates as May 2nd to June 2nd, one day longer.

Membership was still at thirty-eight, no change since the Seventh Exhibition. The Hanging Committee for this exhibition was R.P. Bevan, Roger Fry, D. Fox-Pitt, Harold Gilman, S. de Karlowska, E. McKnight Kauffer, Thérèse Lessore, R. Schwabe and Walter Taylor. They selected up to two works each from fifteen non-members which this year included Sidney and Richard Carline, F.J. Porter, Belle Cramer, Edward Wolfe, Vanessa Bell, Cicely Stock and E.M. O'R. Dickey. There were ninety-five works shown in two rooms. The spartan catalogue gave no sizes, media or prices and the titles again described portraits, flower studies, landscapes and still lifes. Charles Ginner showed five cityscapes of Marseilles, no doubt there as part of his war duties, C.R.W. Nevinson was at Boulogne and Zeebrugge (he was an ambulance driver during the war) whilst the President Harold Gilman exhibited "Gas Light Portrait" and committee member Roger Fry submitted "Self Portrait".

The October 2012 issue of 'The Burlington Magazine' has a well-researched and extremely detailed account, written by John Rolfe, of Harold Gilman's last months. Gilman was to succumb to the Spanish 'flu on the 12th February 1919, but for the previous nine months he had been largely out of the country. The Canadian War Memorials scheme had commissioned Gilman to visit Halifax, Nova Scotia to paint a picture of the harbour, an important war facility for the embarkation of Canadian troops. Gilman sailed from Liverpool bound for New York on 6th May, a few days after the opening of the Eighth Exhibition. Records show that he returned via Montreal and was back in London on the 25th September, a few weeks before the opening of the Ninth Exhibition. In that time Gilman had been working in Halifax making drawings, preparatory sketches and a huge oil sketch, now in Vancouver. (Rolfe describes numerous difficulties faced by Gilman to undertake these preparations, including being challenged as a spy by the Chief of Police). On the 6th December 1917 a huge explosion had devastated Halifax harbour. A collision between two cargo ships, one laden with wartime explosives, had caused 'the most terrible man-made accident to have occurred in Canada' killing over 2,000 people. The resulting finished work was Gilman's largest, and some say his best, canvas. "Halifax Harbour at sunset" was 198 by 335.8 cms, completed in London and first exhibited at the Canadian War Memorials Exhibition at Burlington House on the 4th January 1919 (now in the National Gallery of Canada, Ottawa). 'The Burlington Magazine' of February 1919 declared Gilman's painting as being 'above any of the other landscapes exhibited'. Six weeks later Harold Gilman was dead. Later in the year Wyndham Lewis and Louis Fergusson wrote "An Appreciation" for the ex-London Group President. The affable and much respected Gilman was 'the glue' holding the diverse elements of The London Group together and his absence for much of 1918 and his untimely death could account for part of the reason for the Vorticists' final withdrawal from the Group.

"Ninth Exhibition of The London Group", Mansard Gallery, Heal and Son,

196 Tottenham Court Road W.C., 1st November to 29th November 1918. The group holds a second exhibition six months after the last. Harold Gilman and E. McKnight Kauffer remain in post but Robert Bevan (from a wealthy banking family) takes over as Treasurer. Kauffer designed the poster to this exhibition, an example of which is held in the V&A archive. No change in membership was recorded in the catalogue to this exhibition. A full list of members was printed in each of this 'string' of catalogues which is most useful in terms of knowing who joined and who left at regular six-monthly periods. The Hanging Committee for this second exhibition of the year was R.P. Bevan, D. Fox-Pitt, Harold Gilman, Nina Hamnett, S. de Karlowska, E. McKnight Kauffer, and R. Schwabe. They selected nine non-members with some new faces exhibiting including Elizabeth Bashford, Victor Lorien and F. (Florence) Unwin. In total ninety-one works were exhibited. The catalogue held in the Tate Archive is in a very fragile condition but has been fixed to archive paper. Consequently exhibits numbers 65 to 91 have a title but the artist has been lost. However, the subject matter remains unchanged with outdoor and domestic subject matter. It is frustrating not to have illustrations in the catalogue to actually see what kind of work was supported by The London Group at this time. There seems to be little reference to the First World War. Titles such as "Teapot" by Mark Gertler, "A Posy" by Ethel Sands, "Willow Trees" by Roger Fry and "The Grand Piano" by W. Ratcliffe predominated.

Ezra Pound writing in 'The New Age' continued his invective against Bloomsbury, "Very much the same thing and same group as last year, all a year older, some a year wiser."

1919

The League of Nations is founded. The German High Fleet scuppers itself in Scapa Flow. The 'Weimar Republic' is formed in Germany, based on a democratic constitution. In Italy the Fascist Party is formed by Benito Mussolini. Alcock and Brown complete the first non-stop flight across the Atlantic. British dirigible R34 flies from England to New York and back in July. T. S. Eliot begins writing his poem 'The Wasteland' to be published in 1921. Elgar composes his Cello Concerto Op.85.

In Moscow young revolutionary 'street' artists form OBMOKhU. Tatlin begins work on the Monument to the Third International. In Vitebsk, Malevich establishes UNIVOS (Affirmers of the New Art) replacing Marc Chagall, and publishes "On New Systems in Art". The famous German Expressionist film "The Cabinet of Doctor Caligari" is made by Robert Wiene. In Germany, Kurt Schwitters invents the 'Merz' collage, Max Ernst and Hans Arp form Cologne Dada, Archipenko's studio opens in Berlin and Walter Gropius founds the Bauhaus School in Weimar. In Italy there is the first de Chirico retrospective.

Wyndham Lewis exhibits at the **Goupil Gallery** in February, his first one-man show. The planned publication of "Blast" number 3 is abandoned. Harold Gilman, The London Group's first President, dies in February of influenza in the Spanish 'flu epidemic which kills millions world-wide. Wyndham Lewis returns from his duties as a war artist with the Canadian Corps. In October at **The Leicester Galleries** there was a "Memorial Exhibition of works by the late Harold Gilman (President of The London Group)". Charles Ginner wrote an appreciation. **The Adelphi Gallery**, drawings and woodcuts from Edward Wadsworth. **The Omega Workshops** close. At thirty-eight years old Picasso visits London for the first time to design costumes and sets for "The Three Cornered Hat" performed by Diaghilev's Ballets Russes. The premier was on 22nd July at the Alhambra, Leicester Square. Picasso stayed at the Savoy for ten weeks and worked from a studio in Floral Street, Covent Garden. More than two hundred British pictures are transferred from the National Gallery to the National Gallery, Millbank (Tate Britain).

Exhibition catalogues for this year record no President due to the death of the incumbent Harold Gilman

E. McKnight Kauffer remained in post as Honorary Secretary and Robert Bevan as Treasurer. Some sources have Bevan as President, but this is not supported by catalogue evidence.

"Tenth Exhibition of the London Group", Mansard Gallery, Heal and Son,

196 Tottenham Court Road. 12th April to 17th May 1919. Not surprisingly the first three pages of a ten page A5 sized catalogue were devoted to an Obituary for Harold Gilman written by his colleague Charles Ginner. Here is a short excerpt: "I have never met a man so full of optimism or one who had so great a belief in the final triumph of good painting over bad. Having many admirers but few purchasers of his works, living for many years in the back streets of Camden Town, working under many difficulties, having to waste much time in facing the problem of living, even in these years his optimism never failed, and in spite of seeing art besieged by the insincere and the money makers, he never lost faith in the ultimate triumph of good and sincere art. In his work he never concede an inch of the ground of what he considered right in his art, in pandering to any kind of fashionable taste of the day which might have helped his pecuniary situation. His pictures appeal by their richness of colour, by the feeling they express of his fine observation and by his sincerity.

His friends have lost in him, a man of extraordinary charm, a delightful companion with a keen sense of humour; art has lost by his death many beautiful pictures and much ripeness of knowledge which he would always have been ready to impart. He was one of the most important English painters of our generation."

Membership this year was recorded as being thirty-nine. The Hanging Committee, and thus active and influential within the group, were W.B. Adeney, R.P. Bevan, Roger Fry, E. McKnight Kauffer (who also designed the poster), Thérèse Lessore, John Nash and Paul Nash. The number of Lay Members remained at eight. Twelve non-members were selected for exhibition and, tellingly, included Vanessa Bell, Rupert Lee, Elliot (sic) Seabrooke and Walter Sickert. This first exhibition of 1919 was bigger than previous events with one hundred and eight exhibits displayed in two rooms, the "Mansard Gallery" and the "Water Colour Room". Titles seem to indicate all paintings and no sculpture. Indeed, a quick look at the membership list records Jacob Epstein as the only sculptor member. Curiously, now the war had ended there were more paintings with war as their subject matter in paintings by Roger Fry, D. Fox-Pitt, Rupert Lee, Charles Ginner and E.M. O'R. Dickey.

This exhibition was pivotal to the history of The London Group. The President had died leaving a vacancy for an influential post within the Group's structure (Gilman's "Portrait – Mrs. Mounter" was exhibited here posthumously). The affable and diplomatic Gilman had held the disparate elements of The London Group together during his Presidency. His death led to a crumbling of a number of loose associations which, together, was The London Group at this time. With the election of Bernard Meninsky, the re-election of Duncan Grant to full membership and the selection of Vanessa Bell as a Non-Member exhibitor the Fry/Bloomsbury axis was gaining momentum within the Group. Walter Sickert exhibited "The Future" and "The Past". This was also the last exhibition where Wyndham-Lewis, Edward Wadsworth, William

Roberts and Frederick Etchells were listed as being London Group members. None of these four exhibited work in this exhibition. Lewis, Wadsworth and Roberts last exhibited with The London Group in March 1915 and Frederick Etchells in March 1914. They were heavily involved with the alternative radical movements of English Cubism/Vorticism and the publication of the magazine "Blast" and Lewis in particular had fallen out with Fry and the Omega Workshop over the Daily Mail interior design issue. Two artists chosen as non-member exhibitors in this exhibition were significant for the future direction of The London Group. Rupert Lee and Elliott Seabrooke were to be Presidents from 1926-36 and 1943-48 respectively. Lee was to turn away from painting in favour of making sculpture and the ground breaking 1930 London Group outdoor sculpture exhibition on the roof of Selfridges was very much his doing. There was certainly a feeling of fresh winds of change blowing through The London Group following the First World War.

"Eleventh Exhibition of The London Group", The Mansard Gallery, Heal & Son Ltd., 196 Tottenham Court Road, (The titles and places of these exhibitions are as printed in the exhibition catalogues), 1st November to 29th November 1919. Only R. Bevan was recorded as an officer (Treasurer) at the head of a single sheet catalogue. The Working Committee was R.P. Bevan, D. Fox-Pitt, M. Godwin, Sylvia Gosse, C.R.W. Nevinson and R. Schwabe from a total of thirty-seven members. There had been some membership changes since the last exhibition in May. Edward McKnight Kauffer (who had been the Honorary Secretary) had resigned. Others not listed were Charles Ginner (although he continues to exhibit with the Group through the inter-war years), Wyndham-Lewis, William Roberts, Edward Wadsworth and Frederick Etchells. Lewis only ever exhibited in two London Group exhibitions (March 1914 and March 1915) and in the 1928 Retrospective and Wadsworth has an identical record. Frederick Etchells only showed in the March 1914 first exhibition and the 1928 Retrospective whilst Roberts showed in 1915, 1922, 1925, 1926, the Retrospective, 1937 and 1938 pre Second World War. Walter Sickert appears again on the list as a full member having been first elected in 1916, along with new members Vanessa Bell, Bernard Meninsky, Keith Baynes and Boris Anrep. This was a large exhibition of one hundred and twenty-nine works, much more than previous years. Thirteen non-members exhibited up to two works each, (members were entitled to show five each), amongst them being E.M. O'R. Dickey, Rupert Lee, F.J. Porter, Mathew (sic) Smith, Cicely Stock and E. Wolfe. All of these artists were destined to be voted into the Group as full members, previous selection being a condition of London Group membership. The titles listed in this catalogue were predictable and unchanging, "Portrait", "Landscape", "Interior", "Study", "Still Life", "Flowers", "Trees". By contrast there was "The Hunger Marcher" from David Bomberg and circus themes from Mark Gertler and Boris Anrep. Exhibit number 129 (the last!) was "Brown Bear" (sculpture) by Rupert Lee, the first three-dimensional object in a London Group exhibition for a while. This was not a large sculpture. Denys J. Wilcox in his book "Rupert Lee: Painter, Sculptor and Printmaker" gives "Bear" 1918 as being 7.5 x 13.5 cms in glazed pottery. Sylvia Gosse exhibited a number of etching and lithographic prints. The catalogue was a curious construction of two folded sheets of cheap, beige paper folded A5. Given that there were so many designers in the Group (McKnight Kauffer was Honoraray Secretary), or at least known to group members, the quality of these catalogues was disappointing.

The art critic 'J.B.M.' (J. B. Manson?) headlined the eleventh exhibition in the Daily Herald's 10th November edition as "Monkeying with Art, Dull Eccentricities of London Group's Exhibition." J.B.M. continues, "It is dull because monkey tricks and the desire of smart young men to be original at all costs are fatiguing after much repetition… Most of the exhibitors have invented a personal convention, which is applied with tiresome reiteration. Observation and perception have disappeared . . ." The critic thought Miss S. de Karlowka's portrait of 'Miss N.' was the best picture, "It would be more difficult to say what is the worst. Probably it is 'Anger' (115), by Mr. R.A. Wilson, an imitator of Mr. Wyndham Lewis; or else it is one of Mr. Gertler's exceedingly coarse and clumsy productions… There is little to be hoped for from Mr. Bomberg; one can forgive him for cultivating eccentricity, but one cannot excuse his extreme dullness. His skeleton 'Barges' (31) is really too silly." Others lashed by the pen were Roger Fry, Mr. Meninsky, Mr. F.J. Porter and Mr. W. Ratcliffe. Mr. Matthew Smith, Miss Ethel Sands, Mr. Walter Taylor and Mr. Fox-Pitt formed "a quiet oasis in this neurotic and turgid medley."

The 1920's

Dada was born in Zurich in 1916 with Jean Arp, Hugo Ball and Tristan Tzara founding the Cabaret Voltaire. The only issue of the review 'Cabaret Voltaire' contained contributions from Apollinaire, Arp, Cendrars, Huelsenbeck, Kandinsky, Modigliani, Picasso and Tzara. Picabia also published the first issue of '391'. Dada was a global movement with Duchamp and Man Ray in New York, Max Ernst in Paris, the Berlin Dadaists in Berlin, Schwitters in Hanover and significant activity in Rome and Weimar. By 1924 the movement had largely petered out, marked by the last publication of Picabia's '391' in that year.

Surrealism's main period of activity was between 1924 and 1939. Notable surrealists were André Breton, Luis Buñuel, Salvador Dali, Max Ernst, Alberto Giacometti, René Magritte, André Masson, Joan Miró, Man Ray and Yves Tanguy. The publication associated with Surrealism was "La Révolution surréaliste", publishing several issues. Articles included "Is suicide a solution" and suggestions to the Pope, the Dalai Lama and heads of mental institutions. Its final issue in 1929 contained the "Second Surrealist Manifesto". Freud's "Interpretation of Dreams" had been transalted into English in 1913 and Paul Nash was much influenced by Freud's theory of the 'uncanny' (1919).

Abstraction and Constructivism often characterised by the use of flat planes and pure colour. Russian Constructivism ('Suprematism') featured Kasimir Malevich, Vladimir Tatlin and Alexander Rodchenko. Dutch abstraction under the umbrella titles of 'Neo-Plasticism' and 'De Stijl' involved Piet Mondrian, Theo van Doesburg, Bart van der Leck and Georges Vantongerloo. Wassily Kandinsky and Paul Klee were pursuing their own individual paths within abstraction. Many artists were also making constructions, sculptures and assemblages including Tatlin, Constantin Brancusi, Alberto Giacometti, Joan Miró, Anton Pevsner, Picasso, Kurt Schwitters, Naum Gabo and Laszlo Moholy-Nagy.

Neue Sachlichkeit (New Objectivity) in Germany sort to highlight social inequalities in this inter-war period. Artists connected to this movement were George Grosz, Otto Dix, Max Beckmann and Christian Schad. There was a return to realism and classicism in other countries, Carlo Carrà and Giorgio de Chirico in Italy for example. Other notable individuals working in a figurative mode in this decade were Balthus, Edward Hopper, Alberto Giacometti, Matisse and Picasso.

Architecture responded to these new movements and to new materials available for construction, especially steel, glass and concrete. Working throughout the decade were Le Corbusier, Walter Gropius, Ludwig Mies van der Rohe, Alvar Aalt, Frank Lloyd Wright and Richard Buckminster Fuller.

The medium of **film** became very popular as a form of entertainment and many old music halls were adapted to show film. This was the age of Hollywood, Chaplin and Keaton.

Tate Modern Timeline from 1920-1930 Constructivism continued through into the 1920s. The Mexican Muralists linking Diego Rivera, José Clemente Orozco and David Alforo Siqueiros. New Objectivity with George Grosz, Otto Dix, Max Beckmann, Christian Schad and Albert Renger-Patesch. A huge grouping of Surrealists including André Breton, Man Ray, Joan Miró, Salvador Dalí, André Masson, Max Ernst, Yves Tanguy, Jean Arp, Meret Oppenheim, Dorothea Tanning, Wilfredo Lam, Alexander Calder, Hans Bellmer, Robert Matta, René Magritte, Leonor Fime (?), Leonora Carrington, Paul Delvaux and Pierre Roy.

Individuals Raoul Dufy, August Sander, Amédée Ozenfant, Walter Ruttmann, Brassaï and Tina Modotti.

1920

The Treaty of Versaille brings a formal end to the First World War. The Society of Nations was established - signed on the 4th June, Hungary loses 2/3 of its territory and 60% of its population. The Russian economy collapses resulting in famine, but the Civil War in Russia comes to an end when the Bolsheviks defeat the Whites in the Crimea. A right wing coup, the "Kapp Putsch" attempts to overthrow the new democracy in Germany.

Erwin Piscator forms the Proletarisches Theater in Berlin, including Berlin Dadaists. Josef Albers joins the Bauhaus as a student aged 32. In Russia Kandinsky, Talin, Punin and Malevich continue to hold office in the new Sate art systems. In Moscow VKhUTEMAS (Higher State Artistic and Technical Workshops) is established merging existing Free Art Studios. The state sponsored research institute INKhUK (Institute of Artistic Culture) is set up for the interchange of ideas between painters, sculptors, architects and theorists, continuing until 1924. In November Tatlin unveils his model for the "Monument to the Third International" in St Petersburg. Elsewhere, Gabo and Pevsner publish "Realist Manifesto" and Modigliani dies in France. Puccini starts work on his final unfinished opera "Turandot". First commercial broadcasting in Pittsburg, Pennsylvania.

In March and April at the Mansard Gallery Lewis organises **"Exhibition of Group X"**. Seen as the "swansong" of the Vorticist movement, exhibitors included Jessica Dismorr, Frank Dobson, Frederick Etchells, Charles Ginner, Cuthbert Hamilton, Edward McKnight Kauffer, Percy Wyndham Lewis, William Roberts and Edward Wadsworth. This was an attempt to revive the public's interest in Vorticism but came to nothing. In a catalogue to a Tate exhibition in 1956 Lewis wrote, "Vorticism, in fact, was what I, personally, did, and said, at a certain period" which solicited a huge outcry from surviving Vorticists.

The Seven and Five Society hold their first exhibition at Walker's Gallery in Bond Street, London.

Today's Tate Britain was formally designated **"The National Gallery, Millbank"**.

London Group President (acting): Robert Bevan (1913)

At the head of each of the two catalogues for this year only D. Fox-Pitt as Honorary Treasurer is recorded as an officer and Bernadette Murphy as Secretary.

This year saw a large intake of new members throughout the year: E.M. O'Rourke Dickey, Ruth Doggett, Frederick Porter, Elliott Seabrooke, Matthew Smith and Cicely Stock.

"Twelfth Exhibition of The London Group", The Mansard Gallery, Heal & Sons Ltd., 196 Tottenham Court Road, W.C., 10th May to 5th June 1920. At the beginning of a new decade it is worth recording in full the Membership List printed in this catalogue. Members were W.B. Adeney, Boris Aurep (sic), A.P. Allinson, Phyllis Barron, Keith Baynes, Vanessa Bell, R.P. Bevan, D. Bomberg, B. Coria, E.M. O'R. Dickey, M.C. Drummond, Jacob Epstein, Jessie Etchells, Roger Fry, D. Fox-Pitt, Mark Gertler, Mary Godwin, Sylvia Gosse, Duncan Grant, Nina Hamnett, A.H. Hudson, S. de Karlowska, Jacob Kramer, Bernard Meninsky, John Nash, Paul Nash, C.R.W. Nevinson, F.R. Porter, W. Ratcliffe, Ethel Sands, Randolph Schwabe, Walter Taylor and Ethelbert White. There were only ten women out of thirty-four members and only one sculptor, Jacob Epstein. E.M. O'R. Dickey and F.R. Porter had already been elected before this exhibition, whilst removed from the last exhibition's members list were H. Brodzky, Renée Finch, Walter Sickert, Harold Squire and Harold Sund. Brodzky, however, exhibited with the Group between 1925 and 1932, Finch only exhibited twice in March 1914 and June 1916, Squire only March 1914 and the 1928 Retrospective (he showed mainly with the NEAC) and Sund only once in March 1914. The Hanging Committee for this exhibition was not indicated in the catalogue but seven non-members were shown, D. Brett, Ruth Doggett, C. Gordon, S.E. Greenwood, Elliot (sic) Seabrooke, Matthew Smith and H. Wellington. There were one hundred and thirteen exhibits of mainly painting but also wood engravings from John Nash and block printed linen from Phyllis Baron. Gertler continued with his circus theme and there were drawings from Bomberg, Porter and Jessie Etchells. Titles which caught the eye amidst the usual landscape, portrait, still-life etc. were "Steel and Steam" by C.R.W. Nevinson and "There's a Song my Heart is Singing" by Sylvia Gosse. The catalogue was a new format of a single sheet folded to double A4 buff paper priced at sixpence. Frustratingly, no sizes, media or prices were given.

P.G. Konody writes in the 'Observer' of 16th May, "The secession of 'Group X' has robbed the London Group of its most exciting features. Indeed, for an exhibition of artists who claim to represent the revolutionary advanced guard, the show that has been opened at the Mansard Gallery is singularly tame, though still of a nature to make and academician's hair stand on end." 'The Sunday Times' of the same date is of the same opinion, "Not so exciting as the recent display by 'Group X.', nor containing perhaps any paintings quite so important as have been seen in its previous exhibitions, the collection of works by members of the London Group... contains a number of paintings which testify to the liveliness and talent of our younger independent artists". The 'New Witness' of 14th May had the following, "The exhibition of the Royal Academy at Burlington House and the London group (sic) at the Heal Mansard Gallery are certainly the largest and probably the smallest collective art exhibitions in London at the moment, one representing reactionary and the other modern art. It reminds one of Jack the Giant Killer, a tiny intelligent Jack and a foolish sleepy giant. Little Jack is armed with a sword called Art, while the Giant only possesses a club called Industry, but he is heavily reinforced by an immense artistically ignorant public, which 'knows what it likes' and shows considerable signs of liking anything better than art. Also the giant possesses a magnificent castle and cellars full of money and official grants." The press singled out a couple of members for attention, this from the 'Evening Standard' of 8th May, "Its prevailing defect, if it has one, is priggishness rather than extravagance. The most extreme things in it are the circus scenes by Mr. Mark Gertler, and the 'Ghetto Theatre' and landscapes by Mr. Bomberg. Both these painters make use of distortions and disproportions that do not seem to be necessitated by their artistic aims; but the 'bite' of their work is undeniable." Other opinions expressed were, "Extremist Painters with quite moderate views", "Some 'shockers' in a Moderate Picture Show", "Not so terrible", "Atrocities are on the wane among the futurists" and "Music for the eye".

"Thirteenth Exhibition of The London Group", The Mansard Gallery, Heal & Sons Ltd., 196 Tottenham Court Road W.C., 18th October to 13th November 1920. D. Fox-Pitt is recorded as Hon. Treasurer and Bernadette Murphy as Secretary. Thirty-eight members are printed in this catalogue. Recently elected were Ruth Doggett, Elliott Seabrooke, Matthew Smith and Cicely Stock. No Hanging Committee was recorded in the catalogue. There were only seventy-four works in this second exhibition of 1920. Six Non-Members were invited to show up to two works each, D(ora?) Carrington, Belle Cramer, S.E. Greenwood, Malcolm Milne, A. Thornton and Hubert Wellington. Not all members took part in this exhibition although Paul Nash, Elliott Seabrooke, Boris Anrep (mosaics) and Ethelbert White all put in their full members' quota of five pieces of work. Seven women exhibited in this show, Bell Cramer (2), Ruth Doggett (3), S. de Karlowska (2), Thérèse Lessore (1), Dora Carrington (1), Ethel Sands (2) and Cicely Stock (4). H. W. Palliser showed "The Ant-eater", the only sculpture in the exhibition. There appeared to be a large number of outdoor subjects judging by the titles to most of the paintings ranging from London to the rest of the country and Europe, perhaps indicating that people were travelling again after the restrictions of the First World War. Keith Baynes designed a poster for this exhibition, but the woeful catalogue design prevailed.

The reviewer for the 'Manchester Guardian' wrote on the 23rd October, "Like other revolutionary groups, its direction now seems to be back to the centre. Eccentricity for its own sake is becoming rarer, and landscape is taking the part of apples on plates and the other stale subjects of the day before yesterday". P.G. Konody writing in the 24th October issue of the Observer concurs. "A marked predominance of landscape paintings and complete absence both of distorted portraits and of still life paintings introducing acid-green apples and twisted pottery distinguish this year's exhibition... The secession of the former members who now constitute Group X, and the abstention of Mr. Roger Fry and his inyrmidons (?), contribute towards depriving the show of its revolutionary character, although most of the work is still expressionist in tendency." The 'Daily Herald's' art critic wrote on the 11th November under the banner, "Sparkless Pictures", "The gauntlet which the London Group flings at the feet of the public from its 13th Exhibition at Mr. Heal's Mansard Gallery to-day is, compared with many of its previous challenges, but a very tame 'kid-glove' affair. Indeed, those of us who used to admire the freedom and daring of this set of pioneers cannot but regret the lack of distinction so noticeable in this year's exhibition. The sparkle has gone out of their vision and there is no ginger in their mental recipes." Michael Sadleir writing in the June edition of the Educational Times makes a succinct point, "The London Group at Heals have abandoned Cubism. Some of them are still a little uncomfortable in their new nakedness; others have found freedom and grace. It is desirable to see what is a stimulating and often charming exhibition in order to compare the work of young Englishmen with that of France, which is so largely its inspiration."

Denys Wilcox, in his publication "The London Group 1913-39" (p.17), prints a very illuminating letter dated 23rd November from Roger Fry to Marie Mauron, "I felt they were against me, and since I was completely indifferent whether I did the arranging of the exhibitions or not, I proposed the Jury should be drawn by lot. Everyone was delighted and I did nothing about the exhibitions. The result was that very incompetent people did the hanging and in two years the group had no more funds. Then they asked me back. I reconstructed the constitution of the society, forming rules that would give a certain responsibility to a few elected artists; in fact, I reinstalled government and de-democratized the society. It's the only way to do something. When everyone shares responsibility, nothing gets done... I refused to accept any office in the society, neither President nor Jury nor anything: I don't want them to say I'm out for power, and, besides, I want to remain perfectly free."

1921

A mutiny in the Russian fleet at Kronstadt forces the new Bolshevik government to restore the free market economy in the New Economic Policy as nearly 5 million die in a famine. In Germany, where there is rampant inflation, Adolf Hitler becomes leader of the National Sozialistishe Deutsche Arbeiter-Partei. Communist organisations are founded in Austria, Czechoslovakia, China, Italy, Portugal and Spain. Following the Anglo-Irish War the Anglo-Irish Treaty is signed in which independence is granted to the 26 southern states in Ireland and the province of Northern Ireland is created within the UK. Dr. Marie Stopes opens the first birth control clinic in London.

In Russia El Lissitzky was painting his abstract 'Prouns' in Vitebsk. Constructivism emerges with the First Working Group of Constructivists. In September Exter, Popova, Rodchenko, Stepanova and Vesnin organise "5x5=25" exhibition. Easel painting was decried as outmoded in Russia. George Grosz, with other Dadaists, was fined for libelling the German army. Wittgenstein was writing in Austria. In the UK Wyndham Lewis edits the magazine "The Tyro", a review of the Arts of Painting, Sculpture and Design. The first edition had articles by Wyndham-Lewis and TS Eliot and illustrations by William Roberts, David Bomberg and Frank Dobson.

At the **Leicester Galleries** Picasso and later by Wyndham Lewis were exhibited. Picasso's exhibition was a 'commercial disaster'.

Galerie Druet, Paris Bevan and Ginner organise "Un Groupe de Peintres Anglais Modernes" including Gilman and Karlowska. McKnight Kauffer, John Nash, E.M. O'R. Dickey, William Roberts, Edward Wadsworth and Ethelbert White were also shown.

London Group President: Robert Bevan (1913) began the year, Bernard Adeney (1913) elected at the AGM

Only one new member, Richard Carline, was elected in 1921.

"Fourteenth Exhibition of The London Group", The Mansard Gallery, Heal & Sons Ltd., 196 Tottenham Court Road, 9th May to 4th June 1921. In the catalogue Bernard Adeney is recorded as President, Malcolm Drummond as Hon. Treasurer and Eleanor Rogers as Secretary. No other officer posts were printed. Membership stood at thirty-eight for this exhibition with only twenty-three exhibiting. Of the fifteen none exhibitors the most significant were David Bomberg, Mark Gertler, Charles Ginner, Paul Nash, C.R.W. Nevinson and Matthew Smith. Thirteen non-members were selected for showing up to two works each. They were V. Citron, F. Farleigh, M. Foster, F. Griffith(s), D. Jones, L. Pearson, S. Popovitch, W.L. Shillabeer, H.L. Wellington, R.

Lee, G.W. Widmer, E. Wooden and M. Watson Williams who was elected to the group in 1922 and changed her name to Paule Vézelay. R. Lee is Rupert Lee also to be elected in 1922 and to become the Group's President in 1926. There were one hundred and ten exhibits in the fourteenth exhibition, mainly nudes, landscapes and still lifes with titles indicating travel in Europe, especially France and Italy. John Nash exhibited six wood engravings amongst predominantly paintings, although in all of the Heal's catalogues no media or sizes are given, the only clues are in the titles. The 'shoddy' catalogue format continued, a one sided sheet 60cms high by 25 cms wide which cost the visitor sixpence.

Edward Holroyd in the 'New Statesman' of 4th June was most impressed, "The present exhibition is likely to be a milestone in modern English painting, and it gives rise to the hope that the star of English Arts is in the ascendant." R.H.W. in the 'Athenaeum' of the 14th May writes, "… the artists make the minimum of concession to the demands of the market. We feel ourselves in the company of men who know that their work is worthwhile for its own sake, and such company cannot fail to stimulate… For thanks, largely, to the pioneer efforts of the London Group itself, all serious students have now learnt to accept these creeds and techniques. No one, we imagine, who thinks the London Group's exhibition worth visiting at all will quarrel with the particular varieties of Expressionism and Degas-Sickert-Impressionism which flourish here." The crtitc for 'The Nottingham Guardian' makes a shrewd observation, "Meanwhile Mr. Roger Fry, who is, of course, a moving power in art, has not been deprived of momentum by the formation around him of this too static group." Bernadette Murphy, in an extensive article in 'The New Listener', makes the following points, "The group most in evidence in this exhibition is that which has formed around Mr. Roger Fry, but which draws its inspiration from Vanessa Bell and Duncan Grant; F.J.Porter, Keith Baynes and Elliott Seabrooke are its most active and promising members, and there are indications that others are becoming fascinated – entangled… The second group to be noticed is most interesting, for it is a group in the act of forming itself. It is collecting (whether she likes it or not) around the vivid and distinct personality of Thérèse Lessore. The work of this artist is peculiarly intriguing; her individuality has been vigorous enough to withstand even that of the master (Sickert) with whom she allied herself early in her career… A third group rallies around Mr. R.P. Bevan; it includes the remnants of the London group (sic) as it was originally constituted – the founder members as it were."

"Fifteenth Exhibition of The London Group", The Mansard Gallery, Heal & Sons Ltd., 196 Tottenham Court Road, 24th October to 16th November 1921. Adeney remains as President, Drummond as Hon. Treasurer and Rogers as Secretary. Eleanor Rogers' address was given as 8 Fitzroy Street W1 continuing the Group's links with this particular area of London. Three members had left the Group since the previous exhibition, Phyllis Baron, Nina Hamnett (although she showed with the Group in the late 20s and early thirties) and C.R.W. Nevinson who was to throw his hat into the Vorticist ring. Twenty-one of the thirty-five members exhibited a total of one hundred and ten works. Prices were printed in this catalogue which must indicate an initiative to sell more work. The London Group was set up as an exhibiting society and here it is trying to do exactly that. Was there also pressure from Heals to increase revenues from the Mansard Gallery? The average price for paintings was between £5 and £20 with top prices of £60, £55 and £50 from A.P. Allinson. There was a Preface to this exhibition written by the economist Mr. Maynard Keynes, but it is not held in the Tate Archive catalogue section (although what appears to be the full text is printed in the 'Daily Graphic' of October 19th). Perhaps the most significant aspect of the fifteenth exhibition is an analysis of the twenty non-members selected for exhibiting alongside fully elected members. Ten of the twenty were to be elected to the Group. The London Group liked to "take a look" at prospective candidates hung next to members' work. Sales were also a possible indicator in support of election. It is worth recording in full the twenty non-member exhibitors and where they were elected to the Group at a later date, that date is given in brackets. Gabriel Atkin, A. Baker Clack, F.W.C. (John) Farleigh (1927), S. Fedorovitch, F. Griffith(s), D. de Halpert, R. Lee (1922), Claire Leighton, M. Lilly, M. Mackinlay, Malcolm Milne, Cedric Morris (1927), K.M. Morrison (1924), L. (Lydia) Pearson (1922), S. (Sava) Popovitch (1922), J.W. Power (1923), A. (Alfred) Thornton (1924), F. Unwin, M. (Marjorie) Watson Williams (1922, later Paule Vézelay) and E. (Edward) Wolfe (1923).

'The London Mercury' review of The London Group in December 1921 gives some clue as to what Mr. Maynard Keynes wrote in his Preface. The reviewer wrote "He makes some pertinent remarks on the urgent need of the young painters for patronage. He dismisses the modern plutocrats as being beyond persuasion, but he invites the ordinary run of visitors to the London Group to be less shy about buying. Without patrons art cannot flourish, and the Group 'includes the greater part of what is most honourable and most promising amongst the younger English painters of to-day'". Rather damningly, the reviewer continues, "Yet the charge of eccentricity can scarcely be brought against the London Group exhibition, which suffers rather from an academic dullness than from an excessive and subversive impulse to novelty. The Group has become a little anaemic". Most of the press coverage is focused on Maynard Keynes' introduction which seems to have ignited a debate about the purchasing of art and economic support for emerging artists. Frank Rutter writing in 'The Sunday Times' said, "It is part and parcel, perhaps, of what our Continental critics are apt to describe as 'British hypocrisy' that you may say anything and everything about a picture except, in polite society, to mention the price." Views of the exhibition itself are typified by E.H.R.C. writing in 'The Westminster Gazette' of October 27th, "The fifteenth exhibition... invites serious criticism and can stand it, for when the worst is said good things remain. Roughly half the exhibitors derive their inspiration (it is too strong a word in many instances) from the experiments of certain modern French painters the superficial qualities of whose work are too often accepted by the Englishmen without intelligent examination." The 'Manchester Guardian' printed the following on October 25th, "But every society has a 'tail', and the London Group is not without one. So the people speak of the pictures of this Society and of other modernist work as insolent. Nothing, I think, is now more unfair than that view, although it may have had some truth in the past. The younger artists of this era probably work harder, with greater mental effort, than any of their nineteenth century predecessors, apart from the Pre-Raphaelites." The November issue of Vogue printed eight black and white photographs of exhibited paintings (five of which were landscapes) by Thérèse Lessore, Randolph Schwabe, Bernard Adeney, Paul Nash, Keith Baynes, Elliott Seabrooke, Charles Ginner and William Ratcliffe.

1922

The Union of Soviet Socialist Republics (USSR) is officially established. Gabo, Kandinsky and Pevsner all leave the USSR. In the USSR Vladimir Shukov designs the iconic Shabolovka radio tower. In Italy a fascist regime under Mussolini takes power following his "March on Rome". The group 'Novocento' is founded in Milan with support from the new regime. The Conservatives under Bonar Law win a General Election in the UK in November. For the first time Labour, led by Clynes, receive more votes than the combined Liberal parties, 'National Liberals' following Lloyd George and 'Liberals' following Asquith. In December the BBC begins regular daily news broadcasts. James Joyce publishes "Ulysses" in France. Vaughan Williams celebrates his fiftieth birthday with the first performance of his third symphony, "A Pastoral Symphony".

The second issue of **"The Tyro"** was published including an article by Herbert Read and images from Dismorr, Lipschitz, Dobson, Etchells, Wadsworth and Cedric Morris.
The Whitechapel Art Gallery David Bomberg delivers a lecture on "The Modern Feeling in Painting".

London Group President: Bernard Adeney (1913)

"Sixteenth Exhibition of The London Group", The Mansard Gallery, Heal & Sons Ltd., 196 Tottenham Court Road, WC, 8th May to 3rd June 1922. Malcolm Drummond stepped down as Hon. Treasurer and non-artist R. Stuart Browning took his place. Eleanor Rogers is still recorded as Secretary although at this point it is thought that Diana Brinton became Secretary of The London Group. She came from a comfortable background, her father Reginald Brinton was chairman of a carpet manufacturing company. Roger Fry had put her forward having had experience of her administrative capability during her time as sub-editor at The Burlington Magazine. Denys Wilcox writes, "When Diana took over as the Group's secretary in 1922, the London Group was poorly organised and in financial difficulties. Within only a couple of years of Diana's management the Group was stronger than ever. She had been able to engineer more press coverage and visitors to the exhibitions resulting in significantly more sales. By 1925 the London Group was a superbly organised exhibiting body with an ever-growing membership".

The year 1922 was a shake-up year for The London Group with eight new members elected. Recorded in this catalogue as joining the Group were Mario Bacchelli, Frank Dobson (a sculptor), Rupert Lee, Lydia Pearson (-Righetti), Sava Popovitch and

Paule Vézelay (also known as Marjorie Watson Williams). G.H. Barne and S. (Sidney) Carline who were all elected before the seventeenth exhibition. Three decided to leave the Group, Boris Anrep (who was to be re-elected two years later), E.M. McKnight Kauffer and David Bomberg who was uncomfortable with the direction the Group was heading. Eleven non-members were selected to show, Hilda Carline, Sidney Carline (to be elected later in the year and probably sponsored by his brother Richard Carline, himself only elected in the previous year), S. Federovitch, M.Mackinlay, F.C. Medworth, M. Milne, H.W. Palliser, J.W. Power (1923), Chantal Quenneville (1926), W. Roberts (William Roberts who had been a Founder Member in 1914 but had left the group) and E. Wolfe (1923). There is an anonymous Preface to this catalogue, possibly written by Maynard Keynes, acquainted with the Bloomsbury set. The London Group "wish to encourage … a public by pricing our pictures as low as possible, so that they may be assured that in gratifying their tastes they do not run a risk of serious loss, and indeed may have some considerable chance of incidentally making a sound investment…. He regards them (pictures) as social amenities and he pays for them as he pays for other unnecessary, but flattering evidences of his social standing….We continue in favour of what may be called 'commercial' as opposed to 'genteel' prices." Yet in this exhibition prices are higher than before. Watson Williams was asking £210 for her "Nude, brown & grey", Popovitch £150 each for a nude and a portrait and Dobson £105 for his sculpture "Torso". Duncan Grant priced a landscape at £60 and a still life at £80, but the average was between £5 and £50. Six of the one hundred and twenty-one works on show were not for sale, they were perhaps already sold, commissions or purely for show. Those applying the NFS label were Keith Baynes, Roger Fry, Vanessa Bell, Thérèse Lessore and two from William Roberts.

The financial emphasis on sales from this exhibition was commented on by the press. P.G. Konody writing in 'The Observer': "There is something truly admirable in the frankness with which the members of the London Group – and among them are many artists of great distinction – admit that they are out for business." Frank Rutter, writing in the Arts Gazette, observed "Of the various bodies of independent artists who exhibit in England, the London Group may fairly claim to be the most advanced… for it is in this exhibition that we may learn something of the aims and ideals of the left wing of contemporary British painting". However, Rutter then makes the following statement, "Viewing this collection as a whole, we shall note that it is much less revolutionary in its general aspect that many previous exhibitions of the group have been. Abstract paintings, in which representative elements are superseded by geometrical patterns, have entirely disappeared; of cubism there is hardly a trace… and the majority of the paintings are examples of that new simplified realism which contains little to shock or bewilder the spectator." This 'safe' direction probably resulted in the enormous press coverage for this exhibition. Over thirty reviews have been archived from both

London and regional newspapers, some lavishly illustrated with black & white and colour images, evidence of an effective London Group administrative machine.

"Seventeenth Exhibition of The London Group", The Mansard Gallery, Heal & Sons Ltd., 196 Tottenham Court Road, 16th October to 11th November 1922. The secretary recorded in this catalogue is Eleanor Porter. Could this be Eleanor Rogers who had married London Group member F.J. Porter? Thirty-nine members are recorded here. Douglas Fox-Pitt, a 1913 Founder Member, had died on the 19th of September and six of his works featuring subjects from Dieppe and Cracow were exhibited as a mark of respect. This was a large exhibition of one hundred and thirty-five works with titles continuing to indicate landscape, still life, portrait and nude. Non-members selected were Adge Baker, David Bomberg (back again!), Charles Birchfield, Violet Citron, Vera Cunningham (1927), S. Federovitch, (?) Kottler, Guy Maynard (1923), Winifred Nicholson, J.W. Power (1923), W (William) Roberts, Walter Sickert (in and out of the Group), Marin Studin, A. Thornton (1924) and Edward Wolfe (1923). And some of them were asking the highest prices, Sickert £300 for "The Batchelor Hotel", Roberts £150 for "Dock Gates" and Bomberg £100 for "Grief". The average was between £10 and £50. There were 1167 admissions raising £72.11.2 whilst catalogue sales were recorded at £19.8.0. The inclusion of a Foreword in the catalogue took a rather bizarre turn with this offering from John Middleton Murry.

"The artist is the man who, amid this riot of unmeaning events, strives to pause and possess himself, and by so doing to give us the chance of possessing ourselves also. When you stand before a picture in this Exhibition and ask yourself: Is that now any good? you are at least half-way towards a condition of mind which nowadays has to be snatched from the very teeth of angers and distractions and despairs. If you can say with deep assurance: Yes that is good, you have reached it wholly. That moment of recognition, that consciousness of revelation, is the evidence that still there is a way by which the spirit of man can conquer the world of appearance even though at other moments the signs are legion that the world of appearance has won a final victory over the spirit of man. The artist, whose aim is to awaken this half-forgotten faith, deserves his reward. For remember that the rareness of your belief is a true measure of his difficulty in grasping his".

The Press seemed to be very exercised by Murry's piece, especially, as Rupert Lee writing in 'The New Age', observed, "(Murry) tells us that he has not even seen the pictures." Two newspapers carried photographs of paintings by William Roberts, the 'Daily Graphic' making a thinly veiled dig under the headline, "You can buy this picture for £150". In the 'Observer', P.G. Konody wrote, "If the London Group,... is not exactly teeming with new ideas and epigrams, it is simply that this New Art has ceased to be very new, and because the advanced artists belonging to the Group too often content themselves with quoting each-others' or their French precursors' thoughts and epigrams… With all their diversity of aims, the pictures, or most of them, fall into groups following certain formulas, and the perpetually reiterated formulas of the Post-Impressionists are apt to become as tiresome as those of the Academic School." Charles Marriott writing in the 'Atheneum', was of a similar opinion, "With all the merits there is about the seventeenth exhibition of the London Group… an effect of uneasiness, like that of people not sure of themselves in company. Paradoxical as it may sound, this effect is probably due to the conscious pursuit by the exhibitors of that very virtue which Mr. John Middleton Murry, in his foreword to the catalogue, claims as peculiar to art: the virtue of disinterestedness. One cannot help feeling that these artists, of undoubted talent, do indeed 'strive to pause and possess themselves'." Sickert and Gertler were singled out by most critics with a range of critical opinion. The wonderfully named Tancred Borenius, writing in the 'Saturday Review', offered the following morsel, "Many a time have I been wondering whose stroke of genius it was to think of the name of the London Group. For surely it must be accounted a masterpiece of adroitness by reason of the way in which it succeeds in combining a semblance of something definite with a comprehensiveness so wide as to admit any conceivable artistic aspiration under its hospitable cloak".

1923

In Germany hyperinflation continues to undermine the economy. In Munich Hitler attempts to gain power in the famous 'Beer Hall' putsch, is imprisoned and writes "Mein Kampf". In Spain, a dictatorship under Primo de Rivera gains power (1923-30). After only a year another General Election is held in the UK resulting in a hung parliament and the first time that Labour, led by Ramsay McDonald, form a government although in coalition with the re-united Liberals under Asquith. The Conservatives, led by Baldwin, win 258 seats whilst Labour win 191 and Liberals 158. The first FA Cup Final played at Wembley Stadium. The magazine 'Time' is published for the first time The Walt Disney Company and Warner Brothers are founded in the United States.

Also in the United States, Marcel Duchamp completes "The Bride Stripped Bare by Her Bachelors, Even" (The Large Glass). Albers and Moholy-Nagy were appointed to teach the first year preliminary course at the Bauhaus in Germany. Kandinsky, Klee, Feininger and Jawlensky form 'Die Blaue Vier' which exists for 10 years. Kurt Schwitters publishes his magazine "Merz" until 1927 and George Grosz is put on trial for obscenity. The Ballets Russes perform Stravinsky's "Les Noces" with designs by Goncharova. Malevich moves to Petrograd and is appointed head of the State Institute of Artistic Culture. W.B. Yeats is awarded the Nobel Prize for Literature.

The Whitechapel Art Gallery "Modern British Art".

St. George's Gallery, Hanover Square Bevan and twelve others form the Modern English Watercolour Society.

The National Gallery, Millbank (Tate Britain) commissioned an octagonal mosaic floor from Boris Anrep (1919) depicting "Proverbs of Hell" from Blake's "The Marriage of Heaven and Hell" (1790). Still on view.

London Group President: Bernard Adeney (1913)

"Eighteenth Exhibition of The London Group", The Mansard Gallery, Heal & Sons Ltd., 196 Tottenham Court Road, 21st April to 19th May 1923. In this catalogue the Secretary is recorded as Marjorie Strachey, no mention of Diana Brinton. Membership is at an all-time high of forty-six, an increase of seven since November 1922. New members were Boris Anrep (re-elected), Guy Maynard, Roderic O'Conor, John W. Power, Walter Sickert (re-elected) and Edward Wolfe. Maynard, born in America, was associated with Bloomsbury, Roger Fry and Matthew Smith and had lived and worked in France. O'Conor, a sixty-three year old painter born in Ireland, had lived in Paris and was influenced by Fry and Smith. Australian John Wardell Power was a forty-two year old painter who had also lived in Paris. Twenty-six year old Wolfe, born in South Africa, had worked for Fry's Omega Workshop and was to become very active in The London Group. There is a definite impression of a French hand on The London Group tiller, more specifically Roger Fry's. The eighteenth exhibition was huge, one hundred and seventy-three works in total. 817 admissions were recorded for this exhibition and 754 catalogues were sold. The titles continue to indicate figurative paintings as in previous exhibitions, but drawings from John Nash, Maynard and Lee can be identified. Six figurative sculptures (heads, portrait, torso) appear to have been included from Frank Dobson (" 'Bob' McAlmont" priced at £130), Margaret Hayes, Betty Muntz (1927) and Maria Petrie. Dobson's sculpture and S. Popovitch's painting "Nude" were the only works above one hundred pounds. Prices were noticeably lower than previous exhibitions and it would appear that there was a drive to improve sales. Five, probably small, Sickerts could be purchased for 2 guineas each. In the seventeenth exhibition there were fifteen non-members shown, but here numbers increased by 100% to thirty, including Ivon Hitchens and Maurice Utrillo. Curiously Hitchens's "Farm Buildings" and "Underhill Farm" were not priced and Utrillo's "Street Scene" was price on application. At least fourteen of the thirty non-members were women artists, there could have been more but the catalogue often only gives initials. The London Group appeared to be surging forward but with a strong guiding hand.

However, the art critic for the 'Daily Mail' had a different opinion, "Needless to say, the London Group continues to represent extreme modernism in art, though lately there has been a tendency towards compromise." 'Pall Mall' and 'Globe' were of the opinion that, "On the whole, the exhibition is disappointing. The group which has led us to expect innovation and development in its past exhibitions seems to be standing still. Lack of purpose and the driving force of conviction gives a dull atmosphere of sterility. But if the London Group is to retain the high position it has won for itself in contemporary exhibitions, it must hang pictures of greater individual importance." The 'Morning Post' printed, "The little that the London Group has to say is conveyed in the main with wearisome reiteration", whilst 'The Times' declared, "The new exhibition of the London Group at the Mansard Gallery is not so exciting as the last one. That is not so much because it is a good deal bigger, and large numbers are always depressing; or because there is no Gertler and no Sickert so striking as the picture of the hotel lounge. It is chiefly because everybody seems to have done very much what they did before; and one misses that air of experiment and development which, logically or not, one demands more from the London Group than of any other artistic society."

"Nineteenth Exhibition of The London Group", The Mansard Gallery, Heal & Sons Ltd., 196 Tottenham Court Road, 8th October to 3rd November 1923. By the opening of this exhibition membership had declined to forty-three. Douglas Fox-Pitt had died in 1922 and Mario Bacchelli and Jessie Etchells had left. Thirty year old

Italian Bacchelli had only shown in two London Group exhibitions and 1913 Founder Member Jessie Etchells in only three! Bernard Adeney is recorded as President, R. Stuart Browning as Hon. Teasurer and Marjorie Strachey as Secretary. There were only one hundred and three works in this show, probably either paintings or drawings as Dobson did not exhibit and the titles do not indicate any sculpture. Top price was claimed by Sickert's "Mdlle. Leagh" at £120, the only work above £100. Prices were generally much lower than even a year ago, a work by Bell, Ginner, the Nash brothers or Matthew Smith could be purchased for under £30. Prize for the most outstanding title must go to Hyam Myer's painting "Portrait of a Bloke". Close control of exhibited non-members continued with only thirteen included and of those thirteen, six were to be elected to full membership in the future. They were the illustrator and wood engraver F.W. Farleigh (1927), the painter Cicely Hey, fifty-six year old Kenneth Maciver Morrison (1924 and sponsored by Roger Fry), Hyam Myer (1930, studied at the Slade and in Paris), Alfred Thornton (1924, elected age 61, taught with Sickert) and Allan Walton (1925) who had studied with Sickert. There would appear to be no cuckoos in the nest. Other non-member exhibitors were Violet Citron, Cyril Cole, Mac Diamand, Lesley Keen, Adrienne Mason, Malcolm Milne and F. Spear. Visitors were charged one shilling to enter the exhibition, of which three pence was tax and the 'cheap' looking A4 catalogue sheet was priced at four pence. 594 catalogues were sold and there were 661 paying visitors. In previous exhibitions, visitors were allowed to walk into the exhibition before they paid, so that they understood what they were paying for!

The response of the press was similar to that towards the previous exhibition. The 'Manchester Guardian' wrote, "The London group (sic) of artists is settling down into sober middle age. In its latest show restriction in the number of exhibits has helped to raise the general level, and among individual members the sowing of wild oats is almost over". The November issue of the 'Burlington Magazine' carried the following review by R.R.T., "The London Group has been accused of pushing its big men down our throats. Lately it has seemed juster to charge it with too great parsimony in that respect... Nevertheless, wisdom and taste have seen to it that the walls are not crowded with rubbish. The new-comers have been severely scrutinized and the management have rightly kept a whole wall blank rather than reduce quality... there are the usual interesting contributions from non-members and the usual rubbish from the sentimental section of the elect".

1924

The death of Lenin signals the beginning of a power struggle between Stalin and Trotsky, Petrograd is renamed Leningrad and the UK recognises the USSR. In Italy a Fascist government is elected and the Socialist leader is murdered. A third General Election in as many years is called in the UK after the minority Labour administration suffers a vote of no confidence. The Conservatives sweep back into power led by Baldwin and the Liberals under Asquith lose 118 seats and never recover significant popular support. The Zinoviev Letter, calling for Communist agitation in the UK, could have affected the result but some commentators believe the letter to be a fake and not to have affected the outcome. The letter is printed by the 'Daily Mail' four days before the election. Howard Carter discovers the tomb of Tutankhamun in Egypt.

In France, André Breton issues the 'Manifeste du surréalime', Tzara publishes "Sept manifestes Dada" and Léger makes the film "Le ballet mécanique". In Germany following a right-wing campaign, funding is withdrawn from the Weimar Bauhaus and the school is suspended. In Berlin Heartfield and Grosz form a group of communist artists called the 'Rote Gruppe'. Feininger, Jawlensky, Kandinsky and Klee form "Die Blauen Vier" (The Blue Four) to distance themselves from Bauhaus 'artist-engineers'. Joan Miró holds his first exhibition in Spain. Thomas Mann publishes "The Magic Mountain". George Gershwin writes "Rhapsody in Blue". Pucinni dies.
A Ben Nicholson exhibition at the **Adelphi Gallery, London** made a huge impression on the young Ivon Hitchens (1931).
St. George's Gallery, Hanover Square Society of Printmakers is formed including Robert Bevan (1913).
The British Empire Exhibition takes place at Wembley between April and October. Its official aim was to "stimulate trade and strengthen bonds". Fifty-six countries in the British Empire took part in the exhibition which was the largest in the world to date. It cost £12 million to organise and received 27 million visitors.

London Group President: Frank Dobson (1922) replaces Bernard Adeney

Only two new members, Kenneth Morrison and Alfred Thornton, were elected to The London Group in 1924.

"Twentieth Exhibition of The London Group", The Mansard Gallery, Heal & Sons Ltd., 196 Tottenham Court Road, 14th April to 14th May 1924. Bernard Adeney was replaced by Frank Dobson as President of The London Group. For the first time the Vice President was recorded in the exhibition catalogue, Frederick J. Porter. This was an inexperienced line up, Dobson was elected in 1922 and Porter in 1920.

J. Woodger was the Hon. Treasurer and Marjorie Strachey continued as Secretary. Membership remained steady at forty-four. The twentieth exhibition was a relatively large exhibition of one hundred and thirty-four works. There were 731 admissions and 642 catalogues at fourpence each were sold. For the first time sculpture (seven pieces) was separately identified in the exhibition catalogue, no doubt initiated by the new sculptor President Frank Dobson. Prices were very economical, nothing over £100 although Sickert's and Matthew Smith's prices were not printed! "Young Woman in Blue" by Bernard Meninsky at £80 was one of the highest with average prices between £20 and £50. Prints and drawings could be purchased for less then £10. The London Group were "taking a look" at non-member exhibitors again. Of the eighteen selected for this exhibition, six were to become full members in due course, Alfred Thornton in 1924, Wyndham Tryon and Allan Walton in 1925, Vera Cunningham and Betty Muntz in 1927 and Cicely Hey in 1928. Tryon, Walton and Muntz had all worked or studied in France and the thirty year old figurative painter Vera Cunningham had studied under Meninsky, was in Gertler's circle of friends and associated with Matthew Smith. This was the only time Ben Nicholson exhibited, describing London Group exhibitions as 'the London Group's dog's dinner'.

There is no mention of this being the 10th Anniversary of the first London Group exhibition in March 1914. Later in the Group's history every opportunity is taken to celebrate the passing years, the direct opposite of the occurrence of most members' birthdays!

"Twenty-first Exhibition of The London Group", The Mansard Gallery, Heal & Sons Ltd., 196 Tottenham Court Road, 13th October to 8th November 1924. This was the end of a long run of twice a year exhibitions stretching back to 1918, seven years of double exposure. It was also the last at the Mansard Gallery as in June 1925 the twenty-second exhibition was to open in the Royal Watercolour Society's gallery in Pall Mall East. 819 visitors paid to enter the 21st exhibition and 785 catalogues were sold. Officers remain the same for 1924, apart from the recording of Diana Brinton, finally, as Secretary. Forty-five members appear on the membership list whilst a healthy twenty-one non-members were selected for exhibition. The inclusion, probably by invitation, of Raoul Dufy exhibiting "Seascape" (n.f.s.) underlined the Group's interest in French painting but home grown talent in the shape of David Jones was also selected. Within the twenty-one non-member exhibitors were six future members, René Paresce and Allan Walton were to be elected in the following year, two women artists Jessica Dismorr and Chantal Quenneville in 1926, F.W. Farleigh in 1927 and H.S. Williamson in 1933. One hundred and forty-five works were crammed into the Mansard Gallery with nothing priced over £100. Walter Sickert showed "Banco" but did not give a price. Duncan Grant offered "Red-Hot Pokers" for £80, Mark Gertler "Roses & Tapestry" for £40 and Matthew Smith "Odalesque" for £30. The average continued to be between £10 and £50. The titles and prices of exhibits 100-146 would seem to indicate drawings, gouaches, watercolours and prints, more affordable items for the gallery visitor. Titles of the oil paintings continued to be repetitive, "Landscape", "Head", "Still Life", "Pot of Flowers", "My Hampstead Garden", "Figures in Interior", "Nature Morte" and various overseas locations summed up by E.M. O'R. Dickey's painting, "Doing Europe". Using titles as evidence, only one piece of sculpture, "Portrait, Bronze" by Stephen Tomlin, appears to have been exhibited here. Sculptor President Frank Dobson did not exhibit although he would have been involved in the Hanging Committee. There is a distinct feeling of lack of change or development. If the Group were to be thought of as a sailing ship it would be becalmed in the Doldrums.

1925

King George of Greece is deposed and the country declared a republic. In Germany Albert Einstein joins the Bauhaus board and the school moves from Weimar to Dessau, a 'Neue Sachlichkeit' exhibition is held in Mannheim, Franz Kafka's "The Trial" is controversially published posthumously and the first part of Hitler's "Mein Kampf" is published. In Berlin Berg's opera, "Wozzeck" is premiered. In France the first 'Art Deco' exhibition is held, Breton organises the first Surrealist exhibition including Arp, De Chirico, Ernst, Man Ray, Masson, Miró, Picasso and Tanguy, Léger and Ozenfant establish the Académie de l'Art Moderne, the photographer André Kertész moves to Paris and Josephine Baker appears in "Revue negre". In Russian cinema, "Battleship Potemkin" is made by Sergei Eisenstein. Dmitri Shostakovich premieres Symphony No. 1, Op. 10 to great acclaim. There is increasing government control in all Russian cultural activity. Charlie Chaplin's "Goldrush" is screened for the first time. Salvador Dali's first one-man show is held in Barcelona.

Maynard Keynes sets up a co-operative called the **London Artists' Association** to help support artists and to sell their work. The original group, extremely Bloomsbury in orientation, were Vanessa Bell, Duncan Grant, Roger Fry, Bernard Adeney, Keith Baines and F.G. Porter, all associated with The London Group.
John Cooper formed the **'East London Group'**. Cooper was to become an important figure in London Group history as part of a group determined to end Bloomsbury domination.
There is uproar over the inclusion of a female nude in Epstein's "Rima", a memorial to W.H. Hudson. His sculpture was described by the press as 'The Hyde Park Atrocity'.
The Whitechapel Art Gallery "British Art 1875 – 1925"

London Group President: Frank Dobson (1922)

"Twenty-second Exhibition of The London Group", R.W.S. (Royal Watercolour Society) Galleries, 5a Pall Mall East, SW1., 6th June to 26th June 1925. More exhibits, more members. 1925 sees the Group beginning to develop. Jacob Kramer and Roderic O'Conor had left membership, however Horace Brodzky (1914), William Roberts (1914) and R. McKnight Kauffer (1916) were all, seemingly, re-elected. Roderic O'Conor (1923), a friend of Gauguin's, only showed one work with The London Group in the 1928 Retrospective. Three new members joined the ranks, René Paresce, Wyndham Tryon and Allan Walton. Membership now stood at forty-nine, the highest in the Group's history. A total of one hundred and ninety-seven works were shown to the public this year, no doubt taking advantage of a larger space which enabled the group to almost double the number of non-member exhibitors. In total there were 1,637 admissions and 696 catalogues were sold raising the handsome figure of £17.8.0. Thirty-five non-members were selected to show up to two works each. Seven were members-in-waiting, Jessica Dismorr elected in the following year, John Banting and Betty Muntz in 1927, Cicely Hey 1928, H.E. du Plessis in 1929, H.S. Williamson much later in 1933 and finally president elect J.A. Dodgson later still in 1947! Notable non-member exhibitors were J. Cosmo Clark, Belle Cramer, David M. Jones and Roland Penrose who showed "The Sailor's Return". The exercise of comparing titles takes an interesting turn with G.W. Bissell's "Coal Miners" and Horace Brodzky's "Pit Head" compared with "Chintz Curtains" by Walter Taylor and "Lilies and Iris" by Vanessa Bell. Nine sculptures by President Frank Dobson, Betty Muntz, C. Billing, Margaret Hayes and future president Rupert Lee were given their own section in the exhibition catalogue. Dobson's exhibit attracted much attention. He exhibited "Cambria, Scale model for a National War Memorial" (£525). The exhibition catalogue is heavily annotated by pencil in an indecipherable hand, but the pencil writes, "Times says, 'but comment must end with reference to the noble "Cambria. Scale model for a National War Memorial" by Mr. F Dobson. There is a lesson to painters, here, in the way Mr Dobson has composed his group in the substance of which it is made & simplified his forms in accordance with its nature. In a sense the (?) figure is a translation of one of the Pantheon "Fates" into bronze, or carved into moulded forms.'" The annotator also scrawls, "To understand these artists & to appreciate them, it is necessary to abandon all preconceived notions. The attempt is worth trying". In this more ambitious show overall prices were slightly higher, top price of £175 asked by Mark Gertler for "The Toilet".

Royal Watercolour Society Galleries
6 Pall Mall East, London SW1

The Royal Watercolour Society Galleries were stunningly located next to the National Gallery and Trafalgar Square. Number 6 is just behind the metal railings where tourists now wait to board their tour buses. The R.W.S. was then known as the Royal Society of Painters in Watercolour. Its President at this time was Sir Herbert Hughes-Stanton, holding office from 1920 to 1936. Was Sir Herbert related to Blair Hughes-Stanton, a printmaker elected to The London Group in 1933? The R.W.S. is an organisation very much like The London Group. Founded in 1804 the R.W.S. has a President, executive officers, a constitution and eighty members. Previous members included John Sell Cotman, Samuel Palmer, Arthur Rackham, John Singer Sargent, Alma Tadema and Peter de Wint. The London Group held four annual exhibitions at this venue between June 1925 and June 1927. The R.W.S. is now (2013) located in the Bankside Gallery and was opened in November 1980 by Her Majesty Queen Elizabeth. London Group member Trevor Frankland was one of its Presidents in the twenty-first century.

1926

Franco becomes General of Spain. There is a failed assassination attempt against Mussolini in Italy where the Fascists are in power. Unrest rumbles in Greece, Portugal and Poland. Al Capone's headquarters in Chicago attacked. In the USSR output finally reaches that of 1913. Roald Amundsen flies over the North Pole. On May 1st a coal miners' strike begins in the UK. On May 3rd a General Strike is called which lasts ten days. The miners' strike ends in October. Also in October, London is the venue for the 1926 Imperial Conference hosted by King-Emperor George V with the Prime Ministers of the UK, Australia, Canada, Irish Free State, Newfoundland, New Zealand and South Africa. In December Stanley Baldwin, the Prime Minister, ends martial law imposed during the General Strike. There is flooding in some London suburbs earlier in the year. A.A. Milne's "Winnie the Pooh" is released. Fritz Lang makes the futuristic film "Metropolis".

London Group President: Frank Dobson (1922)

"The London Group, 23rd Exhibition", R.W.S. Gallery, 5a Pall Mall East, 9th January to 30th January, 1926. The exhibition catalogue indicates no change in officers or administrators. Membership increases by one to fifty with the election of Jessica Dismorr and Chantal Quenneville and the death of R.P. Bevan, a Founder Member of The London Group from the Camden Town Group. Thirteen of these fifty were women. A paper slip in the catalogue records a Memorial Exhibition at the Goupil Galleries, 5 Regent Street during February 1926 and four Bevan canvases were shown as a memorial in the 23rd Exhibition, all from private collectors including Frank Rutter. One hundred and seventy-three works were exhibited in total, catalogue numbers 1-100 were oil paintings, 101-166 watercolours and 167-173 sculpture. Everything was for sale, apart from Bevan's paintings. Most expensive was W. Roberts' "Esther", a watercolour priced at £200. W. Richard Sickert A.R.A. priced "Battistini" at £150 and Jacob Epstein "Enver" at £120. The average prices were very affordable and at the end of the list of works is printed, "Pictures will be reserved on payment of 10% purchase price, the balance being payable on or before the closing date of the Exhibition". Titles printed in the catalogue continue to indicate figurative work of landscape, flowers, interior, still life and portrait subject matter. Non-member numbers were steadily increasing with thirty-eight selected for this exhibition, at least fifteen of whom were women and included Elsie Barling, Ann Chassal Dallas, Sophia Fedorovitch, May Guinness, Margaret Hayes, Evie Hone, Marjorie Lilley, Marietta Pallis, Anne Estelle Rice and Hilary Stratton. Non-members also included ex-member Jacob Epstein, David Jones (was he being 'groomed' for membership?), Roland Penrose and Christopher Wood.

In 1927 Vera Cunningham, Jon (sic) Farleigh, Cedric Morris and Betty Muntz were all to be elected to full membership and, as before, all were shown in the previous year. Similarly, Cicel Hey (1928), H.E. du Plessis (1929) and Hyam Myer (1930) were also selected. 959 people visited the exhibition raising £47.6.0 in admissions and 710 catalogues at sixpence apiece were sold, bringing in £17.15.0.

The second exhibition of the year was also held at the R.W.S. Gallery between 5th and 25th June 1926. Admissions remained healthy at 943 and 649 catalogues were sold. Officers and administrators were the same as the last show four months previously. "The London Group, 24th Exhibition" had one hundred and sixty-nine exhibits, 1-109 oil paintings, 110-157 watercolours (including prints) and 158-169 sculpture. Abrasha Lozoff exhibited a wooden sculpture entitled "Lot and his two daughters" with an eye watering price of £1,500. Lozoff was one of thirty-nine non-member exhibitors which also included David Jones and Christopher Wood as well as guest artists Jean Dufy and Raoul Dufy (again). Raoul Dufy showed two works "Jardin à Hyères" and a watercolour "Le Paddock à Dauville" both on sale for 6,000 francs. Fourteen non-member exhibitors were women with new names Elsie M. Barling, Constance Lane and Joan Pancheuto appearing. The large number of watercolours must surely indicate an attempt to make sales and generate income for the Group as prices were obviously more affordable than oil paintings. Apart from the Dufys, Paul Nash's "Wood by the Sea" was the highest priced watercolour at £18.18.0 with S.Popovitch and Randolph Schwabe asking 12 guineas for their exhibits. Top price for an oil painting was John Dodgson's "Aphrodite in the Studio" at £157.10 whilst Bernard Meninsky was asking £85 for "Suburban Gardens in the Spring", Roger Fry £65 for "Camelias" and Edward Wolfe £63 for "The Reading Woman". In hard to read margin notes the catalogue owner had recorded 'Judith' writing in the New (Style?) who had attacked Dufy's price tag for "the sort of picture that one sees (?) that only children draw with chalks in the nursery (?)". Most remarkable about the 24th Exhibition was the number of future members shown as non-members. The London Group practice of 'having a look' at candidates before full election to the Group is here writ large! Twelve future members were selected, a figure that including five women. Six artists, Elizabeth Andrews, John Banting, Vera Cunningham, Jon (sic) Farleigh, Cedric Morris and Betty Muntz gained full membership in 1927. Others included Cicely Hey (1928), H.E. du Plessis (1929), Hyam Myer (1930), Elsie Farleigh (1931) and H.S. Williamson (1933). In June 1926 there were 48 listed members, Boris Anrep and Wyndham Tryon leaving since the last exhibition and not replaced although Tryon was shown in January 1929 and November 1934.

1927

The first transatlantic telephone call is made from New York to London. Early television is demonstrated in the USA. Charles Lindbergh makes the first solo non-stop flight of the Atlantic. The Ford Motor Company replaces its Model T with the new Model A. British forces sent to Shanghai, China where various incidents escalate into the Civil War which was not to end until 1949. The Chinese People's Liberation Army is formed. Stalin takes firm control of the USSR as Leon Trotsky is expelled from the Communist Party. In Canberra, the first Australian Parliament convenes. Following the Treaty of Jedda, Saudi Arabia becomes independent of the UK. In the UK there is another serious influenza epidemic. In December a severe cold snap hits London. Following the recognition of the republic of Ireland the Royal and Parliamentary Titles Act 1927 changes the name of the UK to the United Kingdom of Great Britain and Northern Ireland.

Fritz Lang's film "Metropolis" opens in Germany. In the USSR VKhUTMAS becomes VKhUTEIN (Higher State Artistic and Technical Institute). In Hanover Schwitters begins what was to become his 'Merzbau'. In the USA the film "The Jazz Singer" opens marking the end of the silent movies era. The BBC is granted a Royal Charter of Incorporation.

London Group President: Rupert Lee (1922)

"The London Group 25th Exhibition", R.W.S. Gallery, 5a Pall Mall East, 4th June to 25th June 1927. The exhibition catalogue records a change in London Group President from the sculptor Frank Dobson to the sculptor Rupert Lee. The incoming president presided over a membership of fifty-six, seventeen of whom were women. Eight new members had been elected, three sculptors Elizabeth Andrews, Betty Muntz and Alan Durst and five painters, John Banting, Vera Cunningham, John Farleigh, Cicely Hey and Cedric Morris. A total of two hundred and nineteen works were shown in the 25th Exhibition, catalogue numbers 1-198 were two-dimensional images and 1-21 figurative sculpture with elephants, dancing children, acrobats, cats, Paradise fish and virgins appearing in the titles. Bernard Meninsky's "Odalisque" and E.M. O'R Dickey's "Robert Stephenson's Bridge" shared top price at £80. For between £50 and £80 a visitor could buy a Duncan Grant, a Mark Gertler, a Sava Popovitch or a George Barne. Drawings, gouaches, watercolours and prints were for sale beside the oil paintings. Ubiquitous titling continued. In this show alone seventeen works by different artists had the title "Still Life". W. Richard Sickert A.R.A. exhibited the evocatively titled "Laylock and Thunderplump" and both Bernard Meninsky and Matthew Smith were painting 'Negresses'. There were almost as many non-member exhibitors chosen as there were full members. Forty-eight non-members had an exhibiting opportunity with The London Group including E.J.I. Ardizzone, James Boswell, Richard Eurich and David Jones plus sculptors A.J. Pollen, Ola Cohn, Gladys Hynes and Ethel Pye. There are some fresh, new faces in this cohort, had the new president 'put the word out'? At least thirteen women were among the non-exhibitors including Rosamund Borrodaile, Marjorie Hodgkinson, Madge Knight, Mary C. Mason, Mary Melville Foster and Kathleen M. Sauerbeer. The London Group practice of judging prospective candidates continued unabated with 1929 successes H.E. du Plessis, Maresco Pearce and A.J. Pollen exhibited, 1930 Noel Adeney and Hyam Myer, 1931 E. Farleigh, 1933 H.S. Williamson (who was to be the 'Chairman' of The London Group throughout the Second World War), Frances Hodgkins in the 1940s, J.A. Dodgson in 1947 and Stanley W. Hayter in 1953, ten in total.

997 people visited the R.W.S. Gallery and 708 catalogues were purchased. This was the last exhibition at the R.W.S. Gallery. Already events were underway at the next London Group venue, the New Burlington Galleries in Burlington Gardens, W1.

Perhaps as a result of Lee's 'fresh hand on the tiller' the group published a printed set of rules in November, 1927. The Group would now be clear as to what procedures and regulations were in force. In the pamphlet nineteen rules were printed under the headings of, 'Rules – 1927'(1),'Membership'(2-5), 'Officers and Executive Committee' (6-7), 'General Meetings' (8-10), 'Special General Meetings' (11), 'Exhibitions' (12-19). Rule 1 proudly stated, "This body of Modern Painters and Sculptors shall be called 'The London Group' ". Rule 3 set the annual subscription at £3 and Rule 5 sheds light on the 1927 membership selection process, "New members may be elected half-yearly at the General Meetings. Nominations for these may be sent in at any time of the year… Candidates should, by application to the Secretary, submit their works to these meetings, or if that be not possible, photographs of their work; and it shall be the business of the meeting to discuss the work of each candidate in turn. Candidates must poll more than 50% of the votes of those present." Under 'General Meetings', "The Group shall hold at least two General Meetings, one before and one after the yearly exhibition." "An Executive Committee of five members, working with the Officers of the Group shall undertake the organisation and hanging of the Annual Exhibitions or Exhibition… The Members of this Committee shall hold office for one year, but shall be eligible for re-election." Excerpts from 'Exhibitions', "Members may exhibit five works… Non-members may submit not more than two works… Non-members' work shall be judged at the Gallery on the sending-in day by the members in consultation, and they shall record their votes by show of hands… If half the number of members present are in favour of a work, it shall be accepted… The Group shall charge a commission of 20%… No picture or work of art shall be exhibited 'not for sale'… No oil-paintings with white frames will be admitted to Exhibitions." The emphasis on exhibitions firmly underlined the fact that The London Group was an exhibiting society and was seriously in the business of selling artists work to the public.

1928

The Representation of the People Act is passed giving all women over the age of 21 in the UK the vote. Stalin draws up the first Five Year Plan. Trotsky exiled to Alma Ata. Amelia Earhart becomes the first woman to fly the Atlantic. Alexander Fleming discovers penicillin. Chiang Kai-shek becomes the Chairman of the National Military Council in the Republic of China. Republican Herbert Hoover wins the US Presidential election. The International Red Cross is formally established. "The Threepenny Opera" by Bertold Brecht and Kurt Weill opens in Berlin. Ravel's "Bolero" premieres at the Paris Opera. Picasso is taught how to weld by Julio Gonzalez.

The Thames burst its banks on January 6th flooding many areas of London. A large section of the embankment at Millbank collapsed inundating the National Gallery, Millbank (Tate Britain) to a depth of five to eight feet. Some of Turner's works were damaged. Large sections of Millbank had to be rebuilt including Thames House now MI5 HQ. This flood was the last major flood to hit London and resulted in demands for a barrier to be built.

Tooth's de Chirico's first exhibition in England.

London Group President: Rupert Lee (1922)

"London Group Retrospective Exhibition 1914 - 1928", New Burlington Galleries, Burlington Gardens W1, April to May 1928. No exact dates for the exhibition were given in the catalogue which was illustrated (for the first time ever in a London Group catalogue) with black and white photographs of selected work from the exhibition. In the London Group accounts ledger dates of the 27th April to 26th May for the exhibition are recorded. The ledger also records 1,823 admissions with 1,094 catalogue sales, double the recent average figures. The question must be asked as to why the Group wished to organise a Retrospective after only fifteen years? Fry, Lee and Brinton Lee were hugely capable of organising such an event and perhaps they were intent on raising the Group's profile. Notably, non-member submissions in subsequent send-ins increased substantially on the back of this Retrospective. R.R. Tatlock wrote a Foreword to the Retrospective:

"Regarding the London Group from the point of view of an art critic, I feel extremely grateful. Its members have so often given us something worth thinking and writing about. This, I think, is mainly because they have never hesitated to paint with passion, even when that meant painting dangerously. Consequently the written criticisms of their shows have always been far better worth writing and reading than those dealing with the numerous and deadening 'safety first' exhibitions.

I am persuaded that those in whom the spirit of choice dwells at ease and are not overawed by the Goddess of Discretion will be cheered by the realisation that in spite of its remarkable achievement, the London Group is only fifteen years of age, and has the prospect of remaining youthful for many years to come."

There then followed a short history of The London Group written by Alfred Thornton, a member of The London Group and its Executive Committee. A list of "Owners of Works" who loaned examples of the work of past members of The London Group included loans from Arnold Bennett, Lord Ivor S. Churchill, the Contemporary Art Society, Samuel Courtauld, the Imperial War Museum, J. Maynard Keynes, Professor William Rothenstein, Frank Rutter and the Earl of Sandwich, in all a total of fifty-nine lenders. Presidents and Officers for the last fifteen years are then recorded, followed by a list of current officers and members which is worth presenting here in full on this important anniversary for the Group.

Rupert Lee was the President, Frederick J. Porter Vice President, J.S. Woodger Honorary Treasurer and Diana Brinton Secretary. Members of the Executive Committee were A.P. Allinson, Keith Baynes, Roger Fry, Bernard Meninsky, Randolph Schwabe, Alfred Thornton, Allan Walton and Edward Wolfe. In April 1928 membership stood at fifty-four as follows, Bernard Adeney, A.P. Allinson, Elizabeth Andrews, John Banting, George Barne, Keith Baynes, Vanessa Bell, Horace Brodzky, Richard Carline, Sidney Carline, Vera Cunningham, E.M. O'R. Dickey, Jessica Dismorr, Frank Dobson, Ruth Doggett, Malcolm Drummond, Alan Durst, John Farleigh, Roger Fry, Mark Gertler, Charles Ginner, Mary Godwin, Duncan Grant, Cicely Hey, A.H. Hudson, S. de Karlowska, Rupert Lee, Thérèse Lessore, Guy Maynard, Bernard Meninsky, Cedric Morris, K.M. Morrison, Elizabeth Muntz, John Nash, Paul Nash, René Paresce, Lydia Pearson, S. Popovitch, Frederick J. Porter, J.W. Power, W.Ratcliffe, William Roberts, Ethel Sands, Randolph Schwabe, Elliott Seabrooke, Richard Sickert, Matthew Smith, Cicely Stock, Walter Taylor, Alfred Thornton, Allan Walton, Ethelbert White, Paule Vézelay (Marjorie Watson Williams) and Edward Wolfe. No new members were elected in 1928.

Roger Fry followed with a piece entitled, "The Modern Movement in England", He wrote, "To put it briefly, and using convenient, but rather vague, labels, we may say that the London Group has done for Post-Impressionism in England what the New English Art Club did, for a previous generation, for Impressionism." He continued, "If in what follows I have to devote most of the space at my disposal to the various experiments and manoeuvres of the Post-Impressionist branch it must not be forgotten that the others have held the most continuous thread of tradition and have exercised an influence at each successive period of the whole group... Turning now to the other current tradition which came in with the amalgamation of the Camden Town Group with other groups, we note the predominant influence of contemporary French Art."

Later in his piece he rather dismissively wrote, "Others of the group were more affected by the Cubist experiments of Picasso, and some of those who worked in this direction founded under Mr. Wyndham Lewis the Vorticist Group. Some of these, like Mr. Nevinson, developed a special brand of Cubist illustration which had considerable vogue during the war. Evidences of Cubist influence are to be found sporadically throughout most of the period". He summed up recent developments thus, "As years went on indeed the tendency became more marked to revert to construction in depth; to abandon the essentially decorative surface organisation in favour of the more essentially pictorial effects of recession… It would however be an exaggeration to suggest that the period of experiment is altogether over or that pictorial tradition of to-day has attained anything like uniformity, nor is such a condition to be desired. All that we can say is that the experimental field has been narrowed and that most of those artists have found the style within which they can function most freely. One must also admit that something of the adventurous courage of the earlier years has gone and that large-scale compositions have given place to works more suitable to the exiguity of modern apartments". All the images selected to illustrate the exhibition catalogue were figurative. Of the twenty-four reproductions, three were of sculpture and only one was of a Vorticist nature, "The Love Song" by William Roberts. The overwhelming majority of reproductions were still life and landscape.

The exhibition was organised in three sections, Paintings, Sculpture and Drawings and Watercolours. There were one hundred and eighty oil paintings, twenty-three sculptures and sixty-two drawings and watercolours. Title, date and price (of those for sale) were printed in the catalogue. Listed here are the oil painters followed by the number of paintings exhibited, Bernard Adeney 5, Adrian Allinson 4, John Banting 1, George Barne 1, Phyllis Baron 1, Walter Bayes 1, Keith Baynes 4, Vanessa Bell 3, Robert Bevan 4, David Bomberg 6, Henri Gaudier-Brzeska (pastel) 1, Horace Brodzky 2, Richard Carline 2, Sidney Carline 1, Benjamin Coria 3, Vera Cunningham 1, E.M. O'R. Dickey 2, Ruth Dogett 2, Malcolm Drummond 4, Frederick Etchells 3, John Farleigh 1, Douglas Fox-Pitt 1, Roger Fry 5, Mark Gertler 5, Harold Gilman 5, Charles Ginner 4, Mary Godwin 4, Spencer F. Gore 5, Sylvia Gosse 2, Duncan Grant 5, C.F. Hamilton 1, Nina Hamnett 3, James Hamilton Hay 2, Cicely Hey 1, A.H. Hudson 2, S. de Karlowska 5, E. McKnight Kauffer 2, Jacob Kramer 4, Rupert Lee 1, Thérèse Lessore 5, J.B. Manson 1, Guy Maynard 2, Bernard Meninsky 4, Cedric Morris 1, K.M. Morrison 2, John Nash 3, Paul Nash 4, C.R.W. Nevinson 3, R. O'Conor 1, René Paresce 1, Lydia Pearson 2, Lucien Pissarro 1, S. Popovitch 2, Frederick Porter 4, J.W. Power 1, William Roberts 2, Ethel Sands 2, Randolph Schwabe 1, Elliott Seabrooke 3, Richard Sickert A.R.A., P.R.B.A. 4, Matthew Smith 3, Harold Squire 4, Cicely Stock 2, Alfred Thornton 2, Edward Wadsworth 2, Allan Walton 1, Ethelbert White 4, Paule Vézelay (M. Watson-Williams) 2 and Edward Wolfe 2. Percy Wyndham Lewis is conspicuous by his absence! Seven sculptors exhibited, Elizabeth Andrews, Henri Gaudier-Brzeska, Frank Dobson, Alan Durst, Jacob Epstein, Rupert Lee and Elizabeth Muntz. Drawings and Watercolours were from both oil painters and sculptors. Notable works exhibited were David Bomberg's "In the Hold" of 1914, Mark Gertler's "Merry-go-Round" of 1916, Harold Gilman's "Mrs. Mounter" of 1915, "We are Making a New World" from Paul Nash in 1917, "Bird Swallowing Fish" by Henri Gaudier-Brzeska in 1915, "Head of Paul Robeson" by Jacob Epstein in 1928 and President Rupert Lee's stone sculpture "The Owl" made in 1920. Adverts for the Leicester Galleries (who showed many of The London Group), St George's Gallery, the Morris Singer Art Bronze Foundry, Messrs. Vincent Brooks, Day and Son (Lithographers) and Winsor and Newton helped subsidise the printing of the catalogue.

No annual exhibition was held in 1928 as no doubt all the Group's energies were devoted to this retrospective exhibition. The Group's Pass Book with Drummonds Branch, Royal Bank of Scotland, dated 25th October 1928 recorded debits of £1,090.1.6, credits of £1,209.13.9 and a balance of £119.12.3. Membership fees appeared to be £3 annually and hanging fees were also charged. On May 3rd, for example, P. Nash was charged £1.8.5, M. Gertler £1.11.2 and E. Seabroke £1.7.6.

The New Burlington Galleries
6 Burlington Gardens W1

Number 6 Burlington Gardens was the address of the New Burlington Galleries where The London Group held many exhibitions into the 1930s.

The following is from a press cutting dated 6th December 1928 published in 'The Times' newspaper, "THE BRITISH EMPIRE ACADEMY. HOME AT NEW BURLINGTON GALLERIES. The necessary funds for the establishment of the British Empire Academy having now been collected, that body is to make its headquarters at the New Burlington Galleries in Burlington-gardens, (sic) W.1. The objects of the Academy, which has been brought into existence by the efforts of Mr.

W. Howard Robinson, whose portrait of Lord Dysart is on exhibition in the galleries, are to promote, aid and unite all the arts throughout the Empire. The galleries, which were formerly the Bristol Hotel and the Ladies' Army and Navy Club, have now been adapted as an art gallery and centre for social gatherings.

The British Empire Academy will move into its new quarters forthwith, but up to June various other events already arranged will be held there. A programme of art exhibitions, concerts, and recitals of a wholly British character will take place later. At Easter there will be an important exhibition of pictures, to which British artists living reasonably near London will be invited to contribute, and in the autumn there will be another such exhibition of a more comprehensive character. Meanwhile a number of evenings will be set aside for concerts of British musical works to be performed by British musicians. Membership of the Academy is to be offered to all Empire artists, whether painters, sculptors, writers, musicians, or any other kind, who would thus have a centre in London with adequate exhibition space."

Linked with the above information, the "Survey of London, Volume 32, Parish of St. James Westminster" indicates that number 6 Burlington Gardens was newly built and opened in 1870 by Queen Victoria as an examination centre for the University of London before the University moved to the Imperial College site in South Kensington in 1900. Number 6 was then briefly occupied by the National Antarctic Expedition until 1902 when it was made over to the Civil Service Commission and still occupied by them in 1963. And then this paragraph: "Since 1928 the British Academy has occupied rooms in the building which were reconstructed and adapted for their use to the plans of Arnold Mitchell". If the "British Academy" was a shortened version of the "British Empire Academy" and "their use" was art exhibitions, then this places the New Burlington Galleries in number 6 Burlington Gardens. London Group catalogues show that up to five galleries were used to exhibit over 300 items to the public. There are no other premises big enough in (present day) Burlington Gardens to accommodate such galleries. 1928 is also the year when The London Group left the Royal Watercolour Society's gallery and held their retrospective exhibition at the new venue, the New Burlington galleries, at Easter, 1928 (the "important exhibition of pictures" mentioned in the Times press-cutting?). The only other significant building with an entrance on to Burlington Gardens was number 7, also known as Queensbury House, owned during this period by the Royal Bank of Scotland.

**The staircase at
6 Burlington Gardens**

The imposing staircase beyond the entrance to what were the New Burlington
Galleries. Halfway up the stairs is a small, mezzanine gallery which is called the
Staircase Gallery in The London Group catalogues. This also firmly identifies
number 6 Burlington Gardens as the New Burlington Galleries.

1929

In a UK General Election Labour under Ramsay MacDonald form the second Labour government in coalition with the Liberals. It was dubbed the "Flapper Election" as women over 21 voted for the first time. Italy and the Vatican sign the Lateran Treaty in which the Vatican is recognised as a sovereign state. Many are killed on both sides in the 1929 Palestinian Riots. Saint Valentine's Day Massacre in Chicago. At the Bell Telephone Laboratories in New York, H.E. Ives demonstrates the first colour television pictures. Following an all-time high the American Wall Street Stock Market collapses in October (Black Thursday) and heralds the beginning of the Great Depression. "All Quiet on the Western Front" published, written by Erich Maria Remarque. First appearance of the cartoon characters Tin Tin and Popeye.

Royal Academy Exhibition of Dutch Art 1450 – 1900 including de Hooch, Rembrandt and Vermeer.
The Whitechapel Art Gallery "Contemporary British Art".
The Museum of Modern Art in New York opens to the public.
The Stedelijk Museum in Amsterdam holds a Neue Sachlichkeit exhibition.

London Group President: Rupert Lee (1922)

"The London Group, 26th Exhibition", New Burlington Galleries, Burlington Gardens W1, 5th January to 26th January 1929. Officers remained the same as the previous year. No new members had been elected at this time. Fifty-four members were recorded in the catalogue with sixty-five non-members chosen to exhibit with them. Notable non-members exhibiting were James Boswell, William Coldstream, John Dodgson, R.O. Dunlop, H.E. du Plessis, Richard Eurich, E. (Elsie) Farleigh, Edna Ginesi, Nina Hamnett, S.W. Hayter, Frances Hodgkins, James Holland, Lynton Lamb, Morland Lewis, Edna Manley, Robert Medley, Maresco Pearce, Mary Potter and Wyndham Tryon. Two hundred and twenty-three two-dimensional works were shown and thirteen sculptures. Again, only titles, names and prices were printed in the unillustrated catalogue. Titles continue to indicate figurative subject matter, still life, landscape, interior, portrait and flowers, of which there were an abundant profusion, chrysanthemums, dahlias, anemones, stocks, tobacco plant, lilies, gladiolus, fuchsias and laburnum. A.H. (Nan) Hudson's "Mid-day Cassis" seems to sum up the rather sleepy, soporific, comfortable feel of the subjects depicted. The sculptures appeared to be much more vital using a wide range of materials, bronze, mahogany, marble, stone, alabaster, wood, ebony, cedarwood, plaster and lead. Prices overall were very reasonable averaging between fifteen to fifty pounds. Duncan Grant was asking £525 for his "Pierrot Lunaire", Matthew Smith £262.10 for "Dahlias and Pears" and Mark Gertler's "Sleeping Girl" was priced at £200. A total of £828.17.0 for sales of work was recorded in the Accounts book. Duncan Grant made £420, Matthew Smith £93 (less 1929 sub..) and A.P. Allinson £33.12.0. 893 admissions were also recorded and 646 catalogues were sold. One of the advertisements in the catalogue, headed "A Problem Picture", gives a snapshot of the times. Visitors to the exhibition were asked to make a donation to the London Association for the Blind in order to purchase new knitting machines for "skilled blind girls that are face to face with unemployment and its attendant miseries".

"The London Group, Twenty-seventh Exhibition", New Burlington Galleries, Burlington Galleries, W1., 14th October to 1st November 1929. There was no change in officer structure since the January exhibition. Sidney Carline had died and four new members were elected, Charles Maresco Pearce, Roland Vyvian Pitchforth, H.E. du Plessis and Arthur Pollen. There were eighty-nine non-member exhibitors for this exhibition. In addition to most of the non-members selected for the January exhibition, Quentin Bell, Edward Burra, Jacob Epstein, Julian Trevelyan, Gabriel White and H.S. Williamson exhibited work in this second exhibition of 1929. Two hundred paintings were hung along with thirty-five watercolours and drawings and twenty sculptures. Epstein showed four pieces which by their titles appear to be portrait busts. No sizes or media were printed in the exhibition catalogue. Twelve sculptors were exhibited in total and of these twelve, ten were to be shown in the next London Group exhibition which would be totally devoted to sculpture. Only Clare Balfour and Eric Schilsky were not shown in the 1930 Sculpture Exhibition. With the President Rupert Lee having moved from painting to sculpture in the last few years, no doubt his new found interest was influencing policy. Epstein's prices were very high compared to others, asking £200 and £300. Duncan Grant was asking £183.15s for "The Doorway" and £131 5s for "Still Life and Guitar". Horace Brodzky was asking £100 for "Allegory" as was Paul Nash for "Northern Adventure". Otherwise prices were held at between £15 to £50 on average. The pervading style was still figurative according to title.

At the back of the catalogue is an advert for Alex. Reid & Lefévre, Ltd. (The Lefévre Galleries) who inform the reader that British and French Modern Masters are "always on view". The British Modern Masters always on view were the Scottish Colourists, Cameron, Fergusson, McBey and Peploe. French Modern Masters included Cézanne, Degas, Derain, Daumier, Manet, Matisse, Picasso, Renoir, Sisley, Seurat, Utrillo and Van Gogh. This advert indicated the tastes of the time and, at the end of the decade, the prevailing influences within The London Group.

There were 1,544 admissions to the 27th Annual Exhibition raising £74.4.0 and 1,175 catalogues were sold for a total of £29.7.6. Nineteen works were sold bringing in £455.19.5 with Grant and Allinson, again, making good sales. Group finances were not as healthy as in the previous year. The Pass Book at Drummonds dated 13th September 1929 recorded debits of £1,597.15.4, credits of £1,657.18.11 and a balance of £60.3.7.

Burlington Gardens, running parallel to Piccadilly behind the Royal Academy, became well known to London Group members. It was here that the Group held their Annual Exhibitions from 1928 to 1938. The commemorative stone below the street sign bears the date 1925 testament to the developing economic importance of this area of Piccadilly.

The 1930's

Herbert Read, published "**The Meaning of Art**" in 1931 followed by a series of lectures explaining the importance of abstract or 'plastic' components that can be found in earlier artists' work and developed by contemporary visual artists. He was a great champion of the Surrealists, "contemplate with wonder objects which civilisation has rejected but which the savage and surrealist worship". In 1933 Read published "Art Now", an international survey of modern art. Roger Fry, painter, writer and critic, was a powerful influence supporting French Art and European developments. Very influential in The London Group for two decades, Fry died in 1934.

In 1931 **Abstraction-Création** was founded. Members included Alexander Calder, Robert Delaunay, Naum Gabo, Piet Mondrian, Barbara Hepworth, Ben Nicholson and Edward Wadsworth. The group put out five annual publications in which members made statements about their work, for example, in 1933 Kurt Schwitters and his Hanover Merzbau were featured.

The Artists International Association was formed in 1933. James Fitton, elected to The London Group in the following year, was a founder member and later also became a member of the Royal Academy. The AIA was described as an exhibiting society, much like The London Group, an artists' forum and focus for left wing political activity. The original declaration of political intent was signed by Eileen Agar, Merlyn Evans, Rupert Lee (who was President of The London Group from 1926–1936 and must, therefore, have signed 'in office'), Henry Moore, Paul Nash and Julian Trevellyan all at some time members of The London Group. The declaration continued, "Intervene (against Fascism) as poets, artists and intellectuals by violent or subtle subversion and by stimulating desire". Almost one thousand joined the AIA including Duncan Grant, Vanessa Bell and Carel Weight who was to be elected to The London Group in 1949. James Boswell, satirical illustrator and chairman from 1944, and Francis Klingender, an art historian, were prominent in the AIA.

Unit One the Modern Movement in English Architecture, Painting and Sculpture. Founded in 1933 by Paul Nash. An important exhibition took place at the Mayor Galleries in April 1934. Those taking part were: Paul Nash (1914), Edward Burra (1949), Edward Wadsworth (1913), Ben Nicholson, Barbara Hepworth (1930), Wells Coates (Architect) and the writer/critic Herbert Read. Unit One brought new European developments (Surrealism, Constructivism, etc.) to British art which influenced and informed young British artists. "The advent of Unit 1 in 1933 deprived the London Group of a number of its most gifted members, as Group X (The Vorticists) had done in 1920. The large and rambling character of the London Group was not attractive to certain artists". (Denys Wilcox "The London Group 1913-1939"). Apart from Edward Burra, all founder members of Unit One were already members of The London Group when Unit One was formed. There was dissatisfaction with the direction of The London Group at this time and allegiances were transferred to this new grouping.

Seven and Five Society, "purged" to become 7 & 5 in April 1934. The Seven and Five Society started exhibiting together from April 1920 at Walker's Galleries in Bond Street. The house style was non-prescriptive and espoused faux-naïve St.Ives artists. To begin with the Society was purely an exhibiting group, just like The London Group. A 1934 purge, however, left a hard core of ten radical abstract artists, Francis Butterfield, Barbara Hepworth (1930), Ivon Hitchens (1931), Arthur Jackson, David Jones, Henry Moore (1930), Staite Murray, Ben Nicholson, Winifred Nicholson and John Piper (1933). In 1934 Laszlo Moholoy-Nagy left Germany following the closure of the German Bauhaus. He spent three years in Britain meeting, among other modernists, Moore, Nicholson and Hepworth. Shortly before the outbreak of war, Adrian Stokes and his wife Margaret Mellis moved to St Ives in Cornwall to escape the expected bombing. They then invited Ben Nicholson, Barbara Hepworth and their children to join them. They, in turn, invited Naum Gabo to come down to Cornwall where they formed the influential nucleus of the visual avant-garde. The 7&5's October 1935 exhibition at Zwemmers was the first all abstract show seen in London. It was also the group's last exhibition, existing for sixteen years and holding fourteen exhibitions.

In 1928 the **East London Art Club** exhibited at the Whitechapel Art Gallery. The club grew from classes taught by John Cooper at the Bow and Bromley Evening Institute in East London. John Cooper founded the **East London Group**, a development of the East London Art Club, at about the time he was elected to The London Group in 1930. The East London Group were a group of up to thirty-five artists whose work was based in the East End of London. Most had no formal training or education and worked at menial jobs for a living. Their style was uncompromisingly realist and they were exhibited at the Whitechapel Art Gallery, the National Gallery Millbank (Tate Britain) and in eight exhibitions at the Lefèvre Gallery through the 1930s. Cooper was a charismatic teacher and friend of Sickert. His wife and fellow East London Group member, Phyllis Bray was elected to The London Group in 1933 along with William Coldstream, another exhibitor with the ELG. Indeed, the East London Group had a very similar structure to The London Group. John Cooper was President, Morroe FitzGerald was Chairman, Archibald Hatemore Honorary Secretary and W.J. Steggles Honorary Secretary. Could there have been some "cross-fertilisation" here? Elsie Farleigh was also a member of both The London Group and the East London Group. There's an interesting pattern to London Group elections emerging here, John Farleigh (Elsie's husband) was elected in 1928, John Cooper in 1930, Elsie Farleigh in 1931 and Phyllis Bray (Cooper's wife) and William Coldstream in 1933. This 'group within a group' were to become instrumental in prising The London Group from the grip of the Bloomsbury members in the middle thirties. Other exhibitors with the

East London Group were B.A.R. Carter, Harold Steggles, Elwin Hawthorne, George Board, Grace Oscroft, Lilian Leahy, Cecil Osborne, Henry Silk and Alan Turpin. Many literary, political and social figures supported the ELG, with extensive press coverage of their exhibitions and sales to public collections. The last exhibition of the East London Group took place at the Lefevre Galleries in 1936. John Cooper died in the Second World War. David Buckman has written a comprehensive history of the ELG entitled, "From Bow to Biennale: Artists of the East London Group". Buckman believed that the East London Group could have survived the Second World War and been revitalised had "overworked" Cooper survived.

AXIS, A Quarterly Review of Contemporary 'Abstract' Painting and Sculpture The first issue, AXIS 1, was published in January 1935 and edited by Myfanwy Evans (Piper). It contained articles and reviews on contemporary visual issues and published its last issue, AXIS 8, in the winter of 1938. AXIS fought for, "what could be called the Modern Movement" (John Craxton).

The International Surrealist Exhibition London, June 1936 Graham Sutherland (1937), Rupert Lee (1922) and Eileen Agar (1933) took part as some time London Group members. Other exhibitors included Arp, de Chirico, Duchamp, Ernst, Klee, Miro, Picasso, Roland Penrose, Herbert Read and Salvador Dali. Surrealism was a movement initially formed by Andre Breton in 1924. It grew out of the anarchic Dada movement of the previous decade. Dada intended to shock and shake the foundations of respectability and convention. Surrealism used the dream and subconscious image in the Freudian era to unsettle the observer. Collage and Frottage, notably Max Ernst, were a chosen media, as was hyper-realism from Salvador Dali and Yves Tanguy. Andre Masson worked through intuitive abstraction based on automatism laying the foundations for Abstract Expressionism. Rupert Lee and Diana Brinton Lee organised the exhibition held in the New Burlington Galleries behind the Royal Academy.

The Euston Road Group was formed in October 1937 as a reaction to the extremes of the avant-garde, especially Surrealism. The Euston Road Group looked back to classical figuration and more analytically objective artists, especially Cézanne and Sickert. The figurative tradition was imported into Camberwell School of Art between 1943 and 1949 and was continued in the Slade School of Fine Art from 1950 onwards. There were four original 'Principals' forming the Euston Road Group: Graham Bell, William Coldstream (1933), Victor Pasmore (1934) and Claude Rogers (1938), four 'pupils': BAR Carter, Denis Daway (?), Lawrence Gowing (1940-43) and Basil Rocke, and one 'associate' William Townsend (1951). Other exhibitors with the Euston Road Group were John Dodgson (1947), Anthony Eyton (1961), Elsie Few (1940-43), Andrew Forge (1960), Anthony Fry (1955), Patrick George (1957), Barbara Harris, Philip Matthews, Rodrigo Moynihan (1933) and Christopher Pinsent. Coldstream, Pasmore, Rogers, Few and Moynihan were all London Group members before the Euston Road Group was formed. Claude Rogers was The London Group President in the 1950s and 60s and was also heavily involved with education at the same time (Slade, Professor at Reading). Coldstream was Professor at the Slade from 1949. In 1959 he was Chairman of the National Advisory Council on Art Education and published the Coldstream Report on Education in 1960 changing the structure of art education in this country and introducing compulsory art history studies for all art students. Lawrence Gowing was Professor at the Slade in the 1970s whilst Andrew Forge was Professor at Reading University at the same time.

314 Euston Road
London NW1

This was the address of the Euston Road School's premises established in October 1937. There were four original 'Principals', Graham Bell, William Coldstream, Victor Pasmore and Claude Rogers. Coldstream, Pasmore and Rogers were all members of The London Group at some point in their careers. The School was forced to close at the outbreak of the Second World War. As can be seen, the site, close to the Euston Road underpass, has now been extensively redeveloped.

Coldstream was also involved with **Mass Observation**, a social research organisation created in 1937 to record and reflect upon the opinions of "the man in the steet". Mass Observation was set up by the anthropologist Tom Harrison, poet Charles Madge, film maker Humphrey Jennings and photographer Humphrey Spender. Untrained researchers were encouraged to keep diaries and to record people's behaviour at work and in the streets. Julian Trevelyan (1949) and Graham Bell also made contributions to the work of the movement. The difficulty with such an institution was that it was felt to be 'spying' on people and to be scientifically 'skewed'. A Tate Britain 2013 information label states, "Critics saw the project in terms of middle class intellectuals from southern England observing the northern working class as if it were another breed".

Picasso's **"Guernica"** was shown in Britain in 1937. The painting arrived in the country un-stretched and rolled and was delivered to Manchester where no gallery or big enough venue could be found to show it. However, a group of art students discovered a disused car showroom and "Guernica" was unceremoniously nailed to its wall for exhibition.

Yet another new periodical was published in 1937, **"Circle: International Survey of Constructive Art"**. The onset of war prevented the second edition being printed. Contributors from Great Britain were Ben Nicholson, John Piper (1933), John Cecil Stephenson as painters, Barbara Hepworth (1930) and Henry Moore (1930) as sculptors and Herbert Read as a writer. Other contributors were European Constructivists, Architects and Writers. In this first publication Mondrian had written "By the unification of architecture, sculpture and painting, a new plastic reality will be created".

Adolf Ziegler, as Head of the Reich Chamber of Visual Art, curated the **'Entarete Kunst'** exhibition in Munich in 1937, the infamous degenerate art exhibition. Emil Nolde, despite being a member of the Nazi Party, and Max Beckmann had works shown in this notorious exhibition, Beckmann eventually fled to Amsterdam. Hans Feibusch, elected to The London Group in 1934 having fled Germany, also had work included in this exhibition. At the end of the process, 16,558 works were declared 'degenerate' and many were destroyed.

Tate Modern Time Line from 1930-40 "Group f/64" including Ansel Adams, Imogen Cunningham, Willard Van Dyke and Edward Weston. Individuals André Kertész and Georgia O'Keefe. "Harlem Renaissance" including Jacob Lawrence and Romaine Bearden. "Unit One" including Barbara Hepworth (1930), Henry Moore (1930) and Paul Nash (1914). "Socialist Realism" including André Fougeron, Renato Guttuso and Boris Taslitzky. "British Surrealist Group" including Eileen Agar (1933), Edward Burra (1949), David Gascoyne, Paul Nash (1914), Roland Penrose, Herbert Read and Edward Wadsworth (1913). "Photo-Journalism" including Robert Capa, Henri Cartier-Bresson and Lee Miller. Individuals Manuel Alvarro Bravo, Frida Kahlo, Edward Hopper, Balthus, Julio González and Stanley Spencer (1914).

1930

Mahatma Gandhi embarks on a programme of civil disobedience in India. Whilst on its way to India on its maiden flight, British airship R101 crashes in France. In Germany the National Socialists become the second largest party in parliament. US President Hoover asks Congress for millions of dollars for a public works programme to support the economy. Amy Johnson becomes the first woman to make a solo flight from England to Australia. In the first ever football World Cup Uruguay beat Argentina 4-2. First publication of the cartoon strip Mickey Mouse. Minor planet Pluto discovered.

Cooling Galleries 92 Bond Street, London Artists' Association exhibiton in which Vanessa Bell had a "major triumph", reviewed by a young John Piper.
Agnew and **Lefevre** were important London galleries during the thirties.

London Group President: Rupert Lee (1922)

Noel Adeney, John Cooper, Barbara Hepworth, Maurice Lambert, Edna Manley, Henry Moore, Hyam Myer and John Skeaping were elected this year.

London Group Exhibition of Open-air Sculpture, The Roof Gardens, Messrs. Selfridge & Co., Ltd., Oxford Street, London, W.1., 2nd June to 30th August 1930. Twenty sculptors, nearly half women, took part including A.P. Allinson, Elizabeth Andrews, Priscilla Baumer, Frank Dobson, Lavender Dower, D.C. Dunlop, Alan Durst, Jacob Epstein, Barbara Hepworth, Arnrid Johnstone, Moses Kotteler, Maurice Lambert, Rupert Lee, Edna Manley, Henry Moore, Elizabeth Muntz, Arthur Pollen, Ethel Pye, John Skeaping and Anne Strauss. The exhibition was organised by Adrian Allinson and Rupert Lee supported by garden architect Mrs. Marjory Allen and the Group's Secretary, Miss Brinton. Five sculptors, Barbara Hepworth, Maurice Lambert, Edna Manley, Henry Moore and John Skeaping were elected to The London Group in order to take part in this exhibition designed to raise the profile of sculpture in the Group and in the art world as a whole. A number did not continue exhibiting with the Group after 1930 and their membership lapsed. Barbara Hepworth only showed once again in the October 1931 London Group exhibition. In the same year she met Ben Nicholson and formed a relationship with him. Between 1932 and 1935 she exhibited with the 7&5 Society and in 1933 joined Unit One. John Skeaping, Hepworth's husband (they married after meeting as students), only put work into one more London Group exhibition in October 1931. He then became a member of the 7&5 Society from 1931 to 1932. Maurice Lambert showed twice with the Group after 1930, once in October 1930 and again in November 1934. Lambert had been a member of 7&5 from 1928 and left in 1932. Edna Manley showed in five subsequent London Group exhibitions up until November 1938. For many years Manley lived and worked in Kingston, Jamaica showing a number of mainly portrait busts in London Group exhibitions. Henry Moore supported the Group beyond 1930 serving on a number of London Group Hanging Committees in the early 1930s. Moore at the same time was a member of 7&5 from 1932 to 1935 and of Unit One, joining in 1933. Sixty-one sculptures in a wide variety of materials, including plaster, were shown in the roof gardens. Work was for sale with Maurice Lambert asking the highest price of £500 for "Group on a Hill" in lead. John Skeaping priced "Torso" in marble at £200, Henry Moore was asking £157.10s for "Standing Girl" in stone and Edna Manley £157.10s for "Eve" in wood. Jacob Epstein showed his bronze "Head of Paul Robeson" (lent by Hugh Walpole). It was possible to buy a Moore or a Hepworth for about £30 from this exhibition. A debit sum of £105 is recorded in the Accounts ledger for, "Damage Selfridge a/c Moore". The media was printed next to the title in the exhibition catalogue and the titles indicate a largely figurative approach in which animals figure prominently, owl, buffalo, bear, monkey, squirrel, ape, elephant, pigeon, swan and numerous cats all represented. Materials used by the sculptors included stone, lead, bronze, wood, marble, concrete and pottery. Roger Fry wrote an introduction to the catalogue, "The years covered by the existence of the London Group comprise one of the most eventful episodes in the history of British Art. It has been a period of searching inquiry into the principles of design, of criticism of all the accepted standards, of daring experiment in the search for new possibilities. Throughout this period the London Group has been the home of those English artists in whom the ferment of new ideas was working".

Selfridge & Co
Oxford Street, London W1

Selfridge's department store was opened in 1909 and by the 1920s the roof gardens were very popular comprising a terraced garden, cafes, a mini golf course and an all-girl gun club. The roof gardens were often used for fashion shows. Following a bombing raid causing extensive damage in 1940, the gardens were permanently closed.

"Twenty-eighth Exhibition of The London Group", New Burlington Galleries, Burlington Gardens, W.1, 13th October to 31st October 1930, billed as "The English 'Salon d'automne'". Officers continued in office, Rupert Lee as President, Frederick J. Porter as Vice President, J.S. Woodger as Honorary Treasurer and Diana Brinton as Secretary. Sixty-four members are recorded and one hundred and eleven non-members selected for this exhibition, a huge number of non-members. The catalogue lists four separate sections to the exhibition, 'Catalogue', numbered 1 to 181, 'Small Room', numbered 182 to 223A, 'Drawings and Water-colours' 224 to 262 and 'Sculpture' 263 to 291. Notable non-members selected for exhibition included Edward Ardizzone, Quentin Bell, Edward Burra, William Coldstream, Lynton Lamb, Morland Lewis, Robert Medley, Rodrigo Moynihan, Margaret Nicholson, Victor Pasmore, Mervyn Peake, Mary Potter, Claude Rogers, Helen Saunders, Geoffrey Tibble and Julian Trevelyan. Apart from Arnrid Johnstone, all of the Selfridge sculptors were represented in this exhibition too. Sculpture was the most expensive section with Lambert, Schilsky, Pollen, Muntz and Allinson all asking over £100 for work. Two-dimensional work was much more affordable and noticeably lower in price with only Matthew Smith, Brodzky and Farleigh asking sums over £100. With no illustrations in the catalogue only titles indicated content of the works on show. There seems to be a predominance of landscape and cityscape in the painting section with the ubiquitous portrait, flower and nude subjects in close support. 921 admissions brought in £43.11.6, whilst £19.8.6 was raised from the sale of 777 catalogues.

In a foreword to the British Empire Academy's Second Exhibition, Section 1 (17th April to 7th May 1930) in the New Burlington Galleries, Burlington Gardens, Charles Peers wrote, "As nearly altruistic as possible, the British Empire Academy uses the profits which accrue from the lettings of the Burlington Galleries in order to keep it subscriptions as low as possible." The London Group was hiring the New Burlington Galleries from the BEA for their annual exhibitions. A possible link was C.R.W. Nevinson who, as one of twelve, was a member of the BEA's Painting Selection Committee for this exhibition, Charles Peers being the Chairman of this committee. Peers continues in a style redolent of the 1930s, "The BEA Club Meetings on Wednesday evenings provide excellent entertainment in song, dance and drama. At these gatherings one gets those little chats with brother artists which are often so useful and always pleasant - exchange of views is good. Then there is another side of the Club: the Artist can entertain his clients and give them a really good evening for a ridiculously small fee. Art teachers also are taking advantage of this as a means of entertaining their students".

On the 24th September 1930 The London Group had a balance of £136.9.1 at Drummonds. Sub..s had brought in a figure of £105.10.3 still set at £3 a year per member.

1931

Many large scale building works continue in the US, the Hoover Dam, the San Francisco - Oakland Bay Bridge and the Empire State Building. In one of the world's greatest natural disasters, between 850,000 and 4,000,000 people are killed in Central China in the Huang He floods. The Chinese Soviet Republic is proclaimed by Mao Zedong whilst in Madrid the Second Spanish Republic is declared. A financial crisis developes in Europe with the near collapse of the European banking system and the US attempts to shore up the European banks. In the UK a National Government is formed to tackle the Great Depression replacing Ramsay MacDonald's Labour government. MacDonald was expelled from the Labour Party for supporting a National Government and in a General Election later in the year the Conservatives win a landslide election. The UK abandons the gold standard. On the 31st December the Statute of Westminster brings into being the British Commonwealth of Nations.

In film, Bela Lugosi stars in "Dracula" and Charlie Chaplin makes "City Lights". Salvador Dali's "The Persistence of Memory" is exhibited for the first time in Paris. Herbert Read, publishes "The Meaning of Art" in 1931 followed by a series of lectures. Picasso was shown at the Lefevre gallery.

London Group President: Rupert Lee (1922)

Raymond Coxon (as an Honorary Member), R.O. Dunlop, Elsie Farleigh and Ivon Hitchens were elected to The London Group this year.

"The London Group Twenty-ninth Exhibition", New Burlington Galleries, Burlington Gardens W1, 12th October to 30th October 1931. Roger Fry wrote the following piece as part of a Preface, "The years covered by the London Group comprise one of the most eventful episodes in the history of British Art. It has been a period of searching enquiry into the principles of design, of criticism of all the accepted standards, of daring experiment in the search for new possibilities. Throughout this period the London Group has been the home of those English artists in whom the ferment of new ideas was working". In the catalogue to this exhibition Rupert Lee is recorded as President with Frederick J. Porter as Vice President, Diana Brinton as Secretary and J.S. Woodger as the Honorary Treasurer. There is no indication as to who was serving on the Working Committee this year although there were sixty-eight members, twenty-one of whom were women and included Vanessa Bell, Barbara Hepworth and Thérèse Lessore. There were three hundred and thirty-two works in the exhibition, twenty-nine sculptures, forty-one drawings and watercolours, the rest, presumably, oil paintings. Of the one hundred and twenty-one non-members exhibiting at least fifty-five were women. It is difficult to accurately ascribe gender because many exhibitors only gave initials, only the artist, title and price were printed in the catalogue. Prices generally ranged from £10 to £30. Top asking price was £250 for Elliott Seabrooke's "Hampstead Heath" followed by Matthew Smith's "A Model" at £180. Barbara Hepworth priced her sculpture "Half Figure" in Hamhill Stone at £100, as did John Skeaping for his "Male Torso" in Ancaster Stone. Notable non-member exhibitors were Edward Ardizzone, James Boswell, Nina Hamnett, Kenneth Martin, Rodrigo Moynihan, Barbara Nicholson, John Piper, Ceri Richards, Claude Rogers, Geoffrey Tibble, William Townsend and John Tunnard. Hamnett had been a member and many of the others were to be elected to The London Group in the future. Titles in the catalogue indicate a figurative exhibition with landscapes, figure paintings, portraits, flowers and still life predominant.

An anonymous introduction informed the catalogue purchaser that, "The London Group is a society that arose from a definite need. It was founded internally by the action of those who became its members, and not by outside agents who wished to do something for it. At the time of its inception – 1913 – there were a few small groups of painters who felt that the new ideas fermenting in the arts were of such importance as to require the foundation of a new society. They formed themselves into the London Group, which may politically be regarded as a revolutionary body. It gave the first exhibition at the Goupil Galleries in March 1914. Later it moved to Heal's in Tottenham Court Road, from there to the R.W.S. (Royal Watercolour Society) in Pall Mall, and from the R.W.S. to Burlington Gardens.

It has held twenty-eight exhibitions since its foundation in March 1914, one Retrospective Exhibition and one special exhibition of Outdoor Sculpture.

It has been asked by a critic what principle it is that holds the London Group together. The scientific explanation is "pressure from outside", and the natural answer that "they do hold together". Further, one could say that they do not pretend to have discovered a formula which will make their works uniformly excellent or exactly alike. They have neither gospel nor creed, but endeavour to foster vital talent in whatever pictorial form it presents itself, remembering that art is a personal expression and not a mass produced article."

The small A5, yellow catalogue priced at sixpence had a stylised image of a vase of flowers, reversed vertically and this same format was used for the next five annual exhibition catalogues. Could this indicate a desire for stability or a lack of fresh ideas? Sponsorship advertisements in the catalogue were paid for by the Morris-Singer Bronze Foundry, The Leicester Galleries and Windsor & Newton. Printing costs were 10 guineas.

1,253 people visited the exhibition and 992 catalogues were sold. The cost of hiring the New Burlington Galleries was £180 and twelve sales were transacted, V. Bell earning £36.12.0 and R. Fry £17.0.0. The balance of accounts as at the 26th September 1931 was £145.13.6.

1932

In July the Dow Jones Industrial Index reaches its lowest point at 41.2. Unemployment reaches at least 33% in the USA and Germany and few countries can afford to pay their unemployed any benefits. In November Democrat Frankiln D. Roosevelt defeats Herbert Hoover in the US Presidential election. In India Gandhi continues to peacefully confront British rule. There is conflict between Japan and China where the League of Nations broker a peace. Paul von Hindenburg is elected President of Germany and negotiates with Adolph Hitler to form a new government in troubled Germany, whilst in Paris the French President is assassinated. The BBC begins its World Service broadcasts as the BBC Empire Service. Aldous Huxley publishes "Brave New World". In the USSR Stalin 'outlaws' Constructivism and urges artists to return to more classical, social realist forms. Johnny Weissmuller stars in "Tarzan the Ape Man".

In America photographers formed **"Group f/64"**, including Ansel Adams, Imogen Cunningham and Edward Weston. The left-wing British artists group called **Artist International** was set up in London with the aim of achieving "the unity of artists against Fascism and war and the suppression of culture". As with The London Group, there were thirty-two founder members, mainly commercial artists and designers and avowedly Marxist. Misha Black was the first Chairman and the AIA produced posters, pamphlets and other propaganda materials. Founder member James Fitton, elected to The London Group in 1934, used the Central School of Art printing facilities where he taught lithography. For the first time the title **'Tate Gallery'** becomes official.

London Group President: Rupert Lee (1922)

This year three new members were elected, R.P. Bedford, David Low (as an Honorary Member) and Morland Lewis.

"Thirtieth Exhibition of The London Group", New Burlington Galleries, Burlington Gardens, W.1., 10th October to 28th October 1932. Officers were unchanged since the 1931 exhibition. Sixty-nine members were recorded at the beginning of this year's exhibition catalogue whilst ninety-five non-member exhibitors were listed, at least thirty-nine being women. John Piper, Ceri Richards, Graham Sutherland and John Tunnard were selected this year, a whiff of British surrealism. Perhaps more so than in previous exhibitions there seem to be more 'unknowns' than in previous years with such evocative names as Prince Albrecht Urach, Evelyn Clutton-Brock, M. D'Arcy Thompson and Vsevolod Sozonov. This year work was hung in four rooms including the 'Large Gallery', 'Small Gallery and 'Staircase Gallery'. Looking for sales in excess of £100 were Elliott Seabrooke, Richard Sickert, F.H. Huhsam and sculptors Edna Manley and Rupert Lee. As there seemed to be more unknowns selected this year, prices were lower than in previous exhibitions. Elizabeth Watson was only asking 3 guineas for her "Hagar and Ishmael" whilst Elizabeth Andrews priced her lead sculpture "Cat" at only £3. Almost all of the other prices were below £30. A figure of £246.9.6 is recorded in the accounts ledger under 'sales', whilst £48.6.6 appears under 'Entrance and Catalogue' (just over 1,000 visitors). It is unfortunate and frustrating that, as in all recent exhibition catalogues, no sizes or media were given.

A preface written by Roger Hinks alludes to the relationship between artist and buyer: "It is the business of the intelligent modern artist to extract aesthetic virtues out of economic necessities. He has to realise that the public requires few pictures, and those small; and he has to regulate his output to satisfy not only the extent but also the kind of demand now made upon him.

In the nineteenth century the fortunate artist could afford to imitate the wasteful processes of nature, and paint just as the spirit moved him...

Times have changed. The modern buyer, if less lavish, is more intelligent and more exacting. A picture is not, to him, just a picture: a decent covering for so many square feet of wall, which pays an incidental tribute to his purse and his culture. He buys a picture for quite different reasons, and especially because he thinks it will look well in a certain position in one of his rooms". Hicks continues, "... the most that an artist can do is to evolve a style which is likely to harmonise with the kind of domestic interior now in favour". How comfortably this view would sit with the more avant-garde artists in the Group at the time would be interesting to discover. The shadow of Roger Fry, founder of the interior design business Omega Workshops in the 1910s, looms large.

Denys J Wilcox writes informatively of this period in his book "Rupert Lee, Painter, Sculptor and Printmaker". On page 104 he sums up Diana Brinton's contribution to The London Group, "Diana proved herself to be a master organiser and Roger Fry, amongst others, witnessed her qualities at Group meetings. 'Here I noticed her accuracy and firmness in drawing up minutes, her businesslike exactitude in every detail and, what came out most in such meetings, where rather heated discussions not infrequently occurred, was her admirable tact, patience and firmness in dealing with even the most unreasonable objections'. In fact Diana relished the challenge of keeping a volatile band of artists on a constructive course and the evidence would suggest that she was one of the most outstanding exhibition organisers in London during the inter-war period. She must be credited with helping the London Group become a dominant force in modern British art." On page 105 Wilcox continues, "The London Group exhibition in 1932 was greeted with newspaper headlines such as, 'London Art Group Romance' and 'Romance Among The Artists', as the couple (Lee and Brinton) used their engagement to attract extra publicity for the exhibition. In addition, Lee had completed a larger than life-size head of Diana carved in sycamore and the couple posed either side of it for press photographs. Lee's carving was a most dramatic and heartfelt statement of his love for Diana. The press seized on the emotional power of the work, with Frank Rutter in the Sunday Times picking it out as one of the highlights of the show".

On the 22nd July 1932 the Group's balance at the bank was £97.14.7. On November 13th, 1932 the Group records seventeen sales presumably from the October exhibition, including R.Fry £17.0.0, R. Coxon £22.10, A. Allinson £21.0.0 and R.O. Dunlop £28.7.6.

1933

Events gather pace in Germany. Adolf Hitler is appointed Chancellor of Germany and delivers his "Proclamation to the German People" in Berlin. On February 27th the Reichstag is set on fire opening the way for many civil liberties to be withdrawn. In March the National Socialists gain nearly half the vote and the Enabling Act effectively makes Hitler dictator of Germany. The Gestapo is set up and in May the infamous event of the burning of books takes place. All opposition parties and Trade Unions are banned and Germany indicates that it will leave the League of Nations. In March in America Franklin D. Roosevelt succeeds Herbert Hoover as President. Later in the year prohibition comes to an end. Congress brings in the "New Deal". There is political instability in France as five coalitions fail during the year. In London the London Economic Conference is held at the Geological Museum. Sixty-six countries attempt to find solutions to the global economic crisis but the USA puts up barriers and the conference implodes. Also in London the London Passenger Transport Bill is introduced bringing into being "London Transport". Ninety-two separate transport businesses were placed under the authority of the LTPB. First printing of Harry Beck's London Underground diagram, "arguably the most successful and influential map design of the twentieth century". The original film of King Kong starring Fay Wray is released. Albert Einstein leaves Germany travelling to the USA where he is given a post at Princeton University. The British Interplanetary Society is formed.

Ben Nicholson and Barbara Hepworth visit Picasso in his Paris studio.
Mayor Gallery show Max Ernst
Wertheim Gallery 3/5 Burlington Gardens, William Townsend exhibition.
Cooling Galleries showed a duo exhibition of John Dodgson and Claude Rogers.
Both artists were to be elected as Presidents of The London Group in the future.
The **Artists International Association** is formed (see 1930s).

London Group President: Rupert Lee (1922)

Nine new members elected this year. They were Eileen Agar, Phyllis Bray, William Coldstream, P.N. (Norman) Dawson, Edna Ginesi (as an Honorary Member), Blair Hughes-Stanton, Rodrigo Moynihan, John Piper and H.S. Williamson, a huge and healthy intake.

"Thirty-first Exhibition of The London Group", New Burlington Galleries, Burlington Gardens W.1., 13th November to 1st December 1933. Officers remained the same as last year, a settled and consistent period of administration. Membership hits seventy with the large influx of nine new members. Similarly, exhibiting non-members hits a near record high of one hundred and fifteen. Some well-known names are sprinkled throughout the list, Edward Ardizzone, Quentin Bell, Richard Eurich, F.E. McWilliam, Kenneth and Mary Martin, Mary Potter, Brian Robb, Claude Rogers, William Townsend, Julian Trevelyan and John Tunnard. These are heady days for The London Group fulfilling its role as an exhibiting society. Prices continue to be highly affordable and reasonable, only Gertler, Muntz, Sickert and Wolfe in this huge exhibition require more than £100 for their work. (Mark Gertler exhibited, "Passage of Time" at £200, and Sickert showed "Peggy Ashcroft as Lady Teazle" at £300). It's illuminating to list others' prices too, Vanessa Bell asking £45, Bernard Meninsky £25, John Nash £60, Ivon Hitchens £16, Kenneth Martin 5 guineas, Roger Fry £25, John Piper 15 guineas, Edward Ardizzone 7 guineas and the sculptor F.E McWilliam 12 guineas. McWilliam is recorded as making £14.5.6 from this exhibition, whilst A. Allinson made £38.8.0, Mrs V. Bell £36.0.0 and Mrs Bevan £21.12.0. A total of eight sales were recorded. A glance through the titles reveals a continuing focus on figurative subjects, "Still Life", "Flowers", "River scene", "Nude study", "Girl reading", "Girl with Turban" and "Girl asleep" but a few. Two hundred and eighty-two two-dimensional works were on sale to the gallery going public, as well as fourteen sculptures, an enormous exhibition which gives the impression "pack 'em in and hang 'em high". 972 visitors were admitted and 530 catalogues were sold earning the Group £76.9.6 in total.

Frank Rutter writing in the Sunday Times was "strongly of the opinion that what the London Group needs now is, not reviewing, but wreaths". (David Buckman, 'From Bow to Biennale: Artists of the East London Group', page 187)

One of the adverts sponsoring the exhibition catalogue was for "The Modern Room Exhibition" at the Adams Gallery in Orchard Street W.1. The advert informed the reader that, "Artists of THE LONDON GROUP are now exhibiting paintings and sculpture in conjunction with new furniture designed by Maurice Adams at the Modern Room Exhibition". This ties in with the preface to the to the thirtieth London Group exhibition, written by Roger Hinks, setting the modern painter firmly within a domestic and decorative environment.

The Rule Book was tidied up in 1933. The last rules were printed by the Group under Lee's presidency in 1927. No rules appear to have been amended; there were still nineteen rules, even "No oil-paintings with white frames will be admitted to Exhibitions". The annual subscription remained at £3 as did the non-members exhibiting fee of 12/6. There must have been some reason for the reaffirmation of these rules. Could it be found in the section 'Special General Meetings' bearing in mind the rumblings of disquiet beginning within the membership? "The President and Executive Committee may at any time call a Special General Meeting, and shall do so on a requisition in writing signed by five members of the Group, and specifying the object of such meeting. The discussion at this shall be confined to the object for which the meeting was called. Members shall be given six clear days' notice of a special general meeting. Unless called by the Executive Committee for urgent business reasons the quorum at a special general meeting shall be twelve." Was Lee indicating to his critics that they needed to muster at least twelve votes against him?

The Group's Pass Book with Drummonds Branch, Royal Bank of Scotland was made up early this year. On the 27th January 1933 the Group's balance was £68.14.10. Sub..s this year remained at £3 for the year and raised over £237.

1934

Far right rallies in France attempt to destabilise the Third Republic. In Germany Himmler takes control of all police forces. June 30th, "Night of the Long Knives" incident in which the SA (brown shirt secret police) was purged. In August Hitler becomes Fuhrer or Head of State of Germany. The Austrian Chancellor is assassinated by Austrian Nazis. Chinese Communists begin the "Long March". The Soviet Union joins the League of Nations. Kipling and W.B. Yates win the Gothenberg Poetry Prize. F.Scott-Fitzgerald publishes "Tender is the Night". The 'British Committee for Relations with Other Countries' to develop cultural links is established– this body will eventually become the British Council. Stanley Matthews makes his first appearance in an England shirt.

At the **Tate Gallery** Hugh Willoughby's collection of Picasso paintings and drawings was exhibited between 23rd November and 31st December.
Mayor Gallery shows Paul Klee.
Zwemmer Gallery "Objective Abstractions" including Ivon Hitchens (1931), Rodrigo Moynihan (1933), Victor Pasmore (1934) and Geoffrey Tibble (1944).
Leicester Galleries in November Richard Sickert RA exhibited recent paintings. Lucien Pissarro showed paintings and drawings earlier in the year.

London Group President: Rupert Lee (1922)

In this year's elections Hans Feibusch, James Fitton, Victor Pasmore and John Tunnard became London Group members.

"Thirty-second Exhibition of The London Group", New Burlington Galleries, Burlington Gardens, W.1., 12th November to 30th November 1934. Even though officers remained the same as last year there is a feeling of change in the introduction to this year's exhibition catalogue with an appreciation for the recently deceased Roger Fry written by Rupert Lee.

"Those of us who remember the aesthetic battles of pre-war days and who took a wider interest in the arts than our studio activity demanded, will appreciate the debt which the modern artist owes to Roger Fry. In the dual activity of painter and critic he was the man to whom all the younger artists looked for light and guidance. Even those who disagreed with him were always anxious to know 'What does Fry think about it?' His judgement counted more, may we say 'cut more ice' than those of any other artist or critic of his day. He had perception, scholarship, sympathy, experience and generosity. In the work of unknown painters he often recognised values which his colleagues had passed over. We like to remember the occasion of his staying the condemnatory judgment of a work by saying, 'There is something to be said for this picture,' and Mr. Sickert's affectionately malicious retort, 'Say it Roger, say it'. The laugh was against him but the victory was his. Roger was always willing to say it, and to say it with unforgettable genius.

His paintings and writings we possess; his brilliance as a lecturer and impromptu speaker and his personal kindness are memories we value, and in the sadness of the loss there lingers the pride of association."

Six paintings by Fry were shown as a memorial to him. The titles seem to sum up the figurative style of most of the paintings shown in London Group exhibitions in previous years, "The Entrance to S. Pol", "Dieppe", "J. Maynard Keynes, Esq.", "Miss Nina Hamnett", "Peonies and Poppies" and "Oliveyard in Spring".

Membership remained at seventy. Another near record one hundred and twelve non-members were exhibited this year, at least fifty-eight of them women. In the First Gallery, Second Gallery, Staircase Gallery and the Small Gallery three hundred and two works were exhibited to the public. Nineteen of these were sculptures. Prices were still restrained, Raymond Coxon requiring £120 for "Bull-fight", Richard Sickert £100 for "Prima Donna and Soubrette", and sculptor Lionel Leslie £100 for a bronze, "Senegalese". Which means that two hundred and ninety-nine works were all under one hundred pounds! Out of nine recorded sales Jessica Dismoor sold a work for £16.16.0 whilst Quentin Bell received £12.0.0. Exhibit numbers 221 to 283 were all water-colours priced anywhere between £3 and £25 with the average price of £10 to £15. Most of The London Group members had produced work is this medium at this time and as well as the expected landscape subject matter, titles such as "Venus and Adonis", "Avian Discussion" (by John Tunnard) and "Mother and Child" suggested a wider range of subjects.

The catalogue carried adverts for a number of art books, especially those from the pen of Roger Fry published by Chatto & Windus, "Characteristics of French Art" illustrated at 12s 6d, for example. Herbert Read had recently published "Henry Moore, Sculptor. An Appreciation", the first monograph devoted to the work of Moore showing work from 1928 to 1933 and priced at 6s. All for sale at A. Zwemmer, 76-78 Charing Cross Road.

The death of Roger Fry signalled a change within The London Group. Rupert Lee and Diana Brinton Lee were out of the country for extended periods of time and some of the membership felt that the Gropu was being neglected and that the Presidency should change.

On the 1st June 1934 the Group had debits of £261.19.3, credits of £454.13.11 and a balance of £192.14.8, quite a healthy financial position. Membership fees had raised £121.15.0. Admissions (1,025), catalogues and hanging fees had brought in a total of £73.10.0 and sales from the exhibition were recorded at £94.16.0.

1935

Germany rearms in contravention of the Versailles Treaty. Britain agrees to limited expansion of the German Navy. In the UK King George V celebrates his Silver Jubilee. In a general election held on November 14th existing Prime Minister Stanley Baldwin retains power within the National Government but with a reduced majority. This parliament was to sit until 1945 until the outcome of the Second World War was clear. Clement Atlee becomes leader of the Labour Party. Later in the year Anthony Eden becomes Foreign Secretary. Alfred Hitchcock's "The 39 Steps" is released. Penguin Books paperbacks are introduced by Allen Lane. The De La Warr Pavilion in Bexhill on Sea is opened.

Artists International changed its name to **Artists International Association (AIA)** and organised the exhibition "Artists against Fascism and War". Robert Medley (1937), Henry Moore (1930) and Paul Nash (1914) were amongst the exhibitors. By the end of the Second World War the AIA had more than a thousand members. They also published a number of journals beginning with "Artists International Bulletin" in 1934-35 and a book of essays entitled "5 on Revolutionary Art" in 1935.

London Group President: Rupert Lee (1922)

Only one new member was elected this year, the sculptor Gertrude Hermes.

There were rumblings of discontent within the Group. The President Rupert Lee and his partner Diana Brinton Lee were dealing with complicated issues to do with Lee's former wife. Lee and his partner were frequently out of the country and certain members in the Group felt that the Group was being neglected and that Lee should be replaced as President. The two main protagonists were John Cooper, elected in 1930, and John Farleigh, elected in 1927. Cooper had experience of organising artists' groups; he was a Founder Member of the East London Group in 1928. 'Bloomsbury' was still the power broker within the Group but there was growing discontent and division. Vanessa Bell in particular actively backed Lee by organising tea parties in support of the incumbent President. Other notable Lee supporters were Keith Baynes, Duncan Grant, Morland Lewis, Rodrigo Moynihan and Maresco Pearce.

"Thirty-third Exhibition of The London Group", New Burlington Galleries, 11th November to 29th November 1935. Lee remained as President, Porter as Vic-President, Woodger as Honorary Treasurer and Diana Brinton Lee as Secretary. Seventy-two members were recorded in the catalogue including Honorary Member David Low. One hundred and four non-members were selected to exhibit including Roger Hilton, Brian Robb, Claude Rogers and Julian Trevelyan. The large majority of names could be considered in today's terms, unknowns, but at least thirty-nine of the non-member exhibitors were women. There were two hundred and ninety works listed in the catalogue, hung in the First, Second, Staircase and Small galleries. Fifteen watercolours were shown, all by non-members apart from one by R.V. Pitchforth. Twenty-two sculptures were exhibited, the most expensive being "Design for Garden Figure in Lead" by Stephen Tomlin at £400. Sickert was asking £250 for "Sketch for Raising of Lazarus", Gertler's "Composition" was priced at £200 and Duncan Grant's "Jar and Melon" could be bought for £105. Walter Bayes, John Maxwell and Thérèse Lessore were all around £100 but the majority of prices were pitched between £10 to £50. Titles suggested a predominance of landscape with subjects ranging from close to home (London) to S. de Karlowska's "Dabrownik, The Mill" and Ethelbert White's "The Port, Kyrenia, Cyprus". Roger Hilton's contribution was entitled "La Belle Elaine" and only priced at £2.

This was the last of the sixpenny yellow, A5 sized catalogues which further illustrated the changes within the Group. The catalogue format had not changed for nearly ten years and was becoming distinctly tired. Catalogue sales, admissions (1,138) and hanging fees made the Group £91.2.0.

A snapshot of life with The London Group appears in "The Townsend Journals" (William Townsend's diaries), entry dated 22nd November 1935, "Geoffrey (Tibble), after a stern fight had been put up by (Victor) Pasmore and Rodrigo (Moynihan), got his picture hung at the L.G., and has since shared abuse with Rodrigo in almost every review that has appeared. He was delighted with a notice from Frank Rutter in the 'Sunday Times' – the first time any-one has said what he wanted to hear, and it was indeed a triumph for praise of their honesty followed immediately on a paragraph in which Ben Nicholson was accused of practising deception, cheating by compromise with a third dimension in his reliefs. Rodrigo has sold a drawing (£14.5.0) and Pasmore a painting (£30) to Kenneth Clark…" (my italics). This is an example of how The London Group could help bring artists' work to the attention of critics. Tibble was not a member but was elected to the Group in 1944, unhappily dying at the age of 43 in 1952. Tibble's work "Painting", priced at £42, was numbered 2 in the exhibition catalogue. E. White sold a work for £33.6.0 whilst J. Fitton received £23.5.0. and the Group records a total of £146.1.6 for 12 sales. On the 7th August 1935 the Group's balance was £246.14.9, an increase of about £50 on last year's figure.

1936

Germany reoccupies the Rhineland. The Summer Olympics are held in Berlin and Jesse Owens wins the 100 metres. In July the Spanish Civil War breaks out. In January in the UK King George V dies and is succeeded by King Edward VIII. In October Wallis Simpson gains her divorce in order to marry Edward. Government and the country refuse to accept Simpson as Queen and Edward is forced to abdicate. On the 11th December Edward abdicates and his brother, the Duke of York, becomes King George VI. Also in October anti-fascists fight with Moseley's supporters in the Battle of Cable Street. The Jarrow Marchers (207 miners) walk from the North to London in protest against unemployment. In the US Roosevelt is re-elected as President. The GPO Film Unit makes the legendary "Night Mail" with music by Benjamin Britten and poetry by W.H. Auden. Maynard Keynes publishes "The General Theory of Employment, Interest and Money". Cunard's 'Queen Mary' sets sail from Southampton on her maiden voyage to New York. The BBC begins the first public broadcast television service from Alexandra Palace, London. Fire destroys The Crystal Palace.

Prokofiev's "Peter and the Wolf" premieres in Moscow. Margaret Mitchell's "Gone with the Wind" is published in the US.

New Burlington Galleries "International Surrealist Exhibition" 11th June to 4th July 1936, including Salvador Dali and Roland Penrose. Eileen Agar (1933) and Rupert Lee (1922) also exhibited. Lee was, in fact, the Chairman of this venture. It should also be noted that Lee's term of office as London Group President ended and the position of Chairman to replace the position of President occurred during the year.

E.L.T. Mesens moves to London. He ran the **London Gallery** and edited the Surrealist magazine "London Bulletin".

Peoples' Palace in the Mile End Road Phyllis Bray's (1933) murals were formally opened in July. She was 26 years of age.

Museum of Modern Art New York "Cubism and Abstract Art", Mondrian and Ben Nicholson paired together as leading exponents of 'geometrical abstraction'. They had also taken part in the exhibition "Abstract and Concrete" in England.

Venice Biennale London Group members Duncan Grant, Barbara Hepworth and John Skeaping had representation at the event. Work by East London Group members Walter Steggles and Elwin Hawthorne was also included.

London Group President: Rupert Lee (1922), Chairman, R.P. Bedford (1932)

Ethel Walker was the sole artist elected to the Group this year.

Events were moving against the incumbent president, Rupert Lee. David

Buckman in his book "From Bow to Biennale: Artists of the East London Group" (pages 188-189) records a crucial meeting whilst Lee was still president "... he planned his speech for the crucial meeting at which matters would be decided and where he hoped 'to strangle the buggers', he had been alarmed to learn from Keith Baynes that 'the plotters are now planning to put Sicket up as President!' and that Ethelbert White and Raymond Coxon had driven to St Peter's-in-Thanet, Kent, where Sickert had accepted 'on condition that the the present Secretary and Treasurer are retained'. After the crucial meeting, on January 18, 1936, Lee had to cable despondently to Diana in Barbados: 'Sunk all hands president secretary outvoted 26 20'". In an extract from Denys J Wilcok's book, "Rupert Lee (1887-1959), Painter, Sculptor and Printmaker" Wilcox writes, "during the middle of January 1936 they (Lee and Brinton Lee) were outvoted 26 to 20 at the London Group meeting. Vanessa Bell stood up at the end of the meeting and publicly thanked Lee and Diana for their distinguished service to the Group over many years and insisted that a formal letter of thanks be written to them. Bell and Grant subsequently resigned in protest and began plans to form another exhibiting group, but the 'Bloomsbury' heyday was coming to an end and a new generation of artists was emerging."

"London Group", New Burlington Galleries, Burlington Gardens, 12th November to 28th November 1936. This was the 34th annual exhibition as written in ink in the top right hand corner of the Tate Archive catalogue. Furthermore, even though Rupert Lee began the year as President, the sculptor R.P. Bedford had become Chairman by the time of this exhibition in November. Other officers were Mrs D. Hall Macpherson as Secretary and J.S. Woodger as Honorary Treasurer. The Working Committee this year was R.P. Bedford (sculptor), Raymond Coxon, Alan Durst (sculptor), John Farleigh, Rupert Lee (sculptor), Henry Moore (sculptor), Rodrigo Moynihan, John Piper, Ethelbert White and H.S. Williamson. The catalogue lists sixty-three members of whom at least nineteen were women. Of the one hundred and twenty non-member exhibitors at least fifty-six were women. The three hundred and twenty-six member and non-member exhibits were shown in the 'First Gallery' (65), the 'Main Gallery' (86), the 'Little Gallery' (51), the 'Staircase Gallery' (26) and the 'Long Gallery' (72). Despite the Working Committee being heavy with sculptors, only twenty-five sculptures were exhibited. Henry Moore, who served on the Working Committee, did not exhibit. Non-member exhibitors of note were David Bomberg (ex-founder member), Sam Carter, Nina Hamnett, Roger Hilton, Morris Kestelman, Lynton Lamb, Anthony Lousada, F.E. McWilliam, Kenneth Martin, Mary Potter, Ceri Richards, Brian Robb, Claude Rogers, Kenneth Rowntree, William Townsend, Julian Trevelyan, Leon Underwood and Gerald Wilde. Titles in the catalogue indicated mainly landscape painting with subjects ranging from "Orizaba, Mexico" by Edward Wolfe to "Sussex Wood' by Ivon Hitchens. There were no illustrations, sizes or media printed in the catalogue, only number, artist, title and price. The average price was about 15 to 40 guineas, sculptures being the most expensive with Gertrude Hermes, Elizabeth Muntz and Alan Durst asking 100 guineas whilst F.J. Kormis was asking 300 guineas.

Some of the most interesting aspects of this catalogue were not the exhibition content. There was an extraordinary pen and ink drawing on the cover by H.S. Williamson of a marine landscape on a three-legged easel with somewhat bizarre 'fairground' style lettering on mauve paper. Inside there was an advertisement for Lynton Lamb's "The Purpose of Painting" published by the Oxford University Press at 3s 6d. (Lamb was an exhibitor in this exhibition). The Burlington Magazine had written of this book, "An intelligent and well-written essay which does much to clarify the aims of the modern painter", whilst Time and Tide had opined, "He writes with intelligence and no little wit, without either superior aims or demotic grovelling". But of great interest was the large number of sponsorship advertisements throughout the catalogue falling into a number of categories. First of all, 'colourmen', Rowneys, Reeves (170 years of experience), Lechentier Barbe (since 1827) and for the sculptors Tiranti & Co., 'the Sculptor's Shop'. Secondly, London commercial galleries. Alex. Reid & Lefevre "Paintings by the leading British and French artists always on view", (telegrams to 'Drawing'), Adams Gallery currently showing Bonnard and the Leicester Galleries currently showing Henry Moore (probably why Moore did not show with The London Group this year) and "Six French Painters", Bonnard, Matisse, Paul Maze, Segonzac, Utrillo and Vuillard. Then came Zwemmers Fine Art books in Charing Cross Road and an advertisement for the Imperial Arts League which was a body set up to advise and represent artists for which they paid a fee, similar in some ways to The London Group. Finally, an Obituary to Kenneth Morrison who was sponsored for election to The London Group by Roger Fry in 1924, written by 'R.S.', probably fellow London Group member Randolph Schwabe. And all this in twenty pages and for only sixpence!

On the 15th November the 'Sunday Times' reviewer wrote, "The outstanding feature of the 34th exhibition of the London Group at the New Burlington Galleries is the number of well known 'Groupers' who are conspicuous by reason of their absence. Indeed the names of Ketih Baynes, Vanessa Bell and Duncan Grant no longer appear in the list of members; while members not exhibiting include E.M. O'R. Dickey, Mark Gertler, John Nash and Matthew Smith. The absence of these artists inevitably affects the exhibition and diminishes its interest." Graham Bell wrote a long piece in the 21st November edition of 'The New Statesman and Nation'. "As the London Group in 1936 contains no great artists and only a few polite ones, the chromatic uproar is tremendous. Large pictures by members punctuate the walls of the main rooms, hints of a rather timid Surrealism lurk in the corners." He gives special mention to Ethel

Walker, Ivon Hitchens, Rodrigo Moynihan's abstracts (which drew a lot of hostile rhetoric from other reviewers), Adrian Stokes and, not surprisingly given his links with the Euston Road School, Rogers, Pasmore and Coldstream. The 'New English Weekly' reviewer penned the following on 19th November. "The London Group has in the last decade quietly displaced the Royal Academy... Under Roger Fry's leadership, this group first gathered to pick the masterpieces of Cézanne to pieces and put the pieces together again as small vegetable allotment plots. Some of the members are still doing that. Others, now schoolmaster Fry has gone, are overcome with ideas of mischief and daring, and take to parodying all the periods of Picasso. But of course they are all very individual painters indeed, very indignant indeed to find themselves hung next to X, Y, and Z in this exhibition. Still, one has to be 'in' the London Group show, to be 'anybody'."

A contemporary painter's view on this exhibition is recorded in William Townsend's diary entry, dated 9th December 1936, "He (Geoffrey Tibble) tells me that the L.G. exhibition has put a damper on many peoples' interest in modern developments in painting, and that there is a decided swing back from the problems of abstraction, even from the orgies of Surrealism, to the possibility of making a new start from the Post Impressionists. Bill Coldstream and Graham Bell have for instance renounced Picasso and all his works and in despair proclaim there is nothing to do but sit down in front of a landscape and paint it. I think too that is a much better thing to do than what most of the L.G. members are doing. Bill conceives himself to be the new Degas, Graham is Bonnard over again . . ."

A further significant event began to unfold in December 1936, the Professor Hellwag affair. Professor Hellwag was a German official who had a genuine interest in contemporary art. Hellwag indicated that he would like to tour The London Group exhibition to Berlin, all expenses paid. When the official invitation from the German authorities arrived it came with a number of conditions that The London Group found unacceptable, particularly the anti-semitic nature of their demands. In his book "The London Group 1913-39" (p.26), Denys Wilcox prints a letter from Jacob Epstein to 'The Evening Standard' dated 4th December 1936, "Every decent-minded artist in England ought to reject the offer to exhibit. It is nothing more than an attempt to enlist the support of the British artists in the cause of Nazi propaganda. The London Group of artists have already officially rejected the invitation. They were invited to exhibit subject to the exclusion of certain works which would not be accepted for political reasons. The Germans have banned Jewish exhibitors, and have badly treated German artists in exile. The works of several British artists have been destroyed. Now they are attempting to disguise propaganda as a love of culture. All British artists should do their utmost to check this attempt." In 1937 the German authorities organised the famous degenerate art exhibition where many important avant-garde artists were mocked and defiled. The London Group had many Jewish members both at this time and in the past, notably Epstein, Bomberg, Gertler and Meninsky and elected exile Hans Feibusch in 1934. At the 1937 London Group Annual General Meeting, David Bomberg put forward the motion that: 'the London Group members... be prohibited from exhibiting with reactionary groups: that the London Group... consolidate with the Artists International Association and Surrealist Groups in their support of Anti-Facism in politics and art; and that Honorary membership in the London Group... be extended to certain left-wing poets and writers', but his motion was voted down.

On the 5th June 1936 the Group records the highest balance of the decade at £350.6.9. Credits stood at £615.9.6. whilst debits were only £265.2.9.

1937

Heavy fighting in the Spanish Civil War. Germany is implicated in the bombing of Guernica on April 26th. Spanish Republican forces and foreign nationals suffer huge losses and lose ground. Japanese forces invade China and reach Beijing and Shanghai. In the UK in May King George VI is crowned at Westminster Abbey and the ceremony is transmitted to the nation by the BBC's first outside broadcast. Neville Chamberlain becomes Conservative Prime Minister as Baldwin retires. On the 24th June at the Albert Hall, there is a large gathering against Fascism. William Townsend said of the activist and singer Paul Robeson's speech, "It was a brave and truly noble speech: the battle front is everywhere, he said, and every artist must make his stand one side or the other..." Also in June the abdicated King, now the Duke of Windsor, marries Wallis Simpson in France where in the country itself social and political unrest continues. In Ireland the new Constitution of Ireland gives birth to the Irish Free State and Eamon de Valera becomes the first Taoiseach (prime minister). In July the IRA had attempted to assassinate King George VI during a visit to Belfast. Will Hay appears in the film comedy "Oh Mr. Porter", J.R.R. Tolkien publishes "The Hobbit", George Orwell writes "The Road to Wigan Pier", whilst the first issue of the comic "The Dandy" goes on sale. Walt Disney releases the first feature length animated film, "Snow White and the Seven Dwarves". Between May and June Picasso painted "Guernica" in his Paris studio for the Spanish Pavilion at the Paris International Exhibition. Roland Penrose and Henry Moore visited whilst the work was in progress. In July the Nazis organise the "Entartete Kunst" (Degenerate Art) exhibition in Munich showing 650 works by avant-garde artists held in German state collections. After this exhibition some works were destroyed or others sold off. Mass Observation is set up as an instrument to record social interactions in the UK.

Rosenberg & Helft Ltd 31 Bruton Street, Matisse paintings.
London Gallery show Oskar Schlemmer.
Agnew's contemporary painting chosen by Duncan Grant and Vanessa Bell including Coldstream, Rogers and Pasmore.
Artists International Association were based in Constable's old house at 76 Charlotte Street, and held an exhibition of Chinese woodcuts and cartoons, "left wing and popular".
Faber & Faber publish **"Circle: International Survey of Constructive Art"** co-edited by J.L. Martin, Ben Nicholson, Naum Gabo and Mondrian.
A copy of Vogue from March 1937 listed the following exhibitions in **London galleries**: Bloomsbury showed French Graphic Art, Lefèvre Ben Nicholson, Leger Nudes, Leicester The London Group, London Musical Instruments, Redfern Christopher

Wood, Storran James Thurber, Tooth Jongkind and Zwemmer Modigliani. The London Group also toured an exhibition to Wakefield, Sunderland, Hull and Manchester beginning this year.

Chairman: R.P. Bedford (1932), H. S. Williamson (Harold Sandys) (1933) who was to be the Chairman of The London Group from 1937 to 1943

Robert Medley and Graham Sutherland were elected to the Group in this year.

"The London Group Exhibition of Works by Members", The Leicester Galleries, Leicester Square, March 1937. In the Tate Archive catalogue the number '35th' has been written in ink in the top right hand corner which would indicate that this was considered to be one of the annual exhibitions. Only members showed in this exhibition which was held in one of the foremost commercial galleries in London at the time. R.P. Bedford is recorded as being Chairman of the Group in March 1937, Mrs. D. Hall Macpherson as Secretary and J.S. Woodger as Honorary Treasurer. There were sixty-three exhibitors showing one work each. The nine sculptors are notable, Alan Durst, Rupert Lee, Elizabeth Muntz, Gertrude Hermes, R.P. Bedford, Henry Moore, Elizabeth Andrews, Arthur Pollen and Edna Manley. Four women, one past President, the current Chairman and H.M.! Sixty-three is likely to be almost the full complement of members as no one was going to give up the chance of a sale in this prestigious and commercially successful gallery. The exhibition was presented in two rooms, the Reynolds Room and the Hogarth Room. Of the fifty paintings, three watercolours and one drawing, virtually all were landscape images. No prices, sizes or media were recorded although "the Directors of the Leiscester Galleries are prepared to accept payment for purchases on hire-purchase terms". Notable entries were Matthew Smith's "Winter Landscape", David Bomberg's "Plazuela de la Paz, Ronda", Ivon Hitchens' "Chinese Bowl", Mark Gertler's "Still Life Design", Charles Ginner's "Flask Walk, Fifth November" and possibly two early abstracts, "Procession of Forms" by John Piper and "Stationary Forms" by Jessica Dismoor.

There is a notable anonymous introduction printed in the catalogue.: "The London Group, perhaps the most stimulating and exciting of the many societies which go to form the art life of London, dates directly from 1908 when the pioneer Frank Rutter started the Allied Artists' Association in a mood of dissatisfaction with prevailing conditions. The outcome of many meetings at the Café Royal was the formation in 1911 of the Camden Town Group which had as its first President the late Spencer Gore, and as its secretary J.B. Manson, now Director of the Tate Gallery. This Group absorbed other small societies such as the 'Cumberland Market Group' and 'Nineteen Fitzroy Street' and in its turn developed into the London Group under the Presidency of the late Harold Gilman. The thirty-two members of the new Group held their first exhibition in March 1914, at the Goupil Gallery in Regent Street. In this exhibition was to be seen the work of many artists who have now an established position. Mention may perhaps be made of that wayward and ill-fated genius. Gaudier-Brzeska, who was soon to be killed fighting in France, and who, in the pages of the provocative publication 'Blast', enunciated principles which have had a profound influence on the modern movement in sculpture in this country.

By 1916 the work of non-members was shown in the annual exhibitions, and it is perhaps the admission of such work which has tended to obscure the basic aims of the London Group. From its beginnings the Society had a revolutionary and anti-academic character which it has been able to retain by the frequent addition of new members whose art has a virile and personal quality. It is hoped that the present exhibition, confined as it is to the work of members, will demonstrate that the London Group is a vital force in contemporary art."

The Leicester Galleries trumpeted their commercial success in this catalogue. They had made sales to The Louvre (Sickert), Tate Gallery (Gill, Epstein), British Museum (Sickert), London Museum (Nevinson), the Victoria and Albert Museum and many other national and international galleries. Their recent exhibitions were a mixture of home grown talent (Moore, Winifred Nicholson, Sickert, Lamb, Dobson, Gertler, John) and also international, mainly French, heavies (Tissot, Camille Pissarro, Gauguin, Van Gogh, Morisot, Cézanne, Degas and Picasso).

'The Observer' of 21st March supported the idea of a members only London Group exhibition. "For some time the exhibitions of the London Group, have suffered from more than a hint of nepotism, and in consequence this exhibition at the Leicester Gallery, in which only members are showing but one work apiece, comes as a timely refresher." The 'Studio' in May was of a like mind. "Recent exhibitions of the London Group have been so overcrowded by the admission of work by non-members that the basic aims of the artists forming the group, which is essentially revolutionary and anti-academic, have tended to become obscured. This year's exhibition, at the Leicester Galleries, has been confined to the work of members, and does, I think succeed in demonstrating that the London Group is a 'vital force in contemporary art'." Frank Rutter, writing in the 14th March edition of the 'Sunday Times' wrote a long article correcting what he saw as historical inaccuracies in the origin and provenaces of The London Group as written by the anonymous writer in the catalogue. Rutter contends that The London Group came about because of objections from William Marchant of the Goupil Gallery. "He did not like the title of the society (the Camden Town Group as it then was) – which had been chosen by Sickert chiefly because a sensational murder had made Camden Town notorious in 1911 – and he thought more members would be required to fill adequately his larger gallery. This was why in March 1914, the name was changed to 'London Group' for the first exhibition at the old Goupil Gallery, and why the membership was enlarged."

Press cuttings also indicate that selections from the 1937 exhibition toured to the provinces. The first venue was Wakefield City Art Gallery in April. 'E.P.H.' contributed two long and thoughtful articles in the 'Wakefield Express' illustrated with John Nash's "Trees" and Hans Feibusch's "Reading in Bed". Next port of call was Sunderland Art Gallery from late May to 18th July. Headlines in the local press read, "Surrealism comes to Sunderland", "Exhibition by 'The Academy Of The Moderns'" and "Revolutionary Pictures at Sunderland". It was reported that "about 1,300 persons have visited these exhibitions daily", although The London Group's exhibition was toured with Royal Photographs and Regalia! In August The London Group toured to the Ferens Art Gallery in Hull. There appears to have been a skirmish at Hull, indeed the Ferens Director V. Galloway had a letter defending The London Group's exhibition printed in a local paper. Even so, Director Galloway wrote in his defensive letter, "Although most of the artists represented are men of repute, I don't pretend to admire everything. Frankly, there are works which I don't understand – they have no appeal to me – and there are one or two I don't like; but on that account I don't follow your action in condemning everything." Finally, on October 1st, 1937, the exhibition opened at Platt Hall, Manchester. The Manchester Guardian's reviewer, identified as 'N', wrote, "The London Group, which came into being just before the war and held its first exhibition in 1914, has no longer the same air of stark rebellion that it had twenty years ago. Unit One (now defunct) and the Surrealists have since then raised their horrific heads in this country, and the London Group seems to-day a little less uncompromising than it did. But that is all to the good. This exhibition is a welcome reminder that experimental work can still be done by artists who neither turn their backs on the spectacle of life nor take refuge from it in a world of dreams."

The balance with Drummonds on April 2nd was nearly £140 less than 1936, standing at £214.10.2 with credits of £395.13.11 and debits of £181.3.9.

The Leicester Galleries
20 Leicester Square,
London WC2

The Leicester Galleries were situated in the two buildings to the immediate left of the telephone box. Capitol Radio London overlooks the three and four storey buildings now (2009) occupied by Garfunkel's Restaurant and The Terrace, Bar, Café and Pancake House. What would The London Group give to mount an exhibition in this teeming London square today? Across Leicester Square is another bar, "All Bar One". Sir Joshua Reynolds lived and died in a house which used to stand on that spot at 48 Leicester Square.

"The London Group Thirty-sixth Exhibition of Painting and Sculpture", New Burlington Galleries, Burlington Gardens W1, 30th October to 20th November 1937. H.S. Williamson was Chairman by November replacing R.P. Bedford, no Vice President (or Vice-Chairman) was recorded, the secretary was Mrs. D. Hall Macpherson and the Honorary Treasurer was J.S. Woodger. On the Working Committee for this exhibition were Noel Adeney, R.P. Bedford, Raymond Coxon, R.O. Dunlop, Alan Durst, John Farleigh, Gertrude Hermes, Rupert Lee (ex-President), Rodrigo Moynihan and John Piper. Last year there were sixty-three members recorded, but this year it had declined to fifty-five, a loss of eight members. The fifty-five recorded here were 'Member Exhibitors' which may not have been the full list of actual members. If there were only fifty-five members then that would mean that 100% of members had put work forward, an unlikely scenario. In fact one Member Exhibitor was "Fry, Roger (the late Mr.)". There were one hundred and twenty-one non-member exhibitors of which at least thirty-nine were women. Notable non-member exhibitors were Elsie Few, Roger Hilton, Lynton Lamb, Kenneth Martin, Bateson Mason, Margaret Mellis, Mary Potter, Ceri Richards, Claude Rogers, Kenneth Rowntree, A. Stokes, Wm. Townsend, J. Trevelyan and Gabriel White. There were three hundred and thirty-nine exhibits in total, twenty-three of which were sculptures, seventy-seven works in the First Gallery, ninety-eight in the Main Gallery, fifty-seven in the Long Gallery, forty-nine in the Small gallery and in the Staircase Gallery, sixty-five. There were no illustrations, no sizes nor media given in the catalogue. The average selling price was between 25 to 50 guineas with top price of £165 asked by George Churchill for his sculpture "Carvings" followed by Adrian Allinson's painting "Attic Life" at £157 10s 0d. A shrewd purchase would have been William Coldstream's portrait of "W.H. Auden Esq." at £50! Other titles indicate mostly landscapes from South East England, Wales, Cornwall, Ireland, France and even a few from London. Other painting subjects were mainly still lifes and flowers. The sculptors, however, seemed to have a thing for animals and insects this year, titles included, "Raven", "Butterfly", "Eagle", "Dog", "The Kid", "Cat" and "Penguin (Destroying Angel)".

The Tate Archive catalogue, a green A5 publication, has copious and intense notations written by pencil in a tiny hand, comparing the influences apparent on various painters' work. Obviously a very committed exhibition visitor (or LG member). The catalogue carried a large number of advertisements again this year, but two caught the eye. Firstly one for the Wertheim Gallery which "specialised in First One-Man shows" and secondly one for the School of Drawing and Painting at 12 Fitzroy Street run by Messrs. Rogers, Pasmore and Coldstream.

Press cuttings for this exhibition have a wealth of press photos. 'The Daily Mirror' have a wonderful photograph of Miss Gertrude Hermes with her sculpture inspired by butterflies (headlined "Madame's Butterfly"!), whilst other journals chose Ethel Walker's bust "Gabriell Von Schnall", a photograph of Robert Medley at work, "Installation" by John Tunnard, "The Black Bull" by Raymond Coxon (from 'Country Life'), Coldstream's portrait "W. H. Auden" and "Attic Life" by Adrian Allinson. On the whole, the winter exhibition was well received by the critics. T. W. Earp of 'The Daily Telegraph' wrote, "The liveliest London Group show of recent years is presented at the New Burlington Galleries… In which the work of the younger members, which always sets the prevailing tone, imitations of Cézanne and exercises in abstract art have yielded to first hand impulse." 'The Times' critic thought that "The present exhibition of the London Group at the New Burlington Galleries is agreeably unconventional and a large proportion of the 339 works in it look as if they were there on their artistic merits, irrespective of doctrine." "This is a jolly show, bright, care-free, spirited. It actually looks a lot better than it is. It is no less academic in its different way than the R.A. or the New English; but it is a younger and 'newer' brand of academicism." said the 4th of November edition of 'The Scotsman'.

1938

Foreign Secretary Anthony Eden resigns over policy disagreements with Neville Chamberlain. In March Germany annexes Austria in the "Anschluss" (link up). There is tension along all of Germany's borders. Hitler makes demands to annexe the Sudetenlands on the Czechoslovakian borders. Following a summer of intense diplomatic negotiations, German, Italian, French and British governments agree to the annexation of the Czechoslovakian Sudetenlands to Germany and at the end of September Chamberlain returns to London declaring "Peace for our time" following the Munich Agreement. The next day German troops enter the Sudetenlands. Winston Churchill, amongst others, warns of the dangers of appeasing Germany. On November 9th Jewish businesses in Germany are destroyed in the "Kristallnacht" (night of broken glass). In Italy Benitto Mussolini makes demands for French territories to be ceded to Italy. France is rocked by a general strike and social unrest. The Spanish Civil War continued with limited agreement to withdraw foreign nationals from the fighting. The Vatican recognises Franco's government. In the UK the first Green Belts are set up around Sheffield and London. The British locomotive "Mallard" sets the world steam locomotive speed record at 126mph. The largest ship in the world at the time, Cunard's "Queen Elizabeth", is launched. The comic "Beano" is first published and in the US the first Action Comic featuring Superman is published. Hitchcock directs "The Lady Vanishes".

New Burlington Galleries shows "Exhibition of Twentieth Century German Art" in July organised in protest against the 'degenerate art' exhibition in Germany. The British Press supported the anti-nazi stance, but still found the exhibits to be of "extraordinary ugliness". In October Picasso's "Guernica" and 67 other works were exhibited. Graham Sutherland described the exhibition as "a moving experience". William Townsend wrote in his diary, dated 4th October 1938, "Met Rob for lunch and in the afternoon went to the Burlington Galleries to see Picasso's 'Guernica' which Roland Penrose has got over here and which is being exhibited for the Spanish Aid fund. All Picasso's drawings for it are here too, drawings in crayon and pencil and ink, engravings, etchings, oil paintings, an immense amount of preliminary work." The studies were toured to Oxford and Leeds and met up again with "Guernica" at the Whitechapel Gallery where 15,000 visited in two weeks. Picasso's work was also toured to Scandinavia and the United States.

The Modern Architectural Research Group (MARS) also exhibited in the NBG. This British Architectural 'think tank' lost a large sum of money as a result.

A.I.A. Debate 16th March 1938, between the Surrealist and the Realists. Penrose, Julian Trevelyan (1949) and Humphrey Jennings represented the Surrealists and

Graham Bell, Coldstream (1933) and Peter Peri the Realists.

Wildenstein's March to April, "Cross Section of English Painting", said to be important in the formation of the Euston Road School. Included G. Bell, W. Coldstream, R. Moynihan and V. Pasmore.

In September **Mondrian** moves from Paris to London to live close to his friend and supporter Ben Nicholson. Two years later Mondrian was to move to New York to escape the blitz whilst Nicholson moved to Cornwall.

The Artists Refugee Committee was formed, an emergency committee whose "object is to help these artists to some security in this or other countries. Three things are needed: money, guarantors and hospitality". Signators to an emergency letter were, amongst others, sometime London Group members Vanessa Bell, Jacob Epstein, Mark Gertler, Duncan Grant, Augustus John, E. McKnight Kauffer, David Low (Honorary Member), Henry Moore and Paul Nash.

H. S. Williamson (1933), Chairman of The London Group from 1937 to 1943

Ceri Richards was elected this year and possibly Claude Rogers (see below).

In February the Leicester Galleries had three small exhibitions at the same time, one of which was an exhibition of London Group members' work, forty-nine watercolours, drawings and sculptures, one work from each member. 'The Times' of February 2nd wrote, "The chief effect is to show the variety of talents included in the group.", presumably because there were no oil paintings. Exhibitors included, Noel Adeney, David Bomberg, R.O. Dunlop, Alan Durst, Hans Feibusch, Charles Ginner, Bernard Meninsky, John Nash, Marceso (sic) Pearce, John Piper, Matthew Smith, Graham Sutherland, John Tunnard, H.S. Williamson and Edward Wolfe. Under the sub title of "Modern Cornish Artist", 'The Western Morning News' printed the following on the 8th February, "Mr. Tunnard's representation of the human figure is reminiscent of the modern work of the sculptor Mr. Henry Moore, but his geometrical technique is essentially his own, and it is easy to recognise one of his drawings at an exhibition. It is a pity that Mr. Tunnard's work is so obscure, for even after a long examination of his drawings, many onlookers are unable to extract much meaning from them". Not every reviewer was so perplexed. "The London Group can paint and draw; and drawing is such a forgotten accomplishment with so many artists to-day that their exhibition gives cause for gratitude and pleasure". The 'Birmingham Daily Mail' printed this supportive opinion on the 5th February whilst the 'Sketch' of 9th February reported that "The Leicester Galleries 'suffered' – or, rather, 'enjoyed' – a record 'black-out' at the Sava Botzari, Edward Bawden and London Group private view, for the thousand or so visitors completely prevented one from seeing the exhibits".

"London Group–Thirty-seventh Exhibition of Painting and Sculpture", New

Burlington Galleries, Burlington Gardens, W1, 14th November to 2nd December 1938. There were no officers printed in the exhibition catalogue which was also without its traditional written introduction. There were sixty-six members in total with David Low as an Honorary Member (although there is no mention of Duncan Grant who should have been recorded here. It is unclear in the catalogue whether this was a full list of members or just those exhibiting). Of those recorded eighteen were women. Of the sixty-six members, nineteen did not exhibit including the ex-President Rupert Lee, Robert Medley, John Nash, John Piper, Matthew Smith and Graham Sutherland. However the Working Committee was recorded and was made up of Noel Adeney, R.P. Bedford, Raymond Coxon, R.O. Dunlop, John Farleigh, Gertrude Hermes, Robert Medley, Victor Pasmore and Edward Wolfe. Each exhibiting member could show up to five works whilst the one hundred and twenty-seven non-member exhibitors were allowed only two. There were two hundred and ninety-six exhibits in total, seventy-two in the First Gallery, one hundred and one in the Main Gallery, fifty-three in the Little Gallery and forty-six in the Staircase Gallery. A mere twenty-four sculptures were exhibited this year. Only the exhibition number, artist, title and price were given in the catalogue but no media or size and no illustrations. Prices averaged around 25 guineas whilst 200 guineas would buy Edward Wolfe's "Mrs David Milne". Many prices were affordable and, given the number of exhibits, probably 'domestic' in size. The aim of the annual was to sell work for artists and for the Group to make commission, "Deferred purchase terms may be arranged in some cases". Significant non-member exhibitors were Lawrence Gowing, Adrian Hill, Roger Hilton, Lynton Lamb, Roy le Maistre, Kenneth Martin, Mary Martyn (sic), Margaret Mellis, John Minton and Adrian Stokes. Half (63) of the non-member artists exhibited were women. Titles indicate mainly landscape, still-life, flower and figure paintings. There is a frustrating inconsistency in this catalogue which is quite important for the history of The London Group. Future long-serving President Claude Rogers is recorded both as a member in the members list and also as a non-member exhibitor. Denys Wilcox gives his year of election as 1939 but it must be remembered that Rogers had been exhibiting as a non-member since 1931. Jenny Perry writing in "The Affectionate Eye: the life of Claude Rogers" gives his date of election as 1938.

Perhaps the most noticeable aspect of the exhibition catalogue is the extensive sponsorship advertising throughout the whole publication. To name all of them gives a snapshot into the artists' world on the eve of the Second World War. First of all, paints, from Reeves, Lachentier Barbe Ltd. and James Newman Ltd., framers A.R. Killen and Winterbourne Mallinson & Vokins (frames could also be hired), and commercial London galleries The Spectrum Gallery in Charlotte Street, The Brook Street Galleries at 14, Brook Street, The Leicester Galleries in Leicester Square and The Adams Gallery in King Street SW1. There were miscellaneous advertisements for book tokens, A. Zwemmer Fine Art books, The Imperial Arts League, "The Artist" monthly magazine and one for the "School of Drawing and Painting", 314 Euston Road, under the direction of Rogers, Pasmore and Coldstream.

In the Burlington Galleries exhibition catalogue there is an advertisement for a London Group Christmas Exhibition at the Cooling Galleries, 92 New Bond Street with dates from 29th November to 24th December 1938. There is no exhibition catalogue held in the Tate Archive.

William Roberts seems to have scooped the prize for newspaper illustrations. "He Knew Degas" (a painting of Sickert working in bed) was printed in three newspapers whilst his "Lambeth Walk" appeared in the 30th November 'Bystander' and 'The Evening News' of the 12th November under the headlines, " 'DAFT' PICTURES IN THIS SHOW, SERIOUS ARTISTS HAVE THEIR LITTLE JOKES, 'THE LAMBETH WALK', IT SEEMS TO DANCE AS YOU WATCH IT". Eric Newton wrote a long article in the 20th November's issue of 'The Sunday Times'. "What makes the London Group important is the fact that it is not a group at all. That is to say, it is not held together by a creed. Its laudable desire is to show whatever seems good of its kind, provided the kind is a contemporary kind... In painting to-day there are so many cross currents, so many possible approaches to the main problem – and, indeed, so much doubt as to what the main problem is – that any cross-section through all the layers is bound to present a confused appearance... No doubt in seventy years' time an exhibition like this will have achieved unity. 'It's all very mid-twentieth century.' one can imagine the early twenty-first century spectators saying. They may have found a name for it all, just as we can talk about 'Primitive' or 'Baroque' or 'Oriental' airily covering a whole century or a whole continent in a single word. But to-day there is no such peg to hang our ready-made judgments on. The London Group must be taken in detail or not at all". T.W. Earp, writing in the 'The Daily Telegraph', headlined his article "Key to Painting Today, Growth of Sturdy Independence" and continued, "The London Group... still reflects the advanced tendencies of contemporary art. If the walls present a bright confusion, compared with the decorous uniformity of a few years ago, it is because the younger painting of to-day no longer runs in one direction. The Group's exhibitors, who used to follow almost unanimously in the footsteps of Cézanne, are now an assembly of individuals. Their work provides a key to the various trends of painting to-day, but it is impossible to point to one common or prevailing aim." And finally, 'The Guardian' of 25th November, "Here the traditions no longer rule, but violent movement and the hottest of hot colour. It is to be noted, however, that the oddities of Surrealism are few in number, and that the young people who delight in plenty of paint and the crudest of hues are probably on the right track, in their reaction from the timidity that would almost banish colour from the canvas." The critic D.S. McColl had this year attacked The London Group for 'Fryism' and 'sedulous if dowdy imitation' of Paris fashion.

The financial aspect on the 15th February was 'steady as she goes' with Drummonds reporting a balance of £224.3.9 with credits of £332.7.11 and debits of £108.4.2, very similar results to 1937.

Below is a list of members printed in the Group's December 1938 Annual Exhibition catalogue. On the eve of the Second World War these were the artists who made up The London Group.

Bernard Adeney, Noël Adeney, Eileen Agar, Adrian Allinson, Elizabeth Andrews, Walter Bayes, Richard Bedford, David Bomberg, Phyllis Bray, Richard Carline, William Coldstream, John Cooper, Raymond Coxon, Vera Cuningham (sic), Norman Dawson, Jessica Dismoor, Ruth Doggett, Ronald Dunlop, Alan Durst, Elsie Farleigh, John Farleigh, Hans Feibusch, James Fitton, Mark Gertler, Edna Ginesi, Charles Ginner, Mary Godwin, Gertrude Hermes, Cicely Hey, Ivon Hitchens, Annie (Nan) Hudson, Blair Hughes-Stanton, Stanislowa de Karlowska, Rupert Lee, Morland Lewis, Edna Manley, Guy Maynard, Robert Medley, Bernard Meninsky, Rodrigo Moynihan, Elizabeth Muntz, John Nash, Victor Pasmore, Maresco Pearce, John Piper, Roland Pitchforth, H.E. du Plessis, Arthur Pollen, Frederick Porter, J.W. Power, Ceri Richards, William Roberts, Claude Rogers, Ethel Sand, Randolph Schwabe, Elliott Seabrooke, Matthew Smith, Cicely Stock, Graham Sutherland, Alfred Thornton, John Tunnard, Ethel Walker, Allan Walton, Ethelbert White, Harold Williamson and Edward Wolfe. David Low was an Honorary Member.

1939

The Spanish Civil War is won by the Nationalists, the UK and France recognise Franco's government. The Molotov/Ribbentrop pact is made in which Stalin and Hitler 'divide up Europe'. German troops occupy Moravia and Bohemia. September 1st, World War II begins as Germany invades Poland. September 3rd, Great Britain, New Zealand, Australia and France declare war on Germany. Later Nepal, South Africa and Canada join them. The USA declares its neutrality. The German U-Boat U47 sinks the British Battleship "HMS Royal Oak". Soviet forces attack Finland in the 'Winter War'. An attempt is made to assassinate Hitler. Battle of the River Plate in Uruguay where the trapped German Battleship Admiral Graf Spee is scuttled by her crew in Montevideo harbour. Otto Hahn achieves nuclear fission. Albert Einstein writes to President Roosevelt about the possibility of developing an Atomic Bomb. Gandhi begins his protest fast in India. In the Far East the Sino-Japanese War continues until 1945.

John Steinbeck's "The Grapes of Wrath" is published. James Joyce writes "Finnegans Wake". In 1938 Sergei Prokofiev had written the score to Eisenstein's film, "Alexander Nevsky". Premiere of Shostakovich's sixth symphony in Leningrad. Victor Fleming directs the film "The Wizard of Oz" with a sixteen-year-old Judy Garland. In Atlanta, Georgia "Gone with the Wind", starring Vivien Leigh and Clark Gable, premieres. Charles Laughton appears in "The Hunchback of Notre Dame". Tippett's "Concerto for Double String Orchestra" begun in 1938. The first Batman stories are written, created by Bob Kane. Al Capone is released from Alcatraz.

In August **Mass Observation** asked a number of people to keep accounts of their daily lives in the form of diaries. Four hundred and eighty people responded and these diaries are now housed in the MO Archive.

At **Rosenberg & Helft**, 31 Bruton Street, recent works by Picasso were exhibited. "Picasso in English Collections" was shown at **The London Gallery**, 28 Cork Street, financed by Roland Penrose.

H. S. Williamson (1933), Chairman of The London Group from 1937 to 1943

London Group records during the first years of the war are patchy. Between 1940 and 1943 the following were elected to The London Group: Edward le Bas, J. Buckland Wright, Kathleen Faussett-Osborne, Elsie Few, Henryk Gotlib, Lawrence Gowing, Frances Hodgkins, Augustus John (Honorary Member), Oscar Kokoschka (Honorary Member), Lynton Lamb, Mary Potter, Ruskin Spear, Fred Uhlman and Jack B. Yeats. Fred Uhlman was an émigré artist fleeing the Nazis in Germany. He was co-founder of the Free German League of Culture which sought to maintain a German culture free from Nazi ideology. Uhlman was interned with Kurt Scwitters on the Isle of Man.

"Thirty-seventh (sic) Exhibition of the London Group, Special Wartime Show", 2nd November to 25th November 1939. (This was really the thirty-eighth annual exhibition but in the catalogue held in the Tate Archive the 'seventh' has been struck through and 'eighth' pencilled in). Gallery unknown although the Tate Gallery Jubilee Exhibition Catalogue of 1964 states that one was held at the New Burlington Galleries and one hundred and thirty works were shown. It was an extremely sparse and economical catalogue probably due to the fact that hostilities had only recently commenced in the Second World War. No officers were recorded in the catalogue. Roger Fry (who, it must be remembered, died in 1934!) wrote a 'ghost' one-paragraph introduction, "The years covered by the existence of the London Group comprise one of the most eventful episodes in the history of British Art. It has been a period of searching enquiry into the principles of design, of criticism of all the accepted standards, of daring experiment in the search for new possibilities. Throughout this period the London Group has been the home of those English artists in whom the ferment of new ideas was working". There were one hundred and thirty exhibits (eleven of which were sculptures) from both members and non-members and arranged in three galleries, the Large Gallery, the Little Gallery and the North Gallery. Approximately thirty women were shown. Titles indicated that the work was mainly figurative, still life, landscape or portrait but no media was given. Top price was asked by Gertrude Hermes for her sculpture "Torso" (Carving in Oak) at £105 but the average price was between £20 and £70. Other notable exhibitors included David Bomberg, Duncan Grant, Eileen Agar, Ethel Walker, Ivon Hitchens, Ceri Richards, Graham Sutherland, Thérèse Lessore, Victor Pasmore, Vanessa Bell, Rodrigo Moynihan, Claude Rogers, James Fitton, Robert Medley, Gertrude Hermes, Mary Potter, Kenneth Martin and William Townsend. The exhibition catalogue had a mustard coloured cover with a single sheet inside, A5 in size and cost six pence.

The London Group's balance with Drummonds on 3rd March was £174.9.8, almost £50 down on last year. Subscriptions had brought in £101.7.0, Hanging Fees £118.7.9, Commission on Sales £17.3.8 and Admissions £111.5.6.

According to a short financial summary of each exhibition held by The London Group in the 1930s, every one of them made a deficit which doesn't mean to say that the Group was in debt. It had other sources of revenue notably the members' subscriptions and other income came from admissions, catalogues, adverts in the catalogue, submission and hanging fees and a 15% commission on sales. Expenses were rent (£180 throughout the decade), packing and mens' time, adverts, private view, printing notices, printing the catalogue and a gallery secretary fee. The biggest deficit was for the November 1936 exhibition at £87.9.9 whereas the next year's exhibition deficit was the lowest at £34.3.0. The range of deficit was between 10% to 25% of total costs.

On the 11th of September, a week after war was declared, William Townsend wrote the following bleak outlook in his diary, "Nothing else worthwhile is open in London – no theatres, cinemas, exhibitions, galleries, museums, no children and no friends left".

The 1940's

The Second World War 1939–1945 obviously interrupted the normal course of European society and culture. Materials were hard to come by, especially for sculptors, but out of these adversities grew many flowers whose seeds were set at this time. For example, Adrian Heath (1962) met Terry Frost (1957) in a prisoner of war camp and taught him to draw, which resulted in Frost's following a vocation to become a painter and "pick his brush up every day". William 'Bill' Gear (1953) was a member of the armed forces and as he advanced through Europe with the Allies he met and befriended many local artists and formed a 'European outlook' resulting in his links with the CoBrA exhibition in Amsterdam in 1947. There was also, of course, the War Artists scheme in which many artists took part, notably William Coldstream (1933) and his work with Mass Observation.

Even in war time the British Council organised touring exhibitions. In 1943 "Contemporary British Art" was toured in South America and included, amongst others, work by William Scott (1949).

Similarly there were important and influential exhibitions organised in London, particularly the 1945 Victoria & Albert Museum exhibition of Matisse and Picasso's wartime paintings and the 1947-48 exhibition at the newly founded Institute of Contemporary Arts entitled "Forty Years of Modern Art". William Scott, elected to The London Group in the following year, organised an exhibition including paintings by Picasso, Matisse, Bonnard and Modigliani under the title "20th Century French and English Painting". This seemed to continue and affirm the cultural links between the two countries so strong in the 1920s with Roger Fry and the Bloomsbury Group's influence.

Surrealism Following the success of the 1936 International Surrealism Exhibition the movement was developed by many British artists including the sculptor F.E. McWilliam (1949) and Eileen Agar (1933) who worked with paint, collage and found objects. It is worth noting that Eileen Agar, a Surrealist, and William Coldstream, a founder member of the classically oriented Euston Road Group, were both elected to The London Group in the same year, 1933. The Surrealists and Coldstream had exchanged heated accusations regarding the type of resistance to be mounted against the rise of European Fascism in the early thirties. These debates had been organised by the A.I.A. Their both being elected to The London Group in the same year is a very clear example of the Group's open policy making no discrimination on the basis of school or style. Similarly we have F.E. McWilliam, a surrealist sculptor, and John Minton, a figurative painter, both elected in 1949. Other notable Surrealists working in Britain were Paul Nash (1914), John Banting (1927), Henry Moore (1930), John Tunnard (1934), Ceri Richards (1938), Julian Trevelyan (1949), Roland Penrose,

Humphrey Jennings, David Gascoyne, and Conroy Maddox.

"British Romantic Artists" was published by John Piper (1933) in 1942. In this publication he described the British romantic tradition culminating in the work of Paul Nash (1914) and Frances Hodgkins (1940-43). A broad grouping of artists working at this time were described using the term 'neo-romantic' and included, Henry Moore (1930), Ivon Hitchens (1931), Victor Pasmore (1934), John Tunnard (1934), Graham Sutherland (1937), Frances Hodgkins (between 1940-43), Edward Burra (1949), Robert Colquhoun and Francis Bacon.

Mass Observation continued throughout the War. **The War Artists' Advisory Committee** was set up in 1939. The Committee met once a week and allocated half-yearly salaries for artists to produce 'war related' images documenting the period. Many iconic images were made under this scheme, especially from artists such as Frank Dobson (1922), Henry Moore (1930), Leonard Rosoman (1957), William Scott (1949), Graham Sutherland (1937) and Keith Vaughan (1949).

In 1946, following the granting of a Royal Charter, the **Arts Council** was set up with a grant of £235,000 in support of the arts throughout Great Britain.

The London Group also has a history of smaller groupings of artists associated with The London Group itself. **The Borough Group** was one such grouping. Formed in 1946 and disbanded in 1951 the group came into being following discussions between David Bomberg (1914) and Cliff Holden (1961). Bomberg paid tribute to Cézanne and coined the phrase "The Spirit of the Mass" to describe his approach to perception. The founding members of the Borough Group were Cliff Holden (1961), Peter Richmond, Dorothy Mead (1960) and Edna Mann. The group was later enlarged to include Leslie Marr (1961), Dinora Mendelson, Len Missen and Dorothy Missen. It should be noted that their election to The London Group came after the disbanding of the Borough Group ten years earlier. There were informal links between artists sympathetic to the Borough Group's stringent ideas and practices. Frank Auerbach (1960) and Leon Kossof (1963) worked with David Bomberg (1913) in 1947 and 1952 respectively. Dennis Creffield (1962), then aged only sixteen, was elected to the Borough Group in 1949 after meeting David Bomberg. The term 'Borough Group' came from the Borough Polytechnic where Bomberg was a teacher from 1945 to 1953. It appears that Eduardo Paolozzi and Jo Tilson were briefly excited by the ideas and the work produced by the Borough Group, but they soon "retreated back to the Establishment Schools" (Cliff Holden).

Many commercial galleries such as the Mayor Gallery and the London Gallery shut up shop during the war, but the Leger Gallery, Leicester Galleries, Redfern Gallery and Zwemmer Gallery stayed open. The **Leicester Galleries** played an important role in supporting and exhibiting realist painters later in the decade. The Leicester Galleries showed Lawrence Gowing (1940/43), Rodrigo Moynihan (1933),

Claude Rogers (1939), Walter Sickert (1916+), Ruskin Spear (1940/43) and Carel Weight (1949).

The monthly journal **"Horizon"** was published from 1939 to 1950. The editor was Cyril Connolly who was an admirer of the École de Paris, however other contributors, such as Robert Melville and J.P. Hodin, ensured that the British public and contemporary artists were kept up to date with the latest developments in European culture.

Tate Modern Time Line 1940-50 St. Ives including Patrick Heron (1952), Peter Lanyon, Ben Nicholson. Individuals Joseph Cornell, Jean Hélion, Alberto Giacometti, Lee Krasner. 'Spatialism' from Lucio Fontana. Abstract Expressionism involving Willem de Kooning, Arshile Gorky, Franz Kline, Robert Motherwell, Barnett Newman, Jackson Pollock, Mark Rothko, David Smith and Clyfford Still. 'Art Informel' with Alberto Burri, Jean Dubuffet, Jean Fautrier, Henri Michaux, Anton Tapiés and Wols. Individuals George Morandi, Germaine Richier and Pierre Soulage. CoBrA involving Karel Appel, Constant, Corneille Christian Dotremont and Asger Jorn.

To give a feeling for the period, here is an extract from William Townsend's diaries, "The Townsend Journals", dated 17th May 1940. "Getting difficult to be a landscape painter. Claude (Rogers) who has got all the permits an artist can (from the authorities), unless he is an official artist, is scarcely allowed to open a sketchbook out of doors. Rodrigo (Moynihan) sitting down to draw a farm house, after getting consent of the farmer, has found the police summoned by the same farmer, rounding him up within ten minutes. The farmer was obnoxious, the police intelligent!"

1940

Herman Goering assumes control of all war industries in Germany. Hitler and Mussolini meet to form an alliance. Germany invades Denmark and Norway, then the Low Countries and into France. In May Neville Chamberlain resigns and a National Coalition Government is formed, headed by Churchill, "I have nothing to offer you but blood, toil, tears and sweat". The Home Guard is formed. France falls to the Germans and Rommel reaches the Channel. Dunkirk Evacuation of 300,000 troops, "We shall not flag or fail. We shall fight on the beaches...on the landing grounds...in the fields and the streets...We shall never surrender." Italy declares war on France and UK. The French Government retreats to Bordeaux as Paris is taken. The Soviets invade the Baltic States. On September 7th the Battle of Britain begins, London is subjected to 57 days of relentless Blitz bombing. Germany, Italy and Japan sign a tripartite pact. Italy invades Greece. 568 are killed in a Coventry Luftwaffe attack and the RAF responds by bombing Hamburg. Sheffield is then blitzed. Auschwitz-Birkenau camp opens in Poland. In America Franklin D. Roosvelt is re-elected to become the first third-term President. Wall paintings dating to 17,000BC are found in a cave in Lascaux, South-Western France. The Summer Olympic Games had been awarded to Tokyo but were 'removed' due to the outbreak of War. Finland was then awarded the Games but they were cancelled for the same reason. Trotsky was assassinated with an ice axe in Mexico.

Michael Tippett appointed Director of Music at Morley College. (In 1943 he was to be imprisoned for refusing to join the Armed Forces). "The Philadelphia Story" with Katharine Hepburn, Cary Grant and James Stewart, premieres at Radio City, New York. Walt Disney's "Pinocchio" and "Fantasia" are released.

The Leicester Galleries showed many London Group artists throughout this year, Anthony Gross, Ivon Hitchens (first solo show), Henry Moore, John Piper, Henry Lamb, Claude Rogers, Graham Sutherland and Raymond Coxon. The Galleries were described as "unglamorous and dingy". Hardly surprising given the conditions in London at this time!

Kurt Schwitters flees Germany via Norway and lands in Edinburgh on 19th June. Interned on the Isle of Man as an 'alien'.

H.S.Williamson (1933) was recorded as 'Chairman'

"The London Group, Thirty-eighth Exhibition", Second Wartime Show, Cooling Galleries, 92, New Bond Street, London W1, 31st October to 29th November 1940. No President, Officer or List of Members was printed in the exhibition catalogue.

In total there were one hundred and two exhibits in the exhibition with only two pieces of sculpture by Alan Durst (made from terra-cotta and iroko wood) perhaps due to the lack of suitable material during wartime. The exhibition was hung in three galleries, the First Gallery, the Second Gallery and the Lower Gallery. Most of the exhibitors in the Lower Gallery were women and probably invited to show as most of the male members would be out of the country or heavily involved with the war. Only two pieces of work seem to relate directly (by their title) to the war, "A.R.P." by Grace Matthews and "Air Raid Shelter" by R. Hanson whilst the remainder were figurative paintings as suggested by their titles. Other exhibitors were Hans Feibusch, Phyllis Bray, Tristram Hillier, Mary Godwin, Edna Ginesi, Mary Potter, Edward Wolfe, Kenneth Martin, William Townsend, Raymond Coxon, Patricia Preece, John Tunnard, Victor Pasmore, Lynton Lamb, Ethel Walker, Duncan Grant, Matthew Smith and Vera Cunningham. Only the artist's name, title and price of the work was printed in the catalogue, the highest price was for R.O. Dunlop's "River at Kingston" at £150 followed by Matthew Smith's "Pears and Pomegranates" at £135 (pomegranates in wartime?). Most prices were in the £10 to £40 price range. The following was written as an anonymous introduction in the catalogue, "The London Group is probably the only association of Artists in Britain today to whom young painters, adventuring away from academicism, may submit their work for exhibition knowing that they will receive sympathetic consideration. Nevertheless it attempts, and indeed claims to maintain, a standard of what it believes to constitute 'good painting'". The catalogue itself is one piece of slightly smaller than A4 scarlet paper folded to portrait A5 with black typo. The poor quality paper testifies to the conditions prevalent at the time. The price was one shilling, including admission and, interestingly, was printed by The Women's Printing Society Ltd. Brick Street, Piccadilly.

Exhibition Admissions were recorded at £14.10.9, Hanging Fees at £29.15 whilst Subscriptions brought in £55.18.9.

On December 29th a huge Luftwaffe incendiary bombing raid came to be known as the 'Second Great Fire of London'. Over 1,500 fires were started and many famous buildings were damaged or destroyed. The Guildhall, where The London Group was to exhibit in future, more peaceful times, was one.

92 New Bond Street
London W1

Looking south from the Oxford Street end of New Bond Street towards the
commercial gallery district of Cork Street and the Royal Academy, 92 New Bond
Street was the location of the Cooling Galleries where the second war-time London
Group exhibition was held in 1940. Number 92 is the vacant shop on the immediate
right of the photograph but probably not the original building.

1941

Australian and British forces attack Italian held Tobruk in Libya. Swansea suffers three nights of blitz bombing. The Lend-Lease agreement allows Allies to 'borrow' US war materials. Germany invades Greece and Yugoslavia. The Enigma cryptography machine is captured from German U-boat U110 allowing the UK to translate German secret codes. In the North Atlantic the "Bismark" sinks "HMS Hood" and, in turn, is sunk by a torpedo attack from "HMS Ark Royal" (sunk later in the year by U-81). The USSR is invaded by Germany in Operation Barbarossa, Leningrad is besieged and the German army presses on towards Moscow where "it is frozen". Increasing tension between the US and Japan. Hitler asks his Generals to formulate a plan for "a final solution of the Jewish question". On December 7th at Pearl Harbour Japan destroys the American Pacific Fleet causing the US to enter the war. China officially declares war on Japan. Japan invades Hong Kong, Malaya, Manila and Singapore. Two British battleships are sunk north of Singapore by the Japanese. Germany and Italy declare war on the US. Churchill becomes the first British Prime Minister to address a Joint Session of the US Congress. As the London Blitz continues into 1941 more civilians are killed on the Home Front than soldiers on the battlefield.

Noël Coward's play "Blithe Spirit" premiers in London. Orson Wells makes "Citizen Kane". Shostakovich writes his "Leningrad" Symphony No. 7. First issue of "Captain America" comics. Walt Disney makes "Dumbo".
National Gallery London "War Pictures by British Artists", poster designed by John Piper (1933).
Leicester Galleries showed these London Group artists, Frank Dobson, Vanessa Bell, a Mark Gertler Memorial exhibition, Walter Sickert and Frances Hodgkins.
"Exhibition of Sculpture and Drawings" by the **Artists International Association (AIA)** and the Free German League of Culture (FGLC) with an introduction by Herbert Read.
The **Royal Academy** was still holding Open Submission for their Summer Show despite the war (evidenced by Kurt Schwitters' rejection slip!). Victor Pasmore observed that the war meant there were no longer any "tempting French pictures to imitate".

H.S. Williamson (1933) was recorded as 'Chairman'

"London Group Third War-time Exhibition", gallery unknown, although the room arrangements printed in the 1941 catalogue would seem to indicate the Leger Galleries (where the 1942 exhibition was held). Exhibition dates, 22nd October to 19th November 1941. No record of any officers was printed in the catalogue this year.

The exhibition was hung in five galleries, the First Floor Gallery, the Staircase, the Second Floor Back Gallery, Second Floor Front Gallery and the Second Floor Small Front Gallery. Despite the impressive floor space, there were only one hundred and thirty-three exhibits in total, of which only two were sculptures. Titles indicate mainly landscapes, portraits and still lifes whilst only eleven paintings had 'war related' titles. Members had multiple exhibits and the gender spread was about 80% male to 20% female. Significant exhibitors were Lawrence Gowing, John Tunnard, Edna Ginesi, Mary Potter, Blair Hughes-Stanton, Ceri Richards, Charles Ginner, Bernard and Noel Adeney, Ivon Hitchens, Matthew Smith, Elliott Seabrooke, Eileen Agar, Raymond Coxon, Kenneth Martin, Richard Carline and Rupert Lee. Top price was asked for Oscar Kokoschka's "Caricature" at £300 (Kokoschka was an Honorary Member) but most prices were between £10 and £40. Media and sizes were not given. There was quite an interesting Foreword written by William Mabane M.P., Parliamentary Secretary from the Ministry of Home Security. "In art, the London Group represents the freedom of personal expression. Its founders, in 1913, then anticipated what today we state as a war aim. So it is natural that, in the third year of the second Great War, the London Group should hold its third exhibition. It is natural too that this exhibition should be held in galleries which have been both raided and renovated. The instinct for survival overcomes the will to destroy alike in the galleries and the Group." The catalogue was A5, 8 pages stapled and printed black on drab, low quality paper which gave only the catalogue number, title, artist and price. The catalogue cost one shilling.

A tiny slip of grey paper dated 10th May 1941 gives The London Group balance as £178.1.8 with Subscriptions for 1941 bringing in £59.18.9, Hanging Fees £47.5.0, Exhibition Admissions £16.14.9 and Commission on Sales £12.7.0.

13 Old Bond Street
London W1
Now the home of Daniel Katz European Sculpture but still an art gallery. Probably the third and definitely the fourth war-time London Group exhibitions were held here in 1941 and 1942 respectively, then occupied by the Leger Galleries.
The exhibitions were arranged in four galleries on the first and second floors.
Old Bond Street is now the home to many fashion and jewellery houses at the Piccadilly end of New Bond Street, with the Royal Academy just around the corner.

1942

The first US forces arrive in Europe. The Battle of Stalingrad in USSR turns the tide against Germany, the Battle of Midway and Guadalcanal in the Pacific, the Battle of El Alamein in Africa. The new convoy system in the North Atlantic forces Germany to withdraw its U-boats. Germany tests rockets from Peenemünde. Alan Turing and M.H.A. Newman develop the first programmable computer used to crack German secret codes. The Manhattan Project gets underway in the US. In Amsterdam Anne Frank receives a diary for her thirteenth birthday. Instruments in London detect the first bursts of cosmic rays. The basis of the Welfare State is established by the Beveridge Report.

Arnold Schoenberg writes, "Ode to Napoleon Buonaparte", Op. 41. Shostakovich writes Symphony No 8. The film "Casablanca" premieres in New York.

National Gallery London "The Tate Gallery's Wartime Acquisitions", April – May. Despite this being the darkest period of the War, the business of art acquisition continued. London Group artists in this National Gallery exhibition were Edward Burra, Mark Gertler, Harold Gilman, Charles Ginner, Spencer F. Gore, Duncan Grant, Ivon Hitchens, Frances Hodgkins, Augustus John, Edward Le Bas, John Nash, Paul Nash, Victor Pasmore, John Piper, Vivian Pitchforth, Randolph Schwabe, Walter Sickert, Matthew Smith, Stanley Spencer and Graham Sutherland. Many other London Group artists not in the exhibition, such as Edward Ardizonne and Mary Potter, also had work acquired by the Tate Gallery.

The London Museum, Lancaster House "New Movements in Art, Contemporary Work in England", curated by E.H. Ramsden and Margot Eates with work by Naum Gabo, Kurt Schwitters, Peter Lanyon and John Wells. This was an important exhibition. Herbert Read wrote in the magazine 'Horizon', "the highest point ever reached by the aesthetic intuition of man". The exhibition was to tour to Leicester, Manchester, Birkenhead, Bolton, Hull, Doncaster and Liverpool.

R.B.A. Galleries "Members' Exhibition" by the A.I.A. in February, London Group (at some time in their careers) exhibitors were Eileen Agar, John Banting, Morris Kestleman, Edward le Bas, Kenneth Martin, Paul Nash, Ruskin Spear, John Tunnard and Ethel Walker.

The Leicester Galleries continued to show London Group artists, Jacob Epstein, Ivon Hitchens, Ethelbert White, Walter Sickert, John Minton, Lawrence Gowing, Stanley Spencer and Fred Uhlman.

The Modern Art Gallery, London "Exhibition of Paintings, Sculpture and Drawings" including five works by Schwitters who was resident in London at this time.

Wallace Collection "Artists Aid Russia" organised in July.

H.S. Williamson (1933) was recorded as 'Chairman'

In The London Group press cuttings section held in the Tate Archive there is a cutting from the 'Brighton and Hove Herald' dated 16th May 1942 reviewing a London Group exhibition at the Brighton Art Galleries. This was the "London Group Third War-Time Exhibition" which was toured down to Brighton. The reviewer comments on the introduction in the catalogue by Roger Fry, "the ferment of new ideas" and by Mr. William Mabane MP, who remarked upon the "personal and experimental adventure" evident in some of the work. Regarding "experiments of the mind" the Brighton reviewer writes, "of this kind comes 'Baffle' by John Tunnard, of which one can say "It does"". The review continues in the same witty fashion for six column inches. A tour outside London must mean that The London Group had a functioning and active core at this time during the war.

"London Group Fourth War-Time Exhibition", Leger Galleries, 13 Old Bond Street W1. Exhibition dates, 7th October to 7th November 1942. Neither a list of officers nor members was printed in the catalogue. The exhibition was hung in four galleries, the First Floor Front Gallery, the First Floor Inner Gallery, the Second Floor Upper Back Gallery and the Second Floor Small Front Gallery. There were one hundred and fifty-five exhibits including four pieces of sculpture, one a portrait bust of R.J. Sainsbury Esq. by Jacob Epstein (NFS). After the War the Sainsbury business machine was to support The London Group with secretarial and administrative expertise. Most of the 1941 exhibitors were represented again with some new additions, Claude Rogers, Lord Methuen, Augustus John (Honorary Member), Ruskin Spear, William Scott, Vanessa Bell, Robert Buhler, Nigel Gosling, Ethel Sands and Michael Rothenstein. There were ten paintings, which were not for sale, by Sickert. A simple acknowledgement was printed in the catalogue for the loan of works by "the late W. R. Sickert, which are included in this exhibition in affectionate memory of a great artist and the Father of the Group". Jack B. Yeats was asking top price of £100 each for two paintings on show, but the average price was between £10 and £50. Again, few paintings seemed to be war related, only six had identifiable war titles. Otherwise it was the traditional mix of still life, landscape and portrait. The catalogue shared an identical format with the 1941 version.

On May 18th, 1942 The London Group had a balance of £226.4.4, about £50 more than the previous year. Very-hard-to-read pencilled notes in the accounts ledger recorded a 'Meeting' on the 24th October 1942. John Farleigh put forward a resolution, "That in view of the fact that the original reason for the £500 being held in the names of Alan Durst, D.F. (?) Woodger & Rupert (Lee) no longer maintain, the trustees be requested to authorise the bank to transfer the £500 to the London Group a/c at the

Royal B of Sc", seconded by Bernard Adeney. This was probably sorting out matters left over from the time of Rupert Lee's presidency with The London Group which he vacated in 1936. John Farleigh had been one of the members who had campaigned in the 1930s for a change of president. Phyllis Bray put forward another motion, "The group meeting unanimously agreed that for future shows the submission fee be remitted and that the hanging fee be reduced to 10 (shillings)." The motion appears to have been accepted. And from du Plessis, "The meeting requested the Chairman to make enquiries about attending (?) galleries for future exhibitions, particularly Matheson (?) Knoedler and J.F. M (?) to Wallace Collection."

Walter Sickert, 'The Father of The London Group', died this year at the age of 82. He had chaired a number of the first meetings during the transition from the Camden Town Group to The London Group but resigned soon afterwards not wishing to be part of the same group as Lewis and the Futurists. By 1916 he had been re-elected and exhibited with The London Group virtually every year until 1935. In 1926 he married his third wife Thérèse Lessore and in 1934 became a Royal Academician. His importance to the history of British art is firmly established.

1943

Warsaw Ghetto uprising. The siege of Leningrad is broken. Germany's 6th Army surrenders at Stalingrad. Tank Battle of Kursk in USSR. US forces finally defeat the Japanese on Guadalcanal. Eisenhower is chosen to lead the allied armies in Europe. The Afrika Corps surrenders to the Allies in North Africa. Allied landings in Sicily and Italy. Mountbatten named as Supreme Allied Commander in South East Asia. RAF Dambuster raids. 42,000 civilians are killed in the 'firestorm' bombing raids on Hamburg. Huge air raids on Berlin. Mussolini is arrested. Chiang Kai-shek took the oath of office as President of China. Churchill, Roosevelt, Stalin and Chiang Kai-shek meet throughout the year. The economic depression comes to an end in the US as unemployment tumbles due to war time production and Roosevelt is able to close the Works Progress Administration which had given much support to American artists. In London 173 people are killed trying to shelter in Bethnal Green tube station from an air raid. Rodgers and Hammerstein's "Oklahoma" opens on Broadway. Duke Ellington plays Carnegie Hall. Deborah Kerr appears in "The Life and Death of Colonel Blimp".

National Gallery London recent pictures by War Artists.

Lefevre Gallery Josef Herman (1953) exhibition.

The Leicester Galleries showed Kenneth Martin (1949), Augustus John (1940/43) and John Farleigh (1927), all London Group members.

The Artists International Association opened its Charlotte Street Centre with "Hogarth and English Caricature". A discussion group within the A.I.A. was called the 'Hogarth Group' and, amongst others, included Lawrence Gowing who was also elected to The London Group at this time. Many contemporary writers saw a continuity of traditional English art found in the work of Hogarth and running through Sickert and the Camden Town Group. The A.I.A. also mounted the exhibition "For Liberty" in the basement canteen of the John Lewis department store, sponsored by the News Chronicle. Under the theme 'this is what we fight for', four freedoms were identified, freedom of speech, freedom to worship, freedom from want and freedom from fear. Artists were asked to make responses to these freedoms.

Wallace Collection "Artists Aid China" shown in April and May.

In America Mark Rothko and Adolph Gotlib release their famous 'Statement' to the effect that "pictures for the home; pictures for over the mantel" were completely out-dated and should be ignored. ("Theories of Modern Art", Hirschel B. Chipp (ed.), Berkeley 1968, p.545).

London Group President: Elliott Seabrooke (1920)

"The London Group, Fifth War-Time Exhibition", Royal Academy, Burlington House, W1, 26th October to 25th November 1943. The President this year was Elliott Seabrooke who had, as some sources state, "assumed" the Presidency, but no other officers were identified. There were seventy-three members of which nineteen were women and included six Honorary Members. The exhibition was shown in the Lecture Room, Room 8 and Room 9. There were two hundred and twenty-one exhibits in total with multiple works from most exhibitors. Both members and non-members were included in the show but no selection mechanism was described. The Lecture Room contained oils, watercolours and sculptures and there were seven pieces of sculpture altogether, Siegfried Theroux's "Figure" was priced at a staggering £1,050, as was Henryk Gotlib's, "Mickiewicz Returns to Cracow". New names this year included David Bomberg, Thérèse Lessore, John Piper, Feliks Topolski, Bernard Meadows, William Townsend, Roderigo Moynihan, Duncan Grant and Victor Pasmore Prices this year showed a much greater range from £10 to £200. Perhaps the Academy venue attracted more important artists and prestigious work. The catalogue contained "In Memoriam" to Morland Lewis and John Cooper. Lewis was a painter who had studied at the Royal Academy Schools and with Sickert whilst Cooper, also a painter, had trained at the Slade and been involved with the East London Group between 1929 and 1938. The catalogue this year followed the familiar format but comprised of 12 pages and had been reduced from one shilling to three pence!

The 1943 accounts record subscriptions at £70.12. The 1943 exhibition did remarkably well bringing in £55.3.0 in Hanging Fees, £289.1.9 in catalogues & admissions and £563.6.0 in sales. Ivon Hitchens sold four works for a total of over £310, Bernard Adeney sold three for £68, Edward le Bas made £63, John Piper £40 and J. Tunnard, £33.12.

In Edward Wolfe's Exhibition record there is mention of his taking part in a London Group exhibition at the Victoria Art Gallery, Bath in 1943. There appears to be no other source at present to back this up.

The Royal Academy
Piccadilly, London W1

Despite The London Group's original stance against prevailing RA taste at the beginning of the twentieth century, the Group did exhibit here, albeit in the smaller Diploma Galleries, in 1943, 1944 and 1945.

1944

The siege of Leningrad is lifted. Anzio landings take place. Battle of Monte Casino. Battles of Iwo Jima and Guam in the Pacific. June 6th, D-Day operations on the beaches of Normandy. June 13th, first V1 flying bomb attacks launched from France. London is hit by V1 and V2 rockets killing 9,000 Londoners. Paris and Brussels are liberated. Aachen in Germany falls to the Americans. The Nazis sold off the contents of the "Degenerate Art" exhibition in Switzerland. R.A. Butler's Education Act (1944) which lifed the ban on women teachers marrying. The Summer Olympic Games were to be held in London, but were cancelled due to the War. Laurence Olivier directs the film version of "Henry V".

Francis Bacon paints "Three Studies for Figures at the Base of a Crucifixion". Michael Tippett writes, "A Child of Our Time". Glenn Miller disappears in fog whilst flying over the Channel.

The Lefevre Gallery Lucian Freud exhibits "The Painter's Room" (1943)

The Leicester Galleries showed Frank Dobson, Ivon Hitchens, E. Morland Lewis, Cedric Morris, Jacob Epstein, J.B. Manson and Ethelbert White. All were at some time elected to The London Group.

London Group President: Elliott Seabrooke (1920)

Only one member was elected this year, Geoffrey Tibble. This would seem to indicate that a meeting was held to select Tibble and that the Group was functioning in some form or other.

In 2009 Roe and Moore, the London booksellers, were offering for sale a catalogue to an exhibition of London Group paintings. The catalogue to "Exhibition of Paintings by 'The London Group': a temporary exhibition from 27th July to 3rd September 1944", at the National Museum of Wales in Cardiff is described as a folding sheet with a Foreward (sic) by Geoffrey Grigson. In the forty-six item catalogue the following artists were recorded, Agar, Vanessa Bell, Bomberg, Buckland Wright, Farleigh, Fitton, Duncan Grant, Hitchens, Henry Moore, Pasmore, John Piper, Ceri Richards, Spear, Tunnard, Uhlman and Yeats.

"The London Group, Sixth War-Time Exhibition", Royal Academy, 12th October to 9th November 1944. Elliott Seabrooke was the President of The London Group this year and the exhibition catalogue lists sixty-six members plus six Honorary Members who were Jacob Epstein, Augustus John, Oscar Kokoschka, David Low, Matthew Smith and Jack B. Yeats. One hundred and seventy-one exhibits were shown in Room 8, Room 9 and the Lecture Room showing oils, watercolours and sculpture respectively.

Despite the war there were plenty of 'big names' to draw the crowds, L.S. Lowry, David Bomberg, Ivon Hitchens, Victor Pasmore, Thérèse Lessore, Nina Hamnett, Claude Rogers, Duncan Grant, Mary Potter, Matthew Smith, Vanessa Bell, Charles Ginner and Richard Carline. There was a mixture of members and non-members but no indication as to how non-members' works were selected. Highest prices were asked for works by Bomberg, Pasmore, Yeats, Gotlib, Rogers, Grant, Smith, Tibble, Seabrooke, Uhlman and sculpture by Charoux, but most prices were within the £10 to £50 price range. Perhaps due to limited printing materials there was no foreword in the tiny catalogue, although there was an "In Memorium" for Frederick James Potter, a Vice President for several years from 1924, who died following an illness. He was "well respected as a painter". The catalogue was slightly larger than A6 on flimsy white paper with no illustrations and cost three pence.

London Group accounts show £84.16 as being made by 'sub..s' and an incredibly healthy £1,377.13.0 by sales, Victor Pasmore earning £280, Ivon Hitchens £96, R.O. Dunlop £90, Duncan Grant £80 and J. Tunnard £59. Hanging Fees raised £25.10 and catalogues and admissions £290.4.0. A bank slip dated 6th December 1944 gives The London Group a balance of £963.4.5.

"In the winter of 1944 the Royal Academy revealed that it had invited the New English Art Club, the Royal Institute of Painters in Oil Colours, The London Group and other societies to stage their forthcoming annual shows in its galleries, reacting at one level to Hubbard's attack on the young mandarins of the Council for Encouragement of Music and the Arts (CEMA) and the Tate Gallery, and recognising that many young members were already summer show regulars at Burlington House. It would be difficult for the club (NEAC) to take up such an invitation while Steer and Tonks were alive. Comparisons could now be made and, while the institute contained craftsmen regarded as 'slick', The London Group was 'adventurous' but slightly chaotic, the club (NEAC) displayed 'a patient but spinsterish integrity'. 'Integrity' in post-war Britain was to become a byword for reactionary realism". ("The New English: A History of the New English Art Club", Kenneth McConkey, 2006).

In the "Members Record of Subscriptions 1939–1959", the following are recorded as paying their £2 annual subscription to The London Group throughout or periodically during the war (1939 to 1945), Noel Adeney, Bernard Adeney, Eileen Agar, Elizabeth Andrews, Edward le Bas, Keith Baynes, Vanessa Bell, David Bomberg, Phyllis Bray, John Buckland Wright, Richard Carline, Raymond Coxon, Vera Cunningham, R.A. Dunlop, Alan Durst, Elsie Farleigh, John Farleigh, Hans Feibusch, Elsie Few, James Fitton, Edna Ginesi, Charles Ginner, Mary Godwin, Henryk Gotlib, Duncan Grant, Nina Hamnett, Cicely Hey, Ivon Hitchens, Blair Hughes-Stanton, S. de Karlowska, Lynton Lamb, Kit Lewis, Henry Moore (one £2.2.0 payment in 1941 and then a note next to 1942-1949, "Not to be asked"), Rodrigo Moynihan, Victor Pasmore, Maresco

Pearce, John Piper, R.V. Pitchforth, H.E. du Plessis, Mary Potter, Ceri Richards, Ethel Sands, Ruskin Spear, Geoffrey Tibble, John Tunnard, Fred Uhlman, Ethel Walker, H.S. Williamson, Edward Wolfe and Jack Yeats. Here was a long list of members who kept the Group financially alive during the hostilities. Of the fifty-one members listed fifteen were women. Most monies were "by deduction" which presumably meant the war time equivalent of a standing order arrangement.

1945

By January 1945 half of London's housing stock had been destroyed or damaged. The War ends in Europe. The Big Three, Churchill, Roosvelt and Stalin, meet at Yalta. Battle of Iwo Jima in the Pacific. Hiroshima and Nagasaki in Japan are destroyed by atomic weapons dropped by US bombers. The first computer is built and the microwave oven invented. The United Nations is born. Clement Atlee becomes Prime Minister in a Labour landslide election over war-hero Churchill's Conservatives. Labour promised full employment, a Welfare State and a National Health Service. George Orwell writes "Animal Farm", a satire on the Russian Revolution set in a farmyard. On June 7th Benjamin Britten premieres "Peter Grimes" to world acclaim. The film "Brief Encounter" is released. Shostakovich completes his ninth symphony.

Victoria and Albert Museum: the important "Exhibition of paintings by Matisse and Picasso", organised by the British Council, was extended into 1946. This was the kick-start that British art needed to regenerate British artistic life and to inform and inspire young British artists following the war.

National Gallery London in December there was an exhibition of 137 Paul Klee paintings. Klee was an extremely influential artist at this time and was rated alongside Bonnard, Matisse and Picasso.

Lefevre Gallery in a group show Francis Bacon exhibited, "Three Studies for Figures at the Base of a Crucifixion" (1944), a seminal work now in the Tate collection.

The Leicester Galleries exhibited John Piper, Robert Buhler, Lawrence Gowing, Duncan Grant, William Roberts, Henry Lamb and Jacob Epstein, all members of The London Group at some time.

The **AIA** arranged an exhibition for the Amalgamated Engineering Union called "The Engineer in British Life". AIA member Francis Klingender described it as "the first art exhibition sponsored by a British trade union".

London Group President: probably Elliott Seabrooke (1920) but no accurate evidence

No new members were elected to The London Group this year.

"An Exhibition of Paintings by the London Group", a tour of Scotland organised by CEMA (Council for the Encouragement of Music and the Arts), 1945. Precise venues are not recorded but this was the first exhibition by The London Group in Scotland. A review in "The Scotsman" on 18th January 1945 indicates that the "exhibition of paintings opens today in Edinburgh". Edward Wolfe, elected to membership in 1923, organised and assembled the exhibition that contained forty-nine paintings, one work from each artist and all current members. Paintings were for sale on the tour, the majority for under £100, but Jack B. Yeats' "The Horse Lover" was priced at £250 and Matthew Smith's "The Bright Scarf" at £105. Geoffrey Grigson wrote on his Foreword, dated 25th May 1944, "For all its (The London Group) consciousness of Europe, it has been, to my mind, an exceedingly English affair, a compromise in quite a good sense. It has certainly had some of the weaknesses of not being exclusive or passionate in the way small groups of artists who are closely intimate with one another: but as a free and wide association, it has cramped no artist: it has helped painters to develop and has helped and goes on helping your enjoyment and mine.". Duncan Grant, a founding member of The London Group, and Henry Moore were both members of C.E.M.A. under the Vice Chairmanship of Sir Kenneth Clark. Ex-Chairman of The London Group H.S. Williamson also worked for C.E.M.A. during the 1940s.

"The London Group, 1945 Exhibition", Royal Academy, 12th December 1945 to 16th January 1946. The copy of the catalogue to this exhibition held in the Tate Archive is incomplete as pages 3-4 are missing. If the catalogue were to follow a traditional format, on these pages would have been recorded the President, Vice President and the number of members and perhaps even a short foreword by the President. Two hundred and fourteen works were exhibited including thirteen pieces of sculpture and was probably arranged in four galleries at the Royal Academy including Rooms 7, 8 and 9. Both members and non-members were shown but no indication as to how the non-members came to have their works selected. Titles printed in the catalogue indicate a predominance of landscape, portrait and still life, only four pieces of work seem to make direct reference to the recently ended World War. Among those exhibiting were Charles Ginner, Merlyn Evans, Bernard Meninsky, Duncan Grant, Ivon Hitchens, Eileen Agar, David Bomberg, Edna Ginesi, William Roberts, Lawrence Gowing, Jeffery B. Camp, Monty Sunshine, Quentin Bell, Vanessa Bell, Gertrude Hermes and Karin Jonzen. Highest prices were sought by Grant, Feibusch, Rogers, Victor Pasmore, Wolfe, Meninsky, Gotlib, Ethel Walker, Vanessa Bell and Nina Hamnett with the average price for a piece of work between £25 and £50. The catalogue itself was very small and of poor quality paper, as could be expected with materials being in short supply, smaller than A5 portrait, black typo on plain white paper and costing three pence. There was also a short 'In Memoriam' to Malcolm Drummond in the catalogue, an original founder member who had died in 1945.

Vanessa Bell wrote a letter to Angelica Garnett (her daughter born on Christmas Day, 1918, fathered by Duncan Grant) on the 10th March 1946. Bell and Duncan Grant were members of the Selection Committee and had hoped to get Angelica's painting into the London Group's 1945 exhibition, "but invariably they were lunching with Edward le Bas at the crucial moment." Bell's letter continues, "We left them in full swing at nearly 6 but were saved from collapse by the wonderful tea produced by

Mrs Seabrooke, a very stout and good-natured Dutch lady who gave about 30 people tea and sandwiches with cress and some sort of fish filling and very good cakes. I ate all I could get. Everyone was quite wild and no one attempted to do anything according to the rules. Pasmore got wilder and wilder till he looked exactly like a monkey with hair flying in all directions and beard also. What it all amounted to I don't know but we enjoyed it very much in spite of the incredible slowness of everything." ("Vanessa Bell", Frances Spalding, Weidenfeld & Nicolson Ltd., 1983, p.341).

The November 1945 issue of "The Studio" had an article on the Camden Town Group written by Charles Ginner. At the end Ginner writes, "The formation of The London Group and its subsequent history was the subject of an article in 'The Studio' in February 1945, now entirely out of print".

1946

Nuremberg war trials. Churchill invents the phrase 'Iron Curtain'. In July the USA begins an extensive programme of nuclear bomb tests based on Bikini Atoll in the Pacific Ocean. The first General Assembly of the United Nations Organisation meets in Central Hall, Westminster, London with 51 nations sending representatives. UNESCO is also established in November. In the UK the New Towns Act is passed. Twenty-eight new towns will eventually be built re-housing people displaced by the war. National Health Service Act (1946) passed. David Lean directs "Great Expectations".

The Arts Council was set up following the granting of a Royal Charter with a budget of £235,000. **The Arts Council Collection** was charged with purchasing works by modern British artists. (In the year 2005/6, sixty years later, the Arts Council's budget was £410 million from Government and £160 million from the National Lottery).
Leicester Galleries exhibition by Thérèse Lessore, a founder member of The London Group in 1913 and Sickert's widow. Also Kenneth Martin, Rodrigo Moynihan, Ethel Walker, Walter Sickert and Carel Weight.
Lefevre Gallery Summer Exhibition including Macbryde, Colquhoun and Minton.
Redfern Gallery group show including Sutherland and Bacon.
St Ives, Cornwall Mariner's Church, first exhibition of an exhibiting group calling themselves, 'The Crypt Group' including Sven Berlin, Peter Lanyon, Guido Morris, John Wells and Bryan Winter (1955). Critical support from Patrick Heron (1952) in London.
Museum of Modern Art (MOMA) New York Henry Moore (1930).

London Group President: Elliott Seabrooke (1920)

As a repeat of last year, no new members were elected this year.
"London Group, Exhibition of Paintings", David Jones Art Gallery, 19th March to 2nd April 1946. Will Ashton OBE is recorded as the Director of the gallery and the catalogue indicates that there were thirty-four paintings in this exhibition by current members of the Group. The subject matter was overwhelmingly still life and landscape. A Foreword by Cora J. Gordon mentions the "highest official honours" for London Group members and she makes particular reference to the following members and their achievements, Augustus John (Honorary Member), Elliott Seabrooke (current President), Rupert Lee, R.O. Dunlop, Jack B. Yeats, Frederick Porter, Dame Ethel Walker, Mary Potter, Vera Cunningham, Matthew Smith, John Tunnard, Keith Baynes, H.E. du Plessis, Edward Wolfe and Bernard Adeney. There were two black and white, full-page (approximately A5) illustrations in the catalogue of paintings by

J. Buckland Wright and Mary Godwin. Buckland Wright showed "Stalingrad, 1942", a semi-abstract figurative painting in a 'Nash' style showing soldiers in a derelict and devastated landscape whilst Godwin exhibited "Stratton, Cornwall", a straightforward landscape of a view of a typical English village with a church in the background, war and peace. The catalogue itself has quite a beautiful 'modern abstract' design on the cover, cost six pence and a small printers mark on the back for Waite & Bull, Sydney, the only indication in the whole catalogue that this exhibition actually took place in Australia!

A circular to all Committee Members from President Elliott Seabrooke calls for a meeting on September 23rd at 44, Baker Street. On the agenda was discussion "to complete arrangements in connection with the forthcoming exhibition at the Whitechapel Art Gallery. It is earnestly hoped that you will find it convenient to be present at this meeting." This would indicate that officers were once again planning after the disruption caused by the war. A postcard apologising for absence confirms that Duncan Grant was one of the Committee at the time. The Hanging Committee met in July, September, November and December consisting of Elliott Seabrooke, Victor Pasmore, Claude Rogers, Ruskin Spear, R.O. Dunlop, Keith Baynes, Raymond Coxon, Ceri Richards and H.E. du Plessis. The planned show at the Whitechapel Art Gallery could not take place due to repairs underway at the gallery following war damage. "The President pointed out that Ellen Wilkinson, Minister of Education, was extremely keen on the show at the Whitechapel Art Gallery, and had promised to do all she could to ensure its success, including possibly a cocktail party on the day of the opening". Raymond Coxon proposed that a member of the Royal Family should open the show and the President thought that might be a possibility. Other venues considered were Agnews and the Carlton Hotel on Pall Mall. Victor Pasmore was very keen on the Carlton Hotel and suggested it become the permanent London Group home. The Leicester Galleries and the London Museum were also proposed but no Annual Exhibition was held in London in 1946.

However, a new set of Draft Rules were proposed in 1946. The basic rules remained the same as last printed in 1933. The first change was that the membership subscription was lowered from £3 to £2! Instead of the five person Executive Committee organising and hanging the annual exhibition, this task was now to be done by a Hanging Committee of eight members. The only other change was that, "Members may exhibit three works (it had been five) at these Exhibitions. The number of works exhibited by members may be increased at the discretion of the Hanging Committee, in the event of their being sufficient space available for an increased number of works." Obviously exhibition space in London was already perceived to be a problem although non-members were still allowed to submit two works for consideration and exhibition.

There is a heart warming entry in William Townsend's diary dated 27th October

1946, where he calls on William Ratcliffe then living in Wilbury Road. Ratcliffe was a founder member of The London Group in October 1913. The entry reads, "He is a pleasant, tiny old man, with an egg-shaped head; looks like a wise old carpenter or cobbler shuffling about in a littered-up living room, then sitting by an open fire in a cottage armchair, and delighted to talk. He came to Letchworth 40 years ago, was encouraged to paint by Gilman who lived there too. Gilman built a house almost next door but never lived in it, but it was there that Spencer Gore lived one summer and did his pictures of Letchworth. Ratcliffe was one of the Camden Town Group from the start and remembers the gatherings at 19 Fitzroy Street and at Cumberland Market and the exhibition at the Goupil. After the war (1914-18) he deplored the creation of the London Group when the 'cubists' swamped the old crowd completely. Then Gore was dead, and Gilman in 1919, and he confesses he has never painted so happily deprived of their stimulus and encouragement".

1947

The Partition and Independence of India overseen by Mountbatten as the last Viceroy of India. The partition of India gives birth to Pakistan, the first modern Islamic State. 200 million people were displaced and 1 million died in the upheaval. Burma also gains independence. Commencement of Stalin's purges following the formation of the Communist Information Bureau (Cominform). Europe receives aid under the Marshall Plan. Coal and other industries nationalised in UK. The Town and Country Planning Act (1947) is passed.

Victoria and Albert Museum "Braque and Rouault" exhibition. Craigie Aitchison (1962), Frank Auerbach (1960), Patrick Heron (1952) and Leon Kossoff (1963) are on record as expressing how influential this exhibition was in terms of their personal development.

Archer Gallery, London the first Borough Group (see 1940s) exhibition in June.

Leicester Gallery exhibitions by Claude Rogers, Ethelbert White, Jacob Epstein, Ivon Hitchens, Raymond Coxon, C.R.W. Nevinson, Edward Burra and Anthony Gross, all London Group members at some time.

Redfern Gallery Victor Pasmore.

AIA Gallery moves to Lisle Street. Claude Rogers found the new property for them. The AIA was dissolved when the lease ran out on Lisle Street in 1971.

The **London Gallery** "Summer Exhibition" between June and July showed important international Cubists and Surrealists. Roland Penrose and F.E. McWilliam (1949) from the UK were shown.

London Group President: Elliott Seabrooke (1920)

Only one member was elected this year, John Dodgson. A Committee Meeting took place at 44 Baker Street on 20th March attended by Elliott Seabrooke, Victor Pasmore, Ceri Richards, Raymond Coxon and Claude Rogers. "It appears that the (newly formed) Arts Council are very anxious to obtain the use of the New Burlington Galleries which are at present being used as a canteen by the Canadian Army. The Minister promised to contact the Minister of Works in an endeavour to have the canteen transferred to the basement thus leaving the Gallery free for exhibition purposes". It transpired that the galleries were in excellent decoration. The Committee then approved a booking for this year at the RBA Galleries who were asking £330 for 3 weeks hire, but The London Group was only prepared to offer £250 as 'all in' expenses were estimated at £500 to be recouped by hanging fees, gate money, sales of catalogues and sales commission. A pre-war members subscription was £3.3.0, a non-member submission fee was 2/6 whilst a hanging fee was 15/- but the committee discussed changing these charges. Publicity was next on the agenda with notices being sent to newspapers and radio, especially to Basil Taylor on the Third Programme, there were even plans for "sandwich men to patrol Pall Mall East and Haymarket". Pasmore and Rogers suggested all London Art Schools should be sent a stack of 'sending-in forms'. Raymond Coxon had links with friends in New York and suggested a tour to this city across the Atlantic.

"London Group, 1947 Exhibition", RBA Galleries, 6 1/2, Suffolk Street, Pall Mall East, SW1. Exhibition dates, 20th May to 7th June 1947. Elliott Seabrooke was recorded as President with a membership of seventy-four. The exhibition was hung in six galleries containing two hundred and eighty-seven exhibits of which fifteen were sculptures distributed through galleries 2, 3 and 4. Fifty-one of the seventy-four members exhibited, the remainder were non-members but no selection criteria were recorded. Again the subject matter was predominantly landscape, still life and portrait. Media and sizes of works were not printed. Following the war prices were now beginning to rise, the lowest being about 15 to 20 guineas. Three figure prices were asked by David Bomberg, Ethel Walker, P. Norman Dawson, Victor Pasmore, William Roberts, Edward Wolfe, Geoffrey Tibble, Vanessa Bell, Bernard Meninsky, Duncan Grant, Jack B. Yeats, André Masson, T. Potworowski, William Townsend, Henryk Gotlib, Rupert Lee, John Dodgson and Alan Durst (sculpture). P.G.L.Richmond asked the highest price of £682.10.0 for the landscape "Easter Evening: View between St. Paul's and Cannon Street". Some new names begin to appear in the non-members exhibitors' listings including Margaret Mellis, Morris Kestleman, Frederick Brill, Prunella Clough, Roger de Grey, L.S. Lowry, Anthony Eyton, John Minton, Julian Trevelyan and Karin Jonzen. Printed at the front of the catalogue was an 'In Memoriam' to Paul Nash, Thérèse Lessore and Frances Hodgkins. Nash and Lessore were original London Group members and Lessore had been Sickert's third wife. Hodgkins knew Christopher Wood and had been involved with the Seven and Five Society.

Admission to the exhibition was one shilling whilst the 16 page, A5, un-illustrated catalogue cost sixpence. There was a "substantial loss" on the 1947 RBA show, accurate figures were "not to hand". Also from the same source, "The President reported that he had seen Basil Taylor of the B.B.C. who had asked him to give a thousand word talk on the History of the Group, on the 22nd May 1947. Another broadcast, date at present unknown, but to be some time during the exhibition, will be given by an art critic".

1948

Berlin Airlift. The State of Israel is founded. Russia orders the overthrow of Tito in Yugoslavia. Siam changes its name to Thailand. The Summer Olympic Games are held in London's Wembley Stadium. The National Health Service is inaugurated on July 5th by Bevan. Railways and Electricity nationalised. National Assistance Act (1948) replaces the old Poor Law. Universal Declaration of Human Rights. T.S. Eliot wins a Nobel Prize. The Aldburgh Music Festival is founded by Benjamin Britten. Moira Shearer appears in "The Red Shoes".

Tate Gallery hugely influential and well attended exhibition of Van Gogh's paintings.

Institute of Contemporary Art (ICA) "40,000 Years of Modern Art", an exhibition that included Picasso's "Demoiselles d'Avignon".

The Hanover Gallery opens run by Erica Brausen who was born in Germany (how would the general public react, so soon after the war with Germany?). The Hanover Gallery was to support modern international and national art and provide a shop window for new developments. It put British artists in touch with the rest of the world following the isolationism of the Second World War. This year she holds a one-man exhibition by Graham Sutherland (1937). Sutherland was later to introduce Francis Bacon to Erica Brausen.

"The Problems of Painting: Paris – London 1947" was a seminal article written by David Sylvester in the French journal 'L'Age Nouvea'. In it Sylvester used the term 'Ecole de Londres' for the first time, arguing that significant new developments were taking place in British Art and that London and not New York was the successor to Paris.

Gimpel Fils Gallery William Gear (1953) exhibition, catalogue preface by David Sylvester.

The Leicester Galleries Edward Ardizzone, Lawrence Gowing, Augustus John, Louis le Brocquy, Elinor Bellingham-Smith, William Scott and John Piper. All elected to The London Group at some point in their careers.

Delbanco's Sickert drawings.

Lefevre Ben Nicholson

London Gallery Lucien Freud, including "Girl with a White Dog". Freud married Jacob Epstein's daughter Kitty this year but they were divorced four years later. Epstein describing Freud as a 'spiv'.

The Arts Council organise an exhibition of the work of the Euston Road School.

A collection of **Sickert's** writings, "A Free House", was published.

The Venice Biennale This was the first post-war Biennale where Henry Moore (1930) won the Grand Prize for sculpture.

London Group President: Elliott Seabrooke began the year,
Ruskin Spear (1940-43) was elected President at the December AGM

Four new members were elected this year, Anthony Gross (printmaker), Karin Jonzen, Kit Lewis and L.S. Lowry. Committee Members in January were Elliott Seabrooke, David Bomberg, John Dodgson, H.E. du Plessis, Henryk Gotlib, Robert Medley, Ceri Richards, Duncan Grant, Victor Pasmore, Claude Rogers and Ruskin Spear.

"The London Group, 1948 Exhibition", The Academy Hall, 167 Oxford Street, London W1, 21st May to 6th June 1948. The exhibition poster was by Victor Pasmore. This year there were three hundred exhibits, one hundred and sixty-five in the Main Room, fifty-four in the Small Room and twenty-eight in the Watercolour Room. Sculptures were distributed throughout. The Foreword written by Elliott Seabrooke and Victor Pasmore puts forward the familiar historical pedigree of the Group and the historical links to modern French painting in particular. They identified the New English Art Club and then The London Group as agents for showing these new ideas in England. "Today the Group is the only large Society of Painters and Sculptors fully conscious of, and sympathetic with, the developments of Modern Art; consequently it fulfils an important and singular function in that it encourages, and takes a live interest in, all forms of genuine experiment within the medium of Painting and Sculpture". There are many new and (now) unknown names in this show refreshing the annual event with new blood. There is a feeling of the Group beginning to draw new breath and gather its energies. The catalogue has an 'ideas' oriented Foreword and many new exhibitors, artists such as Brian Robb, Patrick George, Henry Inlander, B.A.R.Carter, William Gear, Robert Medley, Jeffery Camp, Roger Hilton, Cliff Holden, Gustav Metzger, Anthony Fry, Anthony Gross, Dorothy Mead and Peter Startup. The catalogue gives only the artist, title and price of each work. Prices seem down on the previous year the average being £10 to £50, perhaps these were smaller works to fit into the Academy Hall which was possibly a limited space venue. Matthew Smith's "Still Life with Clay Figure" was most expensive at £500.

This new spirit of optimism was reflected in the increase of admission from one shilling to one shilling and sixpence and a rise in the catalogue price to sixpence. The sixteen page, A5 black and white catalogue had a new London Group logo and typeface, another indication of the Group moving forward.

A Special General Meeting was called on 14th October at 44 Baker Street. Not surprisingly the agenda for the Special General Meeting circulated to all members had one item, "Discussion of Financial Situation and Future Shows". The President Elliott Seabrooke read a prepared statement admitting that figures and sums of money "have always proved elusive and a mystery to me". He accepted full responsibility for the debts incurred, especially from the last exhibition, and the meeting discussed ways of raising funds to pay off the debt of £288.8.11. There were many ideas put forward including members donating works for a sale, but finally exhibition fees were raised and the subscription fee raised from £2 to £4. It seems that the £500 reserve held in trust under the names of Durst, Woodger and Lee had still not been released, but the Group hoped to deal with the debt without breaking into this sum.

Baker Street was also the venue for the AGM on Monday, December 20th. Nineteen members in attendance elected Ruskin Spear as President with Seabrooke falling back to Vice President. The Hanging Committee was E. Le Bas, R. Medley, B. Meninsky, H. du Plessis, E. Wolfe and V. Pasmore. Interestingly "in reserve" were H. Gotlib, A. Gross, C. Rogers and the Bloomsbury artists D. Grant and V. Bell. The Honorary Secretary reported that approximately half of the earlier debt had now been paid off by members' voluntary contributions. Cliff Holden, one of the longest serving members of The London Group, has fond memories of hanging London Group exhibitions with David Bomberg and Victor Pasmore in the late forties.

The Academy Hall
167 Oxford Street, London W1

The London Group held its annual exhibition here from May to June 1948.
The Academy Hall had a Main Room, a Small Room and a Watercolour Room where three hundred works were hung. The exhibition was an open submission showing works from some of the seventy-four members and from non-members submitting work through a selection committee. Admission was one shilling and sixpence.
An image by Victor Pasmore was reproduced on the exhibition poster. In 2008 Oxford Street was a noisy, congested and crowded shopping Mecca. H Samuel jewellers have replaced the Academy Hall. Admission to H Samuel is free, but you will need more than one shilling and sixpence to buy something (or maybe not).

The following comes from the final item of a Committee Meeting held on the 30th September, "H. du Plessis agreed to see Henry Moore in regard to his proposed resignation, which it is felt is only due to non-payment of subscriptions. John Dodgson suggested that we propose that Henry Moore be made an Honorary Life Member of the Group. This was not agreed."

Facing colour plates
Covers from the catalogues to London Group exhibitions

MARCH, 1914

Catalogue
of
The First Exhibition
of
Works by Members
of

THE
LONDON
GROUP

The Goupil Gallery

5 REGENT STREET
LONDON, S.W.

1

SIXTH EXHIBITION.

The Mansard Gallery,

Messrs. HEAL & SON.

196, Tottenham Court Road, W.

LONDON GROUP

APRIL 26th to MAY 26th
1917

2

THE
LONDON GROUP

THIRTY-SEVENTH EXHIBITION

November 2nd to 25th 1939

Special

War-time

Show

PRICE SIXPENCE

3

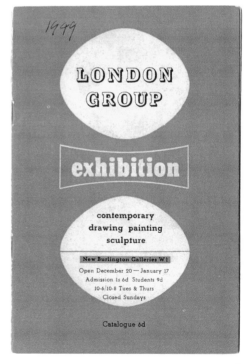

1949

LONDON
GROUP

exhibition

contemporary
drawing painting
sculpture

New Burlington Galleries W1

Open December 20 — January 17
Admission 1s 6d Students 9d
10-6/10-8 Tues & Thurs
Closed Sundays

Catalogue 6d

4

LONDON GROUP

NEW BURLINGTON GALLERIES
OLD BURLINGTON STREET W.1

	10—6 Mons. to Sats.
	10—8 Tues. and Thurs.
	Exhibition closes on
	the 3rd of March
Contemporary	Admission 1s. 6d.
Painting Drawing	Students 9d. ·
and Sculpture	Closed Sundays

1951

Catalogue 1s.

5

SOUTHAMPTON ART GALLERY

A SELECTION
FROM THE
**LONDON
GROUP**
EXHIBITION
1954

February 12th to March 13th, 1955

7

LONDON GROUP

NEW BURLINGTON GALLERIES
OLD BURLINGTON STREET, W1

CONTEMPORARY PAINTING, DRAWING & SCULPTURE

Mons. to Sats. 10-6. Tues. and Thurs. 10-8, Closed Sundays
Exhibition closes on Saturday 24th Nov.
Admission 1s. 6d. Students 9d. Catalogue 1s.

1951

6

London Group. 1968. Royal Institute Galleries. 195 Piccadilly. from 12–28 Nov. Open Mon–Fri 10.0–5.0. Sat. 11.0 5.0
Entrance and Catalogue 2/6

8

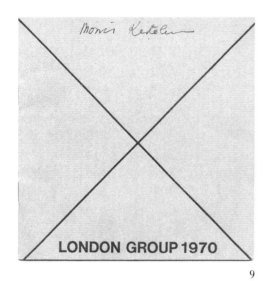

LONDON GROUP 1970

9

THE LONDON GROUP AT THE R.C.A.

11

THE LONDON GROUP

10

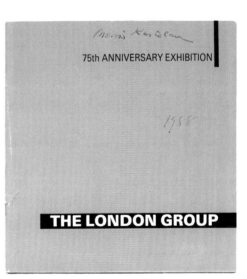

75th ANNIVERSARY EXHIBITION

THE LONDON GROUP

12

13

14

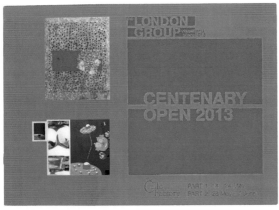

15

1949

North Atlantic Treaty Organisation (NATO) formed. Creation of East Germany. The Peoples' Republic of China declared by Mao Zedong following The Long March. European Convention on Human Rights. The USSR explodes its first nuclear device and the arms race begins in earnest. The Housing Act (1949) was passed. George Orwell published "1984". A classic year for British film releases with "The Third Man", "Whisky Galore" and "Kind Hearts and Coronets". Sir Alfred Munnings delivered his infamous attack on modern art in his address to the Royal Academy.

"**The Visual Arts**" written by Patrick Heron (1952) again put forward the importance of British painting and sculpture. Heron as a painter was more influenced by French art, notably Braque and Bonnard, but still championed not only the School of London but also the St Ives colony of artists in Cornwall. June saw the formation of the **Penwith Society** with Herbert Read as President and Barbara Hepworth (1930), Peter Lanyon and Ben Nicholson in the membership, supported with "informal backing" from the Arts Council.

Whitechapel Art Gallery exhibition of Mark Gertler's (1915) work

Archer Gallery, London the "Third Annual Exhibition" of the Borough Group.

Hanover Gallery sculpture by Reg Butler, catalogue text by David Sylvester. Also a Francis Bacon exhibition and Lucian Freud later in the year.

The Arts Council show "Notes and Sketches by Sickert" accompanied by a large catalogue.

Redfern Gallery Wyndham Lewis (1913) exhibition.

Lefevre Gallery Peter Lanyon's first solo exhibition in London.

The Leicester Galleries showed new work by London Group members in January, followed by Merlyn Evans, Ivon Hitchens, Andre Bicat, Henry Lamb, Edward Burra and William Roberts.

CoBrA exhibition in Amsterdam with William Gear (1953) as the only British artist.

London Group President: Ruskin Spear (1940-43)

Fourteen new members were elected indicating a surge of renewed interest in the Group following the Second World War. They were Robert Adams, Edward Ardizzone, Robert Buhler, Edward Burra, Morris Kestelman, Kenneth Martin, John Minton, F.E. McWilliam, Peter Potworowski, William Scott, Julian Trevelyan, Keith Vaughan and Carel Weight. All men and mostly painters, F.E. McWilliam being a surrealist sculptor. Membership was increased overall by ten to bring more members, and revenue, into the Group.

"The London Group: Exhibition of New Works by Members", The Leicester Galleries, Leicester Square, January 1949. Ruskin Spear ARA was the President but no Vice President was recorded in the catalogue to the exhibition. However, eighty-four artists were listed as members of The London Group, a really healthy and large number of members so soon after the War. Sixty-six members submitted one work each to this exhibition and were displayed in two rooms in the Leicester Galleries called the "Reynolds Room" and the "Hogarth Room", the latter containing the only six pieces of sculpture in the exhibition by Karin Jonzen, Jacob Epstein, Gertrude Hermes, Elizabeth Andrews, Henry Moore and Alan Durst. The other exhibits were mainly paintings and some watercolours. Apart from two works by Victor Pasmore and Norman Dawson, each entitled "Abstract", all the other two dimensional works would appear by their titles to be figurative paintings, portraits, still lifes and landscapes. None of the titles seem to make any reference whatsoever to the recent catastrophe of the Second World War! Life would appear to be getting back to normal. Sixty-six members had new work to exhibit and the Leicester Galleries advertised good sales in their London Group catalogue making significant sales to the Tate Gallery, Arts Council, British Council, Chantrey Bequest, Contemporary Arts Society and the V&A as well as sales to Sheffield, Southampton, Worthing, York and Welsh Public Art Galleries, there were even transactions with a number of Australian Galleries. The catalogue accompanying The London Group new work exhibition was tiny, approximately 15 x 10 centimetres. The poor quality peppermint green paper had rust coloured text with white interior contents, still obviously in need of good quality printing materials. There were no illustrations and no prices, just names and titles and no introduction by the President.

The January 1949 issue of the 'New Statesman' had the following review of the Leicester Galleries show under the banner "Round the Galleries". "Last summer's exhibition of the London Group was a long and tedious compilation of predominantly amateurish efforts sprawled around the badly-lit Academy Hall. The reputation of the Group is retrieved by the current exhibition at the Leicester Galleries of new works by Members proper, no outsiders being present to lower the average level of accomplishment. Style is predominantly Euston Road or New English Art Club, with a leavening of romantic post-Cubism and abstraction and Expressionism".

"London Group Exhibition of Contemporary Drawing, Painting and Sculpture", New Burlington Galleries, London W1, 20th December 1949 to 17th January 1950. Ruskin Spear continued as President supported by Elliott Seabrooke as Vice President. A list of ninety members is also recorded. Two hundred and eighty-five exhibits, including eleven sculptures, were exhibited in four galleries. No media or sizes were given. There were a large number of non-members exhibiting but no indication of how their work was selected. Top price of £400 was asked by Jack B. Yates, £350 by Gotlib with Victor Pasmore and Duncan Grant pricing work at £250. Average prices were between £15 and £80. Titles indicated mostly landscape, still life and figure painting. Victor Pasmore's title was "Abstract: Square Motif" and is the only clue as to what the paintings would have looked like. The very next catalogue entry, for example, was Roger Hilton, a non-member, showing "Lady at Table" which could be a representational image, even though Hilton developed into an abstract painter working within the St. Ives group. Other exhibitors, both members and non-members, were Vanessa Bell, Duncan Grant, Wendy Pasmore, Patrick George, Gerald Wild (thought by many to be Gully Jimpson in Joyce Carey's "The Horse's Mouth"), William Roberts, A. Heath (Adrian?), William Scott, Mary Martin, L.S. Lowry, Matthew Smith, Adrian Stokes, Nina Hamnett, Jameses Boswell and Fitton and sculptors Karin Jonzen and F.E. McWilliam. There were no articles or illustrations in the catalogue that cost sixpence with an admission fee of one shilling and sixpence. It was a twelve page catalogue; slightly smaller than A5 with black type on a rust and buff cover.

The New Burlington Galleries
3-4 Old Burlington Street,
London W1

The New Burlington Galleries were situated on the left hand side of Old Burlington Street just beyond the saplings. The clock visible at the bottom of the street is mounted on the North East corner of the Royal Academy in Burlington Gardens.

The 1950's

The Festival of Britain was celebrated from May to September 1951 to commemorate the 1851 Great Exhibition and to inject a feeling of optimism into post-war Britain. Atlee said it was to be, "a tonic for the Nation". The Arts Council selected artists to show in an exhibition entitled "Sixty Painters for '51'" and even provided canvases for them to paint on. Fifty-three painters were eventually shown and the Arts Council bought five paintings for £500 each, a considerable sum in the 1950s. The five prize winners were Lucien Freud, William Gear (1953), Ivon Hitchens (1931), Robert Medley (1937) and Claude Rogers (1938). This humourous anecdote is from "The Affectionate Eye, the life of Claude Rogers", by Jenny Pery: "The girl at the desk said: 'Well, at four o'clock I have to stick the labels on the pictures chosen by the Arts Council'. 'Good God!' I said 'You don't mean to say you know now, do you?' 'Yes I do' she giggled. 'Well,' said I. 'For heaven's sake, whatever the result, ring me at the Slade at 4 and let me know'...So at four I was in the office and Willy (Townsend) said 'Let's go to tea'. 'I'll just wait for that call,' I told him and at that moment it came through – Golly! Just like a Boys Own Paper School Story, last instalment – my picture had been bought together with Freud, Hitchens, Medley and William Gear... I rushed out to Charlotte Street and got some drink and back to the Slade where we drank out of thimbles and tumblers."

Three of the five prizewinners had already been elected to The London Group and William Gear was to be elected two years later. Only three paintings in the entire exhibition were abstracts, those by Peter Lanyon, Victor Pasmore (1934) and William Gear (1953). (Lanyon's abstracted landscape painting "Porthleven" was purchased by the Contemporary Art Society who then presented it to the Tate Gallery). The London Group still seemed to be supporting progressive painting. Gear's abstract painting "Autumn Landscape" caused quite a furore, led by Sir Alfred Munnings, then President of the Royal Academy. "Autumn Landscape" had a bold abstract design with heavy, jagged, black line heightening the colour scheme of browns, oranges and yellows. Questions were asked in the House and the newspapers and cartoonists had a field day. At the height of all this public controversy and criticism Gear was elected to The London Group. Other radical artists working towards abstraction also gained exposure in the Festival of Britain exhibition. William Scott (1949), for example, painted "Still Life" worked from life but using simplified shape and colour, whilst Ben Nicholson painted "Festival of Britain Mural" now owned by Tate. Battersea Park hosted a sculpture exhibition and sculpture was commissioned for the whole of the Festival site with contracts going to Reg Butler, Lynn Chadwick (1952), Frank Dobson (1922), Jacob Epstein (1913), Barbara Hepworth (1930), Karin Jonzen (1948), Henry Moore (1930), Victor Pasmore (1934) and John Piper (1933).

Artists for Peace organised three exhibitions in 1951, 1952 and 1953. AFP was a loose grouping of active protestors from the Communist Party of Great Britain's Artists Group and the Artists International Association. Independently, Peter de Francia (1977) had helped bring work over from Europe and Picasso had visited, exhibited in and supported the 1953 exhibition.

The Kitchen Sink School, a title coined by David Sylvester in 1954, was a movement born out of the post-war period of depression. Subjects were domestic and every day, hence the title, with drab, muted colour. The Kitchen Sink School artists were largely thought of as the visual equivalent of the "Angry Young Men" 1950s playwrights. Members and exhibitors with the Kitchen Sink School were Jack Smith (1957), John Bratby (1957), Edward Middleditch, Derrick Greaves, Peter Coker and Michael Fussell. In 1956 Smith, Bratby, Middleditch and Greaves were chosen to exhibit as British Realists at the XXVIII Venice Biennale. They were all taught by two London Group members, Ruskin Spear (1940-43) and John Minton (1949) at the Royal College of Art. John Berger was an early supporter of the School in their choosing to depict the everyday lives of people and the mood of post-war Britain at the beginning of the Cold War. One critic coined the phrase, "post-war generation of spiky, morbid aggression." James Hyman writes in his book "The Battle for Realism", "Although since the 1980s supporters of realist painting have given it a reactionary function as an antidote to the perceived excesses of contemporary art, in the 1940s and 1950s realism had a radical position that was neither marginal nor conservative". This grouping of realists was promoted by the Beaux Arts Gallery which, from 1951, was run by Helen Lessore following her husband's death. Helen's husband was brother to Thérèse Lessore (1913) who had been Sickert's third wife. The four most important painters, Bratby, Greaves, Middleditch and Jack Smith came to be known as the "Beaux Arts Quartet". Helen Lessore never exhibited the "Quartet" together as a group in her gallery. She always maintained their individuality as painters, flying in the face of John Berger who was promoting them as a new realist movement. Beaux Arts also exhibited Craigie Aitchison (1962), Michael Andrews (1962), Jeffery Camp (1961), Diana Cumming, John Dodgson (1947) and Cyril Reason (1979). The Beaux Arts Gallery closed in 1965.

Fifties abstraction was rooted in an emotional approach to landscape, centred on the Cornish peninsula surrounded by sea, sky and rock. Ben Nicholson had been living at St Ives since 1939. The St Ives Group continued his abstract approach to painting through the work of Peter Lanyon, Roger Hilton, William Scott (1949), Patrick Heron (1952), Bryan Wynter (1955), Terry Frost (1957) and Alan Davie (1957). Their paintings were essentially abstract paintings, loose and gestural, related to the figure, landscape and natural forms. Their approach related to developments in abstract expressionism in America and Europe. Heron's critical writings underpinned the movement; his series of articles in the 'Guardian' in 1973 are especially memorable.

Heron also organised the "Space into Colour" exhibition at the Hanover Gallery in 1953. Barbara Hepworth (1930) and Lynn Chadwick (1952) were linked to the group but were essentially sculptors.

In 1952 **Herbert Read** published his **"Contemporary British Art"** which included many current London Group members' work. In 1954 Lawrence Alloway wrote the introduction to "Nine Abstract Artists", printed by Tiranti Press, London, promoting the work of Terry Frost (1957), William Scott (1949), Roger Hilton, Adrian Heath (1962), Anthony Hill, Kenneth Martin (1949), Mary Martin (1959), Victor Pasmore (1934) and the sculptor Robert Adams (1949).

In December 1953 the **Second Sao Paulo Biennale** took place. Representing Britain were Merlyn Evans (1953), William Gear (1953), Patrick Heron (1952), Ceri Richards (1938) and William Scott (1949), all members of The London Group and most only recently elected. Three artists were chosen by the British Council for the British Pavilion at the **XXIX Venice Biennale** held in 1958, the printmaker William Hayter (1953), sculptor Kenneth Armitage (1953) and painter William Scott (1949), all three members of The London Group.

The so called **School of London** in the '50s comprised a significant grouping of important painters who often met for drinks in the Colony Room in Soho's Dean Street. They were Francis Bacon, Frank Auerbach (1960), Lucien Freud, Leon Kossof (1963) and Michael Andrews (1962). They had an individual direction as opposed to the "academic naturalism" of the Euston Road Group and the domestic 'Kitchen Sink School'. They believed in the affirmation of the act of painting, especially related to the human figure. Their work often showed the use of and underlined the importance of historical sources, often reworking Old Master paintings in an act of homage. Seemingly Andrews', Auerbach's and Kossof's election to The London Group in the early 1960s was seen as recognition of their achievement in the 1950s. Also linked with the 'School' were John Minton (1949), Tom Craxton, Keith Vaughan (1949) and Edward Burra (1949). In 1958 Andrew Forge (1960) wrote an essay entitled, "Since the War". In it he identified two streams of contemporary realism, firstly the "extreme and stylish" realism of Andrews (1962) and Freud building on the influemce of Bacon and Giacometti and secondly he identified the social realism of the "Beaux Arts Quartet", Bratby, Greaves, Middleditch and Jack Smith who were continuing concerns evident in work by Josef Herman (1953), L. S. Lowry (1948) and Constant Permeke. The School of London was brought to public attention through Helen Lessore's Beaux-Arts Gallery (Helen Lessore inherited the Beaux Arts Gallery in 1951) in the fifties.

The **'first wave' of Pop Art** swept onto the scene with the 1956 exhibition "This is Tomorrow" organised by the **Independent Group** (including Richard Hamilton and Eduardo Paolozzi) which met sporadically at the ICA between 1952 and 1955. Richard Hamilton's enduring image "Just what is it that makes today's homes so different, so appealing?" (1956) was created as a catalogue illustration and a poster for this exhibition. The group saw themselves as reacting to the hegemony of the older taste makers still looking towards Paris as the crucible of progressive art. Reyner Banham declared, "we were against direct carving, pure form, truth, beauty and all that … what we favoured was (sic) motion studies. We also favoured rough surfaces, human images, space, machinery, ignoble materials and what we termed non-art". Other members of the Independent Group were the architects Peter and Alison Smithson, Reyner Banham, John Voelcker, the editor of 'Architectural Design' Theo Crosby and art critic Lawrence Alloway. In 1953 Alison and Peter Smithson, Eduardo Paolozzi and the photographer Nigel Henderson organised the exhibition "Parallel of Life and Art" at the ICA (run by Dorothy Morland from 1951).

The 'second wave' of Pop Art was led by three young artists who were studying at the Royal College of Art in the mid-1950s. They were Peter Blake, Jo Tilson and Richard Smith. None of the three were ever members of The London Group although they did have their work shown in London Group Open Submission Annual Exhibitions, helping them in their career progression.

In 1949 the Young Contemporaries exhibition had been established to show the work of young art students and emerging artists. The following quote is from their website: "The annual exhibition was first set up in 1949 based on an initial idea by Carel Weight (1949) for the British Society of Artists Galleries and known as the Young Contemporaries. In the early years the exhibition went from strength to strength, gathering much critical and audience attention."

Prominent writers on art of this period were David Sylvester and John Berger. Sylvester was a champion of British Realism having lived in Paris and meeting with many leading Parisian artists. Sylvester was seen as a supporter of the Ecole de Paris as articulated earlier by Robert Melville, Roland Penrose and Herbert Read. Berger was an independent Marxist critic greatly influenced by the writings of Frederick Antal when Berger was a student at Chelsea School of Art and Antal a Tutor. However, both Sylvester and Berger supported and heavily influenced the increasing importance of British painting and sculpture in competition with tired and commercially degenerate Paris and, indeed, New York and the claims for American painting made by Clement Greenberg. Berger was himself an artist following in the footsteps of artist-critics Walter Sickert (1913) and Wyndham-Lewis (1913), both founder members of The London Group. David Thompson wrote that in the late 1950s British art was "seriously entering the international lists and winning prestige for itself."

In 1955 John Berger and others set up The Geneva Club (based on the theme of Geneva conferences and the Geneva Convention to bring Cold War countries together in discussion and conciliation) as a meeting place for concerned professionals. The club met between 1955 and 1957 to hold discussions on political and cultural issues.

A number of London Group associates attended informally including Peter de Francia (1977), Claude Rogers (1939), Jack Smith (1957) and William Townsend (1951). The meetings took place in Bertorelli's, an Italian restaurant often frequented by artists in Charlotte Street, West London.

Drama and literature became important in the 1950s with John Osborne's play, "Look Back in Anger" opening in London in 1956. Collectively called 'The Angry Young Men' the literary movement included Kingsley Amis ("Lucky Jim" 1953), John Braine ("Room at the Top" 1957) and Allan Sillitoe ("Saturday Night and Sunday Morning" 1959).

Tate Modern Time Line 1950-60 'Happenings' by John Cage, Merce Cunningham, Allan Kaprow. Individuals Arnulf Rainer, Ed Kienholz, Mark Tobey, Piero Manzoni. 'New York Photography' involving Diane Arbus, Richard Avedon, Rudy Burckhardt, Robert Frank, Weegee and Garry Winegrand. 'Neo-Concrete Group' with Hélio Oiticica and Lygia Clark. 'Neo-Dada' including Jim Dine, Jasper Johns, Claes Oldenburg, Robert Rauschenberg and Larry Rivers. 'Pop Art' including Richard Artschwager, Patrick Caulfield, Richard Hamilton, David Hockney (1963), Eduardo Paolozzi, James Rosenquist and Andy Warhol. 'Situationist International' with Guy Debord and Raoul Vaneigem. 'Hard Edge Painting' including Ellsworth Kelly, Ad Reinhardt and Frank Stella. 'Nouveau Realisme' from Yves Klein.

The New Burlington Galleries
3–4 Old Burlington St,
London W1

The Burlington Car Park is now at numbers 3–4 Old Burlington Street where the New Burlington Galleries were once situated. The London Group organised six consecutive exhibitions at the New Burlington Galleries from 1949 to 1954. The Royal Academy is at the bottom of Old Burlington Street and has, so far, outlived its rivals.

1950

In January India declares itself a republic and the UK recognises the People's Republic of China. June 25th is the beginning of the Korean War when North Korea, backed by China and Russia, and South Korea, backed by the US, UK, Canada and the Philippines, commence hostilities. The United Nations becomes involved in Korea in one of its first peace-seeking missions. Egypt demands that the UK removes all its troops from Suez. In the first FIFA World Cup since 1938, Uruguay beat Brazil in Brazil. In the UK Labour, led by Atlee, wins a General Election by only 5 seats whereas they had won 146 in the 1945 election. Labour had introduced a programme of Nationalisation and a Welfare State. Britain's first self-service store opens but rationing was still in force. Picasso visits the UK for the second time to attend a peace rally in Sheffield. The 'Eagle' comic is launched.

Tate Gallery Fernand Léger, "a complete survey to the present".
Mayor Gallery Paul Klee exhibition.
Redfern Gallery Patrick Heron (1952) including the first showing of his portrait of T.S. Eliot. London Group members Wyndham Lewis and Jacob Epstein also made portraits of Eliot.
Hanover Gallery joint exhibition by Eduardo Paolozzi and William Turnbull (1955) with a catalogue preface written by David Sylvester. Lucian Freud was also shown this year.
Lefevre Gallery an exhibition entitled "Paintings by Some Members of the Camden Town Group".
The ICA moved to Dover Street and put on a series of young artists' exhibitions of modernist realist painting and sculpture. "London-Paris: New Trends in Painting and Sculpture" with London painters Francis Bacon, John Craxton, Lucian Freud, Isabel Lambert and Peter Lanyon and sculptors Robert Adams (1949), Reg Butler and F.E. McWilliam (1949).
Venice Biennale the US exhibition included Willem de Kooning, Arshile Gorky and Jackson Pollock.
John Cage creates his first "chance pieces" influenced by the 'I Ching'.

London Group President: Ruskin Spear (1940-43) followed by John Dodgson (1947)

No new members were elected to The London Group in 1950 and Ruskin Spear began the year as President. No minutes of an AGM for 1950 appear to have been archived, but other evidence points to John Dodgson being elected President and to Ruskin

Spear stepping down to serve as Vice President.

The "London Group Exhibition of Contemporary Drawing, Painting and Sculpture" at the New Burlington Galleries continued to 17th January 1950 (see last entry for 1949).

A report on the Group's financial position stated that "the actual balance of the 1950 Exhibition was £57.8.8 but this included £50 (the balance of the grant from the Arts Council towards the loss on the Academy Hall Exhibition in 1948) and £11.10.0 balance of members' donations made towards the loss. Therefore there would have been a loss on the 1950 exhibition of £4.1.4 if these payments had not been received."

At a Special Committee Meeting on 1st June E.A. Farrell, the Honorary Secretary of The London Group, was instructed to write a letter to Gabriel White of the four-years-old Arts Council of Great Britain. Those giving the instruction were John Dodgson, Ruskin Spear and Julian Trevelyan. The letter notified the Arts Council of cancellation of the normal London Group autumn booking at the New Burlington Galleries (administered by ACGB) because the whole space could not be used due to the Ministry of Works redecorating the premises, hence the reason for no Annual Exhibition during 1950. The letter also confirmed a 1951 booking for the New Burlington Galleries for 6 weeks at £75 per week. Moreover, the officers had asked the Arts Council to cover any losses above this agreement and for future exhibitions too! And finally the letter requested a block booking of the NBG from mid-October to the end of November for the next five years, a model of forward planning. Gabriel White's reply from 4 St. James's Square (ACGB HQ) was business-like and diplomatic, especially regarding the loss cover. The five-year plan was largely accepted, an indication of how important ACGB saw The London Group Annual Exhibitions in the annual art calendar at the time.

In November there was an exhibition entitled "Picasso in Provence" at the New Burlington Galleries. William Townsend, who was to be elected to The London Group the following year, wrote this entry in his diary, "We found out who was making the master's plans for him and when Picasso's train was due from Sheffield. Two of the students, Barbara Braithwaite and Heckford, went off to meet him at St. Pancras. They seem to have done very well. Just as Picasso was alighting from the train Barbara was handed by an unknown lady a bunch of red carnations. 'You give them to him' and she did – as from the 'étudiants de l'école des beaux arts Slade'. The result was they were allowed to accompany Picasso to his taxi while Rodrigo (Moynihan) and a large body of Royal College students couldn't get a look in."

1951

Stalemate in the Korean War, often termed "The Forgotten War", but peace negotiations begin later in the year. UK troops seize the Suez Canal Zone. The United Nations Headquarters open in New York. The US tests numerous atomic devices in the Nevada Desert. Chinese Communists move into Lhasa, Tibet. Greece and Turkey join NATO. The transistor is invented. Vivien Leigh and Marlon Brando star in "A Streetcar Named Desire" and Humphrey Bogart and Katharine Hepburn appear in "The African Queen". The Festival of Britain - King George VI opens the Royal Festival Hall in London. Eighteen months after the last election the Conservatives return to power with Churchill as Prime Minister and Anthony Eden as Foreign Minister. Labour had called the election hoping to increase their fragile majority, but the electorate thought that the Labour government had run out of steam. First colour TV. IBM UK is formed. Benjamin Britten writes "Billy Budd", premiered at Covent Garden.

The Festival of Britain see "The 1950s".
Tate Gallery Henry Moore (1930). "Sculpture and Drawings by Henry Moore".
The ICA influential exhibition by the Chilean surrealist Juan Sebastian Matta Echaurren (Matta).
Whitechapel Art Gallery an exhibition of Bernard Meninsky's (1919) work.
Roland Browse and Delbanco Walter Sickert (1916) exhibition.
Leicester Galleries major one-man exhibition by Ruskin Spear (1940/43).
Hanover Gallery one-man exhibition by Graham Sutherland (1937) and later in the year Francis Bacon and Jean Hélion (a French realist).
The Constructionists issue "Broadsheet 1", essentially a manifesto of pure abstract form celebrating the work of Kenneth Martin (1949) and Victor Pasmore (1934). Other artists who had turned to abstraction were Adrian Heath (1962), Anthony Hill and Mary Martin (1959).
The Ninth Street Show in New York brought together all the New York avant-garde in one huge and important post-war exhibition.

London Group President: John Dodgson (1947)

John Dodgson was recorded in the March exhibition catalogue as President whilst Ruskin Spear A.R.A. was the Vice President this year. Committee Members were Anthony Gross, Gertrude Hermes, Morris Kestelman, Victor Pasmore, H.E. du Plessis, Ceri Richards, Claude Rogers, Julian Trevelyan and Edward Wolfe.

Four new members were elected, Bernard Meadows, Anne Neville, Brian Robb and William Townsend. The catalogue for the March exhibition held in The London

Group archive is annotated with red ink which appears to be a record of how existing members voted for candidates for full membership. At the back of the catalogue is printed a full list of members. An 'X' in blue biro seems to indicate non-voters, there are twenty-six of these. The names Townsend, Medows (sic) and Robb are then written in red biro with one, two and three red dashes respectively against each name. All three had work shown in the March exhibition which must have been used as a means of voting members looking at their work and voting on a one person–one-vote system. Townsend got 12 votes, Meadows 14 and Robb 30. All three appear as fully-fledged members in the November catalogue. Anne Neville was an existing member who had recently changed her name from Elsie Farleigh.

There were two London Group exhibitions either side of the Festival of Britain this year, both at the New Burlington Galleries, one in February/March with three hundred and fifty-five works and the second in November with three hundred and seventy three works. This was the largest post-war showing by The London Group showing a total of seven hundred and twenty-eight works to the public in one year.

"London Group" (Contemporary Painting, Drawing and Sculpture), New Burlington Galleries, Old Burlington Street, W1, unknown date to 3rd March 1951. A membership of eighty-three is recorded and members of the Working Party were Gertrude Hermes, Morris Kestelman, Victor Pasmore, H.E. du Plessis, Ceri Richards, Claude Rogers and Julian Trevelyan. The Foreword to the catalogue contained two tributes written by Morris Kestelman and Victor Pasmore: "The loss through death during the last year, of Elliott Seabrooke and Bernard Meninsky, two of the group's oldest and most distinguished members, will be very much felt." There were twenty-seven sculptures in the three hundred and fifty-five exhibits arranged in four galleries and a Vestibule. Sculptors included Robert Adams, Kenneth Armitage, Lynn Chadwick, Karin Jonzen, Bernard Meadows, Eduardo Paolozzi and Peter Startup. No sizes or media were given in the catalogue. The show contained works by members and non-members. It is not recorded whether the non-members work was by selection or invitation. Judging by the titles most of the work was representational, portraits, landscapes, still lifes, although William Gear exhibited "Black and White Form", Mary Martin "Abstract" and D. Hamilton Fraser "Abstract". Matthew Smith was asking £400 for, "Girl holding a flower" whilst David Bomberg was priced at £300 for "Mediaeval Ruins, Cyprus". The average prices from members and non-members were between £50 and £20. Other exhibitors included Eileen Agar, James Boswell, Harold Cohen, Roger de Gray, Martin Froy, Adrian Heath, Ivon Hitchens, L.S. Lowry, Victor and Wendy Pasmore, Mary Potter, Alan Reynolds, Ceri Richards and Carel Weight. Julian Trevelyan produced the poster whilst Bernard Adeney designed the catalogue cover which cost a shilling. Admission to the New Burlington Galleries was one shilling and sixpence with a 50% reduction for students at ninepence.

The Honorary Secretary reported that "submission fees show an increase as a larger number of works were sent in by non-members and, of course, the hanging fees are well up due to the larger wall space available at the Gallery." Catalogue sales were up 30%. In the 1950 exhibition and this one twenty-one works were sold from each exhibition. Due to more expensive works being sold in the 1950 exhibition commission from that source was £160.19.5 whilst the figure for this show was only £96.14.0.

"London Group" (Contemporary Painting, Drawing and Sculpture), New Burlington Galleries, unknown date to 24th November 1951. Anthony Gross and Edward Wolfe joined the February Working Party for this show. Work was shown in five galleries with sculpture distributed throughout the galleries. There were three hundred and seventy-three exhibits shown, including thirty-one sculptures, in a members and non-members exhibition. Prices were printed in the catalogue ranging from 5 guineas to £450 for a bronze by Gertrude Hermes and "Jugs and Coffee Pot, 1950" by Matthew Smith. The vast majority of prices were around the £50 mark. A full list of eighty-four members was printed, with addresses, at the end of the catalogue, one more than February. Two Honorary Members exhibited, David Low and Jack Yeats. Exhibitors included Dennis Creffield, Andrew Forge, Patrick George, Roger Hilton, Henry Inlander, Albert Irvin, Peter Lanyon, F.E. McWilliam, Dorothy Mead, Robert Medley, John Minton, Claude Rogers, William Scott, Ruskin Spear, Adrian Stokes, Patrick Symons, William Townsend and Evan (sic) Uglow. The exhibition poster was by Edward Ardizzone.

The financial returns for this exhibition were disappointing making a total loss of £30.5.2, exacerbated by "the Party" which had cost "£10.16.6!" Admissions had dropped by four hundred with a corresponding loss of £100 in catalogue sales.

The Rule Book was reprinted this year with a number of changes. The annual subscription was increased from £2 to £4 and rules for non-payment without "extenuating circumstances" were tightened up. There was a significant change in the election of new members through two procedures, firstly at any General Meeting and secondly, "At a General Meeting to be fixed for the election of new members on the day after sending-in day of the Exhibition, or if that be a Saturday, on the following Monday." Also, "Members unable to be present and wishing to vote shall be entitled to do so in writing and shall be counted as 'present' for the purpose of election." These 'postal votes' would then be added to those present and the total number of votes added together. This move made the group far more democratic in its election of new members and paved the way for larger numbers to be elected. The only other notable change was for non-members, "The submission fee for non-members (a new charge) shall be 4/- for each work sent in and the hanging fee for non-members shall be 20/- for each work accepted."

1952

Eisenhower, as US President elect, visits Korea to expedite peace. On October 3rd the first British atomic bomb was detonated on the Monte Bello Islands off Western Australia. In November, in operation code name 'Mike', the USA explodes the first thermo-nuclear Hydrogen bomb at Bikini Atoll. Mau Mau Uprising in Kenya as a protest against white settler land ownership and so Britain establishes a military presence in Kenya. The uprising was to end in 1957 when Kenyans gained many concessions and gained full independence in 1963. The Summer Olympic Games were held in Helsinki, Finland. The death of King George VI. Queen Elizabeth II comes to the throne. The first external pacemaker is fitted to a patient. Jack Hawkins and Donald Sinden star in "The Cruel Sea".

Tate Gallery Jacob Epstein (1913) retrospective.

ICA "Young Painters" exhibition with Michael Andrews (1962), Barbara Braithwaite, Harold Cohen, Alfred Daniels, Richard Hamilton, Edward Middleditch, Anthony Reynolds and Victor Willing.

"Sixteen Young Sculptors" including Robert Adams (1949), Reg Butler, Eduardo Paolozzi and William Turnbull (1955).

"Recent Trends in Realist Painting" included Bacon, Dubuffet, Freud, Giacometti, Gruber, Masson, Minton (1949), Moynihan (1933) and Rebeyrolle.

First meeting of the Independent Group with a 'magic lantern' show by Eduardo Paolozzi.

One-man exhibition of photographs by Henri Cartier-Bresson.

Whitechapel Art Gallery "Looking Forward", an exhibition of realist paintings and drawings by contemporary British Artists organised by John Berger with a political and social message. Exhibiting artists associated with The London Group were John Minton (1949), Rodrigo Moynihan (1933), Claude Rogers (1939), Ruskin Spear (1940/43) and Carel Weight (1949). The Arts Council supported the exhibition and a tour with a catalogue cover design by Josef Herman (1953).

Hanover Gallery an important exhibition of sculpture was shown, enthusiastically supported by the critic David Sylvester, especially "The Square II" by Alberto Giacometti. One man show of Lucian Freud's paintings.

AIA mounted an exhibition entitled, "The Mirror and the Square", an enormous exhibition of nearly 300 exhibits. The title is explained as those artists mirroring nature (representational) and those exploiting shape and geometry (abstract).

Matthiesen Gallery, London paintings by Nicolas de Staël.

Venice Biennale "New Aspects of British Sculpture" written by Herbert Read to accompany the British representatives. Graham Sutherland (1937) showed paintings in the British Pavilion.

London Group President: John Dodgson (1947) followed by Claude Rogers (1939)

Three artists were elected this year, Eleanor Bellingham-Smith, Lynn Chadwick and Patrick Heron. Notably Francis Bacon, Reg Butler, Prunella Clough, John Craxton, Louis le Brocquy, Ben Nicholson, Eduardo Paolozzi, Lucien Freud and Barbara Hepworth declined membership or gave "no definite answer". No reasons for their decisions were recorded.

At the AGM held on Saturday 8th March at Management House, Hill Street, W1, Claude Rogers was elected unanimously as President and the outgoing President, John Dodgson, backed up as Vice President. Dodgson's wife Val had died suddenly in February and John had decided to step down as President to look after his family. Rogers had some new ideas to bring to the Group, amongst them was one to propose "two foreign artists or sculptors to be invited each year to send work without paying (a) hanging fee. 'Foreign' – either from continent, America, the provinces or Scotland or Ireland – not 'names', prefer young, not previously exhibited much in London – so many of our members travel & meet artists this should be easy." Other matters discussed were to do with pressurising members to pay subscription arrears and giving the Hanging Committee greater executive powers. A letter from the Honorary Treasurer, R.J. Sainsbury, records his desire to step down as Treasurer due to pressure of work and to transfer his duties to other members of his staff, Mr.Farrell and Mr.Nash. The meeting supported this move. The Group at this time had a balance of £337.1.3 in the bank.

A further General Meeting was held on Saturday 7th June at 4 St. James's Square with only twelve members in attendance. Hanging Committee members were elected at this GM who were William Coldstream, Anthony Gross, Morris Kestelman, F.E. McWilliam, Bernard Meadows, William Scott, Julian Trevelyan and Fred Uhlman. McWilliam and Meadows were the two obligatory sculptors. More elections followed as Jacob Epstein, Augustus John and Matthew Smith joined Frank Dobson, David Low and Jack Yeats as Honorary Members.

"London Group Annual Exhibition", New Burlington Galleries, 25th October to 22nd November 1952. Catalogues, costing a shilling, adopted a new style which was to carry through the whole of the '50s. It was very simple and can best be described as "school maths book" style. There was an appreciation by Edward le Bas of Charles Ginner who died in January and was one of the founder members of The London Group in 1913. Work was exhibited in two galleries, the Small Room and the Lobby. There were three hundred and six works on display including twenty-seven pieces of sculpture. Matthew Smith was asking the highest price of £1,050 for "The Falling

Model". David Bomberg and Henryk Gotlib could be picked up for half that price, Duncan Grant for £200 and Ivon Hitchens for £136.10 shillings. Apart from 'the regulars', other notable and/or interesting exhibitors were Gillian Ayres, John Bratby, Anthony Caro, Harold Cohen, Anthony Eyton, Elizabeth Frink, Patrick Hayman, Josef Herman, Patrick Heron, Malcolm Hughes, Bruce Lacey, Leonard Rosoman and Bryan Wynter. From notes scribbled in the back of an archive catalogue it appears that there were one hundred and thirteen members' paintings and one hundred and sixty-four non-members'. More annotations at the front of the catalogue estimate that approximately 70% of members exhibited (57 out of 82). The exhibition poster was by William Scott. Myfanwy Piper wrote in the 1.11.52 issue of "Time and Tide", "The London Group at the New Burlington has made a great effort this year to reform itself and we had been led to hope for a show that was both smaller and more vigorously selected than usual. But there are three hundred pictures hung two and three deep of many persuasions – Realist, Abstract, Expressionist – of no group persuasion but strong individual belief – and the rest. Of the rest there are too many; agreeable little works painted in vaguely post-impressionist (London Group variety) style gaily swamping the more serious successes and the more interesting failures".

Twenty-seven works were sold from this exhibition raising £896.7.0 and earning the Group £191.17.4 in commission. As well as the predictable 'big name' sales The London Group helped emerging artists to sell their work, in this case, Albert Irvin, Anthony Eyton, Patrick Symons, Lynn Chadwick, Gillian Ayres and William Townsend. Admissions totalled 2,852 with 1,629 catalogues sold. Statistics show 1,181 submission fees, 108 members' hanging fees and 179 non-members'.

There were some minor rule changes in 1952. Firstly, "There shall also be a Vice President who shall have been the preceding holder of the office of President" and a change in the General Meetings structure with one meeting for "the election of new members prior to the Annual Exhibition, and the other meeting in March and known as the A.G.M..."

In a 1992 interview Morris Kestelman spoke of the following initiative in which The London Group played a significant role. "In 1951 the Director General of Unesco set up a committee of enquiry into the possibility of creating an international association of artists, and as a result there was a conference of artists convened in Venice in 1952. At that time Henry Moore and Graham Sutherland were asked I think by the British Council to represent the UK. Then they decided to have a first General Assembly in order to see how many countries were going to take part. This took place in 1954 again in Venice, and it was done in the first place through the cooperation of the Arts Council under Philip James, not terribly long after the war after all. The London Group put some money up and Richard Carline and myself were asked to go as representatives. It was to cover the fields of paintng, sculpture and graphic art, that and no more... Our original title was IAPA (International Association of the Plastic Arts), but because of plastics we and the Americans changed it to the IAA – the International Association of Art." In 1957 Kestelman became the Chairman of the UK national committee. "Claude (Rogers) sent me to represent the London Group, and that is how it came about." (Many thanks to Sara Kestelman for access to Morris Kestelman's papers).

Around about this time Claude Rogers' notebook sheds light on his thinking. "Occurred to me that we have an advantage (over other exhibiting societies). Our members have more one man shows in year than members of any other society. I wondered if this fact could not be utilised for the benefit of the Group as a whole". These exhibitions would keep The London Group in the public eye between annual exhibitions. Most of the notebook is taken up by Rogers recording his recollections of a dinner he attended at the Royal Academy. "Buttonholed by Kelly (Sir Gerald Festus Kelly was President of the Royal Academy from 1949 to 1954) after a dinner at which I was guest of my friend Tom Monnington. Kelly made a proposition which somewhat astonished me. To begin with he said he understood and felt himself that the modern section of the RA Summer Show (was) not very good and didn't consist of the best modern work to be got. After beating about the bush a bit he came out with the flat proposition – and repeated it several times in the subsequent conversation – that if we, the London Group, cared to send him enough pictures to fill one or even two rooms of the RA he would see they were hung en bloc and that nobody interfered with them. I was somewhat taken aback as you can imagine... He said he didn't believe once we found ourselves on the walls of Burlington House we'd ever leave it." Rogers ruminates on the possible motives for the offer, "to discredit London Group especially with younger members and those independent artists who sometimes show with us... to cause dissention and break us up a bit – or anyway emasculate us like the New English. Tempting as the offer is I am against it and would like to refuse. The character of our exhibition depends as much if not more on the non-members' work we choose as on the work of our members. As a group we are a geological stratification – a layer of cake of every important movement in England since the 1914 war. We know from experience of the Leicester Galleries show a couple of years back that an average exhibition of members work alone is not particularly remarkable, yet there is no doubt that the average member's work has more staying power, more depth than the average and superficially often more exciting non-member's work. I speak here from long experience of hanging the exhibition. I am agin it. I believe we should stay as we are." It would appear that London Group members attending this meeting agreed with him.

1953

27th July, Korean War ceasefire. De-militarized Zone established on the 38th Parallel. No peace treaty was signed and the DMZ still exists. Stalin and Prokofiev die on the same day, March 5th, in Moscow. The Coronation of Queen Elizabeth II is celebrated and almost on the same day Everest is conquered by Sherpa Tensing and Edmund Hilary. In August the USSR detonates the first 'practical' Hydrogen weapon, surprising the USA and escalating the weapons race. The structure of DNA is discovered at Cambridge University by James Watson and Francis Crick. Shostakovich writes his Symphony No. 10. Ian Fleming writes "Casino Royale", the first James Bond novel. The 'Stanley Matthews' Cup Final takes place at Wembley.

Tate Gallery retrospective exhibition of Graham Sutherland's (1937) work.
ICA "The Wonder and the Horror of the Human Head" installed by Richard and Terry Hamilton, a multimedia exhibition covering images about the human head from prehistory to the present day. Also "Opposing Forces" including Michel Tapié's 'un art autre'.
Beaux Arts Gallery Sickert (1913) exhibition.
Marlborough Gallery a large exhibition of thirty-seven paintings by Gustave Courbet, father of French realism. This was followed by an exhibition of the young French Social Realist, Paul Reyberolle.
Leicester Galleries an exhibition of paintings by Prunella Clough, highly praised by John Berger. At this time Clough was a 'realist' painter and had exhibited with Artists for Peace.
Walker Gallery London stages an exhibition entitled, "Paintings for the Kitchen".
The Arts Council asked David Sylvester to organise an exhibition around the activity of drawing, "to understand the artist's method is to go a long way towards understanding his mind". The exhibition 'Drawing for Pictures' included Andrews (1962), Bellingham-Smith (1952), Buhler (1949), Coldstream (1933), Colquhoun, Freud, L.S. Lowry (1948), Moynihan (1933), Victor Pasmore (1934), Richards (1938), Rogers (1939), Sutherland (1937), Spear (1940/43), Spencer (1914) and Vaughan (1949).
Independent Group (see The 1950s) exhibition "Parallel of Life and Art".
Cornwall after falling out with Hepworth (1930) and Nicholson and resigning from the Penwith Society in 1950, Peter Lanyon is elected to the **Newlyn Society of Artists**.
William Scott (1949) visits the United States.

London Group President: Claude Rogers (1939)

This year five new members were elected, Kenneth Armitage, Merlyn Evans, William Gear, Stanley Hayter and Josef Herman.

The Arts Council of Great Britain allowed The London Group to use its St James's Square offices for the AGM on 16th May. Nineteen members attended who elected F.E. McWilliam, Robert Medley, Bernard Meadows, William Scott, John Piper, Merlin (sic) Evans, William Townsend and H.S. Williamson onto the Hanging Committee. There were two items of note in the minutes. Firstly, an explanation of how artists were actually elected to the Group. Nominees "should not be aware of the fact that their names were going forward. This procedure... was approved by the Group when the rule for election-on-reputation was formulated, as a means of saving the feelings of those artists of good reputation, whom the Group rejected, usually because not enough members were familiar with their actual work." Secondly Rogers reported that the Committee had been looking at inviting "Guest Artists" who could live outside of London and even in other countries. U.N.E.S.C.O. had wanted to set up an 'International Association of Plastic Arts' and with that in mind "Richard Carline then gave the meeting a short description of the Convention which had been held in Rome, and outlined briefly the main points behind the U.N.E.S.C.O. plan. Three British Societies had replied to U.N.E.S.C.O.'s enquiries, i.e. The London Group, the Artists International Association and the Society for Industrial Artists. He thought it might be possible to find common ground so that these societies could act together."

"London Group", Annual Exhibition, New Burlington Galleries, 3-4 Burlington Gardens, Old Burlington Street W1, 3rd November to 28th November 1953, the second exhibition with Claude Rogers as President and John Dodgson as Vice President. The catalogue for this annual show records eighty-five members including six Honorary Members. Galleries 1 and 2, the Small Room, the Corridor, the Lobby and the Entrance Hall of the New Burlington Galleries were all used to show three hundred and thirty-six exhibits, twenty-four of which were sculptures distributed throughout the rooms. Both members and non-members were showing. Non-members were listed and totalled one hundred and seventy-nine, an enormous response which obviously did not include all of the artists who submitted work to the "jury". Exhibitors included Frank Auerbach, Sandra Blow, Prunella Clough, Merlyn Evans, Anthony Eyton, Albert Irvin, Peter Lanyon, Mary Martin, Henry Mundy, John Piper, John Plumb and Euan Uglow. There were a substantial number of women artists selected, although not in the majority. Prices seemed to be determined by size, as works in the Small Room were much cheaper. Top price was asked by Matthew Smith for two figure paintings at £350 and £300 respectively. David Bomberg had work on sale for £262 and Edward Wolfe for £250. Average prices were between £10 and £50. The size and media of the exhibits were not given but titles indicated predominantly landscape, still life and figure painting. William Scott exhibited "Blue, black and white Composition" for £70, whilst titles indicated similar abstract work from Adrian Heath, Mary Martin, Peter Foldes and William Gear. At the front of the catalogue were tributes to Geoffrey Tibble and S. de Karlowska (Mrs Robert Bevan) written by William Townsend and Robert Bevan respectively. The format was similar to the 1952 catalogue, with a turquoise cover and cost 1/-. The exhibition poster was designed by Brian Robb.

The Rule Book got another tweak this year too. Under the heading "Officers and Hanging Committee", rule 7 was rewritten as follows, "The Hanging Committee of eight members, two of whom shall be Sculptors (new), working with the Officers of the Group, shall undertake the organisation and hanging of the Annual Exhibitions or Exhibition, and shall deal with current business not affecting the constitution of the Group. No member of this Committee having held office for two consecutive years shall be available for a period of two years for re-election to the Committee (new)." The rewriting of rule 7 was no doubt to ensure fresh blood on the Hanging Committee and to avoid vested interests and influence.

1954

Withdrawal of British troops from Egypt. Nasser replaces Naguib as President of Egypt. The world's first atomic power station opens near Moscow. The first nuclear powered submarine, USS Nautilus, is launched. US hydrogen bomb test at Bikini Atoll followed by the USSR. Joseph McCarthy investigates whether Communism has infiltrated the US Army. The Geneva Conference partitions Vietnam into North and South Vietnam. The first kidney transplants take place in Paris and Boston. Bill Haley and his Comets record, "Rock around the Clock". Elvis Presley is heard on Memphis radio for the first time. The Boeing 707 and B52 Stratofortress take to the air. West Germany beat Hungary 3 – 2 in the FIFA World Cup Final held in Switzerland. The Queen is the first reigning monarch to visit Australia. Aneurin Bevan (Labour) resigns from the shadow cabinet. Dock workers strike ends. Food rationing comes to an end indicating the improvement in post-war society. Roger Bannister runs the first '4 minute mile'. Richard Todd and Michael Redgrave appear in "The Dam Busters".

Whitechapel Art Gallery Barbara Hepworth (1930) exhibition.

ICA Paul Klee exhibition.

The Arts Council organises an exhibition entitled, "Life in Industry" dealing with subjects from everyday working life. Artists included Edward Burra (1949), Josef Herman (1953), L.S. Lowry (1948) and Stanley Spencer (1914). Following **David Sylvester's** "Drawing for Pictures" he now organised "Recent British Drawings" with contributions from Robert Adams (1949), Armitage (1953), Coldstream (1933), Diana Cumming, Freud, Martin Froy (1954), Isabel Lambert, Medley (1937), Moore (1930), Paolozzi, Victor Pasmore (1934), Matthew Smith (1920) and Sutherland (1937).

Beaux Arts Gallery first one-man show of John Bratby's (1957) paintings.

Leicester Galleries one-man show by Claude Rogers (1939), President of The London Group at the time.

Venice Biennale Francis Bacon, Lucian Freud and Ben Nicholson were the British Representatives.

Patrick Heron (1952) writes "The Changing Forms of Art". **Jacob Epstein** (1913) is knighted.

London Group President: Claude Rogers (1939)

Roy de Maistre and Martin Froy were elected this year.

The 1954 AGM was a grand affair taking place on Wednesday 31st March at Bertorelli's Restaurant, 19 Charlotte Street, W1. After the AGM at 6.15pm members were invited to a dinner at 8pm, a bar being available from 5.45pm. Tickets cost 8/6 per head, excluding drinks. In a circular to members, F.T. Nash, the Honorary Treasurer, wrote, "As members are aware, the names of artists of established reputation may be submitted for election to the London Group at the Annual General Meeting." Thirty-five members attended the event, the dinner obviously attracting a larger number of members than usual at an ordinary AGM. The Treasurer's report was heard and adopted followed by the President's report which informed members that Southampton Art Gallery had requested "that their officials be allowed to select representative works of members from the next Group exhibition and hold an exhibition in their own gallery in Southampton." Following the elections at which all serving officers were re-elected, "The President then reported on the recent document which had been circulated to the Group on future exhibition policy and also in conversation with Bryan Robertson at the Whitechapel Art Gallery. Following a general discussion it was agreed that the Group should hold a mixed show in the Autumn of this year at the New Burlington Galleries and that in 1955 there should be a members only show at the Whitechapel Art Gallery."

"London Group" Annual Exhibition, New Burlington Galleries, 6th November to 4th December 1954, the third annual show with Claude Rogers as President and John Dodgson continuing as Vice President. The Working Party for this year was Lynn Chadwick, Gertrude Hermes, Lynton Lamb, L.S. Lowry, Bernard Meadows, Matthew Smith, William Townsend, H.S. Williamson and Edward Wolfe. Eighty-six members are recorded with six Honorary Members. Last year there were three hundred and thirty-six exhibits, this year three hundred and nineteen, eighteen of which were sculptures with the same rooms used as in 1953. One hundred and eighty-eight non-members were selected to show with members, including Gillian Ayres, John Bratby, Edwina Leapman, Lord Methuen, William Turnbull and Bryan Wynter. There is evidence of inclusion of current approaches to contemporary painting with the Kitchen Sink School (John Bratby and Jack Smith) and abstraction (Adrian Heath and Bryan Wynter). About 20% of selected non-members were women artists. Top price, again, this year went to Matthew Smith, £650 for "Miss Diana Marsh". This painting was by far the most expensive as the majority of prices this year seemed generally lower than in the past. The titles of the paintings indicate more abstract works than in previous years, but landscape, still life and figure painting still made up the overwhelming majority of exhibits. There were no illustrations, sizes or media given. There is an article to the memory of John Buckland Wright, painter, etcher and engraver who died suddenly aged 57 whilst in the post of Head of Etching and Engraving at the Slade. The tribute was written by Gertrude Hermes. The catalogue still cost one shilling and was always "price under review". Ceri Richards made the image for this year's exhibition poster.

In the four weeks that the exhibition was open, 3,957 admissions were recorded and 2,307 cacatlogues were sold, 1,995 at a shilling and 312 at threepence (reduced price for students).

Another dinner was held at Bertorelli's to open the ballot boxes which had been available for members in the exhibition galleries to cast their votes. The voting slips had nine names for election, Katherine G. Hartnell, Marek Zulawski, Patrick Hayman, James Boswell, Kathleen Allen, Bryan Winter, Ned Owens, Mary Feddon and Roger de Grey.

The Group seemed to like their celebrations. As well as the Bertorelli dinner there was a Press view, a Private View and "a Party" for which tickets were sold and a profit made!

1955

April 1st, EOKA campaign calling for the expulsion of British troops, self-determination and union with Greece begins in Cyprus led by George Grivas - Britain increases her military presence in response. The European Union comes into being. Founding of the Warsaw Pact. Conservatives under Sir Anthony Eden win a General Election in the UK. The Labour Party was split between the left leaning 'Bevanites' and the right leaning 'Gaitskellites'. Christopher Cockerell patents the hovercraft design. Fashion designer Mary Quant opens a shop called "Bazaar". V. Nabokov writes "Lolita" and Patrick White writes "The Tree of Man". Michael Tippett premieres "Midsummer Marriage", his first opera composed over six years. "The Ladykillers" with Alec Guinness, Herbert Lom and Peter Sellers is released.

The Tate Gallery the Arts Council organise an exhibition entitled, "Four French Realists" who were André Minaux, Roger Montané, Ginette Rapp and Jean Vinay, all associated with the Adams Gallery. This had a particular resonance with the British 'Beaux Arts Quartet', Jack Smith (1957), John Bratby (1957), Edward Middleditch and Derrick Greaves. The **Tate Gallery** and the **National Gallery** are finally separated "by law".

The Italian Institute organised a discussion, chaired and translated by Ernst Gombrich, between Patrick Heron (1952) in the 'abstract corner' and Renato Guttuso (the Italian realist and Communist) in the 'realist corner'. By all accounts Heron took rather a lot of punishment.

ICA mounted Bob Flanagan, Rebecca Horn, Ama Mendieta and Gina Pane. Performance Art by Bas Jan Ader, Vito Accomci, Laurie Anderson, Gilbert and George. Dubuffet exhibition.

The Arts Council organises an exhibition of Alberto Giacometti's work. Giacometti was a powerful influence on British artists Frank Auerbach (1960), Leon Kossoff (1963) and Euan Uglow (1958).

Beaux Arts Gallery Sheila Fell exhibition.

Hanover Gallery Germaine Richier, sculptress.

The Octagon, Bath exhibition by Paul Feiler, Peter Lanyon, Piotr Potworowski (1949) and Brian Wynter (1955).

The first **'Documenta'** is held in Kassel, Germany.

London Group President: Claude Rogers (1939)

Claude Rogers was re-elected as President as was the Vice President, John Dodgson. This years' Working Party was comprised of Lynn Chadwick, Gertrude Hermes,

Lynton Lamb, L.S. Lowry, Bernard Meadows, Matthew Smith, William Townsend, H.S. Williamson and Edward Wolfe. There were eighty-five members recorded this year.

"A Selection from The London Group Exhibition 1954", Cumberland House, Museum and Art Gallery, Eastern Parade, Southsea, 1st January to 6th February 1955. Eighty paintings and five sculptures were shown selected from the 1954 London show by Curators from Southsea and Southampton. The foreword to the dinky A5 emerald and pea green catalogue declared, "the fact that it (The London Group) has survived the numerous developments of the last 40 years - that we have today difficulty in visualising the perplexity and controversy created by such movements as Post-Impressionism and Cubism, is perhaps some indication of its success". Interestingly, the exhibition following The London Group at Southsea was "The Bayeux Tapestry (Reading Facsimile)".

"A Selection from The London Group Exhibition 1954", Southampton Art Gallery, 12th February to 13th March 1955. M.A. Palmer, the Curator for this exhibition, used rather colloquial language using the term 'pictures' for paintings and assuring visitors that, "The Curator of the Art Gallery will be pleased to make arrangements with intending purchasers". Matthew Smith was asking £650 for "Miss Diana Marsh" but most prices were between £20 and £80. There were one hundred and two 'pictures' in this show and five sculptures from both members and non-members. Exhibiting non-members included Prunella Clough, William Turnbull, Gillian Ayres, Jack Smith, John Bratby, Euan Uglow and Bryan Wynter. P. Lambert designed an eye catching front cover in claret and blue with a jester figure holding an information placard. About one third of the 1954 exhibition was toured to Southsea and Southampton.

"London Group Prints", Zwemmer Gallery, 26 Litchfield Street WC2, 9th March to 2nd April 1955. Subtitled in the catalogue: "The first exhibition of original prints and monotypes by members of the London Group". Seventy-six prints were exhibited with a wide variety of approaches including etching, lithography, monotype, wood engraving, linocut, sugar aquatint and silkscreen. It would appear that some artists who were not natural printmakers were encouraged to take part in this exhibition by producing monoprints. No sizes or prices were given. Taking part were Hermes, Scott, McWilliam, Robb, Trevelyan, Potworowski, Uhlman, Hayter, Meadows, Martin, Lamb, Feibusch, Coxon, Ginesi, Bray, Cunningham, Farleigh, Richards, Piper, Kestelman, Gross, Ardizzone, Pasmore, Bell, Grant, Agar, Buckland Wright, Hughes-Stanton, Gear, Lee, Heron, Adeney and Wolfe. The catalogue was a single sheet of grey card with claret coloured type incorporating two 'print' images on the front, one by Edward Ardizzone of two print collectors looking through a portfolio of prints.

Thirty-three members attended dinner at Bertorelli's on the 16th March, preceded by the Annual General Meeting. F.T. Nash, the Honorary Treasurer, reported that the Group was in good heart financially with the bank balance at £507.0.4. President Rogers informed those gathered that the 1954 exhibition had been "successful in all respects" with a good standard of work form members and non–members. There were problems ahead in finding a suitable venue in London for 1956 and 1957. "In the event of no gallery being available in London during 1956 for the yearly members and non–members exhibition, it was suggested that the exhibition be held outside of London, say, at Manchester. After a long discussion this idea was accepted as a possibility, and the new committee were asked to explore the whole matter and to prepare a report." Rogers then urged the members to make sure that the forthcoming Whitechapel exhibition was of an excellent standard as it was important for the future. "EVERYTHING MUST BE DONE TO MAKE THIS A FIRST-RATE EXHIBITION" the AGM minutes proclaim!

There were two separate voting slips for new members this year, one for sculptors and one for painters. William Turnbull and Mary Martin were put forward as sculptors, whilst Edward Wakeford, Anthony Fry, Brian Wynter, Terry Frost, Louis le Brocquy, Adrian Heath, Roger Hilton, William Johnstone and Cecil Collins appeared on the painters slip. Four new members were finally elected, Louis le Brocquy, Anthony Fry, William Turnbull and Bryan Wynter.

"London Group Member's Exhibition", Whitechapel Art Gallery, 10th November to 9th December 1955. Claude Rogers remains as President supported by John Dodgson as Vice President. Administrative back up was provided by Sainsbury's administrative staff. The Working Party for this exhibition was Kenneth Armitage, Lynn Chadwick, Anthony Gross, Morris Kestelman, Lynton Lamb, Brian Robb, Julian Trevelyan and Edward Wolfe. A list of eighty–eight members was printed in the catalogue including six Honorary Members. This was a members only exhibition (see Preface below). In fact this catalogue was quite informative because for the first time since the War medium, date and size were given. The huge majority of work was oil painting, with eight watercolours, two drawings but surprisingly no prints. The sculptor Lynn Chadwick was using concrete, iron and copper whilst Louis le Brocquy showed a montage and a tapestry. Average size of the paintings was 24 ins. x 36 ins., the largest being Anthony Gross' oil painting, "Girl in Red" at 76.5" x 51". The dates indicated that nearly all of the exhibits had been made within the last three years and mostly the previous year. There were one hundred and five exhibits in total with members putting in one or two pieces of work. Prices were reasonable, between £50 and £100. The impression gained from this catalogue is that there was an emphasis on selling, domestic sized canvases at affordable prices but there is no record of how successful this tactic may have been. A Preface in the catalogue was written by B.R., probably Bryan Robertson of the Whitechapel. "The decision to exhibit this year outside the usual boundaries of the West End is in many ways a courageous and unorthodox one: and the Trustees (of the Whitechapel) hope that a large attendance from a wide and varied public, combined with an encouraging number of sales, may justify this innovation. The London Group today really does not need any kind of explanation as an exhibiting body: like the Boat Race or the Promenade Concerts, these annual exhibitions have become part of English life and one held in affectionate esteem by a large public seriously interested in the arts." Claude Rogers as the President wrote another introduction entitled, "The London Group", giving a brief history of the Group and noting the decision to "experiment" in holding a members only show this year, with the intention of returning to showing non-members work in 1956. Previous shows had been selected by a "jury". He continued, "…the members have always done their best to welcome any work which seemed to be seriously concerned with the problems of painting and sculpture, irrespective of style or tendency or popular appeal. Each movement which has impressed itself on English art during the last forty years has found a welcome home and often its earliest manifestation… And this may in part account for the typical London Group exhibition which, it has been pointed out at times since the war, is almost too varied to preserve unity. If this is so it is the outcome of the ideals which animated the original members: of the varied and individual development of these artists whom we have been proud to elect to the Group: and even perhaps to the way our selection committee is constituted. Unlike other societies who delegate power of selection to a small number of members, the Group has always found it best to allow every member who wishes to attend to be present and to vote." Imagine the scene with a possible ninety members voting for exhibits, true (unworkable?) democracy at work. There was also an "In Memoriam" to the painter Vera Cunningham written by H.E. du Plessis. The exhibition poster image was by Sir Matthew Smith.

In a letter dated 12th December the Whitechapel informed The London Group that attendance totalled 8,553 including the Private View with a daily average of 356. Total catalogue sales were 2,015 raising £100.15.0. Elven works were sold for a total of £614 with The London Group receiving £61.80 from 10% commission. "The Press Cuttings as a whole are lengthy, and decent, in general. The show had a very full press—well spread out."

1955 was a busy year for the Group with organising officers resurrecting the concept of a touring exhibition outside of London.

The Whitechapel Art Gallery
Aldgate East, London E1

The London Group exhibited here in 1955 with a members-only exhibition and again in 1973 with an open submission exhibition. The Whitechapel Art Gallery is overlooked by the City of London and has served as both an East London community gallery and a venue for internationally important exhibitions.

1956

In February Stalin is openly denounced by Kruschev at the 20th Communist Party Conference, causing history to be rewritten, literally. Suez crisis involving UK and France protecting Israeli interests after Egypt nationalises the Suez Canal, invasion and withdrawal. Hungarian uprising put down by USSR. Mao Zedong's Hundred Flowers campaign launched in China which encouraged intellectuals to criticise the government – many were denounced and punished. In October the Queen opens Calder Hall, Britain's first nuclear power station. The Summer Olympic Games are held in Melbourne, Australia. John Osborne's play, "Look Back in Anger" opens in London. Elvis Presley first enters the UK Top Ten with "Heartbreak Hotel".

Tate Gallery January, "Modern Art in the USA" including Willem de Kooning, Robert Motherwell, Jackson Pollock and Mark Rothko.

ICA July, Georges Mathieu's exhibition of 'Action Painting'.

Whitechapel Art Gallery August, "This is Tomorrow" exhibition organised by the Independent Group opens (see "The 1950s"). Also Josef Herman (1953) and Nicolas de Staël exhibitions.

The Arts Council organised an exhibition entitled "New Trends in Painting" including Karel Appel, Bram Bogart, Nicolas de Staël, Jean Dubuffet, Max Ernst, Sam Francis, Paul Jenkins, Jean-Paul Riopelle and Pierre Soulages. Lawrence Alloway wrote an essay for the catalogue "The Challenge of Post-War Painting". Also "Modern Art in the United States" in conjunction with the Museum of Modern Art, New York.

Leicester Galleries an exhibition of ten Italian realists including Guttuso, very influential artists of their time especially in relation to the British 'Kitchen Sink' school.

Beaux Arts Gallery first one-man exhibition of Frank Auerbach's (1960) paintings.

Cornwall Patrick Heron (1952) moves permanently back to Cornwall from London.

Venice Biennale Renato Guttuso wins a prize for his painting, "The Beach", considered by Berger to be his masterpiece. Social realist Derrick Greaves from Britain exhibited, "Sicilian Scene" 1954-55, a huge canvas of an Italian farmer seated in his farmyard. John Bratby (1957), Edward Middleditch and Jack Smith (1957) were also represented (The Beaux Arts Quartet), paintings were selected by Herbert Read. The 'Senior Artist' in the other part of the British Pavilion was Ivon Hitchens (1931).

Museum of Modern Art, New York "Masters of British Painting 1890-1956" including Francis Bacon.

In August **Jackson Pollock** dies in a car crash. He had exhibited at the Venice Biennale.

London Group President: Claude Rogers (1939)

Bertorelli's Restaurant continued to receive good custom from The London Group as the Annual General Meeting was held there on the 8th March, followed by dinner. Only twenty members ate and drank together having previously heard from President Claude Rogers that the Whitechapel Exhibition "could be regarded as extremely successful". There had been 8,328 admissions to the exhibition and twelve works were sold for a total of £864. Although the show had made an actual loss of £59.12.11, the Arts Council had guaranteed to cover any losses up to £100. This year's exhibition at the RBA Gallery only came about because a booking for April had fallen through and the RBA offered it to The London Group. The send in had to take place in the gymnasium at the University College, London and all arrangements had to be hurriedly made. "The President stressed the importance of the selection of works and the 'vetting' by the committee this year in view of the fact that no 'doubtfuls' would be taken on to the Gallery." Finally, Fred Uhlman gave a short report on the possibility of taking an exhibition over to Brussels.

Elected this year were Robert Clatworthy, Elizabeth Frink and Phillip Sutton. Other artists whose names appeared on the voting slips were Edward Middleditch, Terry Frost, John Bratby, Roger Hilton, Jack Smith, Leonard Rosoman, Alistair Grant and Peter Barker Mill. John Dodgson was Vice President at the beginning of the year but did not stand for re-election; E. A. Farrell was the Honorary Secretary and F.T. Nash the Honorary Treasurer. Committee Members were Anthony Fry, Anthony Gross, Morris Kestelman, Bernard Meadows, Ceri Richards, Brian Robb, and Julian Trevelyan. There were ninety-one listed members this year, an extremely healthy figure.

"London Group Annual Exhibition", RBA Galleries, Suffolk Street, Pall Mall East, London SW1, who charged The London Group £800 to hire the galleries. Exhibition dates, 14th April to 4th May 1956. The catalogue was laid out listing Sculpture, Paintings and Drawings. Of the four hundred and five items on exhibition, twenty-eight were drawings, thirty-eight were sculptures and three hundred and thirty-nine were paintings. This was the largest post-war exhibition organised by The London Group. The huge majority of paintings were either still life or landscape, discernable by their title. This must have been a huge exhibition to arrange, there were two hundred and forty non-members exhibiting including Frank Auerbach, Gillian Ayres, John Bratby, Prunella Clough, John Copnall, Anthony Eyton, Patrick George, Roger de Grey, Mary Martin, Dorothy Mead, Margaret Mellis, Henry Mundy, Leonard Rosoman, Hans Schwarz, Yolanda Sonnabend, Adrian Stokes, Michael Tyzack and Euan Uglow. Matthew Smith's "Composition" was top price at £525, closely followed by non-member Leonard Rosoman's "Figure in a Walled Garden" at £500. L. S. Lowry,

Edna Ginesi, Robert Medley and Ceri Richards had top prices for painting whilst F. E. McWilliam and Michael Werner took the sculpture top price. Again, the great majority of prices were around £50. Catalogues still cost only one shilling and there were 'late night openings' until 7pm on Wednesdays and Fridays, otherwise 10 am to 5 pm. Total admissions were 2,322 (including the Private View) with 1,514 catalogues sold. The exhibition poster image was by William Gear.

There is a small ticket in the Tate Archive inviting members and guests to a "London Group Party" on Thursday 26th April 1956 between 8 and 11 pm. A single ticket cost seven shillings for which light refreshments were provided (there was also a bar!). For two shillings party goers could purchase a raffle ticket, the winning prize, "will be a work or works total value £30", presumably of art works from the exhibition.

This plaque is situated just inside the three arches of 6 Suffolk Street, London SW1. It commemorates the development of Suffolk Street by the Crown Estates Commissioners. It also states that this used to be the entrance to the Society of British Artists first galleries.

Six and a half Suffolk Street
London SW1

Formerly known as the RBA Galleries (Royal Society of British Artists), the name was changed to the Art Federation Galleries after 1962. The London Group hired Suffolk Street to hold their annual open submission exhibitions here from 1956 to 1965. They were arguably the most successful series of shows in The London Group's post-war history. This impressive building is currently occupied by the Philippino Embassy. Suffolk Street is literally just round the corner from the National Gallery.

1957

USSR launches Sputnik 1 the first satellite to orbit the Earth and later, in the year Sputnik 2. In Cheshire, Jodrell Bank radio telescope starts operation. Sir Anthony Eden resigns as Prime Minister and Harold Macmillan replaces him and later in the year delivers the immortal "You've never had it so good" speech. Britain's biggest nuclear disaster occurs as the core at Calder Hall, Windscale (now Sellafield) burns for two days sending a radioactive cloud across the whole country. Origins of CND in J.B. Priestley's article for the abolition of nuclear weapons in the New Statesman. Decriminalisation of Homosexuality in UK. Shostakovich premieres Symphony No. 11 twelve years after its inception. David Lean directs "The Bridge on the River Kwai".

The first **John Moores Painting Prize** is organised from the Walker Art Gallery in Liverpool, a bi-annual purchase prize first won by Jack Smith (1957) with the painting, "Creation and Crucifixion", a figurative interior painting literally showing a kitchen sink scene. A good year for Smith, elected to The London Group and winning the first John Moores. The stable of artists from the Beaux Arts Gallery were very successful this year too. John Bratby (1957) won the Junior Section with Sheila Fell second whilst Joseph Tilson, Derrick Greaves and Philip Sutton (1956) also received prizes.
Yves Klein exhibits "Monochrome Propositions" at Gallery One.
ICA Victor Pasmore (1934) and Richard Hamilton install "An Exhibit". Later in the year William Turnbull (1955) shows new paintings and sculptures.
The Tate Gallery Claude Monet retrospective organised by the Arts Council.
Beaux Arts Gallery an exhibition of paintings by Leon Kossoff (1963).
Hanover Gallery sculpture by César and a Francis Bacon painting exhibition.
Pushkin Art Museum, Moscow "Looking at People", a largely representational exhibition toured from Britain organised by Paul Hogarth (from the AIA) and including Edward Ardizzone (1949), George Fullard, Derrick Greaves, Betty Rea (sculptor), Ruskin Spear (1940/43) and Carel Weight (1949). John Berger wrote the accompanying text to the exhibition. Greaves, Hogarth and Spear attended the opening in Moscow.
The Catherine Viviano Gallery, New York already represented Alan Davie (1957) and was also showing Patrick Heron (1952), Peter Lanyon, William Scott (1949) and Richard Smith.

London Group President: Claude Rogers (1939)

Attendance at the 1957 AGM was "small" (20) and Bertorelli's did not make as much as in previous years for hosting the Group's 1957 AGM on Friday, 29th March. Finances continued to be reported as strong with £654.15.4 in the bank balance. Claude

Rogers' report on the 1956 exhibition said that "whilst a good one (it) had certain disappointing aspects." Too many pictures had been taken from the UCL gymnasium into the gallery and had to be hung and the catalogue was "unsatisfactory although in the given conditions it was the best we could do." Rogers "then went on to discuss future plans. It had been impossible to obtain a booking at a gallery large enough to hold a mixed exhibition during 1957. In view of this we had taken a booking at the R.B.A. Gallery for five weeks from Monday, 6th January 1958. He appreciated that this was not an ideal time of the year but it was a case of 'Hobson's choice' and if we had not taken this period it would not have been possible to put on a mixed exhibition at any gallery during 1958. In view of the serious position with galleries, a booking has been made at the R.B.A. Gallery during 1959 for the five weeks commencing 6th April." A letter dated 16th October 1956 to FT Nash, Treasurer of The London Group, from the Royal Society of British Artists, Suffolk Street, offered their galleries for two dates in 1957, from the 9th of April to the 30th of April or the 3rd of September to the 3rd of October 1957. None of these dates were convenient to The London Group. On the 18th October 1956 a letter to Nash from The Royal Institute Galleries, 195 Piccadilly stated that there were "no vacant periods during 1957".

The election of the Hanging Committee had to be completed by postal ballot. A Circular to all Members of The London Group on the 10th May informed the members of the result. The Hanging Committee was to be made up of "six artists and two sculptors of their choice". A strange wording in that sculptors were not artists? The six artists elected were Edward Ardizzone, William Gear, Robert Medley, Philip Sutton, William Townsend and Fred Uhlman. The two sculptors were both women, Gertrude Hermes and Karin Jonzen.

This year sees the biggest intake of the 1950s with seven painters elected to the Group. They were Norman Adams, John Bratby, Alan Davie, Terry Frost, Patrick George, Leonard Rosoman and Jack Smith. The AGM minutes recorded that Edward Middleditch, Roger Hilton and Derrick Greaves were also elected to The London Group but seemed to have declined membership.

The U.K. National Committee of the International Association of Plastic Arts (Chaired by Morris Kestelman) based at 277a Fulham Road wrote to The London Group offering membership cards to artists to gain free admission to state museums and galleries in over twenty countries. In the same letter studio exchanges were proposed with artists living in these other countries and if any London Group artists were interested their particulars would be forwarded.

Early in 1957 The London Group was contacted by Mr E.T. Williams from the Dictionary of National Biography at Balliol College, Oxford concerning the history of The London Group. E.A. Farell, the Group's secretary, replied, "From all that I have been told the London Group was founded in 1914 but unfortunately the records were destroyed or lost during the war. However, I am in communication with some of the older members who may be able to help." James Fitton referred Mr Williams to articles in the February and November 1945 issues of 'The Studio'. Fitton also writes, "The first meeting (of The London Group) was on November 15th, 1913 with Walter Sickert in the Chair, Harold Gilman was President, R.P. Bevan Treasurer and J.B. Manson Secretary." Rupert Lee wrote an informative reply, "The meeting at which The London Group came into being is November 15th 1913 (Walter Sickert in the chair). The Camden Town Group originated the meeting and proposed that they and the Fitzroy Street Group should amalgamate and that the new society should be called The London Group. There was another group The Cumberland Market Group which consisted of Harold Gilman, R.P. Bevan, Charles Ginner and John Nash. To the best of my knowledge they amalgamated with the other groups at this meeting. Harold Gilman was the first President of the (sic) London Group, R.P. Bevan was Hon. Treasurer (an obvious choice, having regards to his city connections) and J.B. Manson was Hon. Secretary. . ."

Duncan Grant, Ethel Sands and C. Maresco Pearce were aslo consulted, but their recollections were hazy.

1958

On January 1st the European Economic Community is founded. In China Mao Zedong launches the Great Leap Forward, a hugely ambitious five year economic plan. First American satellite launched. Boris Pasternak was awarded a Nobel Prize but was forced to refuse it by the Soviet authorities. Five thousand attend the first meeting of CND, founded by Bertrand Russell, at the Central Hall, Westminster followed later in the year by the Aldermaston March. There were the first race riots in Notting Hill. Seven Manchester United football players are killed in the Munich Air Disaster. BOAC becomes the first airline to introduce jet flights across the Atlantic using the De Havilland 'Comet'. Prince Charles becomes The Prince of Wales. Christopher Lee and Peter Cushing appear in "Dracula".

ICA January "Five Young Painters" including Peter Blake, William Green and Richard Smith (John Berger writes an attack on the exhibition). February, "Some Paintings from the E.J. Power Collection" (de Kooning, Kline, Pollock, Rothko and Still). November, "Three Collagists" exhibition, including Gwyther Irwin.

Whitechapel Art Gallery Jackson Pollock exhibition. Also Alan Davie (1957) and "Recent Paintings by 7 British Artists".

Marlborough Gallery one-man show by Lucian Freud.

Beaux Arts Gallery Edward Middleditch and Jack Smith (1957) (Smith's last at Beaux Arts before moving with Bratby to Zwemmers).

Artists' International Association 25th Anniversary Exhibition, selectors included Andrew Forge (1960) and David Sylvester.

Hanover Gallery Eduardo Paolozzi.

The Arts Council organise an exhibition entitled "Abstract Impressionism" selected by Lawrence Alloway and also a David Bomberg (1913) retrospective.

The film **"The Horse's Mouth"** (from Joyce Carey's novel) was made using huge paintings by John Bratby shadowing as Gully Jimpson (played by Alec Guinness), the novel's main character. Graham Sutherland had turned down the offer!

Lawrence Alloway and Bryan Robertson visit New York with a grant from the American Embassy.

London Group President: Claude Rogers (1939)

Wendy Pasmore and Euan Uglow were elected to the Group. Claude Rogers was President with Julian Trevelyan as Vice President. Committee Members this year were Edward Ardizzone, William Gear, Gertrude Hermes, Karin Jonzen, Robert Medley, Philip Sutton, William Townsend and Fred Uhlman. This year there were ninety-two members on roll.

"London Group Annual Exhibition", RBA Galleries, 18th January to 7th February 1958. The mustard coloured catalogue begins with appreciations of five members who had died, Nina Hamnett, Francis John Minton, Jack B. Yeats, David Bomberg and Anna Hope Hudson. This exhibition was another members and non-members exhibition in which there were one hundred and forty non-members exhibiting including Roy Ascott, James Boswell, Jean Bratby, Frederick Brill, Nancy Carline, Chien-Ying Chang, Prunella Clough, John Copnall, Robyn Denny, Tom Espley, Anthony Eyton, Mary Fedden, Colin Hayes, Cliff Holden, Brian Hubbard, Mary Martin, Dorothy Mead, Wendy Pasmore, John Plumb, Michael Rothenstein, Richard Smith, Yolanda Sonnabend, Patrick Symons, Joseph (sic) Tilson, David Tindle and Euan Uglow. Two hundred and seventy-seven works were displayed in five galleries with sculpture in rooms 1, 3 and 6 (eight pieces altogether). Two hundred and sixty-nine paintings were hung but Victor Pasmore's "Abstract Construction in White, Black and Cherry Red", Wendy Pasmore's "Oval Motif No1", Mary Martin's "Climbing Form" and Kenneth Martin's "Abstract" all seemed to signal a change from the traditional still lifes and landscapes. Most expensive painting was Michael Salaman's "The Mad Horse" at £1,000, followed by Roy de Maistre's "Mother and Child" at £840. Around £300 would buy you a Victor Pasmore, Ceri Richards, Gertrude Hermes, William Gear or Robert Medley. The R.B.A. Gallery charged a rent of £120 a week for the five weeks of hire and total attendance was 2,680 with 1,700 catalogues sold. The London Group were so pleased with the R.B.A. arrangement that they were reserving exhibition space right into 1959.

Claude Rogers as President of The London Group had also invited ten "Yugo Slav" painters to exhibit in this exhibition. Rogers had seen an exhibition of painting and sculpture in Dubrovnic where he had been an I.A.P.A. delegate. "It was felt that a friendly invitation to show a few of these pictures in our next exhibition would indicate, in small measure, our gratitude for the hospitality we received and our interest in the work we saw." All did not go smoothly as there were problems with late arrivals of crates at Heathrow Airport. A poster for the exhibition was by Phillip Sutton.

There was a new venue for this year's AGM, the Yellow Room at the Arts Council, 4 St. James' Square, S.W.1. The President said that "it had been decided to hold the meeting away from Bertorelli's this year as there was probably a better atmosphere at the Arts Council for a meeting and more conducive to serious discussion." Those attending were invited to attend a dinner at Bertorelli's afterwards as, it seems, old traditions died hard. Only seventeen members attended the AGM on Thursday, 22nd May; there had been a steady decline in AGM attendees over the last few years. Finances, too, were somewhat depleted compared to previous years with the bank balance standing at £495.15.6. Reporting on the last exhibition, non-member submissions were considerably down and the sculpture had been "disappointing", but attendances and catalogue sales were up. The President then went on to "talk of 1963 when we shall be celebrating our 50th Anniversary. He said that, unfortunately, we had no records in our possession for the period prior to World War II. In order to put on a retrospective exhibition of the type and standard we would like, and particularly if the catalogue for such an exhibition was to contain a definitive account of the Group, it was essential that an early start be made to collect necessary information." Older members were to be contacted requesting catalogues, press cuttings, letters etc. and "a small committee would be set up". Morris Kestelman then raised a serious point about "the election period". "He said there had been no consistency of attendance and the number of members present (at selection of non-members for exhibition) had varied considerably from hour to hour." Kestleman and Rogers wanted selection to be made by members who were there all the time which would provide more consistency and quality. The proposal was duly carried.

1959

Castro overthrows the Batista regime in Cuba. In France Charels de Gaulle becomes the first President of the Fifth Republic. The Russians launch Luna 1, the first satellite to pass the Moon. The UK grants Cyprus its independence. The first motorway opens in the UK and the Mini Car is announced. The Conservatives win a third consecutive General Election, this time under "never-had-it-so-good" Harold Macmillan, with an increased majority. The Labour Party was led by Hugh Gaitskell and the Liberals by Jo Grimond. Walt Disney releases "Sleeping Beauty". Buddy Holly and others are killed in an air crash in Iowa ("The Day the Music Died"). In the Congo the first human dying of HIV is recorded.

Tate Gallery February, "New American Painting" touring exhibition organised by the Arts Council with the Museum of Modern Art, New York.

ICA "The Developing Process", an exhibition organised by Richard Hamilton, Tom Hudson, Victor Pasmore (1934) and Harry Thubron (1981) showing the new radical approach to Basic Design art education.

November, Jean Tingueley's drawing machine (goes berserk) assisted by Bruce Lacey.

John Moores Painting Prize 1959 won by Patrick Heron (1952) with the painting "Black Painting (Red, Brown and Olive)". Peter Lanyon won second prize with "Offshore".

Whitechapel Art Gallery Jack Smith (1957), Kenneth Armitage (1953) and Malevich exhibitions.

Beaux Arts Gallery an exhibition of paintings by Leon Kossoff (1963) following on from his 1957 show. Ex-President John Dodgson finally exhibits a substantial amount of work following a lifetime's activity. The Tate, Arts Council and the Ministry of Works purchased work.

Victor Waddington May, 'Middle Generation', an exhibition of works by Terry Frost (1957), Roger Hilton, Patrick Heron (1952) and Brian Wynter (1955).

Anthony Caro meets **Clement Greenberg** in London and later visits New York.

In New York the **Solomon R. Guggenheim Museum** (designed by Frank Lloyd Wright) opens to the public.

London Group President: Claude Rogers (1939)

Three new members were elected in 1959, Mary Fedden, Anthony Hatwell and Mary Martin. The President was Claude Rogers, Vice President Julian Trevelyan and this year's committee members were Phyllis Bray, Terry Frost, William Gear, Gertrude Hermes, Robert Medley, Phillip Sutton and Carel Weight. "Owing to very poor attendance at the recent AGM" another postal ballot was used to elect the Hanging Committee, as in 1957. Terry Frost had a Leeds address whilst William Gear lived in Eastbourne, which must have made for some organisational difficulties but also illustrated the out-of-capital aspect of The London Group. There were ninety-three London Group members this year and five Honorary Members, Frank Dobson, Sir Jacob Epstein, Augustus John, David Low and Sir Matthew Smith.

"London Group Annual Exhibition", RBA Galleries, 18th April to 8th May 1959. The RBA charged The London Group £660 to hire their galleries. 1959 was another large exhibition with one hundred and eighty-eight non-members exhibiting including Derek Boshier, Stuart Brisley, Bernard Cohen, Harold Cohen, Dennis Creffield, William (Bill) Culbert, Mario Dubsky, Bernard Dunstan, Howard Hodgkin, Francis Hoyland, Gerald Hunt, Henry Inlander, Tessie (sic) Jaray, Michael Kidner, Edwina Leapman and Norman Stevens. In six rooms and the Vestibule there were three hundred and fourteen items on exhibition, twenty-seven of them sculptures. Room 1 contained abstract work by Don Foster, Graham Bevan, Wendy Pasmore, Victor Pasmore, Kenneth Martin and William Gear. Room 2 contained more traditional subjects such as landscapes, still lifes and portraits from Vanessa Bell, Euan Uglow, Sir Matthew Smith and Duncan Grant. Room 3 had similar subjects by John Bratby, William Townsend, Mary Potter, Ceri Richards and Raymond Coxon. Room 4 contained mainly landscape and figure painting by, amongst others, Nancy Carline, Andrew Forge, Diana Cumming and Patrick Symons. Room 5 contained a variety of figurative painting including Terry Frost, Howard Hodgkin and Lilian Holt and Room 6 much the same with Edwina Leapman, Derek Boshier, Edna Ginesi, Anthea Alley and Albert Irvin. Robyn Denny and Tessie Jaray were in the Vestibule. Sir Matthew Smith had the top price of £650 for his "Still Life", Roy de Maistre for £450, Henryk Gotlib for £420 whilst S.W. Hayter, Louis le Brocquy, Victor Pasmore, Ceri Richards and Louise Hutchinson (sculptor) were all priced at around £350. The average price seemed to be creeping up this year to about £60 and the catalogue price had also increased this year to one shilling and sixpence. The image on the exhibition poster was by Euan Uglow. The "Four Year Statistics 1959-62" record 1,051 submissions, 1,484 catalogue sales and 2,471 admissions for this year's exhibition.

The Arts Council offices were again the venue for this year's Annual General Meeting but there is no record of the traditional dinner at Bertorelli's. Only thirteen members attended the AGM on the 10th June and the Treasurer's report was equally disappointing. At the beginning of the year the bank balance had stood at £625.13.5, but the April-May exhibition had resulted in a loss of approximately £350 which meant that the present balance was below £300. "Except for a few outstanding subscriptions there was no more revenue due, and it must be borne in mind that we would be holding a further exhibition before the end of the financial year." The President was seeking a meeting with the Arts Council who were, by all accounts, short of funding themselves. Horace Brodzky was also critical of the catalogue "both with regard to the style and the cost". The meeting gave considerable discussion to this topic. Sales of work had been good, reaching almost £1,250, "a figure that has been topped only once during the last 9 years". Finally, "The Party which we held during the exhibition had resulted in a profit of £24. It had generally been agreed that it had been very successful from all points of view, the only disappointing factor being the very noticeable lack of support from members." That phrase, "lack of support from members" seems to sum up the atmosphere in the Group at the end of the decade.

There is a small buff coloured pamphlet in the Tate Archive entitled "The London Group 1959" produced by the Arts Council of Great Britain. Could this be the exhibition "before the end of the financial year" to which the Treasurer made reference at the AGM? In it a 'G.W.' (Gabriel White?) writes the foreword, "In arranging this selection of pictures from the 1959 exhibition of the London Group, the Arts Council has had the fullest help from its President, Mr Claude Rogers, its Vice President, Mr. Julian Trevelyan, and Mr F. T. Nash, its Hon. Treasurer. To them, to the artists and to the owners of the pictures, we should like to extend our sincere thanks." No indication of where this selection of fifty-eight pictures was exhibited, or when. Claude Rogers' signature is on the back of the pamphlet.

In an interview dated 14th February 1992, Morris Kestelman, archivist and loyal, long-serving member of The London Group made the following observation: "We (Kestelman and Claude Rogers) became members of the London Group about the same time in 1951. You had to be elected and it was not easy, I tried several times. Although membership of the London Group didn't exclude you from showing at the Royal Academy, I never showed there and nor did Claude. Their shows were a shambles, each painting killing the other. The London Group shows were very clear, they cohered. As time went on the Royal Academy under Tom Monnington was turned round. The London Group's power changed for a number of reasons, chief among them was the spread of dealer galleries. At the time when it was formed there were very few art galleries and even fewer dedicated to the modern art of that time. After the war a lot of galleries grew up all over London and people who were so to speak avant-garde could get a show. So the attraction of the London Group as a place where if you were a rebel you could show your work gradually died out, probably in the mid-fifties." Kestelman and Rogers were good friends working together in the I.A.P.A. (International Institute of the Plastic Arts, a UNESCO body), C.N.A.A. (Council for National Academic Awards) and The London Group. "Claude had no administrative capacity at all", Kestelman opined, "Claude was not brilliant on committees, he was conscientious but he was not good at controlling a meeting, and had a tendency to let it ramble."

Non-Members Exhibiting

Kathleen Allen
Anthea Alley
Beatrice Arnell
Colette Arnell
John Banting
Colville Barclay
Kit Barker
Graham Bevan
Derek Boshier
James Boswell
Rolf Brandt
Jean Bratby
William Bratt
Pauline Le Breton
Lionel Brett
Frederick Brill
Stuart Brisley
Anne Buchanan
Daniel Burden
Guy Burn
Carol Burns
James Burr
Laurence Burt
Rufus Buxton
Rosemary Cameron
Scott Campbell
Nancy Carline
Derek Carruthers
Chien-Ying Chang
Daphne Chart
Katharine Church
George Churchill
Harry Clarke
Francoise Clarkefort
Bernard Cohen
Harold Cohen
John Cole
Christina Coleman
Elisabeth Collins
Robin Connelly
Vanda Cook
Derek Cooper
John Copnall
Christopher Cornford
Dennis Creffield
Benjamin Creme
Brian Crouch

William Culbert
Diana Cumming
Keith Cunningham
João Cutileiro
Barry Daniels
Olga Davenport
Robyn Denny
Harold Dent
Norman Dilworth
Sannie Drew
Mario Dubsky
Bernard Dunstan
Michael Edmonds
David Emerson
Margaret Evans
Anthony Eyton
Mary Fedden
Hazel Fennell
Brian Fielding
Susan Fieldreld
Thomas Fletcher
Andrew Forge
Don Foster
Gordon Freeman
John Furnival
George Gault
Timothy Gibbs
Jean Gibson
Colin Giffard
Alistair Grant
Hazel Gravatt
Roger de Grey
Kathleen Guthrie
Arthur Hacker
Christopher Hall
Desmond Harmsworth
*Anthony Hatwell
Dennis Hawkins
Daryl Hill
Howard Hodgkin
Trevor Hodgson
Cliff Holden
Lilian Holt
Susan Horsfield
John Hoskin
Gordon House
Francis Hoyland

Brian Hubbard
Gerald Hunt
Louise Hutchinson
Clarke Hutton
Derek Hyatt
Henry Inlander
Albert Irvin
Laura James
Tessie Jaray
Elizabeth Jenkins
Leonie Jonleigh
Vivienne Kernot
Michael Kidner
Anthony Kingsmill
Stefan Knapp
Mary Knott
Geoffrey Konstam
Tadeusz Koper
Halina Korn
Beppo Lamb
Sonia Lawson
Edwina Leapman
R. D. Lee
Pamela Lloyd
Anthony Lousada
Maurice Lovell
Caroline Luttrell
Francis McGill
Anne Madden
Tom Mallin
Eric Malthouse
Mary Martin
Dorothy Mead
Sylvia Melland
Anthony Messenger
Anthony Millar
Paul Millichip
Harold Mockford
Anne Montagu
Joan Moore
Sarah Morison
Ronald Morton
John O'Connor
Patrick Oliver
Peter Oliver
Frederick Packer
Ahmed Parvez

Robert Payne
Christopher Pemberton
Virginia Platen
Richard Platt
Mike Pope
Hugh Powell
Robert Powter
Sheila Pratt
Alma Ramsey
Peter Reid
Will Roberts
Philip Ross
Michael Rothenstein
Avril Rowe
Kamal Roy
Michael Salaman
Margaret Sanders
Maurice De Sausmarez
Jack Simcock
Stanley Simmonds
J. S. Smith
Peter Snow
Michael Southgate
Roy Spencer
Carolyn Stafford
Eric Stanford
Cecil Stephenson
Norman Stevens
Patrick Symons
Muriel Taylor
Margaret Thomas
Margaret Thorp
Joe Tilson
David Tindle
Michael Upton
Edward Wakeford
Frank Walton
Guy Warren
John Watson
Dennis Westwood
Roy White
Geoffrey Willatt
Alan Windsor
John Wolseley
Gordon Wootton
William Young
Marek Zulawski

The back cover of the 1959 London Group Annual Exhibition
held in the RBA Galleries. One hundred and eighty-eight artists' names are recorded
here as Non-Members Exhibiting, a testimony to the service The London Group
provided for young and emerging artists at the end of this decade.

The 1960's

From 30th June to 27th September 2004, Tate Britain held a very informative and timely exhibition, "Art and the Sixties: This was Tomorrow". The exhibition was organised into nine different themes which reflected contemporary historical perspectives. The nine themes were:

Materialism sixties youth had more disposable income than other generations. Artists experimented with different techniques, materials and form. The approach was basically abstract and urban. Artists in this theme were Gillian Ayres and John Latham.

You never had it so good dealing with the impact of contemporary commercial imagery found in pin-ups, science fiction, car design and the cinema. The Independent Group at the ICA with Blake, Hamilton and Paolozzi were included in this theme.

Pop goes the easel centred on young art students from the RCA deriving imagery from contemporary mass culture and commercial packaging. Pop artists themed here were Boshier, Phillips, Richard Smith and Tilson.

Image in revolt artists reacting to the previous generations ideas and continuing experimentation with new materials and technologies. Clive Barker, Bowling (1963), Caulfield and Tucker were included in this theme.

Ban the Bomb Hamilton, Kitaj, Colin Self and Tilson raised awareness of political issues, but developed new approaches, materials and techniques.

A box of pin-ups focusing on the phenomenon of celebrity exemplified by Beatlemania and used by Pauline Boty and Richard Hamilton.

Swinging 60s London was a 'swinging city', with a more open attitude to sexual relationships and identities described as the 'Permissive Society'. Artists in this theme were Anthony Donaldson, Allen Jones, Bruce Lacey and Jo Tilson.

Real and Imagined Cities a section devoted to new architecture including Richard Seifert's Centre Point, London (1961-66) and Alison & Peter Smithson's Economist Building in Ryder Street, London (1959-64).

Destruction in Art Symposium organised at the Africa Centre, Covent Garden, London between the 9th and 11th of September 1966. Major activists in DIAS were Gustave Metzger, Al Hanson and Wolf Vostell.

Richard Hamilton emerges as the most important artist of the 1960s. Other artists included in the exhibition apart from those mentioned above were Anthony Caro, Robin Denny, David Hockney (1963), Philip King and Bridget Riley. Only two artists were elected members of The London Group, Bowling and Hockney, although virtually every other artist had exhibited earlier in their careers with The London Group in open submission exhibitions, even Gustave Metzger!

The **'third wave' of Pop Art**, was the art world's response to the swinging sixties and totally bound up with 'the scene'. The emphasis was on youth formed around teachers and students at the Royal College of Art, and for the first time artists fresh out of Art School were achieving commercial and critical success. Derek Boshier, David Hockney (1963), Allen Jones, R.B. Kitaj and Peter Phillips were its main protagonists. It is worth noting that only David Hockney was elected to The London Group from all of these young and radical artists. Surely the ethos of The London Group should have attracted these young bucks to its annual exhibitions but perhaps the rapid commercial success with galleries such as Kasmin satiated the desire for public exposure. Pop Art was a youthful, energetic and loose movement celebrating popular culture, especially film, magazines and pop music. Earlier, the embryonic **Independent Group** had met at the Institute of Contemporary Art from 1952. This group included Richard Hamilton and the art historian and critic Reyner Banham as well as other artists and writers. The 1956 exhibition **'This is Tomorrow'** at the Whitechapel Art Gallery exposed the first pop images to the gallery going public, notably Richard Hamilton's "Just what is it that makes today's homes so different, so appealing?". Other important Pop artists were Peter Blake and Richard Smith who made colourful paintings exploiting images from contemporary graphic design and packaging.

The 1960s saw the rise of **"Swinging London"** and influential commercial art galleries such as Kasmin, Robert Fraser, Gimple Fils, Rowan, Waddington and Nigel Greenwood. (The phrase "Swinging London" first appeared in the American magazine 'Time' in April 1966). Kasmin operated from 1963 to 1972 first showing Kenneth Nolan's 'Targets', the second show, curiously enough, was John Latham. Other notable artists in the stable were Robyn Denny, Richard Smith (the first to own a loft!) and David Hockney (1963). Robert Fraser traded between 1962 and 1969. His gallery artists were Bridget Riley, Patrick Caulfield, Peter Blake, Derek Boshier, Clive Barker and Colin Self as well as a number of American Pop Artists. Art Dealer Rober Fraser commented, "Suddenly, around 1964, it was all happening. An eruption, you know. A social revolution".

The 1950s and 1960s also saw a loose grouping of **Constructivists** including Kenneth Martin (1949), Victor Pasmore (1934), Anthony Hill, Alan Reynolds and Malcolm Hughes. Their work was to do with a geometric and process based approach eschewing the expressionist and gestural mark. Modern industrial materials like glass, metals and perspex were used in constructions and replaced the traditional media of oil paint. It is interesting to note that in Kenneth Martin's catalogue to the Serpentine Gallery exhibition of his late paintings held in 1985, no mention is made of his, or Mary's, membership of The London Group, even though he was elected at a very formative period of his life (1949) when he had just begun teaching at Goldsmiths, just produced his first abstract paintings and two years later made his first Kinetic Constructions.

Conceptual and Performance Art came to the fore with, amongst others, John Latham and the auto-destruct artist Gustave Metzger. Famously, John Latham and associates had ripped up and chewed a copy of Clement Greenberg's "Art and Culture" on loan from St. Martin's School of Art library where Latham taught part time. The masticated, fermenting remains were returned in a bottle and Latham's teaching contract was swiftly terminated. ("Chew and Still", 10th August 1966).

Op Art with paintings by Bridget Riley and sculpture by Liliane Lijn.

Tate Modern Time Line 1960-70 'Nouveau Realisme' with Arman, César, Niki de Saint Phalle, Daniel Spoeri and Jean Tinguely. 'Fluxus' including Joseph Beuys, George Maciunas, Yoko Ono and Nam June Paik. 'Minimalism' involving Carl Andre, Jo Baer, Dan Flavin, Donald Judd, Sol Le Witt and Robert Morris. 'Vienna Actionism' with Hermann Nitsch. 'Post-Painterly Abstraction' including Helen Frankenthaler, Brice Marden, Joan Mitchell and Robert Ryman. 'School of London' with Frank Auerbach (1960), Francis Bacon, Lucian Freud, R.B. Kitaj and Leon Kossoff (1963). 'Arte Povera' including Luciano Fabro, Jannis Kounellis, Mario Merz, Guiseppe Penone and Michelangelo Pistoletto. 'Conceptual Art' from Marcel Broodthaers and Joseph Kosuth. 'Land Art' made by Hamish Fulton, Richard Long and Robert Smithson. Individuals of the decade were Richard Serra, Anthony Caro, Larry Bell and Agnes Martin.

1960

Sharpville massacres in South Africa. J.F. Kennedy elected as US President. After only two years of the Great Leep Forward in China millions had died of starvation. Cyprus achieves independence from Britain following the EOKA campaign begun in 1955 and two sovereign bases at Dhekelia and Akrotiri are negotiated by Britain. The Summer Olympic Games are held in Rome. 100,000 CND protesters gather in Trafalgar Square. Britain cancels its independent missile programme, "Blue Streak". Hugh Gaitskell, leader of the Labour Party, defeats unilateralists within the party. "Lady Chatterley's Lover" is cleared of obscenity charges. Albert Finney stars in Karl Reisz's "Saturday Night and Sunday Morning" and Alfred Hitchcock makes "Psycho".

The Tate Gallery organises a retrospective exhibition of 270 of Picasso's works in various media, selected by Roland Penrose.
In 1960/61 the "Situation" exhibitions were organised at the RBA Galleries and New London Galleries involving crtitic and theoretician Lawrence Alloway, Gillian Ayres, Bernard Cohen, Roger Coleman, Peter Coriello, Robin Denny (who organised the two exhibitions), Gordon House, John Hoyland, Gwyther Irwin, Bob Law, Henry Mundy, John Plumb, Richard Smith and William Turnbull (1955). The exhibitions showed large scale abstract work emphasising and acknowledging developments in America.
ICA January, Peter Blake, John Latham and Theo Crosby.
March, "West Coast Hard Edge" painting.
May, Morris Louis, 'stained' paintings.
September, Lawrence Alloway leaves his job as ICA Programme Director.
Whitechapel Art Gallery Ceri Richards (1938), Roy de Maistre (1954) and Henry Moore (1930) exhibitions. Three current or ex-members of The London Group.
Leicester Galleries one-man exhibition of Claude Rogers' (1939) work, President of The London Group.
Coldstream Report on the future of art education published in November. Coldstream (1933) had been immersed in art education for many decades and at the same time had been an active member of The London Group.

London Group President: Claude Rogers (1939)

Three artists were elected to The London Group in 1960. They were Frank Auerbach, Andrew Forge and Dorothy Mead. Others nominated and seconded were Adrian Heath, Craigie Aitchison, Jeffery Camp, Michael Andrews, Edward Middleditch,

Dennis Creffield and Anthony Wishaw (sic). Claude Rogers remained as President and Julian Trevelyan as Vice President. Membership this year was put at ninety-two, extremely healthy. The Executive Committee this year was Rogers and Trevelyan, Anthony Gross, Patrick George, Anthony Hatwell, Kenneth Martin, Brian Robb and William Townsend.

"London Group", RBA Galleries, Suffolk Street, 15th January to 5th February 1960. A total of two hundred and fifty-three works were exhibited in four rooms and a Vestibule. Fifty out of ninety-two members exhibited up to three works each and one hundred and thirty-five non-members up to two each. It is noticeable how many of the non-members exhibited were eventually elected to The London Group. Some other exhibiting non-members who were never elected as members of the Group were Mario Dubsky, Alan Green, Howard Hodgkin, Tess Jaray, Edwina Leapman, Terence Scales, Joe Tilson, David Tindle and Karl Weschke. Titles in the catalogue still indicate a preponderance of representational painting but the sculptors seemed to be using more varied, contemporary and unconventional materials. Top price went to Sir Jacob Epstein (who had died recently) for the marble "Arms" at £5,000. The catalogue, following the usual 'fifties format' but with a bright orange cover, contained tributes to three recently deceased members, Sir Matthew Smith, Rupert Lee and Sir Jacob Epstein written by CR (Claude Rogers?), DBL (Diana Brinton Lee?) and RC (Richard Carline?) respectively. The exhibition poster was by Elizabeth Frink this year. The RBA Galleries cost £575 to hire and the "Four Year Statistics 1959-62" indicate 816 submissions, 1,228 catalogue sales and 2,158 admissions.

A document dated 9th June was published as a memorandum on the proposed 1963 Retrospective Exhibition. The Arts Council were the first port of call for this initiative. They were not enthusiastic, requiring that the exhibition should have "point and shape". Bearing that in mind it was felt that Andrew Forge as a painter, critic and exhibition organiser and known to be sympathetic to The London Group, should be approached. He was, in fact, elected to the Group at the next AGM probably to take on this specific project.

In order to give members an opportunity of attending the Group's Annual General Meeting, which had been poorly attended of late, the day was changed to a Sunday. The idea seems to have worked as twenty-eight members attended the meeting on 26th June at the J. Sainsbury Canteen, Blackfriars, S.E.1. Perhaps the three motions put forward by Patrick George and seconded by Euan Uglow attracted a larger audience. The first motion read, "In the eyes of the Hanging Committee all pictures should be considered entirely on their merits. Members' pictures should not automatically and necessarily receive preferential treatment. The Hanging Committee should hang the available pictures to present the best possible exhibition", followed by "One nominated work by each member will be shown in the Exhibition. Other works submitted will be subject to selection by those members present when the selection of non-members works is made for the Exhibition. It is suggested that members' works should be seen at 2p.m. on the first day of the selection" and motion number three, "Every effort should be made to recruit the younger painters and sculptors and to encourage them to feel that the Group concerns them" and quite a shake-up for the comfortable, inherited processes of the 1950s. The second proposal was discussed first and Patrick George said that "while he thought it was a poor proposal he had felt that something had to be done about the London Group (sic) which was now being regarded as a museum piece by three quarters of the London art world." Claude Rogers "expressed delight that some of the younger members were concerned with doing something about enlivening the Group, it was a welcome show of vitality." Understandably there was much discussion on George's idea but on moving to a vote eight were in favour and fourteen against. In true London Group fashion a small committee was formed to look into this matter. The first and third proposals were accepted in full by the meeting and the first meeting of the 1960s had brought a wind of change to The London Group. Tucked away in the minutes was the Treasurer's Report which the President proposed should be "taken as read". What the report showed was that the bank balance as at 28th February 1960 was only £37.18.1. and that the Group needed to husband its resources very carefully.

On the 2nd December the small sub-committee set up to look into issues raised at the AGM published its report. Chaired by Brian Robb and consisting of John Farleigh, Patrick George, Anthony Hatwell and Morris Kestelman, the committee had met eight times and produced a very detailed seven page document. Twenty-four recommendations were put forward under five headings, Obligations of Membership, Recruitment of New Members (Election by Reputation and Election by Submission of Work), Selection of works for Exhibition, Exhibition Policy and Public Relations. The recommendations were described as "in no way revolutionary" and that they were "aimed at developing the traditional character of the Group as the only serious annual cross-section of the more lively currents in English Painting." The most revolutionary idea, Appendix A, was not fully supported by all of the committee but was, nonetheless, given the light of day. Appendix A advocated "the limiting of membership to a fixed period (say five years) after which re-election would be required." The committee felt that this proposal would make the membership "more strenuous".

1961

April 12th, Yuri Gagarin (USSR) orbits the Earth and becomes the first man in space. On May 5th, American Alan Shepherd makes a sub-orbital space flight. Adolf Eichman stands trial on Holocaust charges. A US backed Cuban invasion at the Bay of Pigs fails. The Berlin Wall goes up. In London the decision to demolish the Euston Arch is taken despite opposition from the likes of Pevsner and Betjeman. The Profumo affair with Christine Keeler and Mandy Rice-Davies is revealed. Cliff Richard appears in "The Young Ones", Shostakovich completes Symphony No. 12 and John Cage premieres "Variations II", where the 'score' of eleven transparent sheets is tossed into the air and the resulting patterns used to determine the basic sounds.

In February the **Young Contemporaries Exhibition of 1961** included Caulfield, Hockney, Kitaj and Jones, all students at the Royal College of Art. The critic and writer Lawrence Alloway wrote the catalogue for that exhibition. Ken Russell's programme for the BBC, "Pop goes the Easel" with Peter Blake, Derek Boshier and Peter Phillips was to become an icon of its time.
Whitechapel Art Gallery holds a Mark Rothko exhibition.
John Moores Painting Prize 1961 won by Henry Mundy with the painting "Cluster".
"New London Situation" exhibition opens at the Marlborough Galleries, a second and final exhibition follows on from the previous year's "Situation" exhibition.
Beaux Arts Gallery Frank Auerbach, elected to The London Group last year, shows his London building site paintings.
Lawrence Alloway leaves London for America.

London Group President: Claude Rogers (1939)

Five new members were elected this year, André Bicat as an Honorary Member, Jeffery Camp, Anthony Eyton, Cliff Holden and Leslie Marr. Holden and Marr were part of Bomberg's 'Borough Group' which was gaining significant influence within The London Group bearing in mind last year's election of Auerbach, Forge and Mead. Forge and Mead, in fact, were to become Presidents of the Group in the future; Mead as the first female President of the Group.

"London Group 1961", RBA Gallery, Suffolk Street, 9th March to 29th March 1961. Claude Rogers was President, Julian Trevelyan, Vice President, E.A. Farrell Hon. Secretary, F.T. Nash Hon. Treasurer and Eric Lewis Hon. Assistant Secretary. Committee members were Raymond Coxon, Patrick George, Anthony Gross, Anthony Hatwell, Morris Kestleman, Kenneth Martin, Brian Robb, William Townsend and

Edward Wolfe. There were ninety-three members recoded this year including the three Honorary Members. A total of three hundred and three exhibits under the titles of Paintings and Sculptures were shown in four rooms. Forty-nine members put in up to three pieces each and one hundred and sixty-three non-members up to two pieces. Non-member exhibitors included Craigie Aitchison, Neville Boden, Frank Bowling, Mario Dubsky, Keith Grant, Roger de Grey, David Hockney, Howard Hodgkin, Malcolm Hughes, Albert Irvin, Bryan Kneale, Norman Stevens and Michael Tyzack. Exhibiting Honorary Members were Frank Dobson, Augustus John and David Low. No introduction by the President, only an appreciation of Norman "Peter" Dawson (1934) by Richard Carline. Monsieur Jean Fautrier, winner of the 1960 Venice Biennale, was a specially invited exhibitor (suggested by Anthony Gross) and showing six paintings. Messrs. Bensons and the London Press Exchange promised to purchase work from the exhibition. Prices were not printed in the 18 cm x 25 cm catalogue, printed black type on white and Kenneth Martin produced an image for the exhibition poster. The "Four Year Statistics 1959-62" indicate 1,514 submissions (almost doubled from last year's 816), 789 catalogue sales and 1,301 admissions (last year it was 2,158, nearly halved). Julian Trevelyan, as Chair of the Public Relations Sub-Committee had invited Alec Guinness to open the show. Guinness was 'enthusiastic' but would be 'out of the country' in March. Another innovation was the hiring of Nora Meninsky, Bernard's wife, to be present during the whole exhibition for a fee of £50. She was there to facilitate sales. The London Group's commission on sales was 20%, but Nora was offered 5% by the Group on all sales over £700. The exhibition still made a loss. Last year the exhibition loss was £529.10.7, but this year the loss had risen to £602.2.11. The RBA Gallery cost £575 to hire which was by far the biggest expenditure in the entire exhibition budget. The London Group's reaction to this financial problem was to set up a Financial Sub-Committee which eventually recommended raising the exhibition submission fee to 5/- and to 2/6 for students.

Seventeen members attended the Annual General Meeting on Sunday, 2nd July in Sainsbury's canteen. H.S. Williamson questioned whether the £70 spent on bringing the Fautrier's over from Paris had been worth it. Rogers replied that he thought the public would like to see work from the winner of the main prize at the Venice Biennale. "Fautrier used to exhibit with The London Group, but his work had not been seen in England for a number of years." The President was making the point that The London Group had an important international dimension as well as a London focus. The President's report on the last exhibition had "highs and lows". "There was a substantial increase in submissions, but an alarming drop in catalogue sales and attendances, in addition to a fall in the value of pictures sold." The Arts Council were to be asked to cover losses but comment was made on the two major components of the loss, namely hire of the gallery and the cost of Bourlet's handling fees. Members suggested using student labour to handle the submissions, but it was felt that "students would not be as enthusiastic about handling our work as they were when handling their own works at the Young Contemporaries". "It had always been a problem to get sufficient members at the gallery for the selection of non-members' work. To endeavour to get members to the gallery to handle the works as well would prove almost impossible." At this point in the meeting the elections took place. Rogers was returned as President "unanimously" unopposed, Julian Trevelyan resigned as Vice President and was replaced by Anthony Hatwell whilst Andrew Forge, Patrick George, Anthony Gross, Gertrude Hermes, Kenneth Martin, F.E. McWilliam, Dorothy Mead, Robert Medley and Brian Robb were elected to the Executive Committee. William Roberts was elected as an Honorary Member. The meeting then heard that Alan Bowness had been asked by the Arts Council to organise a retrospective exhibition of The London Group. Fears were raised that the Group would have little control over this process, but Andrew Forge would be involved and represent Group interests. Final discussion at the AGM centred on the size of the annual exhibition. Many members thought that the RBA gallery was too large and that a better quality exhibition could be held on smaller premises. There was much sympathy towards this idea. As the meeting was poorly attended, discussion on the rule changes proposed in the 'Robb Report' were to be held over for a Special Meeting in the autumn.

November 5th was the date of this Special General Meeting in Sainsbury's canteen and fireworks indeed exploded. Thirty-five members attended to take part in this important discussion. Rogers opened the meeting by observing "The art situation, as it has developed in the last two decades, has been most encouraging for artists as a whole. But the effect on the exhibiting societies has been bad. It has become easier for the young and talented painter to have a one-man show or to find a gallery interested in his work... recent London Group Exhibitions have roused little interest. Sales have been bad, the numbers of visitors absurd, as, indeed, have been the length and number of notices in the papers... I believe we must reconsider the way we run the Exhibition and, if necessary, take somewhat Cromwellian steps to improve our method of selecting pictures and of electing new members." The first proposals to raise the subscription from 2 to 3 guineas, to raise the Hanging Fee from 20/- to 25/- and to charge 30/- for paintings over 24 square feet were all accepted. From the Robb Report, "Members who, without sound reason, fail to exhibit for three years in succession be deemed to have relinquished membership" was carried by 24 to 11. Under "Election of New Members" the meeting voted for the setting up of an Election Committee (instead of what Frank Auerbach had called a chaotic and unworkable ad hoc system) consisting of the Executive Committee and five additional members. The five elected to this new committee were Norman Adams, Josef Herman, Morris Kestelman, Lynton Lamb and H.E. du Plessis. Next on the agenda was "Selection of Non-Members" Work for the

Annual Exhibition'. The motion was "That for a trial period of one year the selection of non-members' work be delegated to a small committee representative of different points of view". In favour - 18, Against – 8. Finally the meeting discussed a "Scheme for Reorganisation of the Group: Appendix 'A' of the Robb Report". This was essentially the re-election of new and existing members to the Group every five years to "make membership more strenuous". Unfortunately, many members had drifted away and the meeting was "somewhat depleted". It was agreed to hold this hugely important matter over as item 1 in a further special meeting. The November 5th meeting ended as a bit of a damp squib.

1962

October 18th to 29th, the Cuban Missile Crisis, Krushchev turns his nuclear missile laden ships back from destination Cuba in return for JF Kennedy, secretly, removing US missiles from Turkey as the world is brought to the brink of nuclear war. Dean Rusk, US Secretary of State, famously quotes, "We are eyeball to eyeball, and the other fellow just blinked". The United States sends troops into Vietnam. Marilyn Munroe dies from an overdose. Nelson Mandela is jailed. On May 25th in the UK, Coventry Cathedral is consecrated. The first live television pictures are broadcast across the Atlantic by Telstar satellite. The Beatles release their first hit "Please Please Me" and Benjamin Britten premieres "War Requiem", Op. 66. David Lean makes "Lawrence of Arabia" and Bond film "Dr. No" is released. In the FIFA World Cup held in Chile, Brazil beat Czechoslovakia 3-1.

Tate Gallery hold a major retrospective of Francis Bacon's painting.
"British Painting Today and Yesterday" at Tooths confirms Allen Jones and Howard Hodgkin as the new direction in contemporary painting. Later in the year Elsworth Kelly is shown.
Robert Fraser Gallery opens. In September Harold Cohen is shown.
ICA Richard Smith exhibition of paintings.
Various 'Fluxus' artists organise the **"Festival of Misfits"** exhibition at Gallery One in London including the installation/performance piece 'Living Sculpture' by Ben Vautier.
At Ealing School of Art **Gustave Metzger** gives a talk on auto-destructive art. A young Pete Townshend of "The Who" is in the audience.
John Russell writes an article "Pioneer of Pop Art" on Peter Blake, introducing the new terminology.
In 2013 Bruce Altshuler published **"Biennials and Beyond – Exhibitions That Made Art History 1962 - 2002"**. He focused on twelve exhibitions which he considered seminal in the development of art history. In 1962 he singled out "Dylaby" at the Stedelijk Museum, Amsterdam and "New Realists" at the Sidney Janis Gallery, New York.

London Group President: Claude Rogers (1939)

Six male artists were elected in 1962, Craigie Aitchison, Michael Andrews, Dennis Creffield, Paul de Monchaux, Adrian Heath and Brian Wall.

"London Group 62", Art Federation Galleries in Suffolk Street (changing their name from the RBA Galleries in 1961), 8th March to 30th March 1962. Gallery hire was £575 for the third year running. Claude Rogers was President, Anthony Hatwell Vice President, other officers as 1961. Committee Members were Andrew Forge, Patrick George, Anthony Gross, Gertrude Hermes, Kenneth Martin, Dorothy Mead (who provided the poster image this year), Robert Medley and Brian Robb. There were ninety members including two Honorary Members, Frank Dobson and David Low. Non-members' work was selected by Claude Rogers, Anthony Hatwell, John Dodgson, William Gear, Patrick George, Josef Herman, Kenneth Martin and Dorothy Mead. Notable exhibiting non-members included Roy Ascott, Quentin Blake, Jean Bratby, Prunella Clough, David Hepher, Francis Hoyland, David Oxtoby, John Pasmore, Patrick Proctor, Peter Startup and Isaac Witkin. Non-Members mostly had one work selected and about 5%, two. There were one hundred and eight non-member exhibitors and sixty-one members who showed up to three pieces each. There were a total of two hundred and thirty-two works exhibited in four rooms with a mix of painting and sculpture in each room. Titles seem to indicate a mixture of figurative and abstract painting, sizes not given. No prices were printed in the catalogue which was similar in size and format to the 1961 catalogue. Again there was no introduction from the President but a piece from Lawrence Gowing on Augustus John and Vanessa Bell who had recently died. A separate roneod Price List gives the number of the work against a price, no media, no dimensions. Top price, number 78 at £750, number 168 at £700 and number 37 at £525. Most prices were around the £100 mark. Sales of £1,444 were the highest since 1954 earning The London Group £286.14 in commission. The "Four Year Statistics 1959-62" indicated 1,104 submissions, 1,215 catalogue sales and 2,111 admissions. The exhibition as a whole made a loss on £400 but the Arts Council covered this loss with a grant.

A Press Cuttings album was put together for this exhibition which had been extensively reviewed but contemporary critics including John Russell, ("liveliest by far of our professional Salons"),Terence Mullaly, Neville Wallis, Andrew Forge, Eric Newton, Keith Sutton, William Gaunt and David Sylvester. Writing in the 'New Statesman and Nation', Sylvester stated, "The trends which are decidedly more conspicuous in the London Group than in Bond Street are Constructivism, Bombergism and Coldstreamism. The Constructivist works include beautiful objects by Kenneth Martin and Mary Martin... Dorothy Mead is outstanding among the Bombergers... The leading Coldstreamites are Patrick George and Euan Uglow, who provides what is to me the most interesting piece of painting in the show." The Daily Telegraph's Terence Mullaly wrote, "This year the London Group is showing new signs of virility. A society that since the war has too often seemed to hang what is bad of its kind, now provides a stimulating show . . ." Andrew Forge writing in 'Arts Review' agreed with him, "A few years ago it was said that the Group had had its day – but to judge from the new names that have been added to the membership in the last twelve months it looks as if it is now at the height of a new burst of energy". Eric Newton of the Manchester 'Guardian' fell into line. "The London Group is as good as ever. A little better perhaps, because more varied and more full of enthusiasms." And this from Neville Wallis writing in 'The Observer', "How necessary is the London Group? Granted that it remains our foremost Salon, serious, adventurous, absolutely above any suspicion of diluting its strength with contributions unworthy of its integrity, does this artists' association still serve a purpose when there are commercial galleries galore to seize on artists of quality? I am sure it does."

The AGM took place on Sunday, 1st July in Sainsbury's Blackfriars canteen. The minutes for this AGM listed all the current members of which there were eighty, but only sixteen put in an attendance for the AGM. Those in attendance heard that the Group was in reasonable financial shape with a bank balance of £700 and that the 1962 annual exhibition had been a big improvement on the "catastrophic" 1961 show. Continuing, Rogers then remarked on the appalling standard of work from non-members, "Personally he never remembered seeing such a mass of indifferent work". The experiment with the new Selection Committee had worked "very well". "The President said that the exhibition seemed to him to reflect very well the different kinds of figurative work being done in England but that it was much weaker in non-figurative work." Andrew Forge and Dorothy Mead were congratulated on the publicity for this exhibition which had, no doubt, brought in more visitors. Rogers and Hatwell remained in office whilst Jeffery Camp, Dennis Creffield, Andrew Forge, Josef Herman, Dorothy Mead, Robert Medley, Paul de Monchaux, Philip Sutton, Euan Uglow and Brian Wall formed the Working Committee. Other members elected to the Selection and Election Committees were Frank Auerbach, Anthony Eyton, William Gear, Patrick George, Lawrence Gowing, Adrian Heath, Kenneth Martin and Ceri Richards.

Agenda Item No. 9 was the controversial proposal that all members should be re-elected every five years. The matter was so important and the attendance so small that the proposal was to be sent out as a postal ballot to all members. On the proposal "The election to membership of the London Group should be on the basis of re-election after a given period of years, this principle to apply equally to both present and future members", the voting was 17 for and 38 against; motion defeated.

There were are huge number of departures from the Group this year including Robert Adams, Elizabeth Andrews, Kenneth Armitage, Robert Clatworthy, Alan Davie, Terry Frost, Anthony Fry, Patrick Heron, Ivon Hitchens, Louis le Brocquy, F.E. McWilliam, Elizabeth Muntz, Victor Pasmore, Roland Pitchforth, William Roberts, William Scott and Jack Smith, in part explained by the Treasurer tidying up those who had not paid their sub..s for a number of years but some upset by recent proposals for reform within the Group.

1963

On November 22nd, President of the United Staes John F. Kennedy is assassinated in Dallas. Martin Luther King delivers his immortal "I Have a Dream" speech. The 'Super Powers' sign an agreement limiting nuclear tests to underground explosions to contain the nuclear fallout. Kenya gains full independence from Britain. Britain's application to join the Common Market is vetoed by the French. Harold Wilson is elected leader of the Labour Party following Gaitskell's death. At this year's Labour Party conference Wilson makes his, "White heat of the technological revolution" speech. 900,000 were unemployed in the UK, the highest post-war figure and Harold Macmillan resigns as PM; Sir Alec Douglas-Home replaces him. Stanley Kubrick makes "Dr. Strangelove", Dirk Bogarde appears in "The Servant", Michael Caine and Stanley Baxter in "Zulu" and Richard Harris in Lindsay Anderson's "This Sporting Life".

John Moores Painting Prize 1963 won by Roger Hilton with the painting, "March 1963".

Kasmin Ltd opens with an exhibition of paintings by American Kenneth Noland. Followed by John Latham, Bernard Cohen, Richard Smith and David Hockney.

Whitechapel Art Gallery and the **Tate Gallery** hold the "British Painting in the Sixties" exhbition.

Whitechapel Art Gallery Philip Guston, Serge Poliakoff and Robert Medley (1937) exhibitions. Anthony Caro showed sculpture later in the year.

Many individual exhibitions at **commercial galleries in London** including Roy Ascott, R.B. Kitaj, Billy Apple, Bruce Lacey, Patrick Procktor, William Tucker, Mark Vaux (1990) and Tess Jaray, Bridget Riley and Pauline Boty.

Acrylic paints were first produced in the UK. These new colours were cheap(er), water based, quick drying and could be extended without losing brilliance of colour.

London Group President: Claude Rogers (1939)

This year, five more male artists became members; Frank Bowling (re-elected in 2002), Michael Elliot, David Hockney, Leon Kossof and Evert Lundquist.

"London Group 1963", Art Federation Galleries, 7th March to 29th March 1963. The Federation of British Artists charged £598.9.6 for hire of the galleries, increased from £575 in 1962. Officers were unchanged from 1962 and this year's Committee Members were Jeffery Camp, Dennis Creffield, Paul de Monchaux, Andrew Forge, Josef Herman, Dorothy Mead, Robert Medley, Philip Sutton, Euan Uglow and Brian Wall. Non-members' work was selected by Claude Rogers, Anthony Hatwell, Frank Auerbach, Jeffery Camp, Anthony Eyton, William Gear, Adrian Heath, Robert Medley,

Brian Wall and H.S. Williamson. Some exhibiting non-members this year were Adrian Berg, Neville Boden, Ken Brazier, Guy Burn, Keith Critchlow, Victor Newsome, Paula Rego, Michael Sandle, David Tindle, David Troostwyck and John Wonnacott. There were one hundred and nine non-member exhibitors with rather more artists having two pieces selected than in 1962. Only forty-nine members put in up to three pieces of work out of a total membership of eighty-six. A total of two hundred and thirty-two works were shown in four rooms with sculpture placed with paintings. Prices were printed in this year's catalogue, again similar in design format to last year's catalogue. Gertrude Hermes' sculpture "The Seed" was priced at £800, Frank Bowling was asking £600 for "Painting 1962" and William Gear and L.S. Lowry £400. Titles seem to indicate a healthy mix of landscape, still life, figure painting, abstracts and constructions. No sizes or media were indicated. Peter Snow's title catches the eye - "Thank God for Larry Rivers"! Ethel Sands, one of the Group's oldest members had died during the year. The exhibition poster displayed an image by Josef Herman. The exhibition made a loss of £557.19.6 but the Group expected the Arts Council to award a grant, "not expected to be less than that received in recent years, namely, £400".

The services of a Press Cuttings Agency ensured that a sketchbook of clippings was well filled, quantity, not quality, in this case! For example, the 'London Evening News' makes mention of "hundreds of pieces of firewood" making up Vice President Anthony Hatwell's sculpture, "an arrangement of tablelegs", and "hair on a background of old curtains". The review ends, "Apart from a handful of paintings by serious artists like Professor Carel Weight, L.S. Lowry, William Gear and Philip Sutton, the show, surely the worst in the Group's fifty year history, is aptly summed up by the title of one picture, 'Study For What The Hell'". This critical trend was upheld by Geoffrey Grigson writing in the 'New Statesman' under the headline, "On a Dying Gladiator". After a lengthy and well reasoned argument based on the group's Press Release, Grigson considered that "the London Group (sic) should be reformed. No, groups or societies cannot be revitalized. So this one shouldn't be allowed to bring any further shame on its members, exhibitors, and the act of painting." Andrew Forge wrote a letter in reply arguing that, "Well-exploited hysteria may produce good readable journalism but it makes rotten criticism." Bettina Wadia of 'Arts Review' continued the assault, "The annual exhibition of the London Group is like an unwieldy anthology of some of the best of the season's shows and, unfortunately, a great deal of the mediocre. If such obviously influential artists such as Francis Bacon and Roger Hylton (sic) were included, it would become an event of real interest, a London Salon, instead of the amorphous collection it is at the moment." Positive support comes in the form of John Russell writing in the 'Sunday Times' under the headline "The new wave of sculpture". "In sculpture, the Group this year rejects absolutely the poetic adaption of the human figure which made this country internationally famous in the 1950s."

Russell picks out I. Iardeni, Waldemar D'Orey, Ron Robertson and Anthony Hatwell as good examples. "In painting, the line is markedly Bombergian. With Evert Lundquist and Staffan Hallstrom as guests from Sweden, and Cliff Holden, Andrew Forge, Leslie Marr, Dorothy Mead, Leon Kossof, Frank Auerbach, Dennis Creffield and Peter Richmond all present in strength, the visitor can familiarise himself with a kind of painting which even now does not 'take' with the dealers." George Butcher of the Manchester 'Guardian' also detected, "Somewhat unexpectedly, a strong infiltration of pop sympathy" citing images by Ken Turner, F. Morland, Ronald Robertson-Swann and John Michel. A mixed reaction to the 1963 exhibition. Total admissions were 1,527 (not including the Private View) raising £99.13.6 and 809 catalogues were sold bringing in £60.13.6. By comparison 3,667 people had visited the Young Contemporaries in 18 days.

Recorded as leaving the Group this year were James Fitton, Elizabeth Frink, Lawrence Gowing, Stanley Hayter, Edward le Bas and Leonard Rosoman. Records show that most of these members had either failed to pay their sub..s or had not taken part in an annual exhibition for three consecutive exhibitions and were probably removed from membership.

The minutes of the A.G.M. held in Sainsbury's canteen on Saturday, 28th September reveal something of what other matters were also exercising the Group's membership. "The President continued by saying that this was the second exhibition arranged according to the new directives. That is to say, the work of members was not considered as privileged in matters of hanging, and the Hanging Committee was given complete discretion to make the exhibition look as good as possible; while the selection of the non-members' work was done by an elected Selection Committee instead of by the Group as a whole, or rather by those members of the Group who were able to turn up." So members were not guaranteed to be shown and could not just "turn up" to vote for friends' or students' work sent in. Selection was now in the hands of a dedicated committee and had therefore removed the right of individual members to vote for what was termed "pre-selected work". This new system was an attempt to raise the quality of the send in. The President "still remembered with some sense of surprise the shocking quality of the work sent in by non-members in 1962." It fell to the newly elected Selection Committee to improve the quality of work shown. The following members were given this responsibility, Michael Elliott, William Gear, David Hockney, Cliff Holden, Mary Martin, Brian Robb and Brian Wall.

1964

Nelson Mandela is sentenced to life imprisonment. Brezhnev deposes Kruschchev in the USSR. Gulf of Tonkin attack in Vietnam and anti-war protest grows in the US. Lyndon B. Johnson defeats Barry Goldwater in the US Presidential Election. Jean Paul Sartre refuses the Nobel Prize for Literature whilst Martin Luther King receives the Peace Prize. The Summer Olympic Games are held in Tokyo. In the UK Mods and Rockers slug it out at the seaside. On October 15th the Labour Party is elected to power under Harold Wilson defeating the Conservatives led by Alec Douglas-Hume and Jo Grimond's Liberals. The Beatles get a first number 1 in the USA with "I Want to Hold your Hand", "Bealtemania" ensues. Walt Disney's "Mary Poppins" is released.

The Tate Gallery hosted a huge exhibition presented by the Gulbenkian Foundation called "54:64 Painting and Sculpture of a Decade". Also "The London Group Jubilee Exhibition" (see below).

Whitechapel Art Gallery "Robert Rauschenberg" followed by "The New Generation" exhibition showing contemporary painting by younger artists (Curated by Bryan Robertson). Also an exhibition of paintings by Mary Potter (1940/43).

The **National Gallery** purchases Cézanne's "Les Grandes Baigneuses" for £500,000. Typically, the purchase is not well received by the popular media and the public and is hung, not in the public galleries, but in the Boardroom.

London commercial gallery shows included Philip King, Jules Olitski, Helen Frankenthaler, the Leicester Group (Victor Newsome, Michael Sandle and Terry Setch), Richard Hamilton and Takis (Kinetc art).

Also in 1964 the Centre for Contemporary Cultural Studies opens at the **University of Birmingham**. The Centre was to look at the media and popular culture using new disciplines and academic approaches. Raymond Williams and Stuart Hall were to become well known for their work at the Centre.

Czechoslovakia a British Council exhibition called, "British Painting 1900 – 1962". Lectures by Peter Lanyon where he also had to visit an official Soviet style Socialist Realist exhibition and recorded; "We practised diplomatic rudeness and mutually loathed each other".

London Group President: Claude Rogers (1939)

Two new members were elected this year, Anthony Green and Kenneth Turner. Lynn Chadwick, Leslie Marr, Hyam Myer, John Piper, Ceri Richards, Julian Trevelyan and Harold S. Williamson left the Group during the year.

"London Group 1964", Art Federation Galleries, Suffolk Street, 19th March to

10th April 1964. Gallery hire this year was £588 from a Group total of £1,272.19. Officers remained the same as for 1963 except for the post of Vice President which was to be occupied later this year by Patrick George. Committee Members were Frank Bowling, Jeffery Camp, Dennis Creffield, Patrick George, Anthony Hatwell, Morris Kestleman, Claude Rogers, Euan Uglow and Brian Wall. The non-members selection committee comprised Claude Rogers, Patrick George, Frank Bowling, Michael Elliot, Cliff Holden, Mary Martin, Brian Robb and Brian Wall. Some Non-Member exhibitors were Ray Atkins, Tom Barrett, Ken Draper, Sheila Fell, Peter Greenaway, Mike Kenny, Margaret Mellis, Myles Murphy, Larry Rivers (a portrait of David Sylvester), Terence Scales and Arthur Wilson. Out of a total of two hundred and twenty-two works, ninety-eight non-members had up to four works selected. Anthony Hatwell had suggested that non-members be allowed to submit four works which had increased the overall submission by a large amount and brought in much needed additional revenue. Forty-six out of seventy-seven members exhibited. In 1961 membership stood at ninety-three and within two years it had fallen to seventy-seven. These were testing and stormy times for the older generation of London Group members. There were written tributes to Frank Dobson and Sir David Low (the well-known cartoonist). Evert Lundquist again topped the price list asking £1,000 for "The Field", Anthony Slinn priced his "Homage to the National Gallery" at £787.10 and Cliff Holden's "The Kiss" at £500. No sizes or media were indicated. Catalogue format was the same as 1961 with an exhibition poster image by Jeffery Camp. The exhibition incurred a loss of £388.5.4 but was covered by a grant from the Arts Council and the President reflected on just how long this safety net would be in place.

Press interest in the 1964 annual was much diminished. John Russell writing in the 'Sunday Times' was, as usual, supportive. 'The Times' critic thought the exhibition proved that the group "shows evidence of still being full of life" and "a cross-section of contemporary work in all its variety". Bettina Wadia of the 'Arts Review' thought that "The Group has really shaken itself up for its fiftieth anniversary show: a more stringent selection and better hanging, among other things, make it more like a representative exhibition of what's going on in London than the clutter of pensionable painting it appeared to be last year." Andrew Forge wrote a full page article for the 'New Statesman' based on the Group's fifty year history and in particular on the importance of Bomberg as an artist and teacher. He draws similarities, in fact, between Bomberg and Coldstream, two tendencies within The London Group at the time. "Both painters seem to paint as if to develop their awareness of what they are painting. It is rather that in the instant of looking at the picture one is involved in a self-contained painting process from which an image accrues." Writing in the 'Jewish Chronicle', Peter Stone communicates some interesting detail in his article "Fifty Years of Freedom". "Although the increased number of galleries in London has reduced the significance of group shows, the London Group this year received more entries from non-members, most of them not affiliated to any gallery, than it has ever had. And it has hung fewer than usual in the hope of raising the standard. Another innovation is to increase to four the number of works each artist may submit and to hang those accepted as a group." If only there were large, affordable exhibition spaces in London in the twenty-first century! There were 1,724 admissions totalling £105.18.9 whilst 841 catalogue sales raised £63.1.6. By comparison, those visiting the Young Contemporaries totalled 3,528 in 19 days.

Twenty-six members gathered in Sainsbury's canteen on Saturday 30th May for the Group's AGM, fourteen sent apologies; notable in that these figures indicated that about half of the total membership was 'engaged'. The President's report on the last exhibition was worrying. Attendances, catalogue sales and sales of work had been steadily declining over the last years. London Group shows attracted on average 1,600 visitors whilst the Young Contemporaries achieved 3,500. Furthermore a letter from the Treasurer had warned of financial difficulties and the meeting voted to increase submission fees from 4/- to 5/- (2/6 for students) and entrance fees from 1/6 to 2/6 (1/3 for students). Later in the AGM the meeting also agreed to raise the annual subscription from 3 to 5 guineas and that Hanging Fees be increased to 30/-. The President then moved to a report on the forthcoming Tate Gallery retrospective. It had been "a close run thing" as he had learned that the Group was to be financially responsible for virtually all the costs of staging the exhibition. Two thousand pounds needed to be found and the Arts Council would only provide £250 of this. Over Christmas Rogers had meetings with representatives from the Calouste Gulbenkian Foundation who eventually agreed to underwrite the exhibition to the sum of £1,500, part grant, part guarantee. "There should be ample money to mount the exhibition decently." Patrick George replaced Anthony Hatwell as Vice President.

"London Group 1914-64, Jubilee Exhibition, Fifty Years of British Art", Tate Gallery, Millbank, 5th July to 16th August 1964. This was probably the most important and auspicious exhibition for The London Group since the Second World War. The catalogue to this exhibition is also an important historical document because it contains two lists. The first is of past and present (to 1964) members of the Group. The second is fifty years of London Group exhibitions from 1914 to 1964 giving dates, venues and totals of works exhibited. One would imagine that this research would be totally accurate as the Tate catalogue would have been put together by Tate exhibition organisers using their own archive resources. The catalogue is copiously illustrated with fifty-nine black and white images. It is strictly divided into convenient chronological units, usually a decade. By 1964 a total of two hundred and eight artists had been elected to The London Group but only one hundred and seven were represented in this exhibition with at least one piece of work. Sickert, for example, was represented by three paintings. The exhibition contained one hundred and fifty-eight exhibits, both painting and sculpture. There were some notable, perhaps iconic images in the Tate show, for example: Bomberg's "In the Hold" (1913-14), Epstien's "Torso from the Rock Drill" (1914), Paul Nash's "We are making a new world" (1917) and Mark Gertler's "Merry-go-round" (1916). There are also some illuminating statements at the beginning of the catalogue. Firstly, an extract from the 'Foreword' written by the President, Claude Rogers: "At a General Meeting the Group accepted the view that the Jubilee Exhibition ought to consist as far as possible of work which had appeared in previous (London Group) exhibitions. It was evident that, with the possible exception of the Royal Academy, no galleries existed in London large enough to accommodate the work of every member past and present. This was our first problem (the second being tracking down work). Selection though invidious and distasteful was clearly a necessity. Indeed, despite the generous gallery space allotted at the Tate it will be obvious that many distinguished artists have had perforce to be left out." Secondly, an extract from an 'Appreciation' written by Andrew Forge: "Advanced artists had to find an outlet, and the form it took had somehow or other to accommodate the diversity of these influences". He then continues citing Bomberg and Pasmore as examples of how artists used The London Group, "Victor Pasmore changed his orientation in the late forties and started to exhibit his first abstract works. It was a matter of necessity to show them, to muster support, to indicate affiliations. The London Group functioned on more than one occasion as a rallying ground for the revival of abstract art here after the war." And perceptively remarks, "There are more ways than one for an artist to escape attention. It is the claim of the London Group that it tries to take account of this fact." Finally, from the 'Historical note' written by Dennis Farr and Alan Bowness, "In the later 'forties it was two publically unpopular tendencies - the new rallying cry around Bomberg and the pioneer abstract artists around Pasmore - that found expression inside the Group exhibitions. Most British artists of consequence have at one time or another been members, and very few indeed have never shown a work at the Group's exhibitions".

The 'Gang of Four', Rogers, Forge, Farr and Bowness had formed, "a small committee to help organise and give shape to the exhibition". The Arts Council gave a grant towards expenses and arranged a tour after the Tate showing in London.

The Tate Gallery
London SW1

Now Tate Britain, but formally known as the Tate Gallery,
it was here in 1964 that The London Group celebrated its Fiftieth Anniversary
with "London Group 1914-64, Jubilee Exhibition, Fifty Years of British Art".
The exhibition was presented chronologically, decade by decade, showing important
pieces of work which had originally been shown in London Group exhibitions.
There were 160 exhibits. The catalogue contained a Foreword, written by President
Claude Rogers, an Appreciation by Andrew Forge and Historical Notes by Dennis
Farr and Alan Bowness.

There is a gap in the Committee Meeting minutes held in the Tate Archive. The
last minuted meeting was on Wednesday, 7th October 1964 at the Slade. At this meeting
there was discussion on the appointment of a Selection Committee and on the election
of new members in 1965. A whiff of change in the wind appears in these 1964 minutes,
"Ken Turner … expressed the view that he felt the Group was not really in touch
with present trends, and that a greater effort should be made to make contact with
the artists following these trends, either by getting them to submit (which he thought
rather doubtful) or by some form of special invitation". Discussion followed and the
minutes were initialled by CR (Claude Rogers). Could this 1964 Committee Meeting
discussion account for 1965's large and varied intake of new members?

1965

US air raids in Vietnam, anti-war protests in US and Europe. Malcolm X is assassinated. India invades Pakistan. Britain enacts the Race Relations Act which prohibited discrimination on the basis of race in public places. Sir Winston Churchill dies.

The new Labour Government spent an additional £665,000 on national arts spending, making a total of £2,815,000. Jenny Lee said she sought, "a gayer more cultivated Britain". The BBC decides against showing the film "The War Game". Kubrick begins filming "2001" and Michael Caine stars as Harry Palmer in "The Ipcress File".

"The New Generation" sculpture exhibition at the **Whitechapel Art Gallery** in 1965 was a seminal exhibition for British sculpture. The exhibitors were teaching colleagues at St Martins School of Art and included Anthony Caro, William Turnbull (1955), David Annesley (1990), Michael Bolus, Philip King, Tim Scott, William Tucker and Isaac Watkin.

John Moores Painting Prize 1965 won by Michael Tyzack with the painting "Alesso B" (Clement Greenberg on the Jury).

London commercial galleries showed Bruce Lacey, Derek Boshier, Vasarely and Peter Blake.

The British Council mounted "London: the New Scene" at the Walker Art Gallery, Minneapolis, exporting the swinging sixties to the USA where the Beatles had stormed America a year earlier.

London Group President: Claude Rogers (1939) followed by Andrew Forge (1960)

Norman Adams, Frank Auerbach, Kit Lewis, Mary Potter and Kenneth Turner are all recorded as leaving in 1965. However, this year also saw the sixties' biggest intake with ten new members, Neville Boden, Geoffrey Harris, Albert Irvin, David Partridge, Edwin Pickett, Paula Rego, Matt Rugg, Michael Sandle, Bernard Schottlander and Rachel Tripp; a more varied intake with female members and sculptors too.

"London Group", Art Federation Galleries, 18th March to 9th April 1965. The Federation of British Artists Ltd. charged The London Group £607.18.10 for hire of the gallery from the Group's fund totalling £1,313.14.4, an increase of £20 on last year. Claude Rogers was President, Patrick George Vice President and the Working Committee consisted of Michael Andrews, Frank Bowling, Andrew Forge, Patrick George, Anthony Gross, Anthony Hatwell, Josef Herman, Gertrude Hermes, Kenneth Martin, Claude Rogers and Ken Turner. There were eighty-one members including four Honorary Members. Of these eighty-one only forty-eight members took part in the 1965 exhibition containing two hundred and nine pieces of work, both painting and sculpture exhibited in four rooms. There were eighty-four non-members exhibiting including Douglas Abercombie, Quentin Blake, Stuart Brisley, a J.B. Flanagan, Peter Greenaway, Tina Keane, Myles Murphy, Gerald Newman, Roy Oxlade, Fabian Peake and John Wonnacott. Roy de Maistre's "Sir Robert Adeane" topped the price list at £1,000, whilst Henryk Gotlib was asking £850, William Townsend and Leon Kossof £750 and Cliff Holden £700. Admission to the exhibition at Suffolk Street was 2/6. This year's exhibition resulted in a profit of £123.7.4. despite attendances and sales being the lowest since 1960. "We were fortunate on this occasion to receive from the Arts Council a grant of £500, an increase of £150 on recent years."

Durrant's Press Cuttings service could only find seven clippings relating to the 1965 annual exhibition, the most significant were printed in 'Arts Review', 'The Times' and 'Jewish Chronicle'. "This year, although they are in evidence, the younger artists do not come over especially strongly. No doubt they are busy in other places. Pieces of polychrome sculpture spring from the ground not far from severely frontal nudes and gentle London landscapes, and all these different ways of looking at the world are placed around like scattered links from a chain that only time can piece together into cohesive strength". So wrote 'The Times' critic. In his article "With it or without it", Peter Stone of the 'Jewish Chronicle' wrote a prescient piece, "Everything shouts at the London Group exhibition at the Art Federation Galleries, saying 'Look! I am with it, with it, with it. Can't you see how with it I am?' Behind screens, around corners, are a few older members with quieter pictures, uneasy, afraid of being square and incapable of being 'with it'. Claude Rogers, the president, does not exhibit." 712 visitors paid 2/6 for entry and 509 paid the reduced rate of 1/3. Catalogue sales totalled 516.

On 3rd May Andrew Forge wrote a long "screed" to Claude Rogers over his concerns for the Group. The recent Tate retrospective had given the Group an opportunity to reflect on its role and Forge asked "What is it now trying to do? What ought it to do and what can it do?". He continued, "You will agree that in the past there have been two reasons for artists to form exhibiting societies. It can be to gain acceptance for a single style which is new or unpopular… or it can be a banding together of all sorts of artists of different tendencies… The incompatibility of the two motives has been plastered over in the Group by the blanket intention of making a 'good' mixed exhibition." Following the recent exhibition "Both the selection and the hanging was fundamentally weak because whatever insights or ideas that there were got lost through sheer compromise. Somehow the philosophy of the Group must be clarified. The exhibition must be both intensive and extensive, exclusive and inclusive." Forge goes on to make a number of suggestions for discussion within the Group, the first being a fixed term for the Presidency of between three to one year/s. He was quick to assure Rogers that this was in no way personal bearing in mind the Group's loyalty to the incumbent President. The Working Committee must be slimmed down to four, President, Vice President and a member each for 'printing and publicity' and 'gallery management'. Forge's proposal for the Selection Committee is quite uncompromising. "The basis of these proposals would be that a member would have at his disposal a given amount of wall and/or floor space. He would say 'I want to show my own work and that of my fellow members A, B and C, plus the non-members' work which I shall select specifically for it'". Finally, on the issue of electing new members, Forge thought that "if somebody wants to join, let him produce three consecutive London Group catalogues with his name in them, thus proving that he is interested and that his work is of an acceptable standard... This system should be linked with Pat's (Patrick George) idea of 5-year membership, perhaps." A meaty document for the President and officers to chew on.

The proposals were so difficult for the Group to digest that the AGM was held in two stages. When Forge's proposals for the hanging of the next exhibition and the election of new members were discussed in the first stage it was realised that "they would cause some Constitutional difficulties." "It was then decided to elect a sub-committee, to discover if the proposals could be met without any alteration to the current Constitution." The committee of Richard Carline, Andrew Forge, Patrick George and Claude Rogers decided that they could be accommodated "without undue strain".

The second stage was held on Saturday, 23rd October with twenty-two members in attendance and twenty apologies, a measure of the importance of this meeting for the future of the Group. The first business was the election of President and Vice President. "The Treasurer announced that the President wished to retire" and John Dobson gave a vote of thanks to the outgoing president Claude Rogers who in turn proposed Andrew Forge for the post, seconded by Brian Robb. "There being no other nominations Andrew Forge was unanimously elected as President." Rogers declined the automatic appointment as Vice President "owing to his own commitments" and Frank Bowling was elected in his place. With Forge as the new President his proposals were discussed by the meeting with Morris Kestelman and Ken Turner making important points. Kestelman wanted assurances that the President would appoint "members for the Selection Committee who had completely different outlooks" and that the committee would change from exhibition to exhibition. Ken Turner's proposal was even more radical than Forge's. Turner proposed a "Group Within A Group" with the intention of making the shows "more livelier" and appointing "a Controller" and a "Vice-Controller". "A great deal would depend on pre-selection and, therefore, submissions as such would be very few in number." The meeting felt that these ideas "could not be adopted without due notice of them being given on the agenda." Forge's proposals were then fully voted in by the AGM.

1966

Mao Zedong initiates the Great Proletarian Cultural Revolution in China, sweeping away anything to do with the West, capitalism, religion and tradition. The Black Panthers movement is established in the US. The Labour Party calls a General Election under Harold Wilson and wins an increased majority. Edward Heath led the Conservative campaign, Jo Grimond the Liberal's. There is a Seaman's strike, Wages and Prices freeze, cut-backs in public sector spending and currency speculation. England beat West Germany 4-2 after extra time at Wembley in the FIFA World Cup Final.

Tate Gallery June, Marcel Duchamp retrospective.
Whitechapel Art Gallery Bryan Kneale (1987) sculpture, Richard Smith retrospective and another "The New Generation" exhibition.
Venice Biennale the UK representatives were Richard Smith, Robyn Denny, Anthony Caro, Harold Cohen and Bernard Cohen.
August 10th, **"Chew and Still"** event by John Latham and Barry Flanagan.
September, **"The Destruction in Art Symposium"** opens at the Africa Centre and the Jeanetta Cochrane Theatre organised by Gustave Metzger. DIAS was composed of a number of performance/installation/action artists.
Indica Gallery a Yoko Ono exhibition where she first met John Lennon.
Individual exhibitions at various venues from Gustave Metzger, Jim Dine ("Tool Box" prints and collages), Brian Wall (1962), John Latham, Mark Boyle, John Plumb, Jim Dine/Eduardo Paolozzi, Barry Flanagan, Maurice Agis and Peter Jones "Space Place" installation. Some smaller commercial galleries close due to the economic downturn.
January, Andrew Forge interviews Anthony Caro for 'Studio International'.
"Biennials and Beyond – Exhibitions That Made Art History 1962 - 2002" Jewish Museum, New York, "Primary Structures".

London Group President: Andrew Forge (1960)

No new members were elected this year and no London Group Annual Exhibition took place either (see Forge's preface to the 1967 exhibition: "It is two years since the last London Group exhibition"). The Group experienced a major body blow this year as described by Andrew Forge in the minutes of the 1966 AGM held on the 11th June in Sainsbury's Headquarters Canteen in Blackfriars. Sainsbury's had provided the Group for many years with administrative support in the form of Mr. Farrell as the Secretary, Mr. Nash as the Treasurer and Miss Truss who took "extraordinarily accurate notes at Group meetings". Andrew Forge reported, "However, Robert Sainsbury now feels that for a variety of reasons this help can no longer continue: Mr Nash has moved to a new post within Sainsbury's which allows him very little time for anything else. Therefore, as he is no longer personally responsible to Robert Sainsbury our relationship with his firm must be wound up; this will be the last meeting we can hold on these premises and also the last meeting at which Mr Nash will be functioning as our Treasurer". A long discussion ensued as to how the Group could now organise itself. Worst of all, Sainsbury's had provided venues and administration for free and the Group were now faced with having to pay for these services, a major drain on limited finances. However, by the end of the meeting a Mrs Maria Snow was offered the temporary post of Secretary at the princely sum of 150 guineas per annum. She accepted. Another major change had also occurred recently in the resignation of Claude Rogers as President after serving a record fifteen years. Andrew Forge, an unknown quantity, was elected by the Group to replace him. A number of experienced members left the Group at this time too, fearing radical change.

Finance was relatively healthy. The financial report as of the 31st January 1966 showed a profit of £358. 16s. 7d (it does not say what this was the profit from) and a balance of £694. 0s. 11d. Later, with the 1967 sub..s paid in, the Group had "in the region of £1,000". However, in January 1966 the Group still had free administrative support. The FBA was now charging a rent of £125 a week, £600 a month. There then followed an interesting discussion on the Federation of British Artists (FBA). Maurice Bradshaw, who ran the FBA and the Art Exhibitions Bureau, had been talking to Forge about a possible merger, a 'super group'. Forge, and many other members especially Dorothy Mead, were very suspicious of Bradshaw's intentions and were fearful of losing London Group autonomy and independence in a merger. To many it looked as though Bradshaw "was trying to squeeze the Group out" of its traditional annual slot at the FBA if it did not agree to the merger. Claude Rogers had been talking to the ICA (but they were not interested) whilst Forge wanted to approach the Arts Council to discuss the Group's difficulties. At this meeting the Group did finally agree to an offer of a booking at the Royal Institute Galleries at 195 Piccadilly for an exhibition in January 1967, the first time in ten years that they had not rented the FBA Galleries.

With all these changes, difficulties and new proposals perhaps there was some excuse for the Group not being able to organise an annual open submission exhibition in 1966.

1967

June 5th, the Six Day War begins, Israel seizes Middle East lands. The first heart transplant takes place. San Francisco's 'Summer of Love' is enjoyed by the Hippy community. In the UK in February, gallery owner Robert Fraser, Mick Jagger and Keith Richards are arrested for possession of drugs. In November "the pound in your pocket" is devalued by 14.3%, the Abortion Act is passed and colour television transmissions begin.

Whitechapel Art Gallery Tim Scott followed by Gertrude Hermes (1935) sculpture exhibitions. John Hoyland painting exhibition. This year the Whitechapel held its first "East London Open" exhibition, the first in what was to be the Gallery's thirty year commitment to open submission exhibitions showcasing artists living and working in East London.
John Moores Painting Prize 1967 won by David Hockney (1963) with the painting "Peter getting out of Nick's pool".
Artist's Placement Group (APG) founded by John Latham to place artists in industry.
February, Mark Boyle projects a light show at a Soft Machine gig. Archigram's exhibition "Beyond Architecture" opens.
March, The Beatles' "Sergeant Pepper" album is released with a cover collaged by Peter Blake and Michael Cooper.
November, writing in 'Studio International' Norbert Lynton attacks performance and event art forms.
Individual exhibitions in London include Liliane Lijn, Mark Lancaster, Bernard Cohen (White Paintings) and Anthony Caro.

London Group President: Andrew Forge (1960)

A second year with no new members elected. Neither is there a record of any Annual General Meeting held this year.

"London Group '67", Royal Institute Galleries, 195, Piccadilly (right opposite the Royal Academy), 9th February to 3rd March 1967. The Royal Institute Galleries received two payments of £500 and £609.5.8, £1109.5.8 in total, for hire of the galleries, a huge increase on the 1965 hire fee by the FBA of £607.18.0. The total costs of the 1967 exhibition were £1915.18.8 with an income of £960.19.0 from admissions, catalogue sales, sale commission and fees, making a loss of £954.19.8. In November 1967 the Group was overdrawn by £235.16.5 for the second time in four years. Andrew Forge was President, Frank Bowling was Vice President and Raymond Coxon was Treasurer. Committee Members were Frank Bowling, Edward Bullmore, Raymond Coxon, Anthony Eyton, Andrew Forge, Patrick George, Geoffrey Harris, Cliff Holden, Morris

Kestleman and Claude Rogers. This year there were seventy-five members recorded in the catalogue. Andrew Forge, the newly elected President, wrote the following, "It is two years since the last London Group exhibition. Much has happened since. Claude Rogers who was our President for fifteen years found that he was too busy to carry on; Sainsbury's who had given us endless secretarial help for years had to call a halt; we found ourselves in a new gallery." There was an experimental arrangement of the exhibition with four rooms selected and hung by four members (although only three rooms are listed in the catalogue) who were Edward Bullmore, Anthony Eyton, Patrick George and Cliff Holden. The three latter were all figurative painters. Tributes were paid to Bernard Adeney (a founder member), Henryk Gotlib and Mr E.A. Farrell, "an old friend of the Group". There were two hundred and three exhibits, exhibiting but non-members were not identified. Sculpture was arranged by Geoffrey Harris, eleven pieces in Room 1 and thirty pieces in Room 2. Members and non-members were able to exhibit more than one piece of work. According to an annotated catalogue provided by Suzan Swale, which appears to have been the 'desk copy', ten pieces of work were sold totalling about £1,600. Top price (unsold) was Evert Lundquist's "Model" at 1,500 gns, Michael Kenny's sculpture at £800 and Geoffrey Harris's sculpture at £725. The majority of prices were between £50 and £250. The Arts Council purchased four paintings from Cliff Holden, William Gear, Andrew Forge and Euan Uglow for a total of £765.17.6. (The London Group charged 20% commission) and the Contemporary Arts Society based at the Tate Gallery purchased work by Brian Robb and Wendy Pasmore whilst Barry Guntripp, Julian Heaton-Cooper, Buchannan, Paraskos and George made private sales. The catalogue was a triple folded Imperial sheet with black '60s' typography.

There were eleven reviews of the exhibition found by Durrant's, including pieces from John Russell in 'The Sunday Times', Guy Brett in 'The Times', Paul Overy in 'The Listener' and Bruce Laughton in 'Arts Review' which printed a list of every exhibitor. John Russell writes, "In principle, the London Group is an association of friends who like to show together. It has a tradition, also, of hospitality to non-members, and especially to non-members who are casualties of current fashion… But this year's show does us all a service. Few exhibitions in recent years have offered a greater variety of work; in both painting and sculpture, contributors have gone their own way in the belief that art is one thing and impersonation quite another." He picks out the Beaux Arts Gallery artists ("several have not had a show since the Beaux Arts Gallery closed"), the Bomberg/Lundquist faction and the, "straightforward figurative paintings of an educated kind by Claude Rogers, Patrick George, Anthony Eyton and Edward Wolfe". Guy Brett thought that "… the general standard is low. There are no exceptionally good paintings to lift the Group's chin up, and the large amount of work by younger artists, on the whole, gives the impression of having been thrown out rather casually. It could be that while older painters have nurtured and sustained minor talents in this atmosphere, young artists have opportunities elsewhere. One might say, in fact, that what is coming out strongly in the galleries at any time will come out weakly in the London Group and exhibitions like it." Paul Overy commented, "A new method of selection has been employed for the London Group's current exhibition… Four members of the committee were responsible for choosing four sections of the exhibition; the remainder was selected jointly. This has resulted in coherence within the individual sections and a welcome variety over the show as a whole, including work as different as that of the Bomberg painters and that of art students similar to that shown at the 'Young Contemporaries'." Bruce Laughton continues with this theme, "One of the most lively exhibitions that the London Group have put on for several years. Instead of the usual jumble apparently selected by a bingo system, a healthy measure of autocracy has been introduced by having individual members to select and hang certain walls." Laughton records that the four walls were selected by Patrick George, Cliff Holden, the President Andrew Forge and Anthony Eyton whilst the sculpture was chosen by Geoffrey Harris. Keith Sutton, writing in 'Galleries', was of the opinion that, "… if the London Group didn't exist we might have to invent one. And that was not true ten years ago… But the real plea, and a justifiable one if the rest of the group really believe in what its President says, is directed towards artists of quality and mettle to take the London Group seriously again".

The Royal Institute Galleries
195 Piccadilly, London W1

Originally the home of the Royal Institute of Painters in Watercolour, some of whom gaze out onto traffic-choked Piccadilly almost opposite the Royal Academy.
The cavernous galleries themselves were on the upper floors with the entrance to the left of the building. The London Group organised two Annual Open Submission Exhibitions here in 1967 and 1968 and fell heavily into debt, so much so that in 1969 no annual exhibition could be mounted at all.

1968

The Tet offensive explodes in Vietnam. The USSR invades Czechoslovakia. Martin Luther King is assassinated. Student protests in Paris. The Summer Olympic Games are held in Mexico City. "I'm backing Britain" campaign is launched in the UK to support the nation's morale. In Grosvenor Square there are anti-US demonstrations outside the US Embassy on October 27th. The musical "Hair" opens in London. Malcolm McDowell appears in Lindsay Anderson's "If…".

Artists Information Registry (AIR) formed by Peter Sedgley in January.

In February **Space Provision Artistic Cultural and Educational (SPACE)** is proposed by Sedgley and others. In May St. Katherine's Docks are identified as the first SPACE studio site.

Tate Gallery March, César 'happening' disrupted by Stuart Brisley and Bill Culbert.

"The Obsessive Image" was the opening exhibition at the **Institute of Contemporary Arts (ICA)** at Carlton House Terrace from 10th April to 29th May 1968. The exhibition was organised by Mario Amaya which set the international flavour of the exhibition. There was a strong international presence in the exhibition, including Jean Arp, Balthus, de Kooning, Dine, Dubuffet, Ernst, Giacometti, Klein, Lichtenstein, Magritte, Matta, Miró, Oldenburg, Picasso, Warhol and Wesselmann. Representing Great Britain were Bacon, Blake, Caulfield, Hamilton, Allen Jones, (Bruce) Lacey, (Raymond) Mason, Paolozzi, Phillips, Self and Tilson. There were a number of present and past members of The London Group taking part too, Frank Bowling (1963 and re-elected 2002), David Hockney (1963), F. E. McWilliam (1949), Henry Moore (1930) and Graham Sutherland (1937). At the time the President of the ICA was Sir Herbert Read, Director Michael Kustow, Deputy Director Julie Lawson and Assistant Director Jasia Reichardt. There was also a Council chaired by Sir Roland Penrose and including Dorothy Morland as Deputy Chairman, Leonie Cohn, Theo Crosby, Stephen Plaistow, John Tandy and Michael White.

May 28th, picking up on student protest in Paris, art students at **Hornsey School of Art** occupy their buildings following a 'teach-in' on art education. Other art schools are disrupted as students "come out in sympathy".

Venice Biennale June, Bridget Riley wins first prize for painting. Philip King was another representative. Riots close the event early.

The Hayward Gallery, administered by the Arts Council of Great Britain, opens on London's South Bank with its first show, a Matisse exhibition, on July 22nd.

ICA Jasia Reichardt curates "Cybernetic Serendipity".

Mark Boyle tours America with Jimi Hendrix projecting light shows. Later in the year

Boyle begins the "World Series" identifying sites around the globe by throwing darts at a map.

"Biennials and Beyond – Exhibitions That Made Art History 1962 - 2002"
Amalfi town, Arsenale and surrounding area, "Arte Povera + Azioni Povere".

London Group President: Andrew Forge (1960)

The Annual General Meeting took place on July 13th at the Royal Institute Galleries attended by fifteen members. The President reported that the 1967 exhibition "had paid for itself with the exception of the gallery rent". In fact a loss of £1,005.15.3 had been made and "the President expressed a hope that the Arts Council would continue with (financial) help". Andrew Forge was re-elected as President, Dorothy Mead was Vice President, Valentine Ellis Treasurer and Margaret Courtney as Secretary. A further indication of hard times was that Miss Courtney was to be asked "to accept a temporary arrangement whereby she would be paid by the hour for her work as Secretary, rather than an all-over retainer". Albert Irvin, Nevil (sic) Boden, Denis (sic) Creffield, Geoffrey Harris and Cliff Holden were elected to the Working Committee. It is very noticeable how the quality and detail of minutes of meetings had declined over the last years. Mr Fred Nash had produced thirty page minutes in great detail, but now he had retired. The Group thanked Mr. Nash for his years of administrative support by offering him the choice of any work in the 1967 exhibition. Nash chose a landscape by André Bicat "who had kindly agreed to let the Group buy this work over a period of time". Finally "It was agreed that it was a matter of urgency to open the Group to new members and an election was arranged for the 26th October". A healthy seven new members, all male, were elected at some time this year. They were Basil Beattie, Brian Fielding, Michael Kenny, Stephen Lobb, Barry Martin, Stass Paraskos and Arthur Wilson. Records show that Alan Green and Margot Perryman had been invited to join but had probably declined.

"London Group '68", Royal Institute Galleries, 195 Piccadilly, 12th November to 28th November 1968. The Galleries charged £1470.0.0. for the hire of the space. It should be remembered that the Group was in financial difficulties at this time and this exhibition was largely covered with a grant of £1,000 from the Arts Council and a generous loan of £1,000 from Andrew Forge. The exhibition itself made a deficit of £456. Four rooms were used to exhibit the work, the North Room, West Room, Long Room and Hallway. There were one hundred and eighty-two exhibits with both painting and sculpture being shown together in all four rooms. Of the total number of works, seventy-five of them were exhibited by thirty-four members (up to three each) whilst one hundred and seven works were shown by seventy non-members. No media or sizes were given, but the titles indicate a mixture of figurative and abstract work.

The Foreword in the catalogue, written by A.F., states, "Last year, hoping to achieve a sharper and more committed presentation, we introduced a system by which individual members took responsibility for particular sections of the exhibition. This year we have repeated the experiment, the artists concerned being Dennis Creffield, who selected and hung the long wall of the West Room, Albert Irvin who did half the Long Room and Neville Boden who did the other half, as well as the sculpture. The rest of the exhibition was undertaken by the Vice President and the President". Non-members exhibiting included Raymond Atkins, John Bellany, Peter Donnelly (4), John Hubbard, Sonia Lawson, Mali Morris, Myles Murphy, Ian Stephenson, Patrick Symons, Susan Tebby, Daphne Todd and Laetitia Yhap. Evert Lundquist asked the top price of £2,500 for "The Arm", but average prices were between £100 and £300. The catalogue itself was a small, six-paged 'roneod' publication with an image by Kenneth Martin on the cover. Entrance with a catalogue cost two shillings and sixpence, half a crown in old money. The exhibition was advertised with a joint poster by Dorothy Mead and Cliff Holden.

1969

Nixon succeeds Johnson as US President. My Lai massacre in Vietnam. Pompidou replaces de Gaulle as French President. The Boeing 747 (Jumbo) makes its maiden flight and in France 'Concorde' flies for the first time. 20th July, American Neil Armstrong becomes the first man to set fov Apple's roof, London and later release "Abbey Road". John and Yoko's "Bed-in" in Amsterdam. "Midnight Cowboy" and "Butch Cassidy and the Sundance Kid" released. Rupert Murdoch purchases "The News of the World". "Monty Python's Flying Circus" screened on BBC One. Ken Loach directs "Kes".

May 1969 saw the first issue of the **Art Language** magazine, the two most important founder members being Terry Atkinson and Michael Baldwin, neither of whom were London Group members. As with many other post-war art movements the artists involved met whilst studying or teaching in art schools, in this case Lanchester Polytechnic (Coventry) in 1966. Other members were David Bainbridge, Ian Burn, Charles Harrison, Harold Hurrell and Mel Ramsden.

May, John Hoyland at **Waddingtons**.

June, **Camden Arts Centre**, an exhibition entitled "Environmental Reversals" including performances by Stuart Brisley.

In August at the **ICA** an important exhibition was put together by Michael Craig-Martin, "When Attitudes Become Form", considered by many to be the first Conceptual Art exhibition in the UK.

1969 also saw joint winners of the **John Moores Painting Prize**, Richard Hamilton with the painting, "Toaster" and Mary Martin (1959) with the construction "Cross".

The Young Contemporaries before 1969 these exhibitions of student work had been selected by artists and art specialists. This year students took over selection, as they also did in the "controversial" exhibition of 1970 at the Royal Academy. 1970 was the last Young Contemporaries until it was revived in 1974.

Stephen Willats "Man from 21st Century" project.

"Biennials and Beyond – Exhibitions That Made Art History 1962 - 2002"

44 East 52nd Street, New York, "January 5-31, 1969" (Conceptual Art).

Kunsthalle, Bern, "Live in Your Head. When Attitudes become Form: Works–Concepts–Situations–Information".

Seattle Art Museum Pavilion and surrounding area "557,087" (Conceptual Art).

London Group President: Andrew Forge (1960)

No new members were elected this year and there is no record of any catalogue related to an annual exhibition. An entry in the Treasurer's Record Book for this year clearly states, "No Exhibition", a low point in the Group's history.

Even so, the Group was organised enough to reprint its Constitution, with some ominous amendments, notably Rule 15 'Dissolution', "The Group may be dissolved by a resolution duly passed by not less than two-thirds of the members present at a General Meeting. Notice of the proposal to dissolve must be sent to all members at least twenty-one days in advance of the meeting. The quorum at such a meeting must be not less than one-third of the total membership of the Group." Was the clarification of Rule 15 the officers trying to scare members into active support, or was it really laying down the 'legal' pathway to extinction? Rule 14 'Constitution' safeguarded the constitution by requiring a similar two-thirds majority of members present at a twenty-one days' notice meeting. Rule 13 'Finance' had a number of notable sections, "In the event of the Group being dissolved, any assets remaining after all liabilities have been discharged, shall be dispersed in accordance with the wishes of the members resolved at the final General Meeting", and, "No expenditure shall be incurred without the previous approval of the Treasurer." There are two other clauses of special interest in the 1969 Constitution. Under rule 11(e), "Special works may be invited for inclusion in the exhibition, subject to the discretion of the Working Committee, and in exceptional circumstances additional work by members may be invited." And under rule 12(f), "If two-thirds of the members of the Selection Committee are in favour of a work, it shall be accepted, if half are in favour, it will be hung at the discretion of the Working Committee, and if less than half are in favour, it shall be rejected." Previously works only needed half of the members of the Selection Committee to be accepted. Even though the Group was in dire straits, standards were not sacrificed.

Andrew Forge wrote to Sir Thomas Monnington, President of the Royal Academy on the 9th June 1969, "Having lost the support of Sainsbury we have got ourselves into very rough water". Sainsbury's had provided secretarial support for the Group, but now this valuable resource had been withdrawn. Forge wanted to meet Sir Thomas to ask for the support of the historical enemy to provide reasonably priced exhibition space in the future. As will be seen, the Royal Academy saved The London Group by leasing the Diploma Galleries to the Group in the early seventies.

The Group's AGM was held on 28th June at the RI Galleries. Eighteen members heard the President's Report; "The exhibition held in the R.I. Gallery in November 1968 had been considered successful from the point of view of appearance but had been disastrous financially". All attempts at reducing costs had been deployed, printing material in Art Schools, not hiring Bourlet's to handle the work and reducing advertising. Rent had vastly increased from £1,000 to £1,470. It was pointed out that members were subsidising non-members instead of the other way round. The next item was "Discussion re. the future of the Group" - "it became clear at the time of the last exhibition that the London Group could no longer continue along the same lines as in the past." Forge had put forward an idea to the Arts Council that its new Hayward Gallery could be a permanent home for The London Group annual exhibition, but after initial interest in the idea the Arts Council would not accept the current membership structure arguing for renewed membership each year. "It would certainly mean the dissolution of The London Group as we know it." Forge's discussions with the Royal Academy had been "warm" and the RA wished to "rediscover the association that they had during the last war." The Camden Arts Centre was considered as a "rear-guard action" but "Mr Carey said he did not want anything to do with The London Group as he thought it was atrocious, when asked why, he said it was because of its members." Bert Irvin suggested a link with the I.C.A., another suggestion was to hand everything over to Maurice Bradshaw, "including our accounts". By the end of the extensive discussion it was decided to support the President's initiative at the Royal Academy, for one experimental year at least. Unfortunately the membership records "were in a mess" and needed to be sorted out. Only thirteen members had replied to a questionnaire which had been sent out.

A letter to Andrew Forge from The London Group Treasurer, Valentine Ellis dated 14th November 1969 stated, "As promised on the telephone this morning, I am enclosing a cheque for £1,000 in your favour in repayment of your loan to the London Group (sic). Another £250 was paid into the London Group account at Drummonds, following an Arts Council grant". Andrew Forge was fighting hard to keep The London Group afloat. Without his generosity and Arts Council grants the Group could easily have collapsed at the end of this decade.

Entry from the Treasurer's Record Book 1969
Copied from The London Group Income Record Book from 1953 to 1969. This is the last entry in the book before another book was started and records the loan from Andrew Forge and the grant from the Arts Council which ensured the Group's survival.

236

The 1970's

Richard Cork tried to define and identify the huge proliferation of new directions in the 1970s. Cork listed Conceptual Art, Post-minimalism, Land Art, Process Art, Theoretical Art, Arte Povera, Neo-Dada, Body Art, Post-Object Art, Impossible Art, Information Art, Art-as-Idea, Language Art and Dematerialised Art. This decade was said to be "The bad-taste decade" (terrible fashion, Abba songs and awful television programmes) and was punctuated by increasing oil prices with many western economies in decline followed by social and political disquiet (IRA bombs, unemployment, industrial unrest and the three-day week in the UK).

Post Painterly Abstraction a number of the most influential painters were John Hoyland, Basil Beattie (1968), Bert Irvin (1965), Alan Gouk, Fred Pollock, John Copnall (1988), and Brian Fielding (1968). There were a healthy number of painters in The London Group from a Post Painterly Abstraction tendency.

Minimalism in the hands of Bob Law, Peter Joseph, Keith Milow, Edwina Leapman and Alan Charlton. The British Minimalists had been influenced by American Minimalism, including Carl Andre, Dan Flavin, Don Judd, Robert Morris and Frank Stella many seen in the Tate Gallery exhibition "The Art of the Real" in 1969.

"New Image" painting neo-expressionism from Steven Campbell and Adrian Wiszniewski. This resurgence of interest in the sub-conscious image brought about a reappraisal of such artists as Paula Rego (1965), Ken Kiff and John Bellany (1973), a Vice President of The London Group.

In sculpture Barry Flanagan, Gilbert & George (the living sculptures), Richard Long and Bruce McLean reacted against The New Generation sculptors, Anthony Caro and Philip King, who were centred on St Martins, none of whom appear in London Group membership records.

Performance Art the first performances took place, most notable were John Fox's "Welfare State", Cosey Fanni Tutti & Genesis P. Orridge and Stuart Brisley.

Gilbert and George met at St. Martins School of Art when they were Gilbert Proesch and George Passmore. Their 'living sculpture' formula was probably in reaction to The New Generation sculptors who had been influential within St. Martins' sculpture department.

Land Art Richard Long, Hamish Fulton.

In 1970 the Arts Council opened the **Serpentine Gallery** in disused tearooms in Kensington Gardens, Central London. The initial role of the gallery was showcase the work of young artists, exposing it to as wide a cross-section of the public as possible. Each year they were invited to submit slides of their work including painting, sculpture, prints, photography, video, installation and performance. Hundreds of applications were received each year and the Arts Council invited established figures in the art world to choose an exhibition from this open submission. The shows were known as the **Serpentine Summer Shows** (the gallery could only be opened during the warmer weather as there was no heating in the building) and gave a significant opportunity to hundreds of artists during this decade. The Serpentine experience was similar to The London Group's open submission process, i.e. selection, presenting, cataloguing and advertising an exhibition in a London public space.

Art Spectrum series, exhibitions of contemporary art organised across the country by the Arts Council of Great Britain and local Arts Associations. In London during August 1971, the Greater London Arts Association organised the local Arts Spectrum London in Alexandra Palace. The GLAA Visual Arts Panel was chaired by Tim Hilton and included Andrew Forge (1960), Peter Sedgley, David Thompson and Peter Townsend. Selectors for Alexandra Palace were Stuart Brisley, John Dunbar, Annely Juda, Jane Morris and Victor Musgrave. Exhibitors who were members of, or were to be members of, The London Group included Philippa Beale (1977), Basil Beattie (1968), John Copnall (1988), David Gluck (1978), David Hockney (1963), Albert Irvin (1965), Stephen Lobb (1968), Barry Martin (1968), Victor Pasmore (1934), Bernard Schottlander (1965), Wendy Taylor (2004), David Whitaker (1990) and Arthur Wilson (1968).

Stockwell Depot Jennifer Durrant, David Evison, Katherine Gili and Peter Hide.

Greenwich Studios Jeff Lowe (2010), Mali Morris, Clyde Hopkins, Geoff Rigden, Marilyn Hallam and Jeff Dellow (2004).

ACME was formed in 1972 to provide affordable studio and living space for artists living and working in London.

Matts Gallery was opened by Robin Klassnik (1981).

Artscribe magazine first issue in 1976. Editor James Faure Walker (2000).

The Artists Union, an organisation to protect and speak for artists rights was formed. As artists began to organise events such as Open Studios for themselves, the attraction of submitting to The London Group understandably began to decline and one of its roles was undermined.

Tate Modern Time Line 1970-80 'Individuals' Daniel Buren, Gordon Matta-Clark, Adrian Piper and Carlee Schneeman. Alighiero and Boetti. 'Conceptual Art' by Art and Language, Michael Craig-Martin, Hans Haacke, Om Kawara, Bruce Nauman and Lawrence Weiner. 'Feminism' with Lynda Benglis, Judy Chicago, Guerilla Girls, Mary Kelly, Barbara Kruger, Marthe Rosler and Hannah Wilke. 'Body Art' from Chris Burden, Bob Flanagan, Rebecca Horn, Ama Mendieta and Gina Pane. 'Performance Art' by Bas Jan Ader, Vito Accomci, Laurie Anderson, Gilbert and George, Gutai Group, Joan Jonas, Yayoi Kusama and Bruce McLean. 'Conceptual Photography' including Victor

Burgin, Dan Graham, Ed Ruscha and Cindy Sherman. 'Photo-Realism' by Chuck Close, Richard Estes and Malcolm Morley. And finally, Paul McCarthy.

Membership card from the Artists Union 1972-73

The image has not been reversed in the printing. The type reverse was part of the card design. There were many left of centre initiatives to support the creative art worker in this decade, Artists Placement Group (APG) for example. A Conservative government had replaced a Labour administration in 1970, and 1972 had seen a Miners Strike in the UK, a National Front march, opposed by anti-fascist protesters, through Lewisham and Enoch Powell's inflammatory speeches.

1970

The 'Space Race' continues as the USSR lands an unmanned spacecraft on the Moon whilst the USA continues with the manned Apollo landings. My Lai massacre in Vietnam. Anti-government demonstrations in Poland. Allende is elected socialist president in Chile. President Nasser of Egypt dies. The age of majority is lowered to 18 in UK. Equal Pay Act passed. There is a surprise result in a UK General Election as Ted Heath's Conservatives replace Wilson's Labour to form the Government (Jeremy Thorpe was the Liberal Leader). Floppy discs were invented. Germaine Greer publishes "The Female Eunuch" and Jenny Agutter stars in "The Railway Children".

Whitechapel Art Gallery David Hockney (1963) exhibition.
Serpentine Gallery the Serpentine's first Season opened with an exhibition of student work from Chelsea, Manchester and Birmingham Colleges of Art. Barry Martin (1968) and David Whitaker (1990) were two young artists out of twenty-three selected artists shown in five exhibitions.
"Biennials and Beyond – Exhibitions That Made Art History 1962 - 2002" The Museum of Modern Art, New York, "Information".

London Group President: Andrew Forge (1960)

No new members were elected this year.

"London Group Member's Choice Exhibition", Royal Academy Diploma Galleries, 1st March to 1st May 1970. Andrew Forge was recorded in the catalogue as the President and Dorothy Mead, Vice President. Committee members were Neville Boden, Karen Jonzen, Michael Kenny, Barry Martin and Ed Tillotson (a non-member sculptor). There were fifty-four members indicated in the catalogue and ninety-three exhibits. Twenty-nine members showed fifty works and thirty-three non-members showed forty-three works. The intention of the "Member's Choice Exhibition" had been for each member to exhibit two works and to invite for exhibition a further two works by non-member artists. Prices were printed in the catalogue, top price being Michael Harrison's, "Entrance to the Temple of Heaven" at £800, but many works were on sale for under £100 and sales were "very healthy". Neville Boden sold a piece to the Tate, an American collector, Dr. Dorfman, bought eleven works and Theo Crosby purchased seven. Sizes and media were not indicated in the catalogue. Bearing in mind The London Group's historical relationship with the Royal Academy, Andrew Forge's preface was grudgingly thankful for the use of the Diploma Galleries. There were appreciations written for John Dodgson and Mary Martin who had died in the past year. The Royal Academy had charged The London Group £750 for hire of the space, a much better deal than the £1,470 charged by the Royal Institute Galleries in 1968 and the RA exhibition made a surplus of £132, no doubt helped by the award of a £500 grant from the Arts Council, as opposed to the 1968 £456 deficit. The "probable" number of visitors was 3,000. "Miss Maxine Molyneux (of the Royal Academy) had helped with public relations and the show had received twenty-two notices, including one on TV and two on radio."

An Extraordinary General Meeting of The London Group was held in the RA Diploma Galleries during the Member's Choice Exhibition. Twenty-four members were in attendance to hear what the President had in mind. Despite the misgivings of some members the exhibition at the Royal Academy had been "successful in as far as sales, attendance and press coverage were all well up on the last few years." Forge was concerned that the Group could not now afford to organise open exhibitions and that he had called this extraordinary meeting to discuss some ideas before action had to be taken at the forthcoming AGM. Four possible courses of action were tabled; to continue and develop relationships with the R.A., to re-open negotiations with Maurice Bradshaw at Carlton House Terrace, to search elsewhere for exhibition opportunities (for example at the Whitechapel), or to consider a proposal from Adrian Heath "for a joint approach by the A.I.A. (of which he was President) and the London Group to the Arts Council for funds to launch an artist's co-operative gallery, giving permanent exhibition space which could be available to members individually. This scheme would involve the dissolution of both the founding bodies, and the establishment of a new membership." "Further consideration was now given to the various proposals" and the meeting decided to pursue the first option of the four. Item two in the minutes concerned the Presidency. "The President explained that he did not wish to continue in office for reasons that were partly personal and partly because he did not think that it was a healthy thing for the Group to become identified with particular individuals." Forge wished to warn membership in advance of the AGM and "Further discussion of an exhortatory nature was ruled out of order." Item three proposed ten new members for election to the Group at the AGM. However, "A date was fixed for the A.G.M. on 9th June. N.B. This was subsequently cancelled at the request of the President."

1971

Nixon resumes the bombing of Vietnam. China joins the United Nations. Russia launches the first Salyut space station. The UK joins the European Union. Internment without trial in Northern Ireland. An IRA bomb explodes at the Post Office Tower, London. The Open University begins in the UK, the 'Oz' Obscenity Trial takes place and video cameras are introduced. Kubrik's "Clockwork Orange" is released with a visceral performance by Malcom McDowell. Equally bloody, Michael Caine in "Get Carter".

Hayward Gallery an exhibition of Bridget Riley's Op Art paintings.
Whitechapel Art Gallery "East London Open" exhibition. The second in the open submission initiative. Also an exhibition by Mary Martin (1959) and Kenneth Martin (1949).
Summer Shows 1971 Serpentine Gallery Seven Summer Shows of young artists work selected by the Serpentine Committee of Professor Lawrence Gowing (1940/43), Professor Kenneth Rowntree and Edward Lucie-Smith. Richard 'Rick' Oginz (1975) was one of forty-six young artists selected who were working with inflatables, photography, prints, sculpture and painting.
Manhattan, New York "The Singing Sculpture" performed by Gilbert & George, their "breakthrough" exhibition.
"Biennials and Beyond – Exhibitions That Made Art History 1962 - 2002" Sonsbeek Park, Arnhem, and sites around the Nertherlands, "Sonsbeek 71".

London Group President: Andrew Forge (1960) followed by Dorothy Mead (1960)

This year the Presidency passed from Andrew Forge to Dorothy Mead, the first female President of The London Group. Vice President was Andrew Forge and the Working Party was Neville Boden, Brian Fielding, Alan Green, Albert Irvin, Morris Kestelman and Euan Uglow. The list at the back of the 1971 catalogue records fifty-eight members. Anne Buchanan, Julian Cooper, Peter Creswell, Michael Harrison and Laetitia Yhap were elected as new members.

The Slade School was the venue for this year's A.G.M. on 11th February. Twenty-seven members were recorded as being in attendance in the minutes. After a report on the success of the 1970 exhibition and the acceptance of the accounts, the meeting moved to the election of a new President. Dennis Creffield proposed Dorothy Mead and Anthony Green proposed Patrick George but Mead was elected. The new President then led discussion on the format of the forthcoming exhibition, numbers of works, sizes, student involvement and the ratio of non-member to member works exhibited. Finally, under A.O.B., "Stephen Lobb said that he thought that The London Group should make some statement as a professional body in opposition to the Government's introduction of entrance charges in National Museums. Members expressed their agreement with this idea."

"London Group 1971, Member's Choice Exhibition" at the Royal Academy Diploma Galleries from 18th March to 18th April 1971, the Royal Academy again charging a reasonable £750 for hire of the galleries. However, the exhibition made a deficit of £1017 (reduced to £517 by an Arts Council 'guarantee'), making only £661 from hanging fees, admissions, catalogue sales and commission. Apart from the £750 Gallery Rent, £312 was spent on advertising and publicity, £165 on the catalogue and £153 on Gallery Attendants' wages. Total costs were £1,678. It was a small exhibition with only eighty exhibits in total, ten of which were 'sculpture'. Some members exhibited two pieces, but sizes and media were not given in the catalogue. The preface was written by Dorothy Mead. "The second exhibition of the London Group at Burlington House takes much the same form as last year, as the limited space of the Diploma Gallery makes it necessary for us to modify our usual plans for an open exhibition. I regret this limitation but suggest that it is offset by the very specific value of the non-member's work here, each one of which has been sponsored by an individual member of the group. We do hope to find ways of promoting a large open exhibition as a regular event in the future." Notable non-members sponsored by members were Colin Cina, Paul Gopal-Chowdhury and Roy Oxlade, although which member sponsored whom is not recorded. Prices were between £100 to £200 with Craigie Aitchison asking the top price of £800 for "Daphne with eyes closed" and both Neville Boden and Patrick George asking £700. The catalogue itself was a compact, square format with brown image and text on yellow ochre paper, graphics by Brian Fielding.

The Royal Academy
Piccadilly, London W1

The London Group held two exhibitions here in 1970 and 1971. It was never far from Group officers' minds that the Royal Academy represented an institution which The London Group had originally been set up to oppose. However, then President Andrew Forge had been instrumental in negotiating an excellent value booking with the R.A. and had accepted it gratefully, but warily, on behalf of the Group.

1972

The Watergate scandal erupts in the USA, five men arecaught braking into the Watergate offices in Washington. Thirteen demonstrators are killed and many injured on "Bloody Sunday" in Derry, Northern Ireland. Miners strike in the UK. The right wing National Front march through Lewisham, South London. Enoch Powell speeches exacerbate the situation. The Summer Olympic Games are held in Munich where eleven Israeli athletes are killed by Palestinian Terrorists.

"The New Art" the first in a series of Arts Council survey exhibitions of contemporary artists, shown at the **Hayward Gallery** and selected by Anne Seymour. Fourteen conceptual artists were shown in the four-year-old Hayward.

Whitechapel Art Gallery "East London Open" exhibition. Leon Kossoff (1963) and Patrick Heron (1952) were also shown this year.

Summer Shows 1972, Serpentine Gallery Between March and September there were six Summer Shows this year selected from an open submission by Professor Lawrence Gowing (1940/43), Edward Lucie-Smith and Paul Huxley. Thirty-five young artists were shown including Stephen Lobb (1968). "Festival at the Serpentine" (May to June) included kinetics, spectator and participatory events.

John Moores Painting Prize 1972 won by Euan Uglow (1958) with the painting, "Nude, 12 vertical positions from the eye".

ACME was set up by Jonathan Harvey and David Panton to provide affordable studio space and housing for artists in London.

"Biennials and Beyond – Exhibitions That Made Art History 1962 - 2002" Kassel, "Documenta 5".

London Group President: Dorothy Mead (1960)

No new members were elected this year, whereas five had been elected last year. Neither are there any minutes of an AGM for 1972.

No catalogue of any show is held in the Tate Archive, although the 1973 catalogue seems to indicate that onew was held about June 1972. However, the 1973 AGM minutes state, in the President's Report, that no exhibition was held in 1972 because a suitably large and affordable space could not be found. The Royal Academy Diploma Galleries were to be made smaller as two rooms had been taken over for the R.A. Library and were therefore not big enough for a London Group members' show or an open submission exhibition. The Fieldbourne Gallery in St. Johns Wood was far too small, the Camden Arts Centre was already booked and the President also approached the G.L.C. and Messrs. Shaw, an Estate Agency, regarding the possibility of hiring premises in Covent Garden, but without success.

Dorothy Mead in a photograph from 1964

courtesy of Cliff Holden

1973

The Arab-Israeli War breaks out. The US pulls out of Vietnam. In Chile General Pinochet overthrows President Allende in a bloody coup. The Sydney Opera House is opened by the Queen, commissioned in 1957 and hugely over budget. Britain finally enters the European Common Market against a background of industrial strikes. An Arab oil embargo against the US brings price rises to the UK which leads to the 'three-day week' from December 1973 to March 1974. The Open University awards its first degrees. Value Added Tax (VAT) is introduced in Britain. IRA bombs explode at Euston and Kings Cross railway stations in London. Patrick Heron (1952) writes a series of open letters to the 'Guardian' putting forward a UK-centric view of recent developments in painting. Premiere of Benjamin Britten's last opera, "Death in Venice" Op. 88 with Peter Pears in the main role whilst Pink Floyd releases "Dark Side of the Moon". Donald Sutherland and Julie Christie feature in Nicholas Roeg's "Don't Look Now".

Whitechapel Art Gallery "East London Open" exhibition. Three London Group members were shown this year, sculpture from Neville Boden (1965) who was to be elected as President of The London Group this year, and painting from Claude Rogers (1939) and Elsie Few (1940/43). The last exhibition of the year was "The London Group Annual", another open submission opportunity for local artists.

Summer Shows 1973, Serpentine Gallery this year's Committee was Edward Lucie-Smith, Paul Huxley and Hubert 'Nibs' Dalwood.

The season opened with the extremely popular "Photo-Realism" exhibition (mainly American artists).

Serpentine Sculpture '73 selected by Hubert Dalwood, five sculptors chosen.

Serpentine Painting '73 selected by Paul Huxley, six painters were chosen.

Serpentine Photography '73 selected by Peter Turner, forty-three photographers chosen.

Serpentine Graphics '73 chosen by Edward Lucie-Smith, prints and drawings from twenty-six artists including Robert Mason (1977).

In October the ACGB extended the Serpentine Gallery summer season for the first time with "William Tucker Sculpture 1970-73" and "Landscape", paintings from Norman Adams (1957), Adrian Berg, John Hubbard and Edward Middleditch.

London Group President: Dorothy Mead (1960) followed by Neville Boden (1964)

The 1973 Annual General Meeting was held in the Slade School on Friday, 16th March. Twenty-one members were present to hear officers' reports. "The minutes of the last meeting held on the 11th February 1971 were taken as read". This meant that there had been little or no formal group activity in 1972. The Treasurer, Valentine Ellis, reported on the loss made on the 1971 RA show. There had been a deficit of £1,017 on the 1971 exhibition although this had been reduced to £517 following a £500 Arts Council guarantee against loss. (The 1970 exhibition had made a surplus of £132, but, again, only after a £500 Arts Council guarantee). The President, Dorothy Mead, introduced discussion under the following headings: the last exhibition (the 1971 RA show), reasons for not holding an exhibition in 1972, the 1973 exhibition (at the Whitechapel) and the Greater London Arts Association to which The London Group had now become affiliated. Mead reported that the last exhibition had considerably lower admissions and sales affected by poor publicity and "The G.P.O. had also been on strike at this time". The Royal Academy galleries had shrunk in size and the Group had gratefully accepted Jenny Stein's offer of a free exhibition at the Whitecapel Gallery for December 1973. Buried in the minutes is a small but important sentence, "The President suggested that as in the past non-members work be selected by the entire membership who were available." This was a scrapping of Forge's selection structure and the return to London Group tradition. Honorary membership was proposed for L.S. Lowry, Ceciley Hay and Mrs Noel Adeney. "This was carried nem con." The Election of Officers resulted in all candidates being elected unopposed, Dorothy Mead as President, Neville Boden as Vice President and Valentine Ellis as Treasurer. Members were elected to the Working Party for the forthcoming Whitechapel exhibition and finally a motion to increase the membership fee, currently standing at £5.25, was defeated.

An Emergency General Meeting was called on the 21st June 1973 at the Slade. Dorothy Mead had been ill and spent some time in hospital. Neville Boden took on the role of President in her absence. His election was proposed by Dennis Creffield and Stephen Lobb, with Geoffrey Harris as his Vice President.

Another Special Meeting on the 4th October, again at the Slade, warned of "decreased membership" (59). Only eight members turned out for this meeting. Existing members were asked to nominate new members and the open exhibition later in the year was to be used to "take a look at them" and invite some to apply for full membership. Detailed discussion on the organisation of the Whitechapel exhibition ensued all designed to deliver maximum success and media attention.

"The London Group at the Whitechapel", Whitechapel Art Gallery, 4th December to 23rd December 1973. Neville Boden was recorded as President and Geoffrey Harris, Vice President. Officers, presumably the working party for this exhibition, were Brian Fielding, Michael Harrison, Morris Kestelman and Arthur Wilson. Thirty-four members were listed in the 1973 catalogue, although this is not a full list. Thirty members exhibited one or two works each. Six artists were invited to exhibit with the Group this year, including three sculptors, Hubert Dalwood, Peter Startup and Jesse Watkins. There were seventy-one non-member exhibitors, some having two works selected. Non-member exhibitors included John Bellany, David Carr, Ben Levine, David Shutt, Stanley Smith and Mary Webb. There were one hundred and seventy-five exhibits in total. Media and size were not indicated in the catalogue, only name, title and price. Top price was Eike Walcz, "Some foot in a Lake" at £5000. At around £1000 were Jeffery Camp, Anthony Eyton, Paula Rege (sic), Edward Wolfe (all members) and Hubert Dalwood, Peter Lanyon and Richard Oginz. Neville Boden wrote a preface to the catalogue stating that it had been a year and a half since the last London Group exhibition. The Whitechapel Gallery had been offered free of charge to The London Group, mainly due to the goodwill shown by Jenny Stein, then Director of the Whitechapel. Despite the free gallery space, the exhibition still made a loss of £188. Income, mainly from Hanging Fees, was £476 whilst expenditure was a massive £1,264, £348 of which was spent on advertising and publicity. Fortuitously, the Arts Council of Great Britain had sponsored the exhibition with a grant of £600 which softened the blow. The free gallery hire and the Arts Council grant had at least allowed the Group to open up submission to all artists. The scarcity of exhibition space and opportunities for young and unknown painters and sculptors was highlighted in the catalogue. The London Group exhibition catalogue was a small A5 landscape booklet with white cover, black typo and yellow ochre contents pages with no illustrations, text only. The poster for the exhibition sported an image by Brian Fielding and was displayed on London's Underground. The Group does not appear to have emphasised 1973 as the sixtieth anniversary year as had been the 'anniversary tradition' in the past. Elsie Few, Claude Rogers' wife and a London Group member, showed collages in the Small Gallery in a one-person exhibition.

Eleven members were elected this year largely from this exhibition. Peter Archer, John Bellany, Peter Donnelly, Heinz Henghes, John Hoskin, Caroline Hoskin, Caroline Jackson, Colin Nicholas, Livia Rolandini, Peter Startup and Jesse Watkins all became members. This was a huge boost to the Group and consequently its bank balance.

1974

Impeachment and resignation of US President Nixon. Turkish forces invade Cyprus, the Greek Military Junta collapses. India detonates its first nuclear weapon. The skeleton of 'Lucy', an upright-walking hominid dated 3.2 million BC discovered in Ethiopia. Alexander Solzhenitsyn is expelled from the Soviet Union. The "Rumble in the Jungle", the epic fight between Muhammad Ali and George Foreman. The world population reaches 4 billion. Miners' strike in UK. There were two General Elections, both won by Labour with Harold Wilson as Prime Minister. The IRA plants bombs in parliament, the Tower of London, a London club and pubs in Guildford and Woolwich, South East London. An accidental explosion at a chemical plant in Flixborough kills 28 people. Clashes between National Front supporters and left wing opposition in Red Lion Square, London, leaves one student dead. Lord Lucan disappears.

1974 "British Painting '74" second in the survey series at the Hayward Gallery with work chosen by a delegated system invented by ex-London Group President, Andrew Forge (1960). Some passages in the Foreword to the exhibition still strike a chord today, "A lot of art is being produced in this country and much of it remains unseen. No one interested in its history will be unaware that the death of painting was announced decades ago: he will also have noticed its refusal to lie down". Forge did not know what the exhibition was going to look like when he wrote the introduction to the catalogue. He speculated, "Certainly there will be extraordinary and superb works in it – I have seen some of them. Equally certainly there will be contradictions, a whiff of chaos". Written as an ex-President of The London Group. It was a large exhibition with one hundred and twenty-two painters of all ages, but only fourteen women. Thirty-five exhibitors were members of The London Group. Only the following declared their membership in their biographies, William Scott (1949), Claude Rogers (1938), Robert Medley (1937), Dorothy Mead (1960), Leon Kossoff (1963), Albert Irvin (1965), Ivon Hitchens (1931), Anthony Green (1964), Duncan Grant (1913 and Founder Member), Jeffery Camp (1961), John Bellany (1973), Basil Beattie (1968) and Eileen Agar (1933). The following declared having shown in non-member open submission exhibitions: David Tindle, Patrick Symons, Myles Murphy, John McLean, John Kiki, Howard Hodgkin, David Hepher, Paul Gopal-Chowdhury, Brian Fielding (1968), Mario Dubsky, Norman Dilworth, Benjamin Crème, Anne Buchanan (1971), Adrian Berg and Tom Barrett.
Whitechapel Art Gallery "East London Open" exhibition. Two London Group members were shown, Euan Uglow (1958) and Ray Atkins (1978).
Summer Shows 1974, Serpentine Gallery This years' Selection Committee was Hubert Dalwood, Paul Huxley and William Feaver. The complexion of the

Serpentine's programme was beginning to change. There were only three Summer Shows for young artists chosen from an open selection. Thirteen young artists were selected including Tony Carter (2002) Julian Cooper (1971) and Mary Webb (1975). Either side of the Summer Shows were exhibitions of more established artists, Roger Hilton and George Fullard, "Five Dutch Artists", "Five from Germany" and Art into Landscape 1, a competition open to the general public inviting ideas for interventions in the landscape.

John Moores Painting Prize 1974 won by Myles Murphy with the painting, "Figure with Yellow Foreground".

The Young Contemporaries is renamed **New Contemporaries** and re-launched. This from their website, "In 1973, tutors from some London colleges - including Gillian Ayres, Paul Huxley and William Tucker - banded together to revive the exhibition. A new constitution was drawn up. The exhibition was renamed New Contemporaries and its first showing took place at Camden Arts Centre in 1974." (The London Group was to show there in the following year).

"Biennials and Beyond – Exhibitions That Made Art History 1962 - 2002" Moscow, "The Bulldozer Exhibition".

London Group President: Neville Boden (1964)

There are no minutes of any Annual General Meeting this year and no new members were elected either. Neville Boden had investigated several spaces for an exhibition this year but without success. Neither the Royal Academy nor the Arts Council had space to offer. Studio International offered a venue for 3 weeks for £900, "but on examination this proved totally inadequate". Boden was rather disheartened by the 1973 Whitechapel exhibition. Despite the Whitechapel not charging any rent, the exhibition made a loss of £338. It had been, "too long since the previous exhibition (in 1971), December was a bad month, there had been too small a send in (art schools on holiday), there was a lack of publicity and the send-in venue had been too expensive". Only half the membership supported the exhibition by sending in work. Not a good year!

Given the opportunities offered to London artists by the Arts Council (Hayward Annuals and Serpentine selection), the Whitechapel Open programme John Moores and other open submission opportunities, it is not surprising that The London Group was struggling both to recruit new members and to find large, affordable spaces in which to organise their own open programme.

1975

The Vietnam war comes to an end with a victory for Communist North Vietnam. First elections in Portugal for 50 years. Microsoft founded. General Franco dies in Spain. Margaret Thatcher is elected leader of the Conservative Party. The Sex Discrimination Act is passed. The IRA bomb the London Hilton, Ross McWhirter is shot dead and IRA suspects are cornered in the Balcombe Street siege, London. The North Sea oil pipeline was opened by the Queen. Stephen Spielberg's "Jaws" and Ken Russell's "Tommy" released. "Fawlty Towers" is screened on television. Kate Millett invented the term "male chauvinist pig" in her book "Sexual Politics" to describe 1960s novelist Norman Mailer.

Hayward Gallery "The Condition of Sculpture", selected by William Tucker, with work from thirty-six male and four women artists. Feminists protest against lack of women participants and a proposal from Liliane Lijn for a women's exhibition at the Tate is considered "not feasible".

Serpentine Gallery Hubert Dalwood, William Feaver and Patrick Caulfield formed this year's Selection Committee. The season opened with Jasper Johns' drawings with John Hoskin's (1973) sculpture outside. As with last year's programme there were only three Summer Shows exhibiting eighteen young artists including William Henderson (1990) and Robert Russell (1990). Other events followed; "The Video Show" - a festival of Independent Video, "Eight Good Reasons to Visit the Serpentine Gallery" a festival of Performance Art, John Panting sculpture 1940–1974, Mark Boyle and Richard Hamilton, five Swedish artists, American Minimal Art and "Drawings of People" selected by Patrick George (1957).

Whitechapel Art Gallery "East London Open" exhibition.

London Group President: Neville Boden (1964)

This year five new members were elected. They were David Haughton, Richard Oginz, Stan Smith, John Watson and Mary Webb. Membership was slowly beginning to recover with more being elected than those leaving.

The Annual General Meeting was held on 25th February 1975 at the Slade. The last AGM had been held on the 16th March in 1973. Twenty members attended and Theo Crosby was there "by invitation". Neville Boden reported to the AGM that the delay to the meeting was caused by the resignation of Dorothy Mead (in 1973), the work load encountered organising the 1973 Whitechapel Open Exhibition and the illness of Valentine Ellis, the Group Treasurer. Robert Coward had temporarily stepped in as Treasurer. Membership stood at sixty with five Honorary Members. However, one third of members were in arrears with their annual fees leaving the group financially weak. Coward presented the financial report in three sections, the 1973 Whitechapel exhibition which showed a loss of £338 (the Arts Council's guarantee against loss had still to be followed up), the year to 31st January 1974 showed a surplus of £141 and £516 in the General Fund and the year to 31st January 1975 where the surplus was £140 and the General Fund stood at £656. "The income from subscriptions had decreased – Members were not resigning but just not paying." Neville Boden continued as President supported by Geoffrey Harris as the Vice President. The Working Party was the President, Vice President, Peter Donnelly, Brian Fielding, Morris Kestleman and Arthur Wilson. Some members had criticised a proposed exhibition at Camden Arts Centre as being "too far from central London" but "The President pointed out that we could not afford another long delay as London Group exhibitions were losing continuity." There were many proposals for exhibition venues put forward at the AGM, but nothing seems to have come to fruition. The Working Party was asked to re-open negotiations with Maurice Bradshaw at the Mall Galleries and to consider small specialist shows to alternate with open exhibitions.

"The London Group", Camden Arts Centre, Arkwright Road, London NW3. 31st July to 24th August 1975. The membership list printed in the catalogue lists sixty-seven members and of these sixty-seven only twenty-eight exhibited work at the Camden Arts Centre. Five artists were invited to show; they were Norman Ackroyd (3 etchings), Ken Draper (2 drawings), William Pye (2 stainless steel sculptures), Norman Stevens (1 oil painting) and Ainslie Yule (2 wooden sculptures), as wide a variety of work as possible. The Group had finally managed to organise an open submission for this exhibition for the first time in a number of years. A total of one hundred and six non-members were selected including Moich Abrahams, Mark Ainsworth, Philippa Beale, Denis Bowen, Gus Cummins, David Gluck, Jane Humphrey, Gillian Ingham, Jeff Instone, Vic Kuell, Christopher le Brun (a future President of the Royal Academy), Robert Mason, William Mills, Keith Reeves, Bruce Russell, David Shutt, Susan Tebby and Richard Wilson. Two hundred and five pieces were exhibited, of which thirty-eight were denoted as being sculpture. The rest were paintings, prints and drawings as media and prices were printed in this catalogue. Bill Pye was asking £4,000 for his sculpture and Norman Stevens £1,250 for his painting. The Introduction, written by Neville Boden, reported that the last group show was the 1973 Whitechapel exhibition. The London Group was continuing its policy of invitation and selection of non-members for exhibition and also of widening the scope of work for exhibition to include prints as well as drawings, paintings and sculpture.

The Arkwright Arts Trust gave the Camden Arts Centre free of charge (although on 31.01.76 a "Gallery Rent" of £75 was paid for the hire of a small connected gallery) and the London College of Printing was used as the send in and selection venue. The total exhibition costs were £2,046 (£543 spent on advertising and publicity) whereas income stood at £816, chiefly from hanging and handling fees. The deficit was £1,230, but after the application of an £800 Arts Council grant the deficit was reduced to £430. A further Arts Council guarantee of £200 reduced the final loss to £230. By the end of the financial year the Group had assets of £616 in total. On a more sombre note it was recorded that Dorothy Mead, the first female President, had died in June and some of her work was shown in this exhibition as a mark of respect. The exhibition catalogue was an A5 landscape envelope with loose-leaf contents. The cover design used white cut out letters spelling "The London Group" on a black background. Correspondence indicates that a poster for this exhibition was displayed on both the London Underground and British Railways. The Group had also taken out advertising in 'Time Out', 'The Guardian', 'The Sunday Times', 'The Observer' and the 'Hampstead and Highgate Press'. The Group was finally getting its act together and gathering momentum.

Camden Arts Centre
Arkwright Road, London
NW3

1976

Soweto massacre of schoolchildren protesting against the imposition of the Africaans language in their schools in South Africa. The death of Chairman Mao Zedong brings to an end the Cultural Revolution in China. Jimmy Carter is elected US President. Apple Computers established. Richard Rogers' Pompidou Centre completed in Paris. The Summer Olympic Games were held in Montreal. Jeremy Thorpe sex scandal. Britain found guilty of torture in Northern Ireland. Twelve small firebombs detonate in London's West End stores. After a hot summer there is drought in Britain. The Sex Pistol's "Anarchy in the UK" heralds the arrival of Punk Rock. Derek Jarman's "Sebastiane" and Scorcese's "Taxi Driver" released.

Hayward Gallery "The Human Clay", figurative works, mainly paintings and drawings by fifty artists selected by R.B. Kitaj.

Summer Shows 1976, Serpentine Gallery the Committee this year was William Feaver, Patrick Caulfield and Derek Boshier.

Tom Phillips, Jeremy Moon and Howard Hodgkin were shown before five Summer Shows this year. The Committee co-opted Eduardo Paolozzi, John Golding and Michael Craig-Martin to select one show each. Colin Nicholas (1973) and thirty-eight others were selected. Prunella Clough, Harry Thubron (1981) and Alf Dunn (1988) were shown in the autumn.

"Prostitution" at the ICA, put together by performance artists Genesis P. Orridge and Cosey Fanni Tutti. It raised a huge outcry in the media and questions were asked in the House as the Arts Council had given financial support.

Whitechapel Art Gallery "East London Open" exhibition.

May, the **Acme Gallery** opens in Shelton Street, Covent Garden with a show by painter Mike Porter.

John Moores Painting Prize 1976 won by John Walker with the painting, "Juggernaut with plume - for P Neruda".

The British Council organise "Arte Inglesi Oggi" in Milan with nearly three hundred and forty exhibits by fifty-five artists including Mark Boyle, Victor Burgin, Bernard Cohen, Rita Donagh, Barry Flanagan, Richard Hamilton, John Hilliard, David Hockney (1963), Paul Huxley, Genesis P. Orridge, Tom Phillips, Bridget Riley, Richard Smith, William Turnbull (1955) and John Walker. Film and Performance Art were also included. Catalogue introduction written by Norbert Lynton covering developments in British Art from 1960.

The **Venice Biennale** is revived with a theme of 'the environment'. Britain is represented by Richard Long.

Art Monthly is founded, a magazine devoted to contemporary art issues.

Norman Foster's Lloyds Building is completed; Foster said he felt "beleaguered" by critics.

London Group President: Neville Boden (1964)

There were no new members elected this year.

The AGM was held at the Camden Arts Centre on the 28th February 1976. Only eleven out of sixty-seven members attended with four apologies. Much of the discussion in the AGM centred around the lack of support and activity from many members. Some paid their annual fees but never exhibited. Neville Boden pointed out that it was a member's right not to show work every year and, besides, their money was still coming in and keeping the Group afloat! The 'balance held' by the Group was £616. The rules regarding 'lapsing membership' were questioned but by the end of the meeting it was agreed not to take any action at the present time. Many prestigious galleries were brought up as possible London Group venues. The Barbican Gallery (as yet incomplete), the Serpentine Gallery (Sue Grayson had given a favourable response), the ICA (who showed no interest), the Hayward Gallery and the Whitechapel Art Gallery were all discussed. The Group was aiming high, the galleries could always say no (and most of them did). Other possibilities were the Guildhall Gallery and Sir John Cass. "Nothing definite" had been arranged for this year. Another low! Under 'Election of Officers', Neville Boden "was prepared to stand for one more year of office", Geoffrey Harris was unanimously re-elected Vice President (there being no other nominations) and the Working Party consisted of Peter Donnelly, Brian Fielding, Morris Kestelman and Arthur Wilson. The President proposed to increase the Working Party from six to eight members by co-opting Stan Smith and Jesse Watkins which was agreed by the meeting. Claude Rogers, André Bicat, Richard Carline and Elsie Few were elected as Honorary Members.

A sub-committee consisting of the President, Secretary, Morris Kestelman and Brian Fielding was set up to deal with the transfer of archive material collected from Andrew Forge. In August 1975 Andrew Forge had passed on a large bundle of material in four tin trunks to Morris Kestelman with the intention of recording and preserving London Group activity. This material was to form the beginnings of The London Group holding in the Tate Archive. Kestelman listed and sorted the material which was eventually collected by the Tate Gallery in December 1977.

1977

The first democratic elections are held in Spain since 1936. Steve Biko tortured to death in South Africa. Charter 77 manifesto issued in Czechoslovakia. Pompidou Centre (Piano, Rogers, Franchini) opens in Paris. Pierre Boulez was appointed director of IRCAM, a government sponsored studio within the Pompidou Centre. Punk Rock becomes fashionable. During the Queen's Jubilee, "God Save the Queen" by the Sex Pistols gets to number 2 in the charts. Elvis Presley dies (and is seen alive for the next two decades). Mike Leigh's play "Abigail's Party" is staged. Films "Saturday Night Fever", "Star Wars", "Close Encounters of the Third Kind" and "Annie Hall" are released.

The first **Hayward Annual** selected by Michael Compton, Howard Hodgkin and William Turnbull (1955), thirty artists including David Hockney (1963). Hayward Annuals were designed by the Arts Council of Great Britain to "present a cumulative picture of British art as it develops". Another competitor for London Group annuals!
Serpentine Gallery The Serpentine Committee this year were Patrick Caulfield, Derek Boshier and Judy Marle.
Bill Culbert & Liliane Lijn, Terry Frost (1957), Michael Kenny (1968) and Arshile Gorky were shown early in the year. Tim Hilton was co-opted to select Summer Show 2, but no London Group members were shown in the Summer Show programme. Art into Landscape 2, ideas from the public to use redundant open spaces, then Ian Hamilton Finlay, sculptor Peter Startup (1973) and de Kooning sculptures.
"British Painting 1952 – 1977" at the Royal Academy, selected by a working party of mainly RAs. Of one hundred and ninety-seven painters in the exhibition, about forty were Royal Academicians but over seventy were past, present or future members of The London Group, many with dual membership. The exhibition was a looking back over the 25 years of the Queen's reign as well as looking forward to the future. For the purposes of this history of The London Group, this exhibition is a convenient summary on recent painting history, but readers must bear in mind that it was written by a Royal Academician. Frederick Gore RA wrote the introduction to the catalogue which was itself based on an introduction written by Norbert Lynton to "Arte inglesi oggi 1960-76", shown in Milan in 1976. Gore identifies ten individual 'categories' of activity and lists major contributors, given here in the order (of importance?) in which they appear in Gore's introduction:
Cubism Sutherland (1937), Colquhoun, McBryde, Minton (1949), Craxton, Bawden and Piper (1933).
Social Realism associated with the Beaux Art Galleries and Zwemmers. Jack Smith (1957), Middleditch, Bratby (1957), Coker, Greaves and Fussell.

Expressionism derived from Bomberg (1913) and taken up by Auerbach (1960) and Kossoff (1963).

Abstract Expressionism imported from America led by Jackson Pollock. In this country abstract expressionism was pioneered by the St. Ives Group, Frost (1957), Heron (1952), Hilton, Lanyon and Wynter (1955).

The **"Situation"** group, Ayres, Denny, Hoyland, Law, Richard Smith, Bernard Cohen and Turnbull (1955).

Pop Art promoted by Ken Russell's BBC film, "Pop goes the Easel" with Blake, Boshier and Peter Philips. Later came Caulfield, Hockney (1963), Allen Jones and Kitaj.

The **"New Generation"** exhibitors which included some of the above plus Riley and Huxley.

Individuals **Richard Hamilton, John Latham** and **Gustave Metzger**.

Constructivism based on Malevitch (sic), the Bauhaus, de Stijl and Ben Nicholson. They were Kenneth Martin (1949), Victor Pasmore (1934), Anthony Hill, Alan Reynolds and Malcolm Hughes.

Figuration and the Royal Academy in particular Norman Blamey RA and John Ward RA. Also Carel Weight (1949), Lucian Freud, Alan Gwynne-Jones, Duncan Grant (1913), Ivon Hitchens (1931), Lawrence Gowing (1940/43), Leonard Rosoman (1957), Norman Adams (1957), Rodrigo Moynihan (1933), Robert Medley (1937) and Ruskin Spear (1940/43). Francis Bacon was singled out for his individual importance. It is interesting to note that virtually all of the figurative and RA contributors were linked to The London Group, whereas Pop Art's only member was David Hockney. Analysis of ages is also indicative of the selectors' backgrounds. Of the 197 exhibitors just under a quarter (21%) were under 40, just over a quarter (28%) for the 40 to 50 age group but a large majority 102 of the 197 were over 50 (51%). Of these 197, 71 (36%) were past, present or future members of The London Group. Their age analysis is also interesting 23% under 40, 23% 40-50 and 54% over 50.

A parallel sculpture exhibition, **"The Silver Jubilee Exhibition of Contemporary British Sculpture"**, organised by Bryan Kneale (1987) was held earlier in the year in **Battersea Park**. Exhibitors included, Kenneth Draper (1981), Barry Flanagan, Ian Hamilton-Finlay, Peter Hide, Philip King, John Maine, Paul Neagu, Nicholas Pope and Brian Wall (1962).

Whitechapel Art Gallery "Whitechapel Open" exhibition. The Whitechapel changed the name of this open submission exhibition from the "East London Open", probably to enlarge the catchment area and bring in larger numbers of hopefuls.

London Group President: Neville Boden (1964) followed by Peter Donnelly (1973)

This year six new members were elected. They were Moich Abrahams, Philippa Beale,

Peter de Francia, Stanislaw Frenkiel, Robert Mason and Keith Reeves.

"The London Group", Camden Arts Centre, 8th February to 27th February 1977. The Working Party for the exhibition consisted of Neville Boden (President), Geoffrey Harris (Vice President), Peter Donnelly, Brian Fielding, Morris Kestelman, Stanley Smith, Jesse Watkins and Arthur Wilson. Following the custom of recent years this was an open exhibition with more non-members than members showing. Neville Boden in his Introduction records the deaths of past members, L.S. Lowry, Peter Startup, Hubert Dalwood and Heinz Henghes. The catalogue gives the names and addresses of sixty-two members, a rather small total, ninety being a contemporary average. Thirty-one members, exactly half, exhibited one, two or three pieces each. Frank Bowling, Peter de Francia, Mary Kessel, Victor Newsome and Mike Pope were invited to show and one hundred and two non-members were given the opportunity of exhibiting to the public. It is interesting to note that twenty-three of these one hundred and two exhibitors then went on to be elected to The London Group in subsequent years. There were not so many 'names' either, many of the selected exhibitors were young artists, some only a few years out of art school. There had been five hundred and sixteen non-member entry fees at £1.50 each which brought in £774, whilst one hundred and thirty-two non-member hanging fees at £3.00 each had raised £396. Exhibitors used a huge range of two and three-dimensional media. As well as conventional media exhibiting artists were using twine, synthetic enamel, formica, wax, xerox, shellac, quilt and cement fondu! Prices were very reasonable as there was probably a size limit to get all one hundred and ninety-four works into the Camden Arts Centre. Top price was £1,500 asked by Claude Rogers for his oil on canvas "Night Approach to London 11". The rental for the galleries and other miscellaneous expenditure was £677.38. The Arts Council made a generous grant of £1,000 to support this exhibition and a guarantee against loss of £200. Peter Bird of the Arts Council had suggested that as most of the artists were from London, the Group should also seek financial support from the Greater London Arts Association, which Boden later did.

The Annual General Meeting was held on the 22nd April 1977 at Chelsea School of Art, Manresa Road. There were fifteen present with four apologies. Neville Boden had stepped down and the new President Peter Donnelly reported that there had been no success in trying to find new venues. Some members had been dissatisfied with the hanging space at Camden Arts Centre and contact with the Royal Academy and the new gallery at the Barbican was proposed. The 1977 Open Exhibition, however, had been successful and despite gallery hire costs of £677.38 the show had just about broken even with Arts Council grant support. At this time the Group had "£950 in hand". There had been much more interest from non-member send-ins and there had been some positive press coverage too.

1978

Pope John Paul 1 dies after 33 days in office and John Paul II becomes the first non-Italian Pope since 1522. In Rhodesia, Ian Smith agrees to black majority rule. The oil tanker Amaco Cadiz runs aground off Brittany causing extensive pollution. President Jimmy Carter postpones production of the Neutron Bomb. Camp David Accords begin the Middle East peace process. China and Japan sign a treaty of 'Peace and Friendship'. Deng Xiaoping comes to power in China, replacing the Gang of Four and empowering Mao's opponents. There are emonstrations against the Shah in Iran. "Winter of Discontent" in the UK, 1978/79. The first test tube baby, Louise Brown, is born. Georgi Markhov, a Bulgarian defector, is murdered using a poisoned pellet injected by an umbrella, allegedly. Production of 'The Times' newspaper is suspended for almost a year due to labour disputes. The Bee Gees have five songs in the top 100.

Hayward Annual '78 selected by Rita Donagh, Tess Jaray, Liliane Lijn, Kim Lim, Gillian Wise Ciabotaru, sixteen women and seven men. This Annual aimed to "bring to the attention of the public the quality of the work of women artists in Britain in the context of a mixed show". Also "Dada & Surrealism Reviewed" and a Jasper Johns exhibition.

Whitechapel Art Gallery "Art for Society: Contemporary British Art with a Social or Political Purpose", selected by a committee including Richard Cork and Nicholas Serota, Whitechapel Director. One hundred artists are shown including Conrad Atkinson, Ian Breakwell, Victor Burgin, Rita Donagh, Peter de Francia (1977), Alexis Hunter, Mary Kelly, David Redfern (2000), John Stezaker and Stephen Willats. Also a "Whitechapel Open" and an exhibition by Artists Placement Group (APG).

Serpentine Gallery the committee this year was Derek Boshier, Judy Marle and Myles Murphy. Jack Smith (1957) was shown early in the year, followed by exhibitions from the open submission, selected by sculptor David Annesley (1990), performance artist Stuart Brisley and critic Richard Cork. London Group member Jesse Watkins (1973) showed on the lawns. Then Bryan Kneale (1987) sculpture and Jeffery Camp (1961) paintings were shown followed by "Henry Moore at the Serpentine", an 80th birthday exhibition in the gallery and throughout Kensington Gardens.

John Moores Painting Prize 1978 won by Noel Forster with, "A painting in six stages with a silk triangle".

The Spirit of London the first showing of an open submission annual exhibition held at the Royal Festival Hall. Judges were James Fitton RA (1934), Peter John Garrard RBA, NEAC and Peter Greenham CBE, PRBA, RP, NEAC, BA. There were a number of prizes, one of £1,000, four of £500 and eight of £250 which were financed from the "GLC Lottery Income". Sponsors also contributed prizes, George Rowney £500,

Inveresk Paper Co Ltd £500 and 'Artists Magazine' £100. Among the prize winners were Frederick Brill and John Lessore. Artists could submit up to three works and one hundred and eighty-three artists were chosen to exhibit.

Venice Biennale Mark Boyle represents Britain.

London Group President: Peter Donnelly (1973)

"London Group at the RCA", Gulbenkian Galleries, Royal College of Art, 31st March to 15th April 1978. The President this year was Peter Donnelly with Neville Boden as Vice President. The Working Party for this exhibition was Moich Abrahams, Brian Fielding, Geoffrey Harris, Robert Mason, Stanley Smith and Arthur Wilson. The RCA was a new venue for The London Group; Stan Smith was the influential go between as he taught at the RCA. If the membership list printed in the catalogue is correct there were sixty-five members in 1978 and thirty-one of them exhibited one or two pieces of work. There were six invited artists, R. B. Kitaj, Tom Phillips, Cyril Reason, Jack Smith, Ian Stephenson and Karl Weschke. In addition there were one hundred and sixteen non-members who were selected (the catalogue makes no mention of the process or criteria) including Ray Atkins, William Crozier, Patrick Jones, Ken Kiff, Ingrid Kerma, Robin Klassnik, Hugh O'Donnell, Carole Robb, Suzan Swale, Shelagh Wakely, Anthony Whishaw and Gary Wragg. There were twenty-nine pieces of sculpture, the rest being a wide variety of work including oils, acrylics, watercolours, mixed media, drawings and prints. The title, media and prices were also printed in the catalogue. John Watson priced his exhibit at £3,500 whilst André Bicat, Albert Irvin, Richard Criddle, Gus Cummins, David Redfern and Gerda Rubinstein were around £1,000. The catalogue had an Introduction by the new President, P.L. Donnelly, focusing on the need to find a large, affordable space to be able to continue the open submission for all non-member artists. Recently, each exhibition had been a "one off", which meant no continuity of planning from one year to the next as the Group had enjoyed in the past. Thanks were given to the Arts Council of Great Britain for financial support (they had granted £1,750 plus a guarantee against loss of £250) and thanks were also extended to Stan Smith for helping to secure the RCA venue. There was a short dedication to Lynton Lamb who had died recently. The catalogue itself was A5 landscape, black background with lurid green lettering on the cover. There were no illustrations. London Transport were paid £114.09 for displaying advertising posters.

This year's AGM was held at Chelsea School of Art in Manresa Road on the 13th June. Eighteen attended with two apologies. There was an evaluation of the recent Open at the RCA which Stan Smith had been instrumental in booking for £1,000. Despite the cramped exhibition space (due to a misunderstanding in the rooms booked) 2,149 people visited, but there was no press interest and disappointing sales. Looking on the bright side, the RCA Bursar had said, "it was a pleasure to do business with professionals". The RCA had offered dates in 1979 and a unanimous vote supported this initiative. In the autumn of this year, however, the Arts Council crushed all hopes of this show by informing The London Group that it would, "receive nothing for 78-79". "The Group, therefore, had no alternative but to cancel the booking made with the RCA" (LG minutes). Despite this setback, Stan Smith had also approached Cyril Reason at the Morley Gallery, Morley College for the loan of the gallery free of charge for a London Group drawings exhibition in September 1979.

Following the RCA exhibition seven new members were elected this year, Ray Atkins, John Barnicoat, Robert Clarke, Tom Cross, John Crossley, David Gluck and Anthony Whishaw.

Finances appeared relatively healthy this year. The Deposit Account held £1,024, whilst in the Exhibition Account income was £1,162; expenditure was £2,768 with a grant from the Arts Council of £1,750, leaving a small surplus of £144. Four hundred and sixteen non-member handling fees and one hundred and forty-two hanging fees had raised £1,050 in total. The Royal College of Art invoiced The London Group for £1,086.48 in respect of hire of the hall and security staff. In addition the RCA charged The London Group £2.49 for the replacement of a specialist hammer which had gone missing during the installation - the electricians were the usual suspects.

Peter Donnelly was re-elected as President with Stan Smith as his Vice President and Bob Mason, Neville Boden, Anthony Whishaw, Bert Irvin, John Crossley, Brian Fielding and Arthur Wilson elected unopposed to the Working Party. Under A.O.B. "Bert Irvin suggested that the Group should meet again later in the year to discuss the ideology of the Group and to re-define the reason for its existence". The meeting backed this initiative and agreed to meet in October. Donnelly wrote to members on 26th October inviting them to an Extraordinary General Meeting at Chelsea School of Art on 30th November to discuss the Group's ideology, although no minutes have been archived. In 2000 Peter Clossick and Tony Carter were to put forward similar initiatives, an indication of the dynamic nature of the Group and the changing art environment to which the Group had to react.

The Royal College of Art
Kensington Gore, London SW7

The London Group hired the Gulbenkian Galleries within the RCA six times from 1978 and into the 1980s. President Stan Smith was a visiting lecturer at the RCA and would have had the contacts to negotiate an acceptable hire fee. The exhibitions also illustrate the strengthening links between The London Group and educational institutions (i.e. London Art Schools).

1979

The Shah leaves Iran, Ayatollah Khomeni returns to form an Islamic Republic. 52 Americans held hostage in the American Embassy in Tehran for 444 days. Pol Pot is convicted of murdering 3 million Cambodians. USSR invades Afghanistan. In a UK general election Jim Callaghan's Labour Government is defeated and Margaret Thatcher leads a Conservative Government. Earl Mountbatten is killed on his boat in Ireland by an IRA bomb. Airey Neave is killed by a bomb in his car as he exits the House of Commons. "Dirty Protest" in the Maze Prison, Belfast. Barbara Hepworth (1930) dies in a fire at her studio in St. Ives. Francis Ford Coppola makes "Apocalypse Now", filmed in the Philippines and Monty Python make "Life of Brian".

1979 The British Art Show 1 was organised as a national touring exhibition by the Hayward Gallery London, and selected by William Packer. One hundred and twelve artists were selected, showing mainly painting with some sculpture. Artists included Norman Adams (1957), Michael Andrews (1962), Martin Ball (1981), John Bellany (1973), Frank Bowling (1963 re-elected 2002), Jeffery Camp (1961), Tony Carter (2002), Dennis Creffield (1962), John Edwards (1989), Anthony Eyton (1961), Terry Frost (1957), Anthony Green (1964), David Hockney (1963), Albert Irvin (1965), Michael Kenny (1968), Leon Kossof (1963), Janet Nathan (1984), Ken Oliver (1990), Michael Sandle (1965), William Scott (1949), Euan Uglow (1958), Anthony Whishaw (1978) and Laetitia Yhap (1971), all London Group members.

Hayward Annual 1979: Current British Art selected by Helen Chadwick, Paul Gopal-Chowdhury, James Faure Walker (2000), John Hilliard and Nicholas Pope. Twenty-four artists are shown plus a programme of Performance Art.

Lives at the **Hayward Gallery** organised by Derek Boshier including David Hockney (1963), David Redfern (2000) and Carel Weight (1949).

Matts Gallery opens in Robin Klassnik's (1981) studio (named after Klassnik's Old English sheepdog).

Serpentine Gallery this year's Committee was Judy Marle, Myles Murphy and Nicholas Pope. The year opened with Barry Flanagan, Saul Steinberg, an exhibition of contemporary French art and Allen Jones. Three Summer Shows selected by Sue Grayson (invited by the Committee), Judy Marle and Myles Murphy. London Group members Laetitia Yhap (1971) and David Redfern (2000) were selected from the open submission. There followed exhibitions by John Hoyland, Tim Head and André Kertesz.

Whitechapel Art Gallery "Whitechapel Open" exhibition. Also, David Bomberg (1913) retrospective.

The Spirit of London Royal Festival Hall, open submission exhibition.

London Group President: Peter Donnelly (1973) followed by Stan Smith (1975)

Only one new member, Cyril Reason, was elected this year.

The AGM was held on the 2nd July in the RCA Senior Common Room and twenty members were present with three apologies. During the year, Peter Donnelly had resigned as President because he had started a new job and hadn't the time to devote to London Group business; and as Vice President, Stan Smith took over the role. Under President's Report, Smith informed the members that he had been talking to Mike Sixsmith of the Arts Council who encouragingly was "prepared to support the Group financially at a prestige venue". Unfortunately, nothing seems to have emerged from this supportive offer but the Arts Council had allocated £400 towards the cost of the forthcoming Morley exhibition, plus a £100 guarantee against loss. Part of the £400 was towards an illustrated catalogue for which members were urged to send in photographs for reproduction. Robert Coward reported that the surplus for the year amounted to £175 and that the account was "in a healthy condition". Assets at 31st January 1979 were £1,358 whereas last year they were £956. Morris Kestelman proposed Stan Smith to be re-elected as President, seconded by John Bellany. As there were no other nominations Smith retained his position. The post of Vice President was contested between John Bellany, proposed by Albert Irvin and seconded by Barry Martin, and Jesse Watkins, proposed by Dennis Creffield and seconded by Stanislaw Frenkiel. "On a show of hands, John Bellany received 13 votes and Jesse Watkins 3 votes." Barry Martin, Bert Irvin, Anthony Whishaw, Neville Boden, Jesse Watkins and Arthur Wilson were elected to the Working Party. The sad news of past President Claude Rogers' death was given to the meeting which resolved to try to set up some kind of Commemorative Award in recognition of Rogers' work over many years for The London Group.

"The London Group at Morley Gallery – an Exhibition of Drawings by Members of The London Group" at the Morley Gallery, 61 Westminster Bridge Road, London SE1 from 20th September to 12th October 1979. Newly elected member Cyril Reason, as Head of Fine Art, had helped set up the show at Morley with assistance from his successor, Adrian Bartlett. The catalogue records Stan Smith as President, John Bellany as Vice President and a Working Party of the two latter plus Neville Boden, Albert Irvin, Barry Martin, Jesse Watkins, Anthony Whishaw and Arthur Wilson. Membership stood at seventy-two this year, but only thirty-four members showed in this exhibition. There were sixty-five drawings in total executed in a wide variety of wet and dry media on paper, a liberal translation of the word 'drawing'. Work was small to medium in scale, 24" x 36" on average. Top prices were from Richard Carline, Julian Cooper and Anthony Eyton all asking £250, but the average was around the £100 to £150 mark. The catalogue introduction from Stan Smith, his first as the new President, contained some interesting statements. The death of past President Claude Rogers is recorded by

Smith. Rogers served and Smith was to serve as president for fifteen and fourteen years respectively, the two longest serving presidents in the Group's history. Smith wrote "A sadder coincidence is that since our last exhibition Claude Rogers has died. Claude Rogers, that long time President of the London Group, great champion of young artists and tireless supporter, worker and helpmate to his fellow Presidents and the group's members. It is hoped to initiate a memorial to Claude through the Group which we feel would be an appropriate and significant gesture". In subsequent correspondence Martin Froy proposed a Claude Rogers Fellowship at Reading University who would provide the space, but Smith would have to find benefactors. The catalogue introduction continued "The London Group, ever struggling for a fixed location for regular open shows, is currently negotiating for a larger gallery, the details of which will be announced when agreements are concluded." In a letter to Stan Smith dated 11th November 1979, Zuleika Dobson from Camden Arts Centre wrote "the Committee were sympathetic in principle to the London Group and would consider offering the galleries in 1981 on a triennial basis". (Underlining in the letter). Exhibitions were held at Camden Arts Centre in the eighties, but the regular slot seems not to have occurred. The catalogue was A5 in size with a silver cover containing 28 pages. There were 50 black and white photographs of drawings from most of the exhibitors showing a wide range of styles and approaches from abstraction to figuration.

The Morley Gallery
Westminster Bridge Road, London SE1

The Morley Gallery is situated on the corner of Westminster Bridge Road and King Edward Walk, London SE1. The gallery is administered by Morley College.
The London Group exhibited here in 1979, 1981, 1982, 1992 and 2009. Cyril Reason, elected to The London Group in 1979, was Director of Art at Morley College from 1972 to 1979 and Adrian Bartlett, London Group President from 1993 to 1995, was Head of Printmaking from 1962 to 1999. Many other Group members have taught there part-time. The street to the right is King Edward Walk where the Walk Gallery was situated at number 23. The Walk Gallery was to mount a series of London Group four member small group exhibitions from 2001 to 2005.

The 1980's

Perhaps the most important influence in the eighties was Postmodernism which can variously be seen as a reaction against modernism (epitomised by Clement Greenbergian philosophy), or as a return to previous ideas before modernism (as the Pre-Raphaelites had looked to the time before Raphael), or even as building on developments within modernism. Eleanor Heartley attempts a description of the postmodern world, "... our understanding of the world is based, first and foremost, on mediated images. Each affirms the notion that we live within the sway of a mythology conjured for us by the mass media, movies, advertisements. Postmodernism is modernism's unruly child."

The most important individual movement of the 1980s in Britain was "**New British Sculpture**", a term coined to categorise the work of Tony Cragg, Richard Deacon, Barry Flanagan, Antony Gormley, Shirazeh Houshiary, Anish Kapoor, Richard Wentworth, Alison Wilding, Richard Wilson and Bill Woodrow.

In the field of **painting** neo-expressionist painters John Bellany, (1973) Ken Kiff and Paula Rego (1965) were considered influential. Howard Hodgkin, John Hoyland and Sean Scully were important in their own rite.

Individuals Helen Chadwick, Sarah Lucas, Julian Opie and Gavin Turk all achieved critical success.

The Constructionists used modern materials such as glass and perspex, moving away from the traditional use of paint on canvas. Constructionists were Terry Pope, Michael Kidner, Malcolm Hughes, Gillian Wise Ciobotaru and Jean Spencer.

Performance Art notably Stuart Brisley and Bruce McLean with "Nice Style".

The New Contemporaries as quoted from their website, "By the 1980s, the exhibition was held regularly at the ICA and a Permanent Committee supported the exhibition management until 1983. Each year, the exhibition was selected and organised by students. The last exhibition, before running out of steam, was racked by financial problems, leaving the student organisers with personal debt. It was finally disbanded in 1986. In 1987 the Arts Council of Great Britain commissioned a feasibility report on New Contemporaries to look into the future viability of the exhibition. The report was published by Richard Shone, who then became the Chair of a Volunteer Board of Directors and a new constitution and new structure for the organisation was established. For the first time, the exhibition was supported by professional administration and adopted a model of curatorial and college independence, inviting an outside team of selectors from the arts profession each year. The exhibition was re-launched at the ICA in 1989 and toured to four regional centres". Students experiencing this exhibiting system would be well placed for active membership of The London Group and its annual quest for an exhibition venue.

The Whitechapel Open Exhibition was an open submission exhibition which took place every year in this decade apart from 1981.

The Spirit of London was another annual open submission exhibition, this one organised by the GLC at the Royal Festival Hall from 1978 until 1985; a very similar process (and competitor) to London Group open submission exhibitions.

In 1981 Robin Klassnik was elected to The London Group. In 1979 Klassnik had set up the influential **Matt's Gallery** in the East End of London and was to show such avant-garde artists as Richard Wilson and Rose Finn-Kelcey. Fourteen years later in 1995, Klassnik was part of the selection panel for The London Group 1995 Biennale Open Exhibition at the Concourse Gallery, Barbican Centre.

Stockwell Depot and Greenwich Studios studio co-operatives run by and for artists. Open Studio programmes provided access for critics, collectors and the art visitor bypassing "the gallery". Artists were increasingly beginning to organise themselves in bringing their work to the attention of the media, critcs, writers and the gallery going public. This meant that The London Group was not as relevant as had it had been in the past regarding providing open submission opportunities for London artists.

Tate Modern Time Line 1980-90 Leon Golub, Peter Halley, Howard Hodgkin, Sherri Levine, Agnes Martin, Sean Scully, Nancy Spero. Then Jeff Wall, Jeff Koons. Grafitti Art including Jean-Michel Basquiat, Keith Haring. Black Art Movement including Eddie Chambers, Keith Piper and Donald Rodney. Video and Film including Garry Hill, Willie Doherty Stan and Bill Viola. Neo-Expressionism by Georg Baselitz, Francesco Clemente, Anselm Keifer, Sigmar Polke, Gerhard Richter and Julian Schnabel. New British Sculpture with Tony Cragg, Richard Deacon, Antony Gormley, Shirazeh Houshiary, Anish Kapoor, Richard Wentworth, Alison Wilding and Bill Woodrow. Individuals Helen Chadwick, Martin Kippenberger, Louise Lawler, Sarah Lucas, Brice Marden, Julian Opie, Richard Prince, Hiroshi Sugimoto, Gavin Turk and Fred Wilson.

1980

Iran-Iraq war. Solidarity trade union recognised by the Polish government. Mugabe establishes a one party state in Zimbabwe. In the US Ronald Regan is elected President and John Lennon is shot dead in New York. Iranian Embassy siege in London, the SAS storms the embassy and frees hostages. The Summer Olympic Games are held in Moscow. Bill Forsyth makes "Gregory's Girl".

Hayward Annual 1980 Contemporary Painting and Sculpture, selected by John Hoyland, eighteen artists with an average age of forty-five. Piet Mondrian's "Pier and Ocean".

Summer Shows 1980 Serpentine Gallery
The Serpentine Committee this year was Judy Marle, Myles Murphy and Nicholas Pope. This was its last manifestation, as selection was taken over by the Exhibition Sub-Committee of the Arts Council. Dennis Creffield (1971) showed drawings in March, Patrick George (1957) showed drawings and paintings in July.
Summer Show 1 selected by Alan Miller, nine chosen including Michael Hiendorff (1981).
Summer Show 2 selected by Tony Carter (2002), eight chosen including Wendy Smith (2001).
Summer Show 3 selected by Stephen Cox, ten artists chosen.
The Spirit of London the third show of an open submission annual exhibition held at the Royal Festival Hall. Judges were Frank Auerbach (1960), Roger de Gray RA, NEAC and Peter Garrard CBE, VPRBA, RP, NEAC. There were a number of prizes, one of £1,000, four of £500 and eight of £250 which were financed from the 'GLC Lottery Income'. Eleven sponsors also contributed £2,500 in prizes. Anthony Whishaw (1978) was awarded a £500 prize. There were two hundred and twenty exhibits.
Whitechapel Art Gallery "Whitechapel Open" exhibition.
John Moores Painting Prize 1980 won by Michael Moon with "Box-room".
Barbara Hepworth Museum opens in St. Ives. Hepworth was elected to The London Group in 1930 along with a number of other sculptors to take part in the 1930 Selfridges Roof Garden Sculpture Exhibition.
Venice Biennale Nicholas Pope and Tim Head represent Britain.
"Biennials and Beyond – Exhibitions That Made Art History 1962 - 2002" New York, "The Times Square Show".

London Group President: Stan Smith (1975)

No new members were elected this year and no Annual General Meeting was held.

No catalogue of any show is held in the Tate Archive for 1980 although the Group was busy organising a big event for January 1981. Sending in dates for the two January 1981 open exhibitions fell at the end of this year on the 15th to 19th of December 1980. This year seems to have been a year of informal meetings and reorganisation with Joan Strickland as Secretary organising the process. The following invitation was sent out by Stan Smith to the Working Committee, "A Working Party Luncheon Party. At 26 Malwood Road (SW12), Joan Strickland, our astonishing secretary, would like to entertain you to lunch on Sunday, 21st December from 12.30 pm onwards. Please bring your wife along. We aim to combine Christmas conviviality with a discussion to prepare for the selection fray on the following two days". It would make interesting reading to hear what officers' partners would have said about these arrangements working up to Christmas Eve for The London Group.

1981

Greece joins the European Economic Community. The Social Democrat Party is launched in the UK splintering from Labour and eventually merging with the Liberal party. Prince Charles marries Lady Diana Spencer. First reports of AIDS. Inner-city unrest in Brixton (London) and Toxteth (Liverpool). Salman Rushdie writes "Midnight's Children", the film "Chariots of Fire" is released and Bob Marley dies.

"Biennials and Beyond – Exhibitions That Made Art History 1962 - 2002".
"A New Spirit in Painting", **Royal Academy of Arts**. Neo-expressionism from thirty-eight painters working in Britain, Germany, America and Italy curated by Christos M. Joachimides, Norman Rosenthal and Nicholas Serota.
"British Sculpture in the Twentieth Century", **Whitechapel Art Gallery** an extensive survey covering eighty years and showing more than three hundred works. (No "Whitechapel Open" exhibition this year).
Hayward Gallery "Picasso's Picassos". No Hayward Annual but Edward Hopper, Michael Andrews (1962), William Johnstone, Phillip King and Raymond Moore were shown instead.
Serpentine Gallery Mary Potter (1940/43) showed paintings in June and Craigie Aitchison (1962) showed over Christmas.
Summer Show 1 selected by Miranda Strickland Constable, six exhibitors chosen.
Summer Show 2 selected by Adrian Henri, nine exhibitors chosen.
Summer Show 3 selected by Tony Cragg, eleven exhibitors chosen including Anish Kapoor and John Virtue. No London Group members were selected this year.
The Spirit of London the fourth show of an open submission annual exhibition held at the Royal Festival Hall. Judges were Frank Auerbach (1960), Roger de Gray RA, NEAC and Peter Garrard CBE, VPRBA, RP, NEAC. There were a number of prizes, one of £1,500, four of £750 and seven of £350 and a prize of £350 for a disabled artist. Eight sponsors also contributed £2,000 in prizes including Jeffery Archer who contributed a £250 prize for an artist under 30. Two hundred and twenty-nine works were chosen from a total submission of one thousand one hundred.
In October the **Acme Gallery** closed after five and a half years in Covent Garden. The gallery had shown many radical, young artists whose work did not fit into a typical commercial gallery framework. Future London Group members exhibited were Albert Irvin (1965), Simon Read (2006) and Anthony Whishaw (1978).

London Group President: Stan Smith (1975)

"London Group in Southwark Exhibition", Morley Gallery and the South London

Gallery, 9th January to 29th January 1981. Stan Smith was President, the Working Party was Stan Smith, John Bellany (Vice President), Neville Boden, Brian Fielding, Albert Irving (sic), Anthony Whishaw and Arthur Wilson. There were sixty-nine members excluding the new intake of twenty-two, totalling ninety-one members. The catalogue was a loose-leaf silver folder containing A4 sheets of printed paper. The first sheet shows a photograph of the Working Party on the steps of the South London Art Gallery. Stan Smith's introduction records the deaths of Duncan Grant (the last remaining founder member), Richard Carline, Brian Robb, Elsie Few and Jesse Watkins. He writes "The recent great interest shown in the London Group has been reflected in the number of submissions for election to membership. As a result new blood has been brought in and all concerned with the group have confidence that the enerjetic persuits of the highest standards will not only be maintained but enhanced." Spelling as in the original. Harry Thubron and Maurizio Bottarelli were invited artists. The exhibition was at two venues, The South London Art Gallery (fifty-three works) and the Morley Gallery (seventy-one works). A wide variety of work was shown from painting to photography, collage, drawings and sculpture. Anthony Whishaw's "Night Garden II" was top price at £1,250 followed by Kenneth Draper, John Copnall and Gerald Marks, all above £1,000. There had been a surprisingly large send in of non-members work, about four hundred in total, but it is unclear from the catalogue how they came to exhibit or what exhibiting criteria may have been used. This, along with thirty members' work, had "enabled the Group to hold a first class mixed open show". The exhibition made a loss of £2,176 which was largely covered by a grant from the Arts Council for £2,000. The most significant debit was Joan Strickland's fee for the organisation and invigilation of the exhibition recorded as being £600.

The South London Art Gallery
Camberwell, London SE5

The entrance to the art gallery is by the tree on the right. On the left is the old entrance to Camberwell College of Arts where many London Group members studied and/or taught. The two-venue exhibition was a further indication of a renewed vigour and enthusiasm within the Group under Stan Smith's Presidency. The South London Art Gallery is still mounting radical contemporary art exhibitions.

The Group held its AGM at the Morley Gallery on the 15th January whilst the two shows were installed. Twenty-three members attended with four apologies. Discussion continued about a Rogers Memorial, but the situation had been complicated by the death of Rogers' widow, Elsie Few, also a London Group member. The deaths of Duncan Grant, Richard Carline and Brian Robb were also announced and that the Secretary, Sheila Watkins, had resigned; rather depressing news to begin with. There were outline plans for future exhibitions at Camden Arts Centre in 1982 and the South London Art Gallery in 1983 supported by two smaller shows at the Morley gallery in 1982 and 1983 with the possibility of a tour to Oxford. Most of the discussion centred on some members not paying their annual subscriptions. Surprisingly, or perhaps because of the low income from subscriptions, the meeting proposed to raise the annual subscription from £5 to £10 per year in 1982! Under 'New Membership', "Stan Smith (President) reported that selection for new membership had taken place on the second afternoon of the selection for the exhibition, but for a variety of reasons not all prospective members had been voted on". This year saw a huge intake of new members injecting fresh blood into the Group. Twenty-two artists became new members of The London Group. They were Martin Ball, Evelyn Ballantine, Adrian Bartlett, Lindsay Davidson, Ken Draper, John Epstein, Keith Grant, Mel Gordon, Jane Humphrey, Michael Heindorff, Gillian Ingham, Jane Joseph, Roger Kite, Robin Klassnik, Victor Kuell, William Mills, Mike Pope, Peter Richmond, John Roberts, Elma Thubron, Harry Thubron and S. Torrents. It would appear that this was how the huge intake of twenty-two new members was accomplished, by electing new members straight from those artists who had been successful in the open submission. This was probably not according to the rules laid out in The London Group constitution, Stan Smith was known for his cavalier attitude to rules and procedures. At least the Group now had twenty-two more annual subscriptions coming in.

1982

The Polish government abolishes Solidarity. In USSR President Brezhnev dies. Israel invades Lebanon. UK declares war against Argentina in the Falklands War as Argentina invades 'Las Malvinas' after seventeen years of negotiations fail and a British Task Force regains the Islands after a short war. Greenham Common protest, 20,000 women camp out in protest at US cruise missile being sited there. Two IRA bombs in London, one at Hyde Park Corner and the other in Regents Park, kill eight soldiers. Channel Four begins transmission. Richard Attenborough releases "Gandhi", Ridely Scott makes "Blade Runner" and Stephen Spielberg, "ET".

Hayward Annual: British Drawing selected by Kenneth Armitage (1953), Gillian Ayres, Frances Carey, Mark Francis and Euan Uglow (1958). This, like most London Group Annuals, was an open submission exhibition. Over two thousand two hundred artists submitted work and two hundred and sixty-two were chosen.

Serpentine Gallery
Summer Show 1 selected by John Lessore, twelve artists chosen including Ray Atkins (1978).
Summer Show 2 selected by John McLean, ten exhibitors including Tricia Gillman (1988).
Summer Show 3 selected by Richard Francis, six exhibitors chosen.

Whitechapel Art Gallery "Whitechapel Open" exhibition. Also a Philip Guston exhibition.

John Moores Painting Prize 1982 won by John Hoyland with the painting "Broken Bride 13.6.82".

The Spirit of London the fifth show of an open submission annual exhibition held at the Royal Festival Hall.

Venice Biennale Barry Flanagan represents Britain.

London Group President: Stan Smith (1975)

After last year's huge intake it is not surprising that no new members were elected to the Group. Phyllis Bray was elected as an Honorary Member following her withdrawal from the Group through ill health.

The Middle Common Room, Royal College of Art, was where twenty-one members met for the Annual General Meeting on Friday, 26th March. Item 4 'Future Exhibitions' discussed Memorial Shows for Claude Rogers and/or Duncan Grant, but Neville Boden thought that the Group did not have sufficient resources to do these proposals justice. Contacts had been made with Sandy Nairn at the ICA, the Museum of Modern Art, Oxford and the Barbican. The Group had long held a desire for a permanent showing place for The London Group at the Barbican, despite the huge costs involved. "Stan Smith assured contacts were being made regarding this". The first item in the President's report stated "Benefactions were brought up by Stan Smith regarding the Claude Rogers Prize. This had been left with Morris Kestelman but to date nothing had been heard. Paul Tutton had been approached, he seems enthusiastic but is yet to follow up the suggestions with appropriate action. Henry Moore was visited with Joan Strickland who showed enormous enthusiasm and recommended that an award be given. Sainsbury had been approached but had shown no interest." Moving on, the notion of touring a London Group exhibition was then put to those gathered, who were most enthusiastic. Venues in Brighton and St. Ives were already interested. Smith was keen to hold the next open show outside London but, following initial enthusiasm, the meeting decided against. Non-payment of sub.s and lack of submitting work to exhibitions was addressed, again, in the Treasurer's Report. Feelings ran high as members took one side or another, some were for punitive measures, others argued for a more liberal attitude. "The President suggested that he write to all the membership (which he did on the 13th July) asking how they felt the problems should be dealt with so that by the next A.G.M. there is an agreed formula to present to the membership". Under 'Any Other Business', "Stan Smith reported that he and Joan Strickland were working on a major venue for 1984 for the Group's 70th birthday: the ICA and the Tate were interested". Smith could not be faulted for his ambition.

"London Group Members Show", Morley Gallery, 61 Westminster Bridge Road, SE1, 20th September to 8th October 1982. The catalogue to this show was two sheets of cream A4 paper in a silver folder with black typography. There is very little information about the Group or the exhibition in this publication. The catalogue has no introduction or indication of Presidency or number of members. There were thirty-three exhibitors showing one piece of work each, mainly two-dimensional painting but also some prints. Prices averaged £200 to £300 with Kenneth Draper's "Ascent" made of aluminium, resin, oil pigment and wood, priced at £1,500. Mike Pope's oil on canvas "Red Socks" weighed in at £800.

"The London Group '82", Camden Arts Centre, Arkwright Road, Camden, 17th October to 7th November 1982. The catalogue to this show has much more information. Stan Smith is recorded as President, John Bellamy as Vice President and the Working Party was Neville Boden, Robert Clarke, Dennis Creffield, Brian Fielding, David Gluck, Mel Gordon, Roger Kite, Barry Martin, Mike Pope and Arthur Wilson. Membership this year stood at eighty-six. The Foreword states: "There are two innovations this year, one the tour to St. Ives and Brighton: the other the prize so generously donated by Henry Moore". The prize donated by the Henry Moore

Foundation was worth £1,000 and would be awarded for an additional two years. There is no record of the prize-winner. In addition, three artists accepted invitations to show with The London Group, David Hockney, John Hoyland and Ken Kiff. Forty-four of the eighty-six members showed one work each, whilst ninety non-members had one work selected. Sixty-five other works had been, "selected but may not all be exhibited". If the catalogue numbering system identified how many artists submitted work to the Group for selection, then the highest catalogue entry number was 999! Many non-members exhibiting at this exhibition were later to be elected to the Group including Victoria Bartlett, Gus Cummins, Hugh Davis, Alfred Harris, Janet Patterson and David Shutt. About seventeen three-dimensional works were shown, two-dimensional work was varied, mostly oil paintings but some prints and drawings as well. Most expensive asking price was John Edwards' oil painting "Considered Departure" at £2,750. John Bellamy was asking £2500 for his, "Song Thrush laments the ship wreck". The catalogue has a photograph of Stan Smith, John Bellamy and some Working Party members on the steps of the Camden Arts Centre. The catalogue was designed by David Strickland as a vertical format using cream paper with black text and the Private View invitation was illustrated with a drawing by John Bellany. Camden Arts Centre charged The London Group £1,500 as a hiring fee for the galleries. After additional costs and the deduction of just over £100 in catalogue and poster sales, the Group were invoiced for £1,773.39 in total.

Part of this exhibition toured to the Penwith Galleries, St. Ives, from the 16th November to the 7th December 1982. The tour of selected work from the Camden Arts Centre show was financially supported by the Arts Council. It then toured to the Gardner Centre for the Arts, Sussex University, Brighton, from the 19th January to the 12th February 1983. There were no new catalogue publications for the tour. It would appear that extra copies of the London show were printed and used at these venues, although separate posters and PV invites were produced.

In a letter to members Stan Smith wrote, "As we discussed at Working Party meetings, we are obliged to make a selection of members' work in order to travel all non-members' work. With great difficulty such a selection has now been made: initially based upon imperatives such as size and thereafter as making a very small representative show of members' work within the show." (my italics). Thirty members' work was toured. It is unclear who the "we" are who made "a selection". No doubt the letter was to defuse any rumblings from those members not selected for the tour. Interesting to note that all non-member's work was toured, how magnanimous was that!

A photograph taken on the steps leading up
to the Camden Arts Centre, from the 1982
exhibition catalogue

Standing in front is Stanley Smith, the President, seated on the steps, John Bellany,
the Vice President and standing behind him from right to left, Philippa Beale, David
Gluck, Arthur Wilson, Mel Gordon, Joan Strickland, Robert Clarke, Brian Fielding,
Neville Boden and Mike Pope.

1983

Solidarity demonstrations in Poland. US backed invasion of Grenada. US installs Cruise missiles on UK soil at Greenham Common and Pershing 2 missiles throughout Europe. November 8th saw the US and Russian Cold War reach a crisis over a series of intelligence misunderstandings which brought the world close to destruction in a Third World War. US President Reagan announces his hugely expensive "Star Wars" defence system thought to be too complex to work. A General Election in the UK returns a Conservative government, with Margaret Thatcher as PM, buoyed by the "Falklands Factor". Maze prison escape by IRA prisoners. An IRA bomb at Harrods store in London kills six people. William Golding wins the Nobel Prize for Literature and Lech Walesa wins the Peace Prize.

Hayward Gallery Raoul Dufy and Hockney's Photographs.
Serpentine Gallery The year opened with exhibitions from Martin Froy (1954) and Tony Carter (2002) followed by Lawrence Gowing (1940/43).
Summer Show 1 selected by John Roberts, six exhibitors chosen.
Summer Show 2 selected by Noel Forster, seven exhibitors chosen including.Julian Cooper (1971) and James Faure Walker (2000).
These were to be the last of the Serpentine Summer Shows showcasing young artists and contemporary British art giving The London Group some of its market back.
"The Sculpture Show: Edges and Shadows" fifty sculptors at the Serpentine Gallery and the South Bank selected by Paul de Monchaux, Fenella Crichton and Kate Blacker including Michael Sandle (1965).
Whitechapel Art Gallery "Whitechapel Open" exhibition.
The Spirit of London the sixth show of an open submission annual exhibition held at the Royal Festival Hall. The judges were Rasheed Araeen, Jean Cooke RA, Peter John Garrard VPRBA, RP, NEAC, Ben Levene ARA and Monica Petzal. There were a number of prizes, one of £1,500, five of £750, eight of £350 and five 'Peace' prizes of £750, £500, £350, £250 and £150. Five sponsors also contributed £1,000 in prizes including Jeffery Archer who contributed a £250 prize for an artist under 30. Two hundred and eight works were chosen from a total submission of one thousand, two hundred and ninety-five.

London Group President: Stan Smith (1975)

The Group still seemed to be digesting the huge 1981 intake of twenty-two as there were no new members elected two years later in 1983.

No catalogue of any annual show is held in the Tate Archive. There was, however, a tour of selected work from the 1982 exhibition to the Gardner Centre for the Arts, Sussex University, Brighton, showing from the 19th January to the 12th February 1983.

This year saw a memorable incident in the Group that still resonates and is retold around the campfires like an ancient Nordic legend. It centred on Dennis Creffield's election as President at the AGM on Friday, 17th June at the Royal College of Art. An unremarkable agenda for the AGM had been circulated on which Stan Smith was recorded as President and John Bellany as Vice President. No minutes have been archived for this meeting. However, at an Extraordinary General Meeting held at Morley College on 5th November and attended by twenty-two members, the following minutes were recorded:

"Minutes of the last meeting:

Due to some confusion at the previous meeting there were no minutes available for the items on the agenda dealt with there.

Matters arising:

Dennis Creffield explained the events at the meeting in May (sic) at which the business was left incomplete. He had recently resigned the Presidency to which he had been elected then because he said that there were doubts in some minds as to the constitutional correctness of the whole thing."

Under AOB, "It was agreed that a copy of the constitution should be sent to each member". Stan Smith then assumed the position of Acting President and the meeting then confirmed his re-election, with Brian Fielding as Vice President and Adrian Bartlett as Honorary Secretary.

Dark rumblings persist to this day as to the power struggle smouldering beneath the cool objectivity of these minutes. Mike Liggins, The London Group Secretary recounts the following story, "While invigilating with Victoria Bartlett last week (Open Exhibition 2009) she regaled me with a splendid anecdote of an encounter (at her and Adrian's own house) between Stan Smith and Dennis Creffield, apparently in regard to the disputed outcome of a Presidential election, in which the two had descended into fisticuffs. Smith, unbeknown to Creffield, had once been a welterweight boxing champion and accordingly got much the better of the bout, which included knocking over the piano."

1984

Mrs Gandhi assassinated in India. USSR boycotts Los Angeles Summer Olympic Games. Bhopal gas escape kills thousands in Central India. Ethiopia experiences serious famine. Miners strike in the UK led by Arthur Scargill, a long, bitter and often violent dispute seen as a face off by the Conservative Government, led by Margaret Thatcher, and the Trade Union movement at large. The Grand Hotel in Brighton was bombed by the IRA during the Conservative Party Conference, killing 5, injuring 30 and narrowly missing Margaret Thatcher. "The Yuppie Handbook" is published, "Yuppie" stood for 'young upwardly mobile professional'.

1984 The British Art Show "Old Allegiances and New Directions 1979-1984" at the Hayward Gallery selected by Marjorie Allthorpe-Guyton (curator), Alexander Moffat (painter) and Jon Thompson (artist and teacher, Goldsmiths). Eighty-one artists using film, video and performance as well as painting and sculpture were selected. Amongst others, Frank Auerbach (1960), John Bellany (1973), Tony Carter (2002), Leon Kossof (1963), Kenneth Martin (1949), Paula Rego (1965) and Michael Sandle (1965) were exhibited.

The Turner Prize was inaugurated at the Tate Gallery. The Turner Prize was to be awarded annually to the artist who had made a significant advancement for British art in the preceding year. Turner Prize 1984 - the first winner was Malcolm Morley and Richard Deacon, Gilbert & George, Howard Hodgkin and Richard Long had been shortlisted.

The Spirit of London the seventh show of an open submission annual exhibition held at the Royal Festival Hall. The judges were Jean Cooke RA, Peter John Garrard VPRBA, RP, NEAC, Ben Levene ARA, Monica Petzal and Aubrey Williams. There were a number of prizes, one of £1,500, five of £750, eight of £350 and four 'Anti-Racism' prizes, one of £1,000 and three of £300. Six sponsors also contributed £1,500 in prizes including Jeffery Archer who contributed a £250 prize for an artist under 30. Susan Wilson (1997) was a £750 prize-winner, David Redfern (2000) won a £300 Anti-Racism Prize and Julie Held (2002) was commended. Two hundred and two works were chosen from a total submission of one thousand, nine hundred and sixteen.

Whitechapel Art Gallery "Whitechapel Open" exhibition. Even though the gallery was closed for a major refurbishment, the Whitechapel honoured its commitment to providing artists with an open submission opportunity by installing the Open Exhibition in nearby buildings.

Venice Biennale Britain's representative this year was Howard Hodgkin.

London Group President: Stan Smith (1975)

Eight new members were elected this year, Victoria Bartlett, Gus Cummins, Joe McGill, Janet Nathan, Janet Patterson, Suzan Swale, Mike Thorpe and Christopher Twyford.

"London Group 84, Open Exhibition", Royal College of Art, 6th November to 23rd November 1984. Stan Smith was President, Brian Fielding Vice President with the rest of the Working Party comprising, Adrian Bartlett, Peter Archer, Philippa Beale, Evelyn Ballantine, John Crossley, Stanislaw Frenkiel, John Epstein, Gillian Ingham, Victor Kuell and Kit Twyford. Joan Strickland was the Exhibition Organiser and ninety-six members were recorded in the catalogue. The catalogue was the same as the 1981 design, A4 silver folder and loose-leaf contents. Two prizes were on offer to be awarded to non-member exhibitors, the £1,000 Henry Moore prize and the "Atlantis Paper Award". Forty-nine members exhibited one piece each and there were one hundred and forty-three non-member exhibits, a total of one hundred and ninety-two objects. Among non-members exhibiting were, Quentin Blake, Peter Clossick, John Copnall, Cathy de Monchaux, Mario Dubsky, Tricia Gillman, Alfred Harris, Timothy Hyman, Lucy Jones, Eric Moody, Colette Moray de Morand, Paul Neagu, Eugene Palmer, Alex Ramsay, Kevin Slingsby and Marc Vaux, many of whom were to be elected in the future. Top price was for Anthony Eyton's "A Kitchen Range" at £5,500. Members' prices were noticeably higher than non-members' prices. This year also saw a scheme whereby members were asked to donate a piece of work to a London Group raffle to raise funds for the Group. Forty pounds purchased a ticket and the first ticket out of the hat got first choice of donated work, second next, and so on. Stan Smith's introduction speculated that a selection from the "Seventieth Anniversary Exhibition" was to be toured to Braintree in January 1985 but there is no evidence of this happening.

No minutes of an Annual General Meeting in 1984 have been archived.

1985

President Gorbachev calls for 'Glasnost' and 'Perestroika' reforms in the USSR. President Reagan sworn in for a second term in office. In November, the two men meet in Geneva for peace talks. Greenpeace's ship, "Rainbow Warrior", is sunk by French agents in New Zealand. Air India flight 182 explodes over the Atlantic killing 329. The hole in the Earth's ozone layer is discovered. RMS Titanic discovered by a joint French-American expedition. Microsoft launches Windows version 1.0. "Live-aid" raises more than £50,000,000 for famine relief with concerts in the US and UK. Mohammed Al Fayed buys Harrods. Football hooligans fight and riot, coming to be known as the 'English Disease'. In the European Cup Final between Liverpool and Juventus at the Heysel Stadium, Brussels, thirty-eight spectators were killed in a football riot. A fire at Bradford football ground kills fifty-six. Riots in Brixton following a Metropolitan Police shooting of Dorothy 'Cherry' Groce.

The **Saatchi Collection** opens in Boundary Road, North London. Donald Judd, Brice Marden, Cy Twombly and Andy Warhol are in the opening exhibition.
Whitechapel Art Gallery "Whitechapel Open" exhibition. The Gallery was still closed for refurbishment but ensured that local artists had an exhibition opportunity.
The Contemporary Art Society's 75th anniversary, formed in 1910, 3 years before The London Group. The CAS purchased contemporary painting and sculpture for distribution to regional and London galleries.
Hayward Gallery an Edgar Degas exhibition.
Serpentine Gallery Kenneth Martin (1949): The Late Paintings
Turner Prize 1985 the winner was Howard Hodgkin and short-listed were, Terry Atkinson, Tony Cragg, Ian Hamilton Finlay and John Walker.
John Moores Painting Prize 1985 won by Bruce McLean with the painting, "Oriental Garden, Kyoto".
Camberwell, St Martins and Chelsea Colleges of Art and Design merge to form the London Institute.
"Biennials and Beyond – Exhibitions That Made Art History 1962 - 2002" Paris, "Les Immatériaux".

London Group President: Stan Smith (1975)

No new members were elected this year and there is no catalogue of any annual exhibition either.

The AGM this year was held on the 25th October at the Central School of Art and Design. In a letter to members dated the 19th September 1985, the President Stan

Smith wrote, "I am sorry for the lateness in the year of the AGM on this occasion but after the constitutional faux-pas last time I am meeting the majority of the members' preferences in setting the date. I apologies to those who have been inconvenienced by the postponement and reconstitution of the meeting and hope that we shall all go into this one (which promises well), with open minds and high expectations". The agenda lists a Presidents Report, RCA exhibition, future plans and possibilities, prizes and benefactions and votes of thanks. Fourteen members were present at the AGM and they elected Stan Smith as President, John Crossley as Vice President, Robert Coward as Treasurer and Gillian Ingham as Hon. Secretary. Martin Ball, Philippa Beale, David Gluck, Vic Kuell, Mike Thorpe, Kit Twyford, Suzan Swale and Anthony Whishaw formed the Working Committee. The fact that there was no annual exhibition this year also seemed to ease financial concerns. Income from members' subscriptions was £623 which, following deductions for expenditure, left a £543 surplus. But "Sundry Debtors" owed the Group £1,040 (which would have included members who were defaulting on their subscriptions). With "Sundry Creditors" providing £2,926 and cash totalling £2,445, The London Group began the year (31st January 1985) with £559 in the General Fund. The treasurer "commented that the financial position of the group was generally healthy."

1986

Sanctions imposed against South Africa. Chernobyl nuclear reactor disaster in USSR. US bombs Libya, some planes take off from US bases on UK soil. Space Shuttle Challenger explodes at launch killing seven astronauts. President Marcos flees the Philippines. In the UK, press disputes lead to a move from Fleet Street to Wapping, angry confrontations. A new newspaper, the 'Independent', is first printed. Westland helicopter scandal in UK Conservative government. The Greater London Council is abolished and Ken Livingstone is out of a job. The Conservative Government introduces gallery and museum admission charges.

Hayward Gallery "Falls the Shadow: Recent British and European Art". This was the last in the series of Hayward Annuals and the first international venture. Thirty-two artists were selected by Barry Barker and Jon Thompson.
Serpentine Gallery Frank Bowling (1963, re-elected 2002): Paintings, and John Bellany (1973): Paintings, Watercolours and Drawings". Two ex-Vice Presidents of The London Group.
Whitechapel Art Gallery "Whitechapel Open" exhibition.
Turner Prize 1986 winners were Gilbert & George. Art & Language, Victor Burgin, Derek Jarman, Stephen McKenna and Bill Woodrow were shortlisted.
Venice Biennale Frank Auerbach (1960) represents Britain.
"Biennials and Beyond – Exhibitions That Made Art History 1962 - 2002" Ghent, "Chambres d'Amis". Cuba, "Second Havana Biennial".
Henry Moore (1930) and Joseph Beuys die.

London Group President: Stan Smith (1975)

No new members were elected this year and for the second year in succession. Stan Smith and other officers did not arrange an Annual General Meeting either. The feeling of consolidation (or procrastination) was further enhanced by the lack of an annual exhibition.

 The Group's financial complexion continued to improve, no doubt aided by the relief of annual exhibition expenses. Income from both members' subscriptions and bank deposit interest was £658.19, down nearly £50 on the previous year. Expenditure was nearly the same, £161.39, leaving a surplus for the year of £496.80. The biggest improvement came in the General Fund figures up from £559 at 31st January 1985 to £1,000.23 at 31st January 1986. It seemed as though the Group was getting itself in good financial shape before organising future exhibitions and was calling in bad debt and outstanding members' contributions.

The Working Committee for the 1987 exhibition
From left to right they are: Alistair Grant, Anthony Whishaw, David Gluck, Suzan Swale, Barry Martin, Joan Strickland, Victor Kuell, Stan Smith, Gillian Ingham and Martin Ball.

1987

Gorbachev criticises the Brezhnev era in the USSR and continues 'Glasnost' and 'Perestroika'. White only elections in South Africa. A Conservative Government led by Margaret Thatcher is returned for a third term following a UK General Election. The Labour leader was Neil Kinnock and David Steel led the Liberals. October 19th, London, "Black Monday", stock market crash, worldwide decline in stock values. Hurricane-force winds hit South East England causing widespread damage and bringing down many trees. Weatherman Michael Fish lives to regret, "There is no hurricane on the way". Thirty-one people are killed in a fire in Kings Cross Underground Station when a wooden escalator catches fire.

Royal Academy "British Art of the Twentieth Century".

Whitechapel Art Gallery "Whitechapel Open" exhibition, also a Jacob Epstein (1913) retrospective.

The **Turner Prize 1987** winner was Richard Deacon. Those short-listed were, Patrick Caulfield, Helen Chadwick, Richard Long and Thérèse Oulton.

John Moores Painting Prize 1987 won by Tim Head with the painting, "Cow mutations".

Museum of Modern Art Oxford "Current Affairs: British Painting and Sculpture in the 1980s". Art & Language, Susan Hiller and Paula Rego (1965) are among twenty-six exhibitors.

The Hayward Gallery, the Arts Council Collection and the National Touring Exhibitions is transferred to the South Bank Centre following the closure of the GLC. Also shown were Le Corbusier, Tony Cragg and Diego Rivera.

Matt's Gallery shows Richard Wilson's seminal "20/50", a reflecting sump oil installation later purchased by Saatchi.

The **Clore Gallery** extension housing much of the Turner Bequest opens at the Tate Gallery.

Peter Fuller edits the new art journal, "Modern Painters".

London Group President: Stan Smith (1975)

Four new members were elected this year, Clive Burton, Harvey Daniels, Brian Kneale and Chris Plowman.

An AGM was finally held on 13th February at the Royal College of Art. Nineteen members attended and six sent apologies. The President reported that progress had been made in terms of funding with the Arts Council offering £2,000 against loss for a proposed tour of the forthcoming Open. The Henry Moore prize was to run for one more Open Show donated by the Henry Moore Foundation. The group's financial position improved again this year. Records completed on the 31st January 1987 show that the General Fund contained £1,480.77 which was an increase of £480.54 on the same time last year. Members' subscription totals were about the same as last year (£543.65) whilst other expenditure remained at the same level. However, the Treasurer reported that only fifty-seven members were fully paid up and that nineteen were in arrears. The meeting voted for a tactful but firm letter to try to recoup this sizeable sum. President Smith then presented information about the forthcoming open exhibition in the Royal College of Art Henry Moore Gallery. The Group had negotiated a very good "fixed fee of £4,000" for the hire of the facility, but in return RCA students were to be allowed to send one work with no submission or hanging fee charged. The Constitution was also to be reviewed because of "certain practical difficulties". Vic Kuell and Morris Kestelman undertook to review the written rules and report back to the Group. In the elections, Alistair Grant replaced John Crossley as Vice President.

"The London Group 1987 Open Show at the Royal College of Art", RCA, Kensington Gore SW7, 24th March to 22nd May 1987. There were eighty-nine members recorded in the catalogue. Officers this year were Stan Smith as President, Alistair Grant as Vice President, Gillian Ingham as Hon Secretary and Robert Coward as Treasurer. The Working party consisted of Alistair Grant, Anthony Whishaw, David Gluck, Suzan Swale, Barry Martin, Joan Strickland (Organiser), Victor Kuell, Stan Smith, Gillian Ingham and Martin Ball. Stan Smith as President penned a foreword in which he wrote, "Through the association of Henry Moore as a past member, the Henry Moore Foundation has given an award of £1,000 for a work (or works) of distinction in the open exhibition." Daler-Rowney and Atlantis Paper also donated prizes and the Mercers' Company made a generous donation. Two memorial shows were also included dedicated to Harry Thubron and Lindsay Davidson. Fifty-one out of eighty-nine members showed one or two pieces of work each. One hundred and twelve non-members were selected including, Gillian Ayres, Peter Blake, John Edwards, Dame Elisabeth Frink, Tricia Gillman, John Hoyland, Allen Jones, Ken Kiff, Bryan Kneale, Alex Ramsay and Gary Wragg. The catalogue gives name, title, media and price. Oil paint still seems to be the preferred paint at this point in history. Member Anthony Whishaw was asking £6,730 for his acrylic collage on canvas, entitled "Reflections. Interior, triptych" whilst non-member Gillian Ayres priced her oil on canvas entitled "A Painted Tale" at £10,000. A healthy number of prints were also selected. The catalogue was A5 landscape on cream paper with a figure drawing by Stan Smith on the cover and the poster carried the same image. A small formal invite invites the recipient to "A dinner on St. Georges' Day celebrating the birthdays of Shakespeare, Turner, Joan Strickland, and the opening of the London Group 1987 Open Show at the Royal College of Art, April 23rd at 7.30 in the Senior Common Room"– at £15 a head!

Invoice number 098671 from the Royal College of Art required The London Group to pay £4,000 for the hire of the Henry Moore Gallery and £200 for the hire of a seminar room. Further correspondence shows financial support to the tune of £1,500 from the Arts Council of Great Britain, "with a promise of a further £500" and, in addition, there was also a guarantee against loss of £2,000 for the exhibition and the tour.

A selection from this exhibition toured to The Old Court Gallery, Windsor Community Art Centre, St Leonard's Road, Windsor, from 23rd August to 5th September 1987 as part of a local Arts Festival and then to the Bede Gallery, Springwell Park, Butchersbridge Road, Jarrow from 7th October to 15th November 1987. The Tate Archive holds three colour photographs of The London Group touring exhibition at the Bede Gallery. The photographs show one large gallery approximately 20 x 5 metres with a large number of works, perhaps one hundred, crowded into the space and mostly double hung. There are three sculptures on plinths. Individual paintings are not immediately identifiable, possibly a Bert Irvin and a Brian Fielding as well as a painting of an enormous meat pie!

1988

Gorbachev puts forward more democratic reforms in the USSR and also withdraws from Afghanistan. George Bush elected President of USA. Iran and Iraq call a cease-fire in a deadlocked war. Al-Qaeda is formed at a meeting in Peshawar, Pakistan. IRA shootings in Gibraltar. Pan Am Flight 103 is brought down by a terrorist bomb over Lockerbie, Scotland, killing 270. Piper Alpha oil platform tragedy, 167 oil workers die. The Summer Olympic Games are held in Seoul, South Korea. The GCSE examination system is introduced in the UK. Salman Rushdie's "Satanic Verses", fatwa declared by Ayatollah Kohmeini for blasphemy, Rushdie goes into hiding.

Tate Gallery Liverpool opens with "Starlit Waters", fifteen British sculptors including Michael Craig-Martin, Tony Cragg, Richard Deacon, Antony Gormley, Anish Kapoor, Richard Long and Alison Wilding.
Tate Gallery London Major Hockney (1963) retrospective.
After 1962 "Whitechapel Open" exhibition. Michael Sandle (1965) exhibition.
Serpentine Gallery Paula Rego (1965).
"Biennials and Beyond – Exhibitions That Made Art History 1962 - 2002".
PLA Building, Docklands, London Damien Hurst curates and organises **"Freeze"**, showing work from Goldsmiths College students, seventeen artists including Angela Bulloch, Angus Fairhurst, Michael Landy and Sarah Lucas in a dilapidated warehouse in London's Docklands. Perhaps the most legendary 'self-help' exhibition, launching the reputations and careers of many Young British Artists (Y.B.A.s).
Turner Prize 1988 winner Tony Cragg. Short-listed, Lucian Freud, Richard Hamilton, Richard Long, David Mach, Boyd Webb, Alison Wilding and Richard Wilson.
Venice Biennale Tony Cragg represents Britain and gets a 'special mention'.

London Group President: Stan Smith (1975)

Three new members were elected this year, John Copnall, Jean Gibson and Tricia Gillman.

The AGM was held at the Central School of Art on Friday, 11th March. A healthy number of twenty-four members attended indicating an upsurge in support for the Group. The President reported on the success of last year's Open with good sales figures but disappointing press coverage. Despite the relative success of the tours to Windsor and Jarrow, discussion about the high costs of touring resulted in the cancellation of future plans. Other members also felt that the RCA was "off the beaten track" and Camden Art Centre and the Whitechapel were floated as potential venues for future exhibitions. Finally, the Henry Moore Gallery at the RCA was agreed at a hire fee of

£3,000 for the 75th anniversary exhibition. In fact the Treasurer reported that last year's exhibition and tour had incurred a deficit of £2,295.66. Despite many members paying off their arrears the Group only had an overall balance of £110.73. Officers remained the same as last year apart from Mike Thorpe being elected as Vice President.

"London Group 75th Anniversary Exhibition", Royal College of Art, 6th August to 28th August 1988. This was a Members and Invited Artists exhibition only. The Group had chosen to celebrate its 75th Anniversary with a "controlled" submission instead of choosing from an open submission. Members of the Working Party were, Stan Smith as President, Mike Thorpe as Vice President, Gillian Ingham as Honorary Secretary, Robert Coward as Treasurer and Philippa Beale, John Crossley, Jean Gibson, Michael Heindorff, Roger Kite, Mike Pope, Suzan Swale and Arthur Wilson as Working Committee members. There were eighty-one members this year. The catalogue records one hundred and forty-three exhibits including paintings, drawings and sculpture. As usual with London Group exhibitions there was a tight schedule, Monday the 1st and Tuesday the 2nd of August were receiving days, then three days to arrange and hang with the Private View on the Friday evening. This was followed by three weeks of public access requiring an invigilation rota. Only two days, one of which was a Bank Holiday, were allowed for dismantling and collection of work. The majority of the work exhibited was oil painting but with as wide a variety of approach as could be imagined. Notable invited artists exhibiting were Tony Carter, Jeffrey Dellow, John Hoyland ARA, Timothy Hyman, Cathy de Monchaux, Mick Moon, Marc Vaux, Glyn Williams and Ken Kiff. No prices were printed in the catalogue that contained a large number of black and white illustrations but gave title, medium and size. The Working Committee had imposed a width restriction of five feet on all work and a commission of 25% on all sales, 15% to the RCA and 10% to The London Group. In addition there was a hanging fee of £20 and a request for a black and white glossy photograph for inclusion in the catalogue. Honorary Secretary Gillian Ingham had the unenviable job of co-ordinating all this information for publication in the catalogue. Stan Smith wrote an appreciation of Brian Fielding who died this year and a Brian Fielding graphic image was printed on the poster for the exhibition.

On Friday, 16th December an Extraordinary General Meeting was called at the Central School of Art with the sole purpose of reviewing the Group's financial situation. Fourteen members attended and heard from the President that "the financial position of the Group was disastrous and that we had run into debt". The situation was so bad that the Treasurer had informed the President "that the Group had to get solvent or wind up". Mike Thorpe proposed raising the annual subscription to £30 which was unanimously agreed. The President was also instructed by those at the meeting to renegotiate the gallery hire fee of £3,000 with the RCA and to organise fund raising and social events. The meeting closed at 8.00pm!

1989

Thousands of students killed in Tiananmen Square massacre in Peking, China. The Berlin Wall is demolished. In Europe the Communist Block begins to crumble, demonstrations in East Germany, the Roumanian leader Ceaucescu is executed and playwright Vaclev Havel becomes Czech President in the "Velvet Revolution". US invades Panama and installs a sympathetic government. Tim Berners-Lee invents the World Wide Web. Hillsborough Football Stadium tragedy where ninety-five fans are crushed to death. Work begins on boring the Channel Tunnel. Ten soldiers are killed by an IRA bomb at the Royal Marines School of Music, Deal Barracks, Kent.

Whitechapel Art Gallery "Whitechapel Open" exhibition, also an exhibition of paintings by Euan Uglow (1958).
Hayward Gallery Leonardo da Vinci, Andy Warhol and "The Other Story: Afro-Asian artists in Post-war Britain" exhibitions
Serpentine Gallery "Blasphemies, Ecstasies, Cries", selected by Andrew Brighton including Frank Auerbach (1960), Jacob Epstein (1913), Peter de Francia (1977), Wyndham Lewis (1913) and Carel Weight (1949). "Fort-five Paintings" by Ivon Hitchens (1931).
The Design Museum supported by Terence Conran opens nearby Tower Bridge.
Turner Prize 1989 the winner this year was Richard Long. Those short-listed were Gillian Ayres, Lucian Freud, Giuseppe Penone, Paula Rego (1965), Sean Scully and Richard Wilson.
John Moores Painting Prize 1989 won by Lisa Milroy with the painting, "Handles". **The New Contemporaries** is re-launched to be a touring exhibition of the best student and recent graduate work. Opening at the **ICA** and then touring to Manchester, Bracknell, Halifax and Kendal.
"Biennials and Beyond – Exhibitions That Made Art History 1962 - 2002" Beijing, "China/Avant-Garde". Paris, "Magiciens de la Terre".

London Group President: Stan Smith (1975)

Three more new members elected, David Carr, John Edwards and Alex Ramsay.

The Central School of Art was again the venue for the AGM held on Friday, 17th March. Only sixteen members attended with six apologies. The President painted a rosy picture of the Group's activities reporting that the Anniversary Exhibition had been "highly successful" and that "the poster and catalogue had been well received". The treasurer painted a different picture with a net deficit of £1,437.10 from the exhibition and that "therefore we were technically insolvent". The exhibition catalogue was responsible for much of this debt and in future the Working Committee "must operate on a shoestring". Under AOB "Morris Kestelman reported that he and Vic Kuell had been compiling the revised Constitution and that it would be put to members 3 weeks before an E.G.M. At this meeting Morris Kestelman accepted the offer of being made an Honorary Member of the Group".

"The London Group Open Exhibition 1989", Royal College of Art, 8th–24th August 1989. The President was Stan Smith this year supported by Mike Thorpe as Vice President. Gillian Ingham was Secretary and the Treasurer was Robert Coward. The Working Party for this exhibition consisted of John Crossley, Jean Gibson, David Gluck, William Henderson, John Hoskin, Morris Kestelman and Victor Kuell. The catalogue indicates a membership of seventy-nine this year, quite healthy figures. Of the one hundred and thirty-one works exhibited, forty-six members showed one work each, the remainder were by non-members and included fourteen pieces of sculpture. The RCA had requested that 10% of the work hung should be RCA student work and required 15% commission on exhibition sales. Despite criticism from some members that the £3,000 hire charge was too high, officers pointed out that the RCA normally charged £1,000 a day and that The London Group were getting a "realistic deal". Exhibiting non-members this year included Tracey Emin (a watercolour of Istanbul), James Faure Walker, Gwyther Irwin, Matthew Kolakowski, Alan Miller and Mark Vaux. There were no illustrations in the exhibition catalogue, only name, title, media and price. As with many previous exhibitions, the sculpture was the highest price and four figure sums were asked for the majority of member and non-member two and three dimensional works. Stan Smith wrote the catalogue introduction that began with an historical account of the Group. Smith continued, "We are now set fair for a great launch into the 1990s" and follows that statement with, "We are searching avidly for regular financial input", apart from the members' annual subscriptions, one presumes. Daler Rowney pitched in with a materials prize worth £500 and the Christopher James Gallery of Bath stumped up a cash prize of £250. There is no record of who won them. The catalogue itself was A4 portrait with discrete black typo on white paper, cover and contents. The large format poster showed a black and white graphic image by Morris Kestelman and advertised sponsorship from Daler Rowney, Michael Lynn, Christopher James and John Purcell Papers who donated the 100% recycled paper on which the poster was printed.

The London Group ended the decade technically insolvent. The cost of hiring the RCA Henry Moore Gallery, even though at a reduced rate, had depleted the Group's funds. Moreover, catalogue costs had further exacerbated the financial crisis. Annual Exhibitions (as required by the constitution) had not been held every year, had they been the Group's situation would have been even worse. Some members were in arrears with their subscriptions and, moving into the next decade, the President and officers were under pressure to organise initiatives to bring in much needed funds.

The 1990's

The nineties saw a new movement towards artists curating their own shows and finding radical new venues, disused warehouses for example. They did not need The London Group to help promote their work, many art students fresh out of college were quickly taken up by young and professional art galleries like White Cube for example.

For the purposes of this book's introduction to the 1990s, Louisa Buck's "Moving Targets: A User's Guide to British Art Now" published in 1997 by Tate Gallery Publishing is an ideal introduction. "Perhaps the most distinctive feature of the artists who are defining British art in the 1990s is the very fact that they do not share a common style or medium. They produce figurative and abstract paintings, ready-made and hand-made sculptures, photography and text, videos, installations and CD ROMs – sometimes simultaneously. Some work in isolation, others operate within interconnected communities, and many are loath to be given any label, whether personal, artistic or national". Buck then continues to analyse the decade under the following headings, The Makers, Current Contenders, Rising Stars, The Players and Dealers. Under each heading she lists those whom she considers most important.

The Makers: Presiding Forces Francis Bacon, Helen Chadwick, Lucian Freud, Gilbert and George, Richard Hamilton, Susan Hiller, Bruce McLean, Paula Rego (1965) and Richard Wentworth.
Current Contenders Brian Catling, Willie Doherty, Anya Gallaccio, Douglas Gordon, Antony Gormley, Mona Hatoum, Damien Hirst, Gary Hume, Cathy de Monchaux, Julian Opie, Cornelia Parker, Fiona Rae, Mark Wallinger, Rachel Whiteread and Richard Wilson.
Rising Stars Simon Bill, Christine Borland, Jake and Dinos Chapman, Mat Collishaw, Melanie Counsell, Tracey Emin, Sarah Lucas, Steve McQueen, Chris Ofili, Grayson Perry, Georgine Starr, Sam Taylor-Wood, Gavin Turk and Gillian Wearing.
The Players: Curators, Gallery Directors and Teachers Iwona Blazwick from the Tate Gallery of Modern Art, London, Michael Craig-Martin from Goldsmiths College, London, Carl Freedman, a curator and writer, Robin Klassnik (1981), of Matts Gallery, London, James Lingwood of Artangel, London, Declan McGonagle from the Irish Museum of Modern Art, Elizabeth A MacGregor from the Ikon Gallery, Birmingham, Julia Peyton-Jones from the Serpentine Gallery, London and Nicholas Serota from the Tate Gallery, London.
Dealers Jay Jopling from White Cube Gallery, London, Nicholas Logsdail from the Lisson Gallery, London, Anthony d'Offay (Gallery), London, Maureen Paley of Interim Art, London, Karsten Schubert, an art dealer from London and Leslie Waddington (Gallery), London.

It is significant that Buck sees fit to mention Curators, Gallery Directors, Teachers and Dealers in her history of the 1990s indicating the sea change that had taken place in the nature of the art world. Note also that most of the artists that Buck lists were Turner Prize winners and candidates, the Turner Prize being the jewel within the Tate's crown!

Young British Artists (YBAs), Rachel Whiteread, Cornelia Parker, Mark Wallinger, Marc Quinn, Sam Taylor-Wood, Jake and Dinos Chapman, Fiona Rae, Tracey Emin, Gary Hume, Chris Ofili, Gillian Wearing and Damien Hirst. In the 1990s, Goldsmiths' College in South East London continued to take the lead in grooming influential contemporary artists.

The New Contemporaries "From 1989 to 1994 the exhibition was sponsored by British Telecom and from 2000 to 2006 was sponsored by Bloomberg. Apart from 1995, due to the absence of a sponsor, the exhibition has maintained an annual presence. In 1996 the exhibition attracted the patronage of James Moores and a commitment to the city of Liverpool, premiering every two years as part of the Liverpool Biennale of Contemporary Art. New Contemporaries is also a revenue client of Arts Council England. Since 1995, the administration has been based in Manchester." (from the New Contemporaries website). Obviously the attraction of a sponsor outside of London could not be lightly dismissed. The New Contemporaries, despite support from Arts Council England and a professional administration, were still finding it hard to exhbit in the capital. The London Group had no regular sponsorship and a volunteer administration, but still managed to organise more than one exhibiton a year.

Tate Modern Time Line 1990-2000 Rodney Graham, William Kentridge, Doris Salcedo, Luc Tuymans, John Currin, Matthew Barney, Eja-Liisa Ahtila. Under Düsseldorf School of Photography - Bernd and Hiller Becher, Thomas Struth, Andreas Gursky, Candida Höfer, Thomas Ruff. Under Young British Artists - Rachel Whiteread, Cornelia Parker, Mark Wallinger, Marc Quinn, Sam Taylor-Wood, Jake and Dinos Chapman, Fiona Rae, Tracey Emin, Gary Hume, Chris Ofili, Gillian Wearing and Damien Hirst. Then Sonia Boyce, Pipilotti Rist, Anya Gallaccio, David Hammons, Thomas Shütte. Under 'Installation' - Cildo Meireles, Ilya Kabakov, Gabriel Orozco, Juan Muñoz, Olafur Eliasson, Mike Kelley, Michael Landy, Steve McQueen, Douglas Gordon, Isaac Julien and Tacita Dean. Then Rikrit Tiravanya, Felix Gonzalez-Torres, Jeremy Deller followed by Paula Rego (1965), Mona Hatoum, Wolfgang Tillmans and Marlene Dumas.

1990

Iraq invades Kuwait and the UN imposes sanctions on Iraq. Later in the year US forces arrive in Saudi Arabia in preparation for the first Gulf War. Nelson Mandela is freed from twenty-seven years in prison in South Africa. Lech Walesa becomes first president of Poland. Helmut Kohl elected Chancellor of a newly reunited Germany. Yeltsin becomes President of the Russian Federation. Gorbachev is awarded the Nobel Peace Prize. In the UK more than four hundred people are arrested at an anti Poll Tax demonstration in Trafalgar Square. Margaret Thatcher is ousted by the Conservatives and replaced as Prime Minister by John Major. In Wales, the last pit in the Rhondda Valley is closed. 'Mad Cow' disease strikes.

British Art Show 1990 (3) selected by Caroline Collier (curator), Andrew Nairne (curator), David Ward (artist), forty-two artists, most aged under thirty-five, includes painting, sculpture, installations, film, video and performance. No London Group members selected.
Serpentine Gallery Albert Irvin (1965), "Paintings".
Whitechapel Art Gallery "Whitechapel Open" exhibition.
Turner Prize 1990 No prize was awarded this year due to withdrawal of sponsorship.
Paula Rego (1965) becomes the **National Gallery's** first Associate Artist.
Venice Biennale Britain is represented by Anish Kapoor who wins the 'Premio Duemila' for the work of a young artist.

London Group President: Stan Smith (1975)

At the start of this new decade there was a huge injection of new members, twenty-one in total, including Sharon Aivaliotis, David Annesley, Ines Buhler, Hugh Davies, John Dougill, Alfred Harris, William Henderson, Ian Hunter, Matthew Kolakowski, Prudence Kurll, Eric Moody, Peter Morrell, Ken Oliver, Robert Russell, David Shutt, Kevin Slingsby, Keir Smith, Philippa Stjernsward, Mark Vaux, David Whitaker and Gary Wragg.

The AGM was held at Central St Martins College of Art (Southampton Row) on the 23rd March with only sixteen members in attendance, seven proffering apologies. Although the last RCA exhibition was a success, the President reported, "it was generally felt that August was not the best time of the year". The AGM voted to accept the rewritten Constitution "for a period of one year in order to iron out any problems that may arise". "The President proposed that Edna Ginesi and Raymond Coxon be made Honorary Members. The group voted in favour and were duly elected". The Treasurer's report was received with a sigh of relief indicating a net surplus of £388.51.

"The President proposed a vote of thanks to the Treasurer which was accepted unanimously". Mike Thorpe then proposed the idea of Associate Membership to The London Group in order to recruit younger members and a small working party was set up to look into the proposal.

There exists a poster for an exhibition which was held in the Central St Martins Gallery, Southampton Row, London WC1 of London Group Members' Work from May 29th to June 1st (4 days?). Minutes from the recent AGM recorded that a Members Exhibition was to be held in the Letheby (sic) Gallery in May. The Poster proclaims in large black type, '30', followed by members' work (presumably thirty members took part) and, '90', (presumably the year of the exhibition). A catalogue for this exhibition (if it took place) has not been archived.

"Open Exhibition 1990", Royal College of Art, 17th September to 4th October 1990. Stan Smith was still President, Mike Thorpe was Vice President, Gillian Ingham Hon. Secretary and Victor Kuell the Treasurer. The catalogue was A5 black text on white and listed one hundred and eighty-nine exhibits, sixty from members. Stan Smith writes, "For those interested in statistics: 226 non-members entered 339 works, out of which 129 were selected for exhibition" and "A rewarding aspect of the 'Open Exhibitions' is that those who slip through the net of gallery exposure despite indisputable quality, are able to hang work beside others known and well seen across the world. We are particularly proud of this aspect of our work, frustrating and difficult as it often is in these days of financial stresses. Often exhibiting with The London Group will prove to be a springboard for a wider recognition. Art must be about tomorrow and we try hard to continue in the long London Group tradition by welcoming the unusual, the outrageous and those things beyond expectation." Daler-Rowney offered £600 as a prize to a non-member and also sponsored the catalogue. Terry Frost wrote an appreciation of John Hoskin and Tim Hilton wrote a piece on Mel Gordon. The poster follows the previous years' design and format with a graphic image by Anthony Whishaw.

One effect of the huge influx of new members was to increase income considerably. Records for the year show that in the previous year members' subscriptions had brought in £755, whereas this year £1,709.40 was harvested from subscriptions plus a £200 donation, giving a surplus for the year of £1,739.94 after expenditure had been deducted.

1991

Collapse of the Soviet Union, Gorbachev resigns as the last President of the USSR. In December, eleven former Soviet republics unite to form The Commonwealth of Independent States. Yugoslavia disintegrates resulting in escalating civil war. Saddam Hussain's Iraq occupies Kuwait. Operation 'Desert Storm' begins the Gulf War, pictures seen by many from the comfort of their own armchair. A suicide bomber assassinates Rajiv Gandhi. Apartheid Laws are repealed in South Africa.

Hayward Gallery shows an exhibition of Richard Long's journeyings.
Serpentine Gallery Victor Pasmore (1934), "1940-1990". "Broken English" includes work by Angela Bulloch, Ian Davenport, Anya Gallaccio, Damien Hirst, Gary Hume, Michael Landy, Sarah Stanton and Rachel Whiteread.
Whitechapel Art Gallery "Whitechapel Open" exhibition. Paintings by Michael Andrews (1962) were also in the programme.
Turner Prize 1991 winner, Anish Kapoor. Those short-listed were Ian Davenport, Fiona Rae and Rachel Whiteread. The Turner Prize was now sponsored by Channel 4.
John Moores Painting Prize 1991 won by Andrzej Jackowski with the painting, "The Beekeeper's Son".
EAST first exhibition of work from an open submission selected by Andrew Brighton and Sandy Moffat shown at Norfolk Institute of Art and Design. A good example of an initiative shown by an educational institution using its buildings for favourable exposure. Yet another competitor to The London Group's support for artists' open submission. This year also saw **BANK** established, an artists' cooperative to help artists organise their own exhibitions.
"Biennials and Beyond – Exhibitions That Made Art History 1962 - 2002" Charleston, North Carolina, USA, "Places with a Past".

London Group President: Stan Smith (1975)

No new members were elected this year as potential membership slots were all filled.

This years' AGM was held at Central St Martins College of Art on 3rd May with twenty-two members present and ten apologies. The President, Stan Smith, welcomed the new intake from last year. There had been a disappointing lack of support from members in hanging last year's show. Equally there had been little press comment and poor sales. The Working Party regretfully withdrew its application for another show at the RCA this year due to increases in rent (from £3,000 to £15,000) and lack of funding from outside sources. Other venues under consideration were the Lethaby Gallery, Morley Gallery, the Barbican and The Economist building. Daler-Rowney had offered a prize of £650. This year the treasurer reported a deficit of £339 and promised a much tougher line in balancing the accounts. New proposals were put forward for amending the Constitution. Firstly, in addition to existing officers, a Deputy Vice President and an Assistant Secretary (to cope with the additional organisational load) should be elected. Secondly, the officers become the Group's Executive to work on policy and strategy, and finally, that a specific Working Party be elected for each exhibition. The following officers were elected: Stan Smith as President, Adrian Bartlett as Vice President, John Crossley as Deputy Vice President, Vic Kuell as Treasurer, Gill Ingham as Honorary Secretary, Matthew Kolakowski as Assistant Secretary and Robert Coward as Auditor.

"Works on Paper", The Economist, 25 St James's Street, SW1, 4th–26th October 1991. Forty-four members each submitted one piece of work each and virtually every conceivable medium that could be used on paper had been deployed, a huge breadth of approach. Prices ranged from £150 for Suzan Swale's mixed media and xerox, "Collateral Damage" to £1,600 for Gus Cummins' pencil and watercolour, "St Mary in the Castle". The catalogue was a rather perfunctory, stapled A4 black-on-white photocopy publication.

Janet Nathan's CV notes record three other London Group exhibitions this year, a "Member's Exhibition", one at the Morley Gallery and another at the "Barbican Redfern Gallery". No more det ails or venues are given and no London Group records exist of these exhibitions.

The Economist
25 St. James's Street, SW1

The London Group organised a small exhibition in "The Economist" office foyer in October 1991. "The Economist" continues to host art exhibitions. When this photograph was taken in December 2006 a large sculpture had been placed in the forecourt by the Contemporary Arts Society. St. James's Street runs north/south between Piccadilly, where the Royal Academy is situated, to Pall Mall. There are a number of 'bespoke' art galleries in St. James's Street and Christies is just around the corner in King Street.

1992

1992 is regarded as the year in which the Cold War ended. Bill Clinton is is elected US President. 'Rodney King' riots break out in Los Angeles. 'Earth Summit' in Rio de Janeiro. The Summer Olympic Games are held in Barcelona. Al Qaeda's first bomb attack kills two people at a hotel in Aden. In a UK General Election the Conservative Government under John Major is returned for a fourth term. Neil Kinnock continued as Labour leader but Paddy Ashdown was the new Liberal leader. In London the Baltic Exchange in the City is destroyed by an IRA bomb and claims three lives. Manchester is also attacked by the IRA. Many Polytechnics convert into Universities.

Hayward Gallery "Doubletake: Collective Memory and Current Art". Plus René Magritte.
Whitechapel Art Gallery "Whitechapel Open" exhibition.
Turner Prize 1992 winner was Grenville Davey. Short-listed this year were Damien Hirst, David Tremlett and Alison Wilding.
Saatchi Collection "Young British Artists 1" which includes 'the Shark' ("The Physical Impossibility of Death in the Mind of Someone Living") by Damien Hirst.
The **Heritage Lottery Fund** is set up to distribute funds to cultural causes. Francis Bacon dies.

London Group President: Stan Smith (1975)

No new members were elected this year for a second year running.

"The London Group and Guests", Morley Gallery, 30th January to 20th February 1992. A very large exhibition with ninety-five works on show, mainly painting but also sculpture, prints, watercolour, collage, gouache, conté, pastel and a photograph of a previously exhibited installation. Fifty-four members participated in this exhibition and obviously not all of them had invited a guest. Frederick Gore CBE RA and Maggi Hambling were amongst the invited guests as well as artists who were to be elected to The London Group in the future, Richard Kemp, Angela Eames, Eugene Palmer, Michelle Avison and Trevor Frankland. Prices were modest and realistic between £200 and £6000. Here is an extract from an anonymous introduction. "A common style or aesthetic purpose has never been a prerequisite for membership (of The London Group): it is shared desire to exhibit freely and without manipulation. Members are elected by the current membership – artists chosen by artists. It can be seen that the Group includes quite a few that are well known and internationally admired; indeed it does engender great loyalty in its members but also has always been perceived by them as a marvellous forum for emerging talent and supported for this very reason".

Twenty-six members attended the AGM held at Central St Martins College of Art on the 23rd March. The President reported an extremely busy year with two successful group shows at The Economist Building and the Morley Gallery, special thanks to Vic Kuell, Matthew Kolakowski and Adrian Bartlett. The latter exhibition had attracted wide interest but little coverage in the press. However, plans were progressing for the 1992 Open Exhibition at the Barbican Centre. The Working Party would need to be, "strong, committed and energetic". The Treasurer Vic Kuell was able to report good news as last year's overall deficit of £339 had been turned into a surplus of £1,350.11. Tight financial control and prompt subscription payments had brought the records up to date. A number of minor amendments to the new Constitution were then debated and passed by the AGM. The following were then elected as officers, President Stan Smith, Vice President Janet Patterson, Honorary Treasurer Robert Coward and Honorary Secretary, Matthew Kolakowski. Adrian Bartlett put forward a proposal to hold an Open Show at the Barbican Centre Concourse Gallery and outlined tasks and deadlines for the Working Committee.

On May 11th another meeting took place at the Chelsea Arts Club to discuss the Barbican Open Show. Alan Boothroyd was introduced to the Committee who would be hired to oversee arrangements. Janet Patterson had met with Anne Jones at the Barbican and she had made suggestions that the Group should make the Barbican its permanent home! Janet Patterson also circulated a document listing the advantages of introducing Associate Membership of The London Group at £10-£15. Advantages would be a new source of revenue generation, promoting a greater awareness of The London Group, a pool of potential applicants and help in organising and hanging exhibitions. Whoever took the minutes of this meeting apologised "if these minutes do not represent a full and concise record of all the debate that ensued, but it is all I heard above the incidental din of the Chelsea Arts Club". Despite the din, another meeting took place there on the 13th July. This dealt with the nuts and bolts of the Show, invigilation policy, transport, publicity etc. There also began discussion of The London Group 80th Anniversary Exhibition. August 3rd was the date of the next meeting at Space Studios, 71 Stepney Green. Dates were set for the receiving of work and collection of rejects. There were many additional events to organise, even providing information for "Spanish Vogue"! Right at the end of the minutes comes, "general feeling that we should be setting up a committee to deal with 1993 Open soon. Worry about lack of time to make a really good 80th show- should we postpone in order to get everything organised properly?" Meeting ends.

"The London Group - Open Exhibition", Concourse Gallery (level 5) and Sculpture Court (level 8), Barbican Centre, 9th October to 28th October 1992. In the minutes of the 1993 AGM, item 7.1 records, "Vic Kuell was critical of the Barbican Show in that there was no catalogue". A Press Release, dated 13th August 1992 and illustrated with Janet Nathan's "Dove Harbour", states that, "around 250 contemporary works by internationally renowned artists, together with the unknown and rarely exhibited" will be shown. The selection panel comprised The London Group Committee and invited member Albert Irvin. The press release continues, "The London Group has continued to be a reflection of changing trends and over the years it has helped many artists present their work. It also aims "to advance public awareness of contemporary art" (from The London Group Constitution) and it is hoped that this year's exhibition will attract greater numbers of artists of all ages and experience and that it will be viewed and appreciated by a wider audience than ever before." A Price List indicates that one hundred and twenty-six works were exhibited but only name, title and price were given. As a tribute to her, six works were included by Jean Gibson who had recently died. It would appear that virtually every member had put in one piece of work for this auspicious location. Highest prices were asked by Anthony Wishaw (sic), Jean Gibson, Mark Vaux, Brendan Neilan (sic), William Utermohlen, Anthony Eyton, Cyril Reason, Jeffery Camp and Gary Wragg.

The Barbican Centre
The Barbican, London EC2

1993

Bosnian civil war. Slovakia separates from Czechoslovakia. Al Qaeda World Trade Centre bombings in New York kill six and injure one thousand. Yeltsin sends in tanks to put down Moscow unrest. 'Black Hawk Down' incident in Somalia. Huge increase in use of the Internet. The Maastricht Treaty ratifies the establishment of the European Union and the creation of the Euro as the unit of currency. In the UK plans to privatise the rail network are published. 3 million people are unemployed. An IRA bomb causes enormous damage in Bishopsgate, London, and claims only one life. James Ivory makes "The Remains of the Day" with Anthony Hopkins and Emma Thompson.

Tate St Ives opens.
The Henry Moore Institute opens in Leeds.
Turner Prize 1993 winner, Rachel Whiteread. Short-listed, Hannah Collins, Vong Phaophanit and Sean Scully.
John Moores Painting Prize 1993 won by Peter Doig with the painting, "Blotter".
Saatchi Collection "Young British Artists 2".
The **White Cube** gallery opens run by Jay Jopling. One of the first exhibitions is "My Major Retrospective" by Tracey Emin.
Serpentine Gallery 10-13 June, "Here and Now: Twenty-three years of the Serpentine Gallery", an exhibition to mark a Gala Dinner in the presence of HRH The Princess of Wales. Twenty-nine international worthies including Ivon Hitchens (1931), Henry Moore (1930) and Paula Rego (1965) were among the exhibitors.
Venice Biennale Richard Hamilton represents Britain and jointly wins the "Leone d'Oro" with Antoni Tapies.
"Biennials and Beyond – Exhibitions That Made Art History 1962 - 2002" New York, "Whitney Biennial".

London Group President: Stan Smith (1975) followed by Adrian Bartlett (1981)

For the third consecutive year no new members were elected to The London Group.

The 8th of March was the date for the AGM held at Central St Martins with twenty-two members present. The President's Report acknowledged the energy and commitment from committee members, especially Janet Patterson. The Barbican Open Show "received critical acclaim but sadly not appearing in print". The finances of the show did better than expected and the Open Show generated enough income to cover expenses although too much work had fallen on too few people (Stan Smith had earlier apologised to the Group for his absence abroad, earning a living). The Treasurer's report, however, contradicts this view saying that there had been a loss and that the handling fee was too low. There had also been a problem with Daler Rowney's prize when the latter's representative had insisted on choosing the prize winner. Member Peter Donnelly, Dean of Graphics at the London College of Printing, offered an exhibition at the London Institute Gallery. In February, Raymond and Edna Coxon, previous members of the Group who had been at the RCA with Moore and Hepworth, had made a donation of £10,000 to the Group and discussions were underway to decide what to do with the money as regards investment. An interest free loan of £800 also had to be repayed to an anonymous member. Time then ran out at this meeting and the continuation was on 31st March at the Morley Gallery. After mundane business the minutes then record, "that really there needed to be more continuity in the Management Committee for the administrative business of the group to be dealt with efficiently". The following posts were then elected, President, Adrian Bartlett replacing Stan Smith, Vice President Philippa Beale, Honorary Treasurer Vic Kuell and Honorary Secretary Matthew Kolakowski.

There then followed more discussion on the 1993 Open Show, it should not make a loss, the handling fee should be raised to £10 and a catalogue was to be an essential part of the show. Finally there were five proposals to amend the Constitution proposed by Vic Kuell and seconded by Matthew Kolakowski. The first was to do with the election of members. Candidates should receive nine votes from a committee of seventeen, ten being the quorum. Amendment carried. The other four proposals, all carried, were to do with Withdrawal of Membership and the Responsibilities of Officers tightening up grey areas of procedure. The number of members was to remain at about eighty. Peter Donnelly expressed thanks on behalf of the membership to Stan Smith proposing the title of Honorary President for Smith which was carried unanimously. Janet Patterson again spoke to the Group about Associate Membership, but no decision appears to have been made.

"Paintings and Sculpture by The London Group Members and Guests", 25th March to 15th April 1993. The venue was not printed on the archived price list but was likely to be the Morley Gallery. A large exhibition with sixty-eight exhibits, mainly oil on canvas but also "car and cooker metal" (Daniel Peel), "cast plastic and P.V.A." (Philippa Beale) and "brick, wood and brass" (Eric Moody). Each member was asked to invite one guest artist to exhibit in this show, an alternative arrangement to a fully-fledged open selection strategy. Thirty-four members took part in this exhibition. There were eighteen women in the invited guests section, but perhaps the most intriguing title was Roger de Grey's "The Artist surprised at finding himself in the London Group" and priced at £6,500. Prices varied enormously, from £200 to £6,500 (de Grey and Stan Smith).

There were three Working Party meetings between April and June. Juliet Williams was introduced to the committee as the next Open Organiser. Detailed discussion by well attended meetings covered a huge range of details for both the London Institute and the forthcoming Barbican Open exhibitions. On a lighter note, item 1.8 of the minutes of the 7th of June meeting records, "A cork was drawn sonorously and wine sloshed into glasses".

A Private View Card with an Anthony Whishaw image exists for "The London Group at the London Institute Gallery", Oxford Street W1, 6th July to 10th September 1993 and Mike Pope and Philippa Beale seem to have sold works from this show. No more information about this probable annual exhibition has been archived.

A final Working Party meeting was held on September 27th where the catalogue, poster and PV card for the Barbican show were finalised. The Group Dinner to celebrate the 80th Anniversary of The London Group was also discussed. The President Adrian Bartlett, and others, organised a celebratory Anniversary Dinner at the Saatchi Gallery in Boundary Road, North London. Adrian recollects, "I had employed a fundraiser to help with that year's open exhibition (on the basis of being paid a percentage of the money she raised). She was called Juliet Williams and had a sister who worked for Saatchi. We employed a caterer who ran a restaurant on a barge at Little Venice. She served roast duck I think which was as hard as rock". It appears that some things never change. From the minutes, "Juliet Williams felt it possible to obtain a wine donation, which could lower the price by as much as 30%. Philippa Beale expressed concern about damage to valuable works at this function. Some policing might be necessary". Insurance was arranged and the meal passed off, relatively, peacefully.

The London Group 80th Anniversary Dinner
Saatchi Collection, Boundary Road, London NW8

The Group celebrated its 80th Anniversary with an open submission exhibition at the Barbican Centre and a dinner held at the Saatchi Collection, Boundary Road, North London. From left to right are Stanislaw Frenkiel, Robert Coward, David Carr, Anthony Eyton, Eric Moody, Matthew Kolakowski, Morris Kestelman, Gillian Ingham, Neville Boden, Robert Clarke, Gus Cummins, Barry Martin, Stanley Smith,

Adrian Bartlett, Arthur Wilson, Vic Kuell, Gary Wragg, Janet Nathan, John Barnicoat, Anthony Whishaw, John Copnall, David Gluck, Bert Irvin, Suzan Swale, Elma Thubron, Victoria Bartlett and Harvey Daniels. Many thanks to Adrian Bartlett for the use of this photograph.

"The London Group", The London Group's 80th Anniversary Open Exhibition, The Concourse Gallery, Barbican Centre, Silk Street, London EC2, 9th December 1993 to 7th January 1994. The President was Adrian Bartlett, Vice President Philippa Beale, Treasurer Vic Kuell, Secretary Matthew Kolakowski. Honorary Members were Morris Kestleman, André Bicat, Edna Ginesi, Stan Smith, Robert Coward and Raymond Coxon. Committee Members for this important show were Janet Patterson, Victoria Bartlett, John Copnall, Gary Wragg and Suzan Swale. The exhibition was sponsored by Unilever plc which helped to pay for the first colour illustrated catalogue for any London Group exhibition. There were twenty pages, A5 portrait format with a Vic Kuell image printed on the cover and containing twenty-one colour illustrations of members' work giving a broad indication of the variety of styles and formats of two and three-dimensional exhibits. There were one hundred and fifty-one artists taking part, fifty-nine of whom were members, the remainder, ninety-two, chosen from open submission. The catalogue gave name, title, media, size and price and was quite comprehensive. The high prices (many in four figures) suggest that artists were putting high quality and important works into this exhibition, knowing that it would be well visited and reviewed. A foreword was written by Adrian Bartlett plus two articles on The London Group by Julian Freeman, a freelance curator, and Andrew Lambirth, contributing Editor to the RA Magazine. Freeman's article focused on the historical aspect of The London Group, laying out the familiar facts and figures. Andrew Lambirth talked to five (male) artists to ask them what The London Group meant to them. Anthony Eyton observed that the Group consistently showed work, "of worth and excellence", Anthony Whishaw liked the fact that it was run by artists for artists, Bert Irvin and Mike Kenny thought that support for young emerging artists was helpful to them in their careers and John Edwards enjoyed the "fellowship" of the Group. The article also makes mention of the newly found venue of the Barbican for open submission exhibitions and that it was hoped that the Concourse Gallery could become a regular venue for London Group annual exhibitions. As history shows, sadly, this was not the case and lack of a permanent exhibition venue continued to be a major issue for the Group's exhibition policy. The President's foreword states "A young artist will naturally try to attract the attention of art dealers, but such a relationship can never replace the acceptance and respect of fellow artists. The London Group's Open Exhibitions offer this opportunity. Many of our members, however established or famous they may now be, had their very first public showing in a London Group Exhibition. We hope always to be able to present the variety of work by painters and sculptors of all generations which has given The London Group its unique reputation." In fact, it is interesting to note the number of future London Group members who had submitted to the exhibition in order to get work exhibited. They included Michelle Avison, Brian Benge, P Cossick (sic), Tony Collinge, Trevor Frankland, Jules de Goede, Oona Grimes, Georgina Hunt and David Redfern. The exhibition was certainly the most ambitious and costly exhibition since the Tate Gallery 50th Anniversary Show and did much to put The London Group back on the map of contemporary art activity. A black and cream poster was printed with a graphic image by Vic Kuell and festooned with the sponsors' logos.

Poster design for the 1993 London Group Open

The poster shows the large number of sponsors which the Group managed to secure to help fund this very expensive Open Submission exhibition at the Barbican

"The London Group 1913-93" at the Michael Parkin Gallery, Motcomb Street, SW1, 20th October to 12th November 1993. There is an article by Julian Freeman in the Private View invitation for "The London Group at Eighty". Freeman writes, "Eighty years on the London Group remains as independent as it was at birth, without an affiliation to any 'school' or 'ism', but not amorphous. It is surely an institution, yet it is neither patrician nor a coterie: the age range of its membership prevents this. The Group's declared aim remains the encouragement and promotion of all non-academic contemporary visual art, and despite two wars and lesser, occasional peaks and troughs, continues to achieve this. Long may it succeed." Michael Parkin was a specialist in 20th Century British Art and the show comprised of eighty-two artists, in particular Roger Fry, Spencer Gore, Harold Gilman, John Minton, C. R. W. Nevinson and a number of current members.

1994

Nelson Mandela is elected President of South Africa. Rawandan genocide, 500,000 killed. US troops invade Haiti. Yasser Arafat returns from exile to Gaza. Russian Federation heavily involved in Chechnya. The Channel Tunnel opens between the UK and France. IRA ceasefire. Tony Blair becomes leader of the Labour Party. The National Lottery is launched which will help fund many cultural projects. Hugh Grant and Andie MacDowell appear in the ever popular "Four Weddings and a Funeral".

Hayward Gallery Salvador Dali exhibition.
Serpentine Gallery "Some Went Mad, Some Ran Away", curated by Damien Hirst. Also, a repeat of last year's fund raiser, "Here and Now: Twenty-four years of the Serpentine Gallery", including Craigie Aitchison (1962), Frank Auerbach (1960), Terry Frost (1957), Ivon Hitchens (1931), Albert Irvin (1965), Kenneth Martin (1949), Victor Pasmore (1934) and Paula Rego (1965). Another Gala Dinner with Lady Diana.
ICA "The Institute of Cultural Anxiety: Works from the Collection". Curated by Jeremy Millar who selected sixty-one artists including Martin Boyce, Liam Gillick, Graham Gussin, Simon Starling and Keith Tyson.
Whitechapel Art Gallery "Whitechapel Open" exhibition.
Turner Prize 1994 winner was Antony Gormley whilst Willie Doherty, Peter Doig and Shirazeh Houshiary were short-listed.
The Jerwood Painting Prize was established this year. The prize aimed "to identify, celebrate and highlight the range of excellence and imagination in painting in the UK". A Panel of Judges shortlisted a number of painters of any age from an open submission. "At £30,000, it remains the most valuable single prize awarded in the UK and will be granted to an artist who is believed by the panel to demonstrate excellence and originality in painting". Craigie Aitchison, the first winner of the prize, had been a member of The London Group. He was elected in 1962, 32 years before winning the Jerwood Prize.
Saatchi Collection "Young British Artists III".
The **Arts Council of Great Britain** becomes Arts Council of England, Arts Council of Wales and the Scottish Arts Council. Also this year the arts begin to receive funding from the National Lottery. In the year 2005/6 the Arts Council was given £160 million from National Lottery funding.
On the Isle of Jura two members of the pop group **KLF** burn £1,000,000 in notes in front of an invited audience.

London Group President: Adrian Bartlett (1981)

Four members were elected this year, Michelle Avison, Bryan Benge, Oona Grimes and

Colin Kerrigan. With the new voting procedures rigorously applied only four out of twenty candidates were elected.

The year began with a well attended Working Party meeting on 31st January. Adrian Bartlett reported good press coverage and good sales, over twenty, from the recent Barbican Open Show. He hoped that the Group would be able to repeat the success, perhaps on a bi-annual basis as the gallery hire was approximately £8,000. Vic Kuell as Treasurer warned the meeting that, given current subscription rates and income, the Group could simply not afford to operate and hold open submission exhibitions. The Ginesi/Coxon gift of £10,000 had helped finance the recent open. Eric Moody was asked to look into funding of these events by public bodies such as the Arts Council and the London Arts Board and also raised the notion of touring the Open Shows, as had happened in the past. The next meeting was 21st February where finance continued to dominate the discussion, but no clear decisions were made. This year's AGM was held on 21st March at Central St Martins. The President's report makes mention of a members' exhibition at the Bird Street Gallery and reflected on the London Institute Gallery and Michael Parkin Gallery shows. He looked forward to another Open at the Barbican, although not this year due to financial restrictions, with perhaps a tour to Bristol and Sheffield. Generating finance occupied the members in attendance and Vic Kuell the Treasurer urged caution, especially where touring shows were concerned as transport costs would eat up valuable resources. Increasing membership fees to £40 or £50 was put forward and the Working Party were asked to look into this proposal. Adrian Bartlett was re-elected unopposed as President, Philippa Beale won a close contest for Vice President from Gary Wragg, Vic Kuell remained as Treasurer whilst the Sectretary's post was to be temporarily staffed by volunteers.

"A collection of work by members of the London Group", The London Institute Gallery, 65 Davies Street, W1, ending on 22nd September 1994 (letter dated 19th July 1994 to Simon Grant at Listings Limited, from Michael Benson the London Institute's Communications and Marketing Manager). From this same letter it would appear that Anthony Whishaw and Harvey Daniels were two of the members in this show. Benson also lists London Institute teachers, Philippa Beale and Colin Kerrigan (Central Saint Matins) and Peter Donnelly and Mike Pope (LCP). The gallery was situated on the ground floor of the London Institute building that housed the administrative centre and the Student Union facilities for many London art schools. The hiring of the this gallery also highlights the growing links between The London Group and art education.

The London Institute
65 Davies Street, London W1

The London Group "Works on Paper", Morley Gallery, 61 Westminster Bridge Road SE1, 6th October to 27th October 1994. Thirty-nine London Group members put in one piece of work each. Media was mostly watercolour or acrylic on paper but members had also used monoprint, collograph, pen & wash, mixed media and ink & silver. Anthony Green's watercolour & pastel, "The Happy Morning" was the most expensive on show at £3,000, followed by Anthony Whishaw's acrylic & crayon, "Trees and Sky" at £2,800. Prices started at £100 with an average of approximately £500. There was, obviously, a price list to the exhibition but no catalogue. This particular members only exhibition followed London Group shows at Morley in the two previous years in which each member had invited a guest to exhibit along with elected members. "Works on Paper" was installed for one evening at Thomas's Preparatory School, Broomwood Road, London SW11 on the 23rd of November from 7 to 9 pm. It was organised by Nicky Russell of the Clapham Art Committee and Philippa Beale and Suzan Swale both made sales here.

1995

Peace Agreement signed between Russia and Chechnyan rebels. Israeli Prime Minister Rabin assassinated in Jerusalem. Oklahoma City bombing in the USA. Sarin gas attack on the Tokyo subway system. Kobe in Western Japan destroyed by earthquake. The first planet orbiting another star in our galaxy is discovered. Rogue trader Nick Leeson brings about the collapse of Barings Bank with losses of £860 million. Danny Boyle makes "Trainspotting", Mike Leigh makes "Secrets & Lies" and Ang Lee makes "Sense and Sensibility".

The British Art Show (4) selected by Richard Cork (critic), Rose Finn-Kelcey (artist) Thomas Lawson (artist/writer), twenty-five artists, included painting, sculpture, installation, film and video. No London Group members were selected. Also at the Hayward Gallery, Yves Klein.

Serpentine Gallery HRH The Princess of Wales hosts another Gala Dinner, this year it's the sculptors' turn including Tony Carter (2002), Henry Moore (1930), Peter Startup (1973) and William Turnbull (1955). In November William Turnbull showed "Bronze Idols and Untitled Paintings".

Tate Gallery "Rites of Passage: Art for the End of the Century", eleven international contemporary artists. The exhibition celebrated the "diversity and fragmentation (which) have characterised the art of the last decade" showing sculpture, video, photography and installation.

Turner Prize 1995 winner Damien Hirst. Short-listed, Mona Hatoum, Callum Innes, Mark Wallinger.

John Moores Painting Prize 1995 won by David Leapman with the painting, "Double-Tongued Knowability".

Jerwood Painting Prize 1995 won jointly by Maggi Hambling and Patrick Caulfield.

Saatchi Collection "Young British Artists IV".

Venice Biennale Leon Kossof (1963) represents Britain. Kathy Prendergast wins the young artist award.

London Group President: Adrian Bartlett (1981) followed by Philippa Beale (1977)

In January the Group was offered a small space at the Art Fair in Islington. The President made an executive decision to show twenty small works from recently elected members and those who had been working on behalf of the Group. This was an "eleventh hour" job that gave good publicity for The London Group and sold two members' works.

The first Working Party meeting of the year was on the 20th February. The President, Adrian Bartlett, said that the main objective was to suggest potential committee members to organise the forthcoming Barbican show. The spirit of the meeting seemed more optimistic as the London Arts Board had offered £3,000 and the Barbican had lowered the gallery fee by the same amount. Other venues such as the Royal Festival Hall and the Atlantis Gallery in Brick Lane were also discussed. A tour of this open exhibition to Southampton City Art Gallery was also muted.

The AGM was held on 9th March at Central St Martins. The President's Report catalogues recent exhibitions and focuses on increasing sales from London Group exhibitions. Adrian Bartlett indicated that he would not be standing for re-election as he "would like a period of rest from the Group's activities" and the meeting proposed a vote of thanks to both Adrian and his wife, Victoria, for all their hard work on behalf of the Group. Two women, Philippa Beale and Gillian Ingham were nominated for the post of President with the former being elected as the second female President of The London Group. Gillian Ingham was then elected unopposed as the Vice President. Vic Kuell continued as Treasurer and Brian Benge was elected unopposed as Honorary Secretary. Finances were healthier than in years gone by; Vic Kuell reported that the Group was in credit to the tune of £6,500. Beale got down to business very quickly with a Working Party Meeting on the 28th March. On the agenda was forthcoming Group Exhibitions at the Lethaby Gallery (inside Central St Martins' Southampton Row building), Angela Flowers and The Economist Building. The biggest item was the arrangements for the Barbican Show planned for later in the year. Records of minutes show six Working Party meetings throughout the year, a period of intense activity organising the "Biennial 1995 Open Exhibition" at the Barbican. Michelle Hoffner had been brought in to raise finance for London Group enterprises and, supported by her father, Charles, she quickly met her target. There was a rigorous professional approach to the planning of this Open with emphasis on a good looking catalogue for sale at the show. Chris Plato was brought in to design and organise catalogue production. Lessons were learned from previous shows, especially the need for a Sales Coordinator and regular, reliable invigilation to meet exhibition visitors and promote The London Group image. New ideas for future exhibitions began to emerge. 'Theme' shows were suggested, with Robin Klassnick selecting a show of Installation Art, Basil Beattie a show of Abstract Painting and Zulieka Dobson, Sculpture from current membership. Despite all this frenetic activity the Working Party did not take its collective eye off the ball and sent out information announcing elections for membership to be held on Wednesday, 10th January 1996. No doubt they had in mind that a prestigious open show at the Barbican would raise the profile of The London Group as a serious artists' organisation. However, no new members were elected this year.

"Biennial 1995 Open Exhibition", Concourse Gallery, Barbican Centre, 8th December 1995 to 7th January 1996. Members of the Selection Committee, chaired by the President Philippa Beale, were Robin Klassnik – Matts Gallery, Angela Flowers

- Flowers East, Jenni Lomax – Camden Arts Centre, Louisa Buck – art critic and William Ling – Fine Arts. There were five prizes, the £1,200 Daily Mail Ideal Home Exhibition Award, the £1,000 Unilever PLC prize, the £300 Joan Beale Memorial Award, the £250 New Covent Garden Market Prize for the best figurative work and the Mel Gordon Award. In the archive are two A2 catalogue/posters, one printed white on black, the other black on white. Images printed on the black on white poster show work by exhibitors Ines Buhler, Harvey Daniels, Philippa Beale, Gary Wragg, Peter Donnelly, Matthew Kolakowski, David Whitaker, Eugene Palmer, Alfred Harris, Jane Humphrey, Anthony Daley, Philippa Stjernsward, David Gluck and Robert Clarke (two three-dimensional pieces, the rest paintings). The black on white poster shows work by Marq Kearey, Bryan Benge, Carl von Weiler, John Barnicoat, Vic Kuell, David Carr, John Crossley, Janet Patterson, Suzan Swale, Laetitia Yhap, Mary Webb, Graham Day, Gus Cummins and Jocelyn Clarke (three three-dimensional pieces, the rest paintings). Both carry an article by Monica Petzal in which she writes "There is a strong history of pedagogy. Many current members are influential teachers who support their own practice by working to pass on ideas and knowledge to students, who are facing an aggressive art world, and little chance of financial success in their chosen career. In the sometimes limited time outside teaching, they return to their studios and their own practice which has developed over a long period. These former young radicals are no longer spring chickens and in these times when youth is seen as virtue, the London Group has, perhaps quite understandably, found it hard to embrace current practices with its instant stars and high price tickets and harder still to select them for their exhibition."

1996

US troops in Bosnia and US missile attacks in Iraq. President Clinton is re-elected for a second term. IRA bombs in London's Canary Wharf and Manchester city centre cause enormous damage and end the 1994 ceasefire. Prince Charles divorces Princess Diana. UK hit by 'Mad Cow' disease. The Summer Olympic Games are held in Atlanta, USA.

Whitechapel Art Gallery "The Open/Open Studios" exhibition. The format is changed this year after the original open formula began to falter. As well as using the gallery to show work, artists were encouraged to open their own studios supported by the Whitechapel media machine.

1996 New Contemporaries opens at Tate Gallery Liverpool and then to Camden Arts Centre, London.

Hayward Gallery Howard Hodgkin paintings.

Turner Prize 1996 winner was Douglas Gordon. Craigie Horsfield, Gary Hume and Simon Patterson were short-listed.

Jerwood Painting Prize 1996 won by John Hubbard. Short-listed were Glenn Brown, Clem Crosby, Jules de Goede (1996), Anthony Green RA (1964), Jason Martin and John McLean. Judges were David Eliot, John Golding, Annely Juda, Patricia Morison and Nick Tite.

"Biennials and Beyond – Exhibitions That Made Art History 1962–2002" Bordeaux, France, "Traffic".

London Group President: Philippa Beale (1977)

Seven new members were elected this year, Steven Foy, Trevor Frankland, Jules de Goede, Sophie Horton, Brian McCann, Hideo Nakane and Eugene Palmer. Seventeen members of the Selection Committee met on 10th January at Eagle Court, an annexe of Central St Martins. Newly elected members were expected to serve on the Working Committee for the first two years of their membership.

Sixteen members attended the AGM on 20th March at Central St Martins. The President, Philippa Beale, reported that despite some concern about the feasibility of large open submission shows, membership had voted for acceptance. Twenty thousand pounds had been raised by the Group and it "had managed to spend all of it". Sponsors were very pleased with the show. Immediately the Group began to discuss yet another Barbican show, enthused by recent events. In addition the Lethaby Gallery and Kensington and Chelsea College Gallery were proposed as venues. Beale also asked the Group to consider funding for its own gallery with possible financial support from the

London Arts Board. Michelle Hoffner was asked to prepare an application to National Lottery funds for a London Group Book which would contain examples of members' work from 1913 onwards which would be used to launch the Group in Europe. The Treasurer's report was also upbeat with funds standing at £9,500, even after the Barbican Open Show. Expenses for the show had been well managed. Vic Kuell was getting a serious reputation for being a safe pair of hands! The President was returned unopposed, Matthew Kolakowski and John Crossley were nominated for the post of Vice President with the former being elected. Vic Kuell as Treasurer and Bryan Benge as Secretary were re-elected unopposed. Under A.O.B. Stan Smith proposed that the older distinguished artist Frederick Gore be made an Honorary Member. Voting was close, in favour 4, against 4, abstentions 5. The President's casting vote against seemed to indicate a change in the wind and the forward-looking posture of the Group as a whole.

Five Working Party Meetings were timetabled for the rest of 1996. The May meeting dealt with Lethaby Gallery dates and issues. London Group promotional packages were to be sent to galleries to try to gain shows for the Group. Once again the Barbican found itself on the agenda with proposals for guest selectors including William Packer, Sacha Craddock, William Feaver, Annely and David Juda and George Melly. MH Associates (the Hoffners) were again engaged to raise funds. The Millennium Publication Project (for an illustrated historical book about The London Group) was pushed forward with researchers being approached and the Tate Archive consulted. There was an interesting spat at the June 4th meeting where the intended group statement for the Lethaby Show was debated. The traditional animosity against the Royal Academy had re-emerged and some members were pushing for a more critical approach to the RA. Other members recommended a more measured and diplomatic stance, especially as some London Group members were also Royal Academy members. In addition dates were proposed for an exhibition of painting in October at Kensington and Chelsea College, perhaps selected by Basil Beattie. Three interesting strategies emerged from discussion conducted in the 12th November meeting. Charity Status would help the Group avoid paying industrial rates if it ever set up a gallery and would also help attract funds and Charles Hoffner was already looking into this on behalf of the Group. Secondly, Bryan Benge was to contact SPACE with a view to renting a gallery space for The London Group. And finally, "most members felt it would be good sense to further develop the Group's exhibition policy to include smaller selected shows".

"The London Group 1996" at the London Institute. A Visitors Book indicates that it was held in the Lethaby Gallery, Central St Martins, Southampton Row. A Private View invite confirms this and gives the exhibition dates as 4th July to 13th July 1996. This exhibition was dedicated to the memory of Neville Boden, President of The London Group from 1973 to 1977, who died suddenly on Monday 24th June 1996. He was admired and respected by all his fellow artists in the Group. The catalogue was an A4, stapled, photocopied production. There were fifty exhibits, with six recent sculptures from Neville Boden and forty-five members showing work. In the catalogue foreword an unidentified officer (possibly Philippa Beale), made the following observation, "William Packer recently wrote in a thoughtful article about The London Group that it was succumbing to political correctness. Brian Sewell accused the Group of adopting 'Serota type orthodoxy' but neither would accuse The London Group Members of preparing for retirement." Prices, media and size were all given, top price Anthony Green's "Gull" (a freestanding oil on MDF 3D piece) at £12,000, Gary Wragg's large oil painting "Kennington" at £11,000 and Janet Nathan's mixed media on wood and resin "Aegean Gateway" at £5,950. There was a noticeable diversity of media whilst still including traditional oil on canvas, especially those employing the new technologies of computer generated images and mixed media.

The Income and Expenditure records for the year ended 31st January 1996 show a healthy situation. Members' subscriptions brought in £2,143.65 leaving an overall surplus for the year of £1,953.47. On the Balance Sheet the General Fund stood at £7,986.22 and even last year's exhibition had made a surplus of £108.67. In 1995 the General Fund contained £5,924 which meant a healthy increase of about £2,000 in the year.

In a letter dated 29th August 1996, MH Associates put more flesh on the idea of a millennium publication discussed in an earlier meeting. "The publication will be a history of this important, ever self-renewing group of artists after nearly ninety years of uninterrupted existence. It will include all members and major contributors from its beginning in 1913 up to the present day and have illustrations of one of their works together with an artistic biography." The proposed publication was to be 500 pages of "the highest quality print production" and to have a print run of 2,500 to 5,000. Three major critics were to be commissioned to write pieces for the book which was to be put together by a large production team of at least eight professionals all on a flat fee. MH Associates were in communication with The Arts Council of England to raise a grant towards publication, but "the deadline for applications for 1997/8 publications is now passed". Although this ambitious project did not deliver for the millennium, the 2003 Yearbook published for the ninetieth anniversary partly fulfilled this worthwhile plan.

**Central St. Martins
College of Art and Design**
Southampton Row, London WC1

This labyrinthine building at a busy junction in Southampton Row houses studios, workshops, print rooms, lecture rooms and, on the ground floor, the Lethaby Gallery where The London Group mounted their annual exhibitions in 1996 and 2000.
In 2007 plans were announced to move CSM to "a state-of-the-art home based in the heart of London's largest regeneration project at King's Cross". The most ambitious capital project that University of the Arts London and CSM have ever undertaken cost £170 million.

1997

Hong Kong handed back to China. Later in the year all chickens in Hong Kong are killed to prevent the spread of 'bird flu'. In Luxor, Egypt, 62 people are killed by gunmen linked to Al-Qaeda. Princess Diana dies in car crash in Paris. Mother Teresa dies in Calcutta. President Clinton is inaugurated for his second term. The Kyoto Protocol is adopted by a UN committee. In the UK there is a landslide victory (418 seats) for Tony Blair and 'New Labour' in a General Election. Scottish geneticists clone 'Dolly the Sheep'. Visit from the comet Hale-Bopp. James Cameron's "Titanic" premieres in the US, the highest-grossing film of all time. "The Full Monty" is released over here.

Royal Academy "Sensation: Young British Artists from the Saatchi Collection" later toured to New York. Artists included Glenn Brown, Tracey Emin, Marcus Harvey, Michael Landy, Sarah Lucas, Jonathan Parsons and Cerith Wyn Evans. Despite causing media apoplexy and public outrage the exhibition was a huge success visited by 284,734 people.

Turner Prize 1997 winner this year was Gillian Wearing. Short-listed were Christine Borland, Angela Bulloch and Cornelia Parker, an all female contest.

John Moores Painting Prize 1997 won by Dan Hays with the painting, "Harmony in Green".

Jerwood Painting Prize 1997 won by Gary Hume. Jane Harris, Louise Hopkins, Maria Lalic, Jason Martin, Claude Heath, James Rielly, Madeleine Strindberg and Rose Wylie were short-listed. Judges were Iwona Blazwick, Charles Esche, Patricia Morison, Bryan Robertson and Dr Raimund Stecker.

Venice Biennale Great Britain was represented by Rachel Whiteread.

Damien Hirst opens a restaurant in Notting Hill called "Pharmacy".

"Biennials and Beyond – Exhibitions That Made Art History 1962 - 2002" Vienna, "Cities on the Move".

London Group President: Philippa Beale (1977)

Bad news greeted a New Year meeting on the 14th January. Michelle Hoffner reported that nine out of twelve funding applications had been turned down. MH Associates had now become a permanent point of contact for London Group business where a database of members' work was also planned. There was consternation when Vic Kuell indicated that he would be resigning as Treasurer at the next AGM. Kuell had been a reliable and wise officer for the Group and now new blood was required. The President's Report, preparing for the AGM planned for 18th March, thanked Vic for all his support during "his incredible term of office". There was also a tribute to Neville Boden who died in June last year and was The London Group President from 1973 to 1977. In a new initiative Charitable Status for the Group was to be sought which would open up eligibility for lottery money. As well as seeking a permanent gallery space the Group was also pursuing future exhibitions at the Barbican Gallery, Bedford Hill Gallery and Danielle Arnaud Gallery.

Four new members were elected this year, Slawomir Blatton, Pauline Little, Mark Povell and Susan Wilson, elected at a meeting of the Selection Committee on the 15th April.

Eleven artists were selected from The London Group for an exhibition at the Bedford Hill Gallery, 202 Great Suffolk Street, SE1 from the 11th to the 28th June with a Private View on Thursday, 12th June. The eleven were Moich Abrahams, Philippa Beale, Bryan Benge, John Crossley, Steven Foy, Trevor Frankland, Oona Grimes, David Shutt, Suzan Swale, David Whitaker and Arthur Wilson. Who made the selection is not recorded, but it is likely to be agents from the Bedford Hill Gallery and not London Group officers.

"The London Group 1997" at Alan Baxter & Associates, The Gallery, Cowcross Court, 77 Cowcross Street' London EC1, from 7th October to 30th October 1997 (information from a Private View invitation card, 3rd October 1997). This exhibition was intended to be the annual Group show for members only. Forty-five members took part and the exhibition was dedicated to the memories of Neville Boden, Raymond Coxon, William Mills and Carel Weight who had died recently. Steven Foy and Adrian Bartlett both sold work from this exhibition and, amazingly, exhibition costs were covered through commission on sales.

"Alan Baxter & Associates was founded in 1974 as an engineering practice. Its range of work is now broad and covers urban design, masterplanning, sustainability, conservation and civil and structural engineering. The highly interactive office creates imaginative but sound design solutions and also hosts over 40 different firms whose work relates to the built environment. The Gallery hosts exhibitions and lively debates, providing a forum for sharing ideas. The ABA buildings not only house 40 different firms, but the Gallery is also a central London venue for lectures and exhibitions. Many of the key issues on architecture, engineering, sustainability and urban design are debated here. The Gallery space has been created in the basement of the ABA building and is used as a venue for the firm's own wide range of in-house training, lectures and social events and also by individuals and organisations with an interest in aspects of the built environment." (Alan Baxter & Associates website)

Alan Baxter & Associates
Cowcross Street, London EC1

The London Group held its annual exhibition here in 1997. The area is alive and buzzing, especially at lunchtime when local workers take to the pubs and cafés. Just down the street is the old Smithfield Market whilst Central St Martins Eagle Court annexe is close by.

An extraordinary General Meeting of The London Group was called for 3rd October where Charitable Status was to be progressed. This would require a revision of the existing constitution, the election of a Deputy Vice President and the support of MH Associates as secretarial support to the Honorary Treasurer and Secretary. When all of this was in place the Group's permanent gallery could then be set up. The revision of the constitution, always a thorny subject, was never voted through the AGM.

The Group's finances were in good shape, members' subscriptions totalled £2,343 and there was a surplus for the year of £1,539 when expenditure was deducted. The General Fund contained £8,408 for the year ending 31st January 1997.

1998

Tension between India and Pakistan as they each test nuclear weapons. President Clinton in 'Zippergate' sex scandal. Al-Qaeda bombings at US embassies in Tanzania and Kenya kill 223. Saddam Hussein allows UN inspectors back into Iraq and then kicks them out again. Russia devalues the ruble by 70% against the US dollar. Widespread use of Internet, mobile phones and digital technology in broadcast media. Cosmologists pronounce that the universe's expansion is accelerating leading to dark matter and dark energy theory. The iMac is unveiled by Apple Computers. The "Good Friday" agreement is signed in Belfast. A few months later, 29 people are killed and 200 injured by a Real IRA bomb in the Omagh atrocity. In the UK, Sky Digital is launched. General Pinochet is put under house arrest whilst in the UK for medical treatment. Deutsche Bank buys Bankers Trust to form the largest financial institution in the world. The film "Titanic" wins eleven Oscars. Gwyneth Paltrow and Joseph Fiennes appear in "Shakespeare in Love".

Hayward Gallery an exhibition of Francis Bacon's paintings plus Anish Kapoor and Bruce Nauman.
Whitechapel Art Gallery "The Open/Open Studios" exhibition. This was to be the last open submission exhibition organised by the Whitechapel. The first "East London Open" had taken place in 1967 giving unknown and young artists a chance to have their work shown to an informed public and press. Was there still a need for open submission exhibitions?
Turner Prize 1998 winner, Chris Ofili. Short-listed, Tacita Dean, Cathy de Monchaux and Sam Taylor-Wood.
Jerwood Painting Prize 1998 £30,000 won by Madeleine Strindberg. Shortlisted were Basil Beattie (1968), Richard Beck, Andrew Bick, Alan Brooks, Claude Heath, David Leapman, Edwina Leapman, Chris Ofili and William Tillyer. Judges were Mel Gooding, Norbert Lynton, Patricia Morison, Noreen O'Hare and David Thorp. Opening show in the **Jerwood Gallery**, Union Street, London. This shows what sponsorship can do, the Jerwood Prize now had a secure home for future exhibitions.
Antony Gormley's "Angel of the North" is erected just outside Gateshead in the North East of England.
In Bilbao, Spain the ultra-modern Guggenheim Art Gallery opens, designed by Frank Gehry.
"Biennials and Beyond – Exhibitions That Made Art History 1962 - 2002"
São Paulo, Brazil, "24th São Paulo Biennial".

London Group President: Philippa Beale (1977) followed by Matthew Kolakowski (1990)

This year five new members were elected to The London Group. They were Ian Parker, Wendy Anderson, Kate Montgomery, Georgina Hunt and Tony Collinge.

On 21st January the first Working Party meeting took place with fourteen members present. Three members were researching exhibitions, Matthew Kolakowski at Lawrence Graham in the Strand, Bryan Benge at Brighton University (also Norwich and Kingston) and Mark Povell at the James Hickey Gallery, Farnham. The biggest spend financially, £1,400, had been on establishing Charitable Status which was still ongoing. A sub-committee was set up to look at the idea of a permanent gallery for The London Group. Moving into the twentieth century, David Carr suggests a website for The London Group, the first minuted record of a crucial information facility.

Philippa Beale's President's Report for the AGM, dated 10th February, reminded the Group that she was only, "holding the fort" for one year in 1995! She continues, "so I am resigning this year– three years later. In the last three years the Working Party have accomplished a lot of goals set out by previous presidencies and these were: to remain in the black, to set up a secretariat (MH Associates), to have an up to date computerised database, to gain charitable status and to update the Tate Archive. All this has now been achieved and the current Working Party aims to get a London Group Gallery and to have a millennium publication." However, a Working Party meeting of 18th February records ongoing problems with Charitable Status. Twenty-three members attended the AGM on 24th March at Central St Martins. Trevor Frankland, the new Treasurer, laid out the case for increasing the membership fee by £5 to £35, however, a motion from the floor suggested £50 which was accepted. Funds stood at a healthy £11,100. This year all the posts were elected unopposed, Matthew Kolakowski the new President, Philippa Beale Vice President, Arthur Wilson Deputy Vice President, Bryan Benge Honorary Secretary and Trevor Frankland Honorary Treasurer.

A Working Party in May plunged four new members into the deep end of London Group activity, particularly Charitable Status. "The main problem remained of how we can prove to the Charity Commissioners and the Inland Revenue that the Trustees and therefore the Group do not make profits from our shows". Matthew Kolakowski was also urging for clear decisions regarding the proposed London Group website. Philippa Beale presented a document which was to be sent out as, "a presentation of all our artists" to potential sponsors and gallery owners.

As the Group did not secure funding for a large open show, the agreed strategy was to curate smaller, selected, 'theme' shows. They were to be held at Lawrence Graham, the Daniel Arnaud Gallery and Brighton University.

"Selected Members Show", Lawrence Graham, a Corporate Law firm based in the Strand, 26th May. It was planned to have a series of shows at this venue. Slides of work were to be sent to Matthew Kolakowski and Clive Jennings (from Artnet) who would select from these submissions. Clive Jennings selected nine artists from a submission of twenty-one, Adrian Bartlett, Victoria Bartlett, Philippa Beale, Trevor Frankland, Oona Grimes, Brian McCann, Eric Moody, Alex Ramsay and Kevin Slingsby. There was also a plan to invite potential new members to exhibit, which would provide exhibition opportunities to non-members, a welcome return to previous London Group open submission policy.

"The Object and the Concept", Daniel Arnaud Gallery, 123 Kennington Road, London SE11, 26th June to 17th July 1998 with a Private View on 25th June showing work by Victoria Bartlett, Philippa Beale, Brian Benge, Matthew Kolakowski, Eugene Palmer, Suzan Swale (curator) and Arthur Wilson. Sophie Horton was invited to show as a guest. This should have been the first of three small group exhibitions, but no archive records exist of the remaining two ever being held.

"Transient", Brighton University, Grand Parade, Brighton, 8th September to 26th September 1998. "Transient" was chosen from a submission of members' work and selected by Matthew Kolakowski, Bryan Benge, Mark Povell, Suzan Swale and critic Mark Currah. Exhibitors were Wendy Anderson, Philippa Beale, Brian Benge, Harvey Daniels, Matthew Kolakowski, Ian Parker, Janet Patterson, Mark Povell and Suzan Swale with guests Mark Currah and Calum MacKenzie. Media ranged from painting and sculpture to video and photography. The exhibition, "revolved around the theme of transition, of change of time and situation." It was an attempt to "confound our critics" by promoting an exhibition in which the work could be, "1. performed within a space, 2. ephemeral, time constrained or in some way of limited life span, 3. produced specifically for the space/context/surrounding environment, 4. installed as to make specific use of or reference to the space/context/surrounding environment." Bryan Benge, the Honorary Secretary, also noted, "This is a challenging invitation not least to curate but also to make work for. I know some members will feel disinclined to submit proposals for such a show."

The Income and Expenditure Account for the year ending 31st January 1998 showed an income of £2,712.69, £2,560.50 of which was raised from members' subscriptions. The biggest expenditure for this period were legal charges in pursuit of Charitable Status, weighing in at a hefty £1,509.88 and secretarial fees of £500. Treasurer Trevor Frankland wrote, "Our major expenditure this year was the result of our drive towards Charitable Status and to date we have incurred costs of approximately £1,500. This is an expense we felt worthwhile as our applications for financial assistance seem to depend upon us obtaining the status of being a Charity". Even so, the Group just about broke even with a small surplus of £25.28. The General Fund remained stable at £8,518.16, an increase of about £100 on last year. Last year's Alan Baxter exhibition even made a surplus of £84.48!

1999

The Euro currency was introduced into most EU countries. NATO forces in Serbia, 'ethnic cleansing' in Kosovo. Boris Yeltsin resigns as President of Russia. Chechnyan situation deteriorates. Mandela retires as President of South Africa. In the UK Hereditary Peers are abolished in the House of Lords. Devolution in Scotland and Wales. Jeffery Archer is 'found out' and barred from standing in the London Mayoral election.

Hayward Gallery Patrick Caulfield.

Saatchi Gallery "Neurotic Realism" exhibition. Charles Saatchi also gives one hundred works to the Arts Council Collection.

Turner Prize 1999 Steve McQueen won and Tracey Emin, Steven Pippin and Jane & Louise Wilson were short-listed.

John Moores Painting Prize 1999 won by Michael Raedecker with the painting "Mirage".

Jerwood Painting Prize 1999 won by Prunella Clough. The following were shortlisted: Stephen Chambers, Jane Dixon, Neil Gall, James Hugonin, Bob Law and Carol Rhodes. Judges were Judith Collins, Michael Harrison, Carryl Hubbard and Andrew Lambirth.

Venice Biennale Gary Hume represents Britain this year.

Mark Wallinger, Rachel Whiteread and Bill Woodrow are commissioned by the Royal Society of Arts to put forward ideas for the empty **plinth in Trafalgar Square**.

London Group President: Matthew Kolakowski (1990)

Only two new members were elected this year, Peter Clossick and Neil Weerdmeester.

On the 31st January 1999 the all-important General Fund contained £8,124 14, a reasonable sum. Income from members' subscriptions was £2,430.50 whilst total expenditure was £1,990.61, including a massive £918.96 for postage, stationery and printing. Worryingly there appeared a minus in the accounts as a deficit of £1,377.18 on "exhibitions held during the year". The General Fund, however, only shrank by £400 on last year's figures.

Matthew Kolakowski's report to the Group, written for the AGM, begins, "It has been a year in which the Working Party has sought to further the principal constitutional aim of The London Group in exhibiting the work of its members." He indicates that he and Philippa Beale were planning an all members and selected guests show at the Lethaby Gallery for later in the year. Mention was also made of individual member's exhibitions, Suzan Swale, Janet Patterson, Eugene Palmer, Ray Atkins, Hideo Nakane (in Japan) and Susan Wilson (in New Zealand). Gus Cummins won first prize in the Hunting Art Prizes and of ninety-four exhibitors, eight were London Group members. The thorny issue of Charitable Status was continuing to run and run, "the issue being one of private benefit for the proposed trustees not just through the potential sale of work but the significant benefit to trustees merely through the exhibition of work." A letter from the Charity Commission signed by Mr William Thomas Fahey dated 2nd March delivered the 'coup de grace'. "I regret that I am unable to invite registration of this organisation. It is clear that the Trustees (the Working Committee) intend to continue exhibiting their own work. The very exhibition of their own work would in itself render a significant private benefit to those Trustees whose own work is exhibited. On the basis of the information provided it is our opinion that the private benefit to trustees and members of the London Group is likely to outweigh any public benefit so as to preclude the organisation from being established for exclusively charitable purposes." The issue of charitable status was to be circumvented by achieving associate membership with the "Friends of Woodlands Art Gallery", enabling The London Group to apply for funding in this manner.

The death of Morris Kestelman was reported, one of the most respected and longest serving members of The London Group. Kestelman was also the Group's archivist and was instrumental in establishing, updating and maintaining The London Group holding in the Tate Archive.

"The London Group", Cranleigh Arts Centre, Broadoak House, Horsham Road, Cranleigh, Surrey, 10th May to 29th May 1999. Private View, Wednesday 12th May. This venue was for three-dimensional works only, restricted to six feet in any dimension.

"The London Group" The Farnham Maltings, Bridge Square, Farnham, Surrey, 11th May to 29th May 1999. Private View, Tuesday 11th May. Thirty-one exhibits from twenty-eight members. Modestly priced work ranging from £2,200 for Julie Held's "Sleeping Couple" to £175 for Prudence Kurrle's "Landscape with Bell". Media is not given on the price list, probably two-dimensional work as the Cranleigh Arts Centre exhibition was for three-dimensional pieces.

The 1990s had contained several important and large open submission exhibitions at the Barbican Centre involving many members in a great deal of voluntary work. But these ambitious exhibitions had come at a large financial cost and could not be sustained into the new millennium.

The 2000's

'The Dome' opened to the public on January 1st, 2000 and was to have a rocky ride from the public and press. Parallels were drawn between this celebration and the Festival of Britain in 1951, almost half a century before. As with the Festival of Britain artists were commissioned to make pieces of work situated both inside and outside. The Millennium Dome was built on the Greenwich peninsula in South East London on ground reclaimed from one of the largest gasworks in Europe and the structure itself was designed by the Richard Rogers Partnership.

Artists Steve Bunn, Tony Cragg, Bill Culbert, Tacita Dean, Rose Finn-Kelcey, Antony Gormley, Anish Kapoor and Richard Wilson were commissioned to make works for outside, whilst inside Richard Deacon, David Mack, Ron Mueck, Gerald Scarfe and James Turrell installed their contributions, a really diverse and idiosyncratic mix of artists obviously selected by a committee.

This history was written in the second decade of the twenty-first century and consequently any patterns or developments were "too close" to identify. However, in 2000 Louisa Buck updated her 1997 publication and published "Moving Targets 2: A User's Guide to British Art Now" which will serve as an introduction at the very least. Since the 1997 publication, she wrote, "the hothouse has cooled down, the palpitations of the 1990s have calmed, and the pulse of British Art at the beginning of the twenty-first century feels strong and steady. These days, the art coming out of the UK is viewed not so much as an isolated national phenomenon, but rather a vigorous and multifarious strand within an interconnected international art world. The era of so-called Young British Artists is over". Buck retains the listing format of Makers, Current Contenders, New Voices, New Players and New Dealers. Most of her 1997 nominations continued to be listed with the following additions:

The Makers: Presiding Forces Patrick Caulfield, Damien Hirst and Bridget Riley.

Current Contenders Peter Doig, Siobhán Hapaska, Georgina Starr, Wolfgang Tillmans and Jane and Louise Wilson.

New Voices Darren Almond, Fiona Banner, Simon Bill, Martin Creed, Angela de Cruz, Jeremy Deller, Rachel Lowe, Paul Noble, Tim Noble and Sue Webster, Grayson Perry, Michael Raedecker, Tomoko Takahashi and Keith Tyson.

New Players Alex Farquharson from the Centre for Visual Arts, Cardiff, Ann Gallagher of the British Council, Matthew Higgs from the ICA, London, Jenni Lomax from Camden Arts Centre, London, Gregor Muir of the Lux Gallery, London, Judith Nesbitt from the Whitechapel Art Gallery, London, and Toby Webster at the Modern Institute, Glasgow.

New Dealers Sadie Coles of Sadie Coles HQ, London, Paul Hedge & Paul Maslin from Hales Gallery, Deptford, South East London, Martin McGeown & Andrew Wheatley from the Cabinet Gallery, London, Jake Miller from The Approach, London, Victoria Miro (Gallery), London and Anthony Reynolds (Gallery), London.

Contemporary art continued to be diverse and fractured, practiced by individuals without any recognizable or deliberate manifesto groupings. New technologies and time-based media became the norm for young artists emerging from art departments across the country. Meanwhile, more traditional visual activity continued to flourish, especially painting and drawing.

"There is no culture of painting any more, or history or tradition or discipline, just many things done by different people – this is our peculiar moment of art." Matthew Collings, University of the Arts Alumni Magazine, Autumn/Winter 2007.

Tate Modern Time Line 2000-10 Pierre Huyghe, Martin Creed, Carsten Höller, Liam Gillick, Ernesto Neto, Christian Marclay, Andrea Fraser, Yinka Shonibare, Jorge Pardo, Lothar Baumgarton, Maurizio Cattelan, Robert Gober, Absalon, Miroslav Balka, Tomoko Takahashi. Then Francis Alÿs, Takashi Murakami, Thomas Demand, Lorna Simpson, Kara Walker, Thomas Hirschhorn, Ellen Gallagher, Susan Hiller, Fischli and Weiss, Cai Guo-Ciang, Elmgreen and Dragset.

2000

'Y2K', fears about serious computer malfunctions as the new millennium breaks. Putin is elected President of Russia. Israel withdraws from Lebanon after 22 years. Israel and PLO meet at Camp David, but fail to reach an agreement. The USS Cole is attacked in Aden harbour by Al-Qaeda. A Concorde aircraft crashes on take off near Paris. The "Kursk" Russian submarine disaster. The Summer Olympics Games were held in Sydney, Australia. The first resident crew enters the International Space Station. Ken Livingston is elected as the first Mayor of London. The Millennium Dome fails to ignite the public imagination and political recriminations follow. Freedom of Information Act and Human Rights Act. Friends Reunited website launched (sold for £25m in 2009). J. K. Rowling publishes "Harry Potter and The Goblet of Fire". Russell Crowe appears in Ridley Scott's "Gladiator".

2000 The British Art Show 5 curated by Pippa Coles (freelance curator), Matthew Higgs (artist/writer) and Jacqi Poncelet (artist) who selected fifty-seven artists including David Hockney (1963), Paula Rego (1965), toured to Edinburgh, Southampton, Cardiff and Birmingham. Lucio Fontana and "Sonic Boom: The Art of Sound" was also shown at the Hayward Gallery.

Tate Modern opened at Bankside. No current LG members in Tate Modern apart from Anthony Eyton RA who was commissioned to paint inside during conversion from a power station to an art gallery. Conversion architects were Hertzog and de Meuron. **The Millennium Footbridge** opens linking north and south banks of the Thames between St Pauls and Tate Modern, which closed for a while to cure a swaying motion. At the same time the Tate Gallery at Millbank became **Tate Britain**. The new millennium saw a huge programme of refurbishing and building new galleries and museums, both in London and in the provinces. In London the **British Museum's** Courtyard, the **National Portrait Gallery's** new wing, the **Dulwich Picture Gallery** extension and the **Somerset House** refurbishment (where the Courtauld Galleries and the Hermitage Rooms were housed) were opened to the public.

Turner Prize 2000 the first winner of the new millennium was Wolfgang Tillmans; Glenn Brown, Michael Raedecker and Tomoko Takahashi were short-listed.

Beck's Futures an art prize and exhibition for the under 35s sponsored by Becks Beer and housed in the ICA, similar to the "Young Contemporaries".

London Group President: Matthew Kolakowski (1990)

The first Annual General Meeting of the new millennium took place on 30th March at Eagle Court, an annexe of the Central School of Art. Eighteen members attended and two sent apologies. Matthew Kolakowski's Presidents Report was short and matter-of-fact as the "meeting must finish by 8pm sharp". He planned to set up three new sub-committees to deal with Publicity, Exhibitions and Charitable Status in an effort to activate more members and to take the load off "a few principle officers". Publicity was to look at locating The London Group on the Internet and was also producing a high quality document to send out to businesses and potential sponsors, "representing the Group, its history and aims in a positive and professional way". There were ongoing problems with achieving Charitable Status, principally that Trustees (Officers) should not be making profit from exhibitions. Officers could change at any time following elections and would also want to sell their work should the opportunity arise! Novel solutions were suggested, but could be seen to be non-workable. Forthcoming exhibitions at the Lethaby Gallery, Walk Gallery (organised by Adrain Bartlett and David Carr) and the Woodlands Gallery (arranged by Peter Clossick) were discussed and more open studio sessions were planned based on the recent successful event in Jules de Goede's studio. Elections then followed and the President was re-elected; Vice President was Tony Collinge, Deputy Vice President Wendy Anderson, Philippa Beale Hon. Secretary and Trevor Frankland was Hon. Treasurer. The Working Committee this year were Brian Benge, Peter Clossick, David Gluck, Oona Grimes, Vic Kuell, Suzan Swale, Neil Weerdmeister and Arthur Wilson. The five additional elected members of the seventeen strong Membership Committee were Clive Burton, Anthony Eyton, Georgina Hunt, Janet Patterson and Mike Pope. Six new members were elected this year at the Membership Committee Meeting at Eagle Court on the 10th May; James Faure Walker, Annie Johns, Colette Moray de Morand, David Redfern, David Tebbs and Bill Watson.

"London 2000", The London Group Members' Exhibition at the Lethaby Gallery, Central St Martins College of Art and Design, 28th July to 15th August 2000. The London Institute was thanked, "for their generous support in donating the Lethaby Gallery for this exhibition". Matthew Kolakowsaki writes in his introduction to the exhibition, "The London Group continues on the principle of exhibiting its members' work regardless of style, format or content. For more than eighty years it has been successful, but what does the millennium hold for us? We are not a union, a club or a friendly society but an exhibiting society." The professionally produced (by Jane Humphrey) full colour catalogue carried thirty-four illustrations of exhibiting member's work. Of these thirty-four exhibits, twenty-one were paintings, seven were (loosely described as) mixed media constructions, two were sculpture, one photoprint, one video installation, one etching and an inkjet print. Prices were not printed in the catalogue but sizes were. The exhibition arrangement within the two rooms of the Lethaby Gallery was overseen by Vic Kuell and an invigilation rota for members was also negotiated.

The catalogue also makes mention of a recent series of exhibitions outside the boundaries of London. "These exhibitions' selective nature has been defined by location and the logic of the co-curators. The Group's most recent exhibitions were at the Alan Baxter Gallery, Daniel Arnaud Gallery, Brighton University, Farnham Maltings and Cranleigh Arts Centre." Alfred Harris pointed out that in future London Group exhibitions all members should be acknowledged in the catalogue and not just those who had chosen to exhibit.

2001

George W. Bush becomes 43rd President of the United States. '9.11' Al-Qaeda terrorist attack brings down the Twin Towers in New York and kill 2,974 people as hijacked planes are flown into a number of buildings. War against the Taliban in Afghanistan. The hunt begins for Osama bin Laden, leader of Al-Qaeda, who escapes capture following the battle of Tora Bora. Bush refuses to sign the Kyoto protocol in global warming. Enron goes bust. Draft of the human genome published. New Labour with Tony Blair as Prime Minister is re-elected in a General Election. William Hague was Conservative leader and Charles Kennedy the Liberal Democrat leader. Some of the last explosive devices planted in the Irish campaign explode in London at the BBC News Centre, Hendon Post Office and Ealing Broadway. Foot and mouth disease outbreak.

Hayward Gallery Malcolm Morley

Victoria & Albert Museum "Give & Take", a joint exhibition with the **Serpentine Gallery** which made connections between contemporary art and art of the past. The exhibition included Hans Haacke, Jeff Koons, Marc Quinn and Yinka Shonibare. Following tax changes in this year's Budget, all national museums were able to reintroduce free entry for all visitors. By 2004, 6 million more visits were made to national galleries and museums than in 2000. Visits to the V&A were up 113%.

Tate Britain exhibitions of paintings by Stanley Spencer (1914) and Michael Andrews (1962).

Turner Prize 2001 Martin Creed won this year. Richard Billingham, Isaac Julian and Mike Nelson were short-listed.

Jerwood Painting Prize 2001 won by Katie Pratt. Those on the short-list were, Peter Archer, Basil Beattie (1968), Ian Davenport, Marte Marce and Tim Renshaw. Judges were Judith Collins, Sacha Craddock, Norbert Lynton, Declan McGonagle and Wilf Weeks.

Venice Biennale Mark Wallinger represents Britain this year.

London Group President: Matthew Kolakowski followed by Peter Clossick (1999)

"As you know I intend to stand down as President." This was the message delivered to the AGM on 19th March by Matthew Kolakowski who did not want to become a "lifetime incumbent". He still had a number of projects in hand including "establishing our own Web domain to publicise and showcase the members of the Group and to advertise our shows and events." Kolakowski also wanted "to begin to organise The London Group's centenary show at Tate Britain. At present Tate Britain are unaware that they are going to be showing The London Group in 2013 but I hope to make it a reality. Obviously many of us will be a little older and greyer by then and some of us might not be there to see it, but I think it is something worthwhile to aim for." In the following elections Peter Clossick was elected as President, Vice President was Jane Humphrey, Deputy Vice President Suzan Swale, Trevor Frankland Honorary Treasurer and Kate Losty Honorary Secretary.

The London Group at the Walk Gallery, 23 King Edward Walk, London SE1. The Group had negotiated a deal with a small commercial gallery, the Walk Gallery, to eventually show every member in 'packages' of four exhibitors in four shows a year. The London Group would pay a flat fee to the Walk Gallery to help with exhibiting expenses. Adrian Bartlett explains, "In 2000 I was beginning to think that due to the difficulties of organizing the traditional big Group Open exhibition that we should start reinventing ourselves. There is no point in being nostalgic about the state of the art world nearly a hundred years ago, or even thirty years ago. Things are different. I had cooperated on several shows with the director of The Walk, Ranabir Chanda, and had indeed become good friends. We were discussing the difficulty of getting the gallery-going public to come south of the river and I thought that if some well-known artists were to show there it would act as an incentive and break the habit of staying north of the Thames. In my mind I had a show which included Bert Irvin and Anthony Eyton and others, to be called LONDON GROUP SOUTH. Ranabir and I had a mutual friend in David Carr, living in Hampstead! Whoops! The three of us discussed all the possibilities and came up with the formula which lasted until the gallery, sadly, had to close. I insisted that if all LG members were eligible then it should mean absolutely all, in rotation. Not in alphabetical order, but in groups of four which would make an interesting mix together. I selected all the artists on this basis, not including myself, for the first four shows and did the hanging myself. I resigned from the Group that year so someone else took over. In the 80s and 90s, when Art Schools introduced Research Returns, there was a rush to join groups which would guarantee an annual exhibition. In my opinion The London Group should have been shrinking at that time to a more manageable size instead of the reverse."

"Part 1", 18th February to 10th March, Michelle Avison, Victoria Bartlett, Albert Irvin RA and Paula Rego RA.

"Part 2", March/April, Tony Collinge, Trevor Frankland, Anthony Green RA and Kevin Slingsby.

"Part 3", April/May, John Copnall, Jules de Goede, Matthew Kolakowski and Suzan Swale.

"Part 4", June, Ray Atkins, Georgina Hunt, Arthur Wilson and Susan Wilson.

On the 27th March the Group received a letter from solicitors dealing with Edna Coxon's (Ginesi) estate. Edna had passed away in the previous year and in her will had left instructions that 10% of the residue of her estate was to be given to The London

Group. Enclosed in the letter was a cheque for £90,000, initial payment from the bequest. Such a generous gift was most gratefully received by The London Group which would enable the group to make ambitious plans for the approaching 90th anniversary in 2003.

In 2001, seven new members were elected to The London Group; they were Philip Crozier, Mark Dunford, Graham Mileson, Kathleen Mullaniff, Tom Scase, Wendy Smith and Philippa Tunstill.

"The London Group at the Woodlands Art Gallery", Mycenae Road, SE3, 26th May to 24th June 2001. Peter Clossick, the new President, had strong links with the Woodlands Gallery and Maria Turner, the Woodlands Coordinator who was determined to put the Woodlands 'on the map'. Thirty-nine members put in work for exhibition plus one invited artist, Lawrence Edwards. There was no catalogue except for the Price List where Vic Kuell's "Traces in the Margins" commanded top price at £12,000, Lawrence Edwards at £8,330 and Collette Moray de Morand at £4,500 (all paintings). Work was arranged by Vic Kuell throughout four galleries, mainly two-dimensional painting. The Press Release stated, "It is with great affection that the Group dedicates this current exhibition at the Woodlands Art Gallery to Stan Smith (Hon. Life President) who died in February 2001. Also to the artist Edna Ginesi (Hon. Life Member) who died during 2000." It continued, "As The London Group continues to exhibit and attract young artists, it not only represents the best in British art but also presents to an increasing egocentric, media frenzied 'art world' a model of what co-operation and altruism can do to support the visual arts for nearly one hundred years." The Press Release also gave a short history of the affectionately remembered Woodlands Art Gallery now closed due to removal of Greenwich Council funding. "Woodlands was the country home of John Julius Angerstein, and was built in 1774 as a retreat from his work at Lloyds. John Julius was reputed to be the illegitimate son of Empress Anne of Russia and Andrew Poulett Thomson. At the age of fifteen years John Julius came from St. Petersburg to work in his father's counting house and became an underwriter at Lloyds. So great was his success that policies underwritten by him became known as Julians. Known as the 'father of Lloyds' he became so wealthy that in his London home at 100 Pall Mall, he was able to collect van Dyck, Claude, Rubens, Caracci, Rembrandt and Raphael. It is appropriate that his 'charming little villa' in Blackheath became the Woodlands Art Gallery."

The Woodlands Art Gallery
90 Mycenae Road, London SE3

The Woodlands Art Gallery, 90 Mycenae Road, London SE3 was run by Greenwich Council and administered by a Board of Governors and staffed by volunteers. The building had a rich history, it being the home of the Earl of Angerstein whose private collection of paintings was to form the kernel of the National Gallery collection. The London Group exhibited here in 2001 and 2002. Peter Clossick, the President, had strong ties with the Woodlands and sought to, "put the gallery on the map". Unfortunately, Greenwich Council were unable to continue funding and this beautiful local (and London) amenity closed a few years later. The Woodlands had four large galleries overlooking lawns from which there were panoramas of the Thames and Docklands.

"The London Group at the Stark Gallery", Lee High Road, SE12, 26th May to 22nd June 2001. The Stark Gallery was a small but energetically ambitious commercial art gallery on the main A20 out of Lewisham. However, their printing of members' names in the price list let them down somewhat, Terry Collinge (Tony Collinge), Peter Clossock (Clossick), James Faure (Faure Walker) and five other hiccoughs. There were thirty-three exhibits, mainly small scale, two-dimensional pieces between £90 to £2,225. The President Peter Clossick lived a few minutes from the Stark Gallery and was easily able to organise this link for the Group in a local gallery.

The Income and Expenditure Account up to the 31st January 2001 showed that in the previous financial year the Group had a deficit of £1,185.87. Income from members' subscriptions had been £3,920.50 but exhibition expenses alone had totalled £3,843.53. Expenditure in total was £5,177.21 including secretarial fees, advertising and postage. In the year before this year the Group had made a surplus of £252.

2002

Euro currency launched in Europe (not UK). Wall Street journalist Daniel Pearl is murdered in Karachi. Tension between the two nuclear powers India and Pakistan over Kashmir. The trial of Slobodan Milosovich begins in the Hague. The United States invades Afghanistan. The first detainees arrive at Guantánamo Bay, Cuba. The UN approves Resolution 1441 ordering Iraq to disclose WMDs. Ground Zero in New York is finally cleared. Jacques Shirac is elected as France's President after beating Jean-Marie Le Pen. Many former USSR states invited to join NATO. Hu Jintao becomes Secretary General of the Communist Party of China. RNA created synthetically by scientists which could revolutionise medicine. Halle Berry becomes the first black woman to win Best Actress Oscar. In the UK the Queen Mother dies. Queen Elizabeth II's Golden Jubilee celebrations in London. The Soham murders. At Sothebys Rubens' "The Massacre of the Innocents" is sold to Lord Thomson for nearly £50 million.

Hayward Gallery Paul Klee, Sam Taylor-Wood and Douglas Gordon.

John Moores Painting Prize 2002 won by Peter Davies with the painting, "Super Star Fucker - Andy Warhol Text Painting". In 2002, of the thirty-eight selected for exhibition, two were members of The London Group, Gary Wragg (1990) and James Faure Walker (2000).

The Jerwood Painting Prize 2002 won by Callum Innes. Short-listed were Paul Morrison, Nicky Hoberman, Lisa Milroy, Graham Crowley and Pamela Golden, none of whom were members of The London Group. Judges were Frank Cohen, Norbert Lynton, Keith Patrick, Andrea Rose and Charles Saumarez Smith.

Turner Prize 2002 winner Keith Tyson. Short-listed were Fiona Banner, Liam Gillick and Catherine Yass.

Ten regional Arts Boards merge with **Arts Council England** to become the single national development agency for the arts.

"Biennials and Beyond – Exhibitions That Made Art History 1962–2002" Kassel, Germany, "Documenta 11".

London Group President: Peter Clossick (1999)

Nine new members were elected this year, Mark Dickens, Anthony Daley, Frank Bowling, Michael Philippson, Lucy Jones, Tony Carter, Julie Held, John Holden and Anne Cloudsley. Frank Bowling was re-elected to the Group after his membership lapsed. Bowling had in fact been Vice President in 1967 when Andrew Forge was President. Membership was fast approaching a potentially unmanageable number and, even though this urge for membership was encouraging, officers needed to consider future policy.

This year the President was Peter Clossick, Vice President was Jane Humphrey and Trevor Frankland was Treasurer.

"The London Group at the Walk Gallery", 23 King Edward Walk, London SE1. For each exhibition four members organised their medium to small scale work to show in the Walk Gallery, a compact commercial gallery opposite the Imperial War Museum. The London Group paid £350 towards each exhibition of four members.

"Part 1", February, David Gluck, Peter Clossick, Anthony Whishaw RA and Kate Montgomery.

"Part 2", March/April, Julian Cooper, Alfred Harris, Pauline Little and Janet Patterson.

"Part 3", April/May, Philippa Beale, David Carr, Anthony Eyton RA and Vic Kuell.

"Part 4", June, Eugene Palmer, David Tebbs, Bill Watson and Laetitia Yhap.

Three members of The London Group, Gus Cummins RA, Anthony Green RA and Anthony Whishaw RA exhibited at the Woodland Art Gallery in March 2002. The "Three Royal Academicians" exhibition was designed to bring The London Group back into focus by highlighting the quality of its members' work.

"The London Group", Trinity Theatre and Arts Centre, Tunbridge Wells, 16th August to 31st August 2002. Jane Humphrey and Vic Kuell organised and hung the exhibition. The work was arranged within a discrete gallery space inside a church building (now used as a theatre).

November 2002 saw the first issue of a regular London Group Newsletter sent to all members with important information and articles of interest. The magazine was designed by the President's wife, Joyce Clossick.

The final amount from the Edna Coxon bequest amounted to £116,907. Added to the £3,800 from members' subscriptions and other monies, the Group's income this year was £121,631 just in time for the 2003 90th Anniversary Exhibition plans. Income and expenditure had more or less been equal up until this timely gift from the estate of a previous London Group member.

2003

In February more than 10 million people around the world protest against the threat of war in Iraq. In March, America, UK and Allies invade Iraq ("Shock and Awe") to depose Saddam Hussein and search for Weapons of Mass Destruction (none found). In December, Saddam Hussein is arrested. NASA's Space Shuttle "Columbia" breaks up on re-entering the Earth's atmosphere killing all on board. Hu Jintao becomes President of China replacing Jiang Zemin. China launches her first manned space mission. Russia holds parliamentary elections amidst Chechnyan terrorist bomb attacks. The World Health Organisation warns of a SARS epidemic. England beat Australia in the Rugby World Cup. The Human Genome Project is successfully completed. Ministry of Defence scientist David Kelly is found dead leading to the Hutton inquiry. Concorde makes its final flight over London into Heathrow. Deputy PM John Prescott gives planning permission for "The Shard" at London Bridge, which will be the tallest building in Europe. The highest UK temperature ever, 38.1°C, is recorded in Faversham, Kent. In Paris the temperature hits 44°C, the heatwave kills over 30,000 in Europe. On December 25th, Beagle 2 lands on Mars and nothing has been heard from it since.

Victoria & Albert Museum "Art Deco", a comprehensive exhibition of the Art Deco movement.
Tate Britain Lynn Chadwick (1952) exhibition.
Turner Prize 2003 won by Grayson Perry. Jake & Dinos Chapman, Willie Doherty and Anya Gallaccio made up the short-list.
Jerwood Painting Prize 2003 won by Shani Rhys James with Suzanne Holtom, John Hoyland, Marc Vaux (1990), Alison Watt and John Wonacott short-listed. Judges were Griff Rhys Jones, Norbert Lynton, Martin Gayford, Duncan Robinson and David Jaffe.
Venice Biennale this year Chis Ofili represented Britain.

London Group President: Peter Clossick (1999)

No new members were elected in the 90th Anniversary Year. The Group was up to eighty-two, maximum agreed numbers.

"Artists of the London Group", Hatton Art Gallery, Newcastle, 18th January to 1st March 2003. The Curator in Newcastle had failed to make contact with The London Group through using an old address and at that time the website was not up and running. The exhibition was an historical survey from the early years of The London Group showing paintings and drawings. There are installation shots and a poster for the exhibition held in the Tate Archive.

The Annual General Meeting was held at the Ethical Society, Conway Hall, on the 11th March. At the elections, Peter Clossick was re-elected as President, Jane Humphrey Vice President, Suzan Swale and Wendy Anderson Deputy-Vice Presidents, Trevor Frankland Treasurer and Philippa Beale as Hon Secretary. Those elected to the Working Committee this year were Annie Johns, Matthew Kolakowski, Anne Cloudsley, Philip Crozier, Janet Patterson, Wendy Smith, Tony Carter, Tom Scase, Clive Burton and Tony Collinge. The Selection Committee was to include Tony Eyton, David Gluck, Vic Kuell and David Redfern.

During the year small group exhibitions were arranged at the Walk Gallery under the title, "The London Group at the Walk", Gallery of Contemporary Fine Art, 23, King Edward Walk, SE1.

"Part 1", 10th February to 1st March, Wendy Anderson, Jane Humphrey, Annie Johns and Kathleen Mullaniff.

"Part 2", 17th March to 5th April, Philip Crozier, James Faure-Walker, David Redfern and Philippa Tunstill.

"Part 3", 2nd June to 21st June, Evelyn Ballantine, Bryan Benge, Hideo Nakane and Wendy Smith.

"Part 4", 7th July to 26th July, Bill Henderson, John Holden, Janet Nathan and David Whitaker.

The exhibitions were a continuation of the 2002 exhibitions and The London Group paid £450 towards each exhibition of four members.

"The London Group at the Woodlands Art Gallery", 16th February to 15th March 2003. No catalogue was printed for this exhibition but a Price List indicates sixty-two members exhibiting at the Woodlands. The majority of the works on show were paintings. Top price was Frank Bowling's "Ducks and Drakes" at £12,000, David Shutt's "Afon Treweryn" at £7,000 and Kathleen Mullaniff's "A Stranger to this Place". Most prices were in the four figure bracket but only one piece of work was sold. Vic Kuell organised the hang in the Woodland's four galleries and volunteer members hung the show in a day.

"The London Group Ninetieth Anniversary Exhibition", The Gallery in Cork Street and Gallery 27, 2nd June to 7th June 2003. The Press Opening and Anniversary Yearbook Launch was on the 2nd June (unfortunately on the same night as the Cindy Sherman Press Preview at the Serpentine Gallery), Private View for the exhibition on the 3rd of June (heaving) and the new website launch on the 4th June. The exhibition was mounted in two galleries, The Gallery in Cork Street and Gallery 27 next door. The cost of hiring the two galleries was £11,000, largely paid for out of the bequest left by Edna Ginesi. There was no catalogue printed for this exhibition as the Anniversary Yearbook took its place.

The Gallery in Cork Street
London W1

A Price List doubled as a catalogue indicating seventy-two exhibitors, a high proportion of a total membership of eighty-two. Mostly two-dimensional, wall mounted work with a variety of media, oil, acrylic, collage, computer generated images and three pieces of three-dimensional, floor standing work. Victoria Bartlett, Wendy Anderson, James Swinson, Janet Patterson, Georgina Hunt, Trevor Frankland and Tony Carter all gave talks about their work or issues related to The London Group. The typographic design of the poster and PV invites included a list of current members to reflect the holistic identity of The London Group and to avoid favouring one individual artist over another.

The London Group 90th Anniversary Yearbook (often referred to as 'The Bluebook' because of the colour of the cover) was a lavish, colour production edited by Jane Humphrey and published by the Group. Peter Clossick wrote an Introduction, William Feaver wrote a Foreward and Philippa Beale wrote an article, "The London Group Inside Out". Each current member had a page showing a colour illustration of their work and a short text in relation to this work, followed by a list of past presidents, members and exhibitions back to 1913. In this way the 90th anniversary was celebrated by a professional and attractive artifact to mark this notable landmark in the Group's history.

Similarly, the Group's new website housed much of what was contained in The Bluebook, but also provided access for communication for those with enquiries and wishing to make contact.

A Working Group Meeting was held at the City Pride pub in Clerkenwell on 23rd June. Items discussed were the forthcoming exhibitions at the Café Gallery, the Highgate Gallery, the programme for the 2005 Walk Gallery series and an auction to help save the Woodlands Gallery from closure. The meeting also looked at issues to do with distributing The London Group 2003 Yearbook and servicing the new website.

"London Group, Works on Paper", Café Gallery, Southwark Park, 9th July to 2nd August 2003. The Café Gallery was a small, recently refurbished, very public space with two galleries inside Southwark Park and run by the Bermondsey Artists Group. Fifty members took part in this exhibition and a copy of the exhibition labels naming the exhibitors is preserved in the Tate Archive. The work on show was extremely varied with members using a paper ground in a traditional and non-traditional way, from pastel and charcoal to colour laser prints and graphite on resin cast. One thousand five hundred people visited the exhibition which the organisers said, for a small gallery was an extremely encouraging figure. Peter Clossick gave a talk on The London Group followed by a debate on the future of the Group.

The Café Gallery
Southwark Park
London SE16

The Café Gallery in Southwark Park, South London was the venue for the 2003 exhibition "London Group, Works on Paper". The recently refurbished gallery was financially supported by a number of institutions including Southwark Council and was run by the Bermondsey Artists Group, a local South London group of artists who had organised themselves into a group for exhibiting opportunities, just like The London Group.

Three large exhibitions had been organised in this anniversary year and, not surprisingly, exhibition expenses this year had been £15,237.39, book production expenses totalled £23,079.32 and website design, £5,875.01, whilst secretarial assistance and postage consumed nearly £2,000. The timely bequest from 2002 had enabled the Group to push the boat out to celebrate 90 years existence.

2004

Al-Qaeda terrorist bombs on the Madrid rail network kill 192 and injure over 2000. Continuing involvement in Iraq for US and UK troops as Spain withdraws. George W. Bush re-elected as US President. Beslan School Hostage Crisis in Russia, 335 killed, 700 injured. The European Union expands by another ten member states. An earthquake and tsunami on December 26th kills or drowns over 300,000 in and around the Indian Ocean. China successfully launches its first astronaut into Earth orbit. NASA lands two rovers, Spirit and Opportunity, on the surface of Mars, they will eventually prove that Mars once had water on its surface. SpaceShipOne becomes the first privately funded spaceship to fly in space. The Summer Olympics Games are held in Athens. Tony Blair meets Colonel Qaddafi in Libya. Boscastle in Cornwall was flooded by a flash flood. The Licensing Act allows 24-hour drinking. Peter Jackson's "Lord of the Rings" sweeps the Academy Awards. Munch's "Scream" is stolen from an Oslo Museum.

Tate Britain "Paula Rego" exhibition. Rego was elected to The London Group in 1965 and is still an exhibiting member with the Group. Also the "Art and the Sixties" exhibition (See "The 1960s").
2004 Hunting Prize Susan Wilson (1997) was a Regional Prize Winner (New Zealand). Other members selected for exhibition were Anthony Whishaw (1978), Janet Patterson (1984), Georgina Hunt (1998) and Peter Clossick (1999).
John Moores Painting Prize 2004 won by Alexis Harding with the paint/material construction "Slump/Fear (orange/black) 2004".
Turner Prize 2004 was won by Jeremy Deller. Short-listed this year were Kutlug Aaman, Langlands & Bell and Yinka Shonibare.
Hayward Gallery showed paintings by Roy Lichtenstein.
In May, a fire at the Momart warehouse in London destroys many important YBA artworks including the Chapman Brothers' "Hell".

London Group President: Peter Clossick (1999)

Later in the year, eight new members were elected to the Group. They were Mark Ainsworth, Jeff Dellow, Tricia Gillman (who was re-elected following lapse of membership), Susan Haire, Marcel Hanselaar, Richard Kemp, Peter Lowe and Wendy Taylor. There were a large number of nominations and hard choices had to be made by the Selection Committee.

The AGM was held on Monday, 8th March in Conway Hall, Red Lion Square. Approximately a quarter of the total membership of ninety turned out, the hard core of London Group supporters, although there were a healthy number of apologies. The mood was optimistic and buoyant, echoed in the meetings' decision to open up membership beyond the ninety ceiling to "infuse some fresh blood". More members than in the recent past were putting work into the annual exhibition, but there was still space for more. The President's Report listed the exhibitions of 2003 and reminded members of the forthcoming "What is The London Group?" debate at Greenwich College, the newly introduced Newsletter, a current members database and the Group joining the Friends of the Woodlands Art Gallery in order to apply for funding through their charity status. The London Group Archive at Tate Britain continued to be updated, publicity was described as, "a slick machine" and the 90th Year Book was considered to be a considerable success. The meeting extended its warm thanks to Jane Humphrey for overseeing its design and printing. The new Website was finally up and running and a new logo about to be finalised. Election of Officers (all unopposed) was as follows, President Peter Clossick, Vice President Jane Humphrey, Deputy Vice President Clive Burton, Honorary Secretary Philip Crozier and Honorary Treasurer Trevor Frankland. The Working Party was elected as follows, Wendy Anderson and Wendy Smith carrying on from last year, Annie Johns, Ian Parker, Suzan Swale, Philippa Beale, Mark Dickens and Tony Carter. The Selection Committee (comprised of seventeen members altogether, five officers, eight Working Party and four elected) was, Tom Scase, Georgina Hunt, John Holden and Vic Kuell.

The small group exhibitions continued at the Walk Gallery with four more shows. The London Group at the Walk Gallery, 23 King Edward Walk, London SE1.
"Part 1", 2nd February to 20th February, Clive Burton, John Crossley, C. Morey de Morand and Neil Weerdmeester.
"Part 2", 8th March to 26th March, Julie Held, Ken Oliver, Alex Ramsay and Philippa Stjernsward.
"Part 3", 19th April to 7th May, Tony Carter, Mark Dickens, Ian Parker and Mike Phillipson.
"Part 4", 7th June to 28th June, Martin Abrahams, Slavomir Blatton, Anne Cloudsley and Tom Scase.

"The London Group at the Menier Chocolate Factory", a Members and Guests Exhibition from the 26th April to 14th May 2004. The Menier Chocolate Factory, 51 - 53 Southwark Street, London SE1 was hired for three weeks at a cost of £850 per week. The Menier (not a working factory anymore but a gallery/theatre conversion complex) was situated close to Tate Modern and the popular Borough Market ensuring a good location for visitors. Hanging the show was a tricky affair as the gallery space was fragmented using long and short run white screens and brick wall columns. Tony Collinge was given the unenviable task of arranging the sixty-six exhibits, only two of which were not wall hangings. Twelve guests, who were to be put forward for full membership of The London Group, also submitted work. This was a deliberate decision to bring fresh blood into the Group and to try to return to the concept of member and non-member exhibitions which had lain dormant for a while due to restrictive sizes of recent venues. Fifty-four members out of ninety total membership supported this annual showing. All of the wall mounted work showed a wide range of approaches and sizes, from traditional oil or acrylic paintings to computer prints and mixed media. Prices averaged £1,000, top price £9,000 from Frederick Gore RA for his oil painting "A Farmer in his Vineyard", followed by Tricia Gillman asking £7,000 for her oil painting "April". Both of these artists were guests and both were seeking re-election to The London Group, having been members in the past. Top members' price came from Frank Bowling, asking £6,500 for his acrylic abstract, "Swing" and Susan Wilson asking the same amount for her representational oil painting, "Rachel Windsor (Kuia)". The Private View on Tuesday, 27th April from 6-9pm was well attended despite torrential rain and thunderstorms, a suitable fanfare for the new annual show.

The Menier Gallery
51–53 Southwark Street
London SE1

The Menier Gallery, 51–53 Southwark Street, London SE1, is situated on the ground floor and in the basement of the Menier Chocolate Factory, an arts complex with a theatre and restaurant just southeast of Tate Modern. This architecturally rich building was hired by The London Group for "The London Group: a Members' and Guests' Exhibition" in 2004, the "London Group Open Exhibition, Parts 1 and 2" in 2007 and the 95th Anniversary Exhibition in 2008.

"Small Works", at the Highgate Gallery, The Highgate Literary and Scientific Institute, 11 South Grove, Highgate, London N6, 14th May to 27th May 2004 with a Private View on Friday, 14th May. An exhibition with a size restriction organised for the Group by Tom Scase. One member described the exhibition as like "The London Group in Lilliput"! Roger Fry, elected to The London Group in 1917 and influential critic, designer and artist, spent his early childhood at numbers 5 and 6 The Grove, Highgate, just a stone's throw from South Grove. Fry had fond memories of these imposing houses and his father encouraged the young Roger to recognise the importance of science in late Victorian society. London is a small place too.

London Group members also enjoyed success at this year's Royal Academy Summer Show. Philippa Stjernsward won the Duprée Family Award for a Woman Artist valued at £3,500 for her painting, "Mosaic". Tricia Gillman, invited to show in the Menier Gallery, was commended for her painting, "Silver Lining" and eighteen London Group members had work selected and hung.

In October, Newsletter 5 was sent to members. It contained information about the forthcoming exhibition in April 2005 at the Bankside Gallery, as well as the new programme for the Walk Gallery, "where we have, overall, made more sales than at any other exhibition." It also contained articles on the updating of the website, a welcome to the eight new members, an article by David Carr, Members' Recent Exhibitions, a report from the Archive and from the Menier Exhibition. There was also a copy of a very interesting letter from Cliff Holden, living in Sweden, to Sir Nicholas Serota concerning the long overdue comprehensive retrospective of David Bomberg's life, especially in relation to his "legendary" reputation as a teacher. On November 19th The London Group website was linked to the BBC Arts website, enabling the Group to link with members of the public interested in the visual arts.

Income this year totalled £6,347 but expenditure was £9,090 leaving a nasty deficit of £2,743. The biggest expenditure was website maintenance followed by meetings expenses and postage. However, the Group still had the cushion of a large part of the 2002 bequest, leaving a healthy balance of £81,616 in the General Fund.

2005

'7/7' terrorist attacks on London's tube and bus system kill 56 including 4 suicide bombers, the biggest terrorist attack ever committed in the UK had been carried out by British-born Muslims 'trained' in Pakistan. Shortly afterwards, J.C. Menezes is shot by police at Stockwell tube station as a suspected suicide bomber. Continued US and UK involvement in Iraq and Afghanistan. Yasser Arafat, Leader of the PLO, dies. YouTube is launched. Pope John Paul II dies. Hurricane Katrina floods New Orleans killing nearly 2,000 people. Ahmadinejad becomes president of Iran. 'New Labour' is returned in a General Election but with a much reduced majority. Michael Howard was Conservative leader and Charles Kennedy the Liberal Democrat's. England regain the Ashes. Civil Partnership Act comes into force. MG Rover goes bust. Trafalgar Square's fourth plinth is occupied by Mark Quinn's "Alison Lapper".

Tate Britain "Degas, Sickert and Toulouse Lautrec: London and Paris 1870 – 1910" exhibition.
Turner Prize 2005 winner was Simon Starling and those short-listed were Darren Almond, Gillian Carnegie and Jim Lambie.
Royal Academy "China: The Three Emperors", an exhibition of Chinese artifacts dating from 1662-1795.
Venice Biennale Gilbert and George represent Britain.
Steven Cohen, a hedge-fund manager, buys Damein Hirst's "The Physical Impossibility of Death in the Mind of Someone Living", from Charles Saatchi for $12 million.

London Group President: Peter Clossick (1999) followed by Philip Crozier (2001)

Only one new member was elected this year, Susan Skingle, a sculptor/object maker. There had been eleven nominations. Two or three nominees had come close to election and would be encouraged to seek nomination again. Membership was "creeping towards 100" and might become "unmanageable". (Quotes from President Philip Crozier in the November Newsletter No. 6).

Just before this year's AGM the President, Peter Clossick, wrote to the members proposing an increase in the annual subscription from £50 to £80. With ninety-five members this would raise another £2,700 which would help pay for a part-time paid secretary to help run the Group and take the load from many officers, especially the President. This new person would help to organise meetings, exhibitions, publicity, the newsletter and to keep the website up to date. Clossick also informed the Group that after four years as President he was stepping down due to pressure of work. "It has been an exciting time, the 90th celebrations, numerous exhibitions (twelve in all, plus fourteen at the Walk), the website and book, newsletter, plus a new catalogue for Bankside."

The AGM itself was again held at Conway Hall on Monday, 14th March 2005 between 7 and 9 pm. Minutes of last years' AGM were previously circulated and contained written reports by the Treasurer and President for the year 2003/4. At the AGM the following were elected to office, the new President was Philip Crozier, Vice President Clive Burton, Deputy Vice President Wendy Smith, Honorary Secretary Susan Haire and Honorary Treasurer Robert Coward (who was himself an Honorary Member). Trevor Frankland had stood down at the AGM due to pressure of other commitments. The Working Party this year was to be Philippa Beale, Tony Carter, Peter Clossick, Tony Collinge, Mark Dickens, Jane Humphrey, Annie Johns and Ian Parker.

The newly elected President, Philip Crozier, subsequently wrote an introductory letter to membership laying out his vision for the future. "My priorities are to keep the annual exhibition and the smaller shows, although these may not be linked to a particular gallery, to develop a regional and if at all possible an international presence, and to have an aspiration to an LG Open exhibition. The main problem with this is the enormous change in the economics of gallery space: spaces affordable in the past are prohibitively expensive now without significant sponsorship from outside the Group. This is something else to be pursued." The letter explains the proposal to raise the annual subscription by £30 to help pay for a part-time administrative assistant. The previous president's wife, Joyce Clossick, had put in a tremendous amount of unpaid work, dealing with emails, setting up the Newsletter and dealing with exhibition administration. Crozier's letter ends, "Finally, my favourite quote from W.R. Sickert on how to achieve success in the Art World: 'These things are done by gangs'. Let's be a good gang."

Exhibitions in 2005 began with two shows of the eight newly elected members at the Walk Gallery. "The London Group at the Walk Gallery", 23 King Edward Walk, London SE1. "Part 1", 3rd February to 25th February, Mark Ainsworth, Jeff Dellow, Tricia Gillman and Marcelle Hanselaar. "Part 2", 3rd March to 24th March, Susan Haire, Richard Kemp, Peter Lowe and Wendy Taylor.

"Systems of Creativity", The Green Space Gallery, 58-60 East Dulwich Road, London SE22, 15th March to 17th May 2005 with a Private View on Wednesday, 16th March. Exhibitors were Jane Humphrey, Georgina Hunt, Kathleen Mullaniff and Wendy Smith, four female London Group members brought together and curated by the second female London Group President, Philippa Beale. "The exquisitely honed aesthetic pursued by each artist is both innovative and alluring." (PB)

"London Group Annual Exhibition", The Bankside Gallery (next door to Tate Modern), Hopton Street, Southwark SE1, 8th April to 17th April 2005. Over three hundred and eighty people attended the Private View on Thursday 7th April. A fully illustrated colour catalogue, designed by member Jane Humphrey, accompanied the exhibition. In the Introduction the outgoing President Peter Clossick wrote, "The London Group is unusual in its ability, as one of the few remaining exhibiting societies from the early twentieth century, to sustain its original principles and structure. It has survived through ninety years of art historical transience. Unchanged since 1913, the open nature of the group and its inclusiveness encourages opportunities for all members through the vehicle of the group's mission, 'The object of the group shall be to advance public awareness of contemporary visual art by holding exhibition/s annually'. As a member, you know that you are within a body of artists who are interested in, and prioritise, other's aesthetic qualities – regardless of your own personal direction. This is the strength of the group, to make space for another, because we all have chosen to elect and be elected by, to exhibit together as a whole regardless of the different factions that compose the group. For an artist to become part of The London Group will be to value a plurality of viewpoints and to join in its illustrious history. A history that is ahistoric in outlook, as it is always part of the present, part of now. The group does not have hierarchies or notions of linear progression, but is rooted within the democratic principles of care and equality and is prepared to collaborate with any other organisation." There were other written contributions from Nicholas Usherwood (Features Editor of Galleries Magazine), Philippa Beale (a previous president) and David Redfern (Archivist). Seventy-one members exhibited one piece of work each. Forty works were two-dimensional paintings in oil or acrylic, sixteen of which were figurative, whilst the remainder were three-dimensional wall or floor mounted, photographs, computer prints, drawings, video or combinations, in other words as varied as contemporary art activity could be at this time. Albert Irvin, Matthew Kolakowski and Suzan Swale sold their work from this show. The catalogue lists ninety full members and four Honorary Members. Five Royal Academicians were also recorded, Gus Cummins, Anthony Eyton, Anthony Green, Albert Irvin and Anthony Whishaw. In the financial accounts, the total exhibition expenses for the Bankside Exhibition were £7,533.72, a large amount of money but thought worth paying by officers and membership, given the Banksides' close location to Tate Modern and its art going public.

Bankside Gallery
Hopton Street, London SE1

The Bankside Gallery near Tate Modern is a well situated but expensive location, used for the 2005 and 2006 Annual Exhibitions. The gallery is situated on the ground floor of a block of flats.

SoCo Gallery, St Mary-in-the Castle, Pelham Place, Hastings from the 1st October to the 30th October 2005. Exhibition entitled "To the Limit", a joint venture between SoCo (South Coast Artists) and The London Group. Participating London Group members were Mark Dickens, Tony Carter, Gus Cummins, Philip Crozier, Susan Haire, Vic Kuell, Graham Mileson, David Redfern, Wendy Smith, David Tebbs, Neil Weerdmeester and Laetitia Yhap. The SoCo gallery was situated on the front at Hastings and seems to tunnel back into the cliff itself, a warren of small galleries rising up from the main entrance. This was South Coast Artists annual exhibition (similar to The London Group's annual) and was made possible by President Philip Crozier's links with the town and local artists. This exhibition was seen as a forerunner to more exhibitions with SoCo in the future in which every London Group member would eventually have an opportunity to exhibit.

In November, the sixth Newsletter was distributed to members of the Group. In "Matters Arising", Crozier reported on the success of this year's Bankside show and confirmed the 2006 Annual Exhibition would be held at the same venue. Membership news was that Susan Swingle had been elected to the Group, Jane Humphrey unanimously ratified as an Honorary Member and that ex-President Philippa Beale had retired from the Group to concentrate on independent curating. Tamara Thomas was introduced as the Group's new P.A. helping officers with day-to-day administration. Tony Carter speculated on the purpose of The London Group, suggesting that, "we will need to see our own make-up more clearly" creating "subgroups within the whole".

Carter also urged the membership to consider a European or International role in the future. A list of recent and forthcoming London Group exhibitions followed with a detailed list of individual members' exhibitions and successes, especially in the RA Summer Show where nineteen members were exhibited.

November also saw an Extraordinary General Meeting called by member Alfred Harris to discuss small group exhibitions and their selection process. Harris' letter to members began, "We frequently allude to the Group's ethos as being routed in artists of different persuasions having equality of membership. This concept is eroded by arrangements for Small Group Exhibitions".

A Working Committee Meeting was held on Wednesday, 14th December in the City Pride pub, Clerkenwell. Fourteen members attended and discussed final details concerning the 2006 Bankside exhibition. The exhibition was to be dedicated to Kevin Slingsby who had died recently. Five brief reports followed on exhibition opportunities as follows; links with a similar organisation in Amsterdam curated by Peter Clossick, an exhibition at the Guildhall Art Gallery in 2007 curated by Annie Johns and Janet Patterson, a sub-committee of Mark Dickens, Peter Clossick and Susan Haire to look into exhibition possibilities with Radisson/Portman Hotel chain, small shows at Sassoon Gallery organised by Clive Burton and Philippa Beale and another SoCo show in Hastings in September 2006. The meeting also concluded that the issue of small group exhibitions without changing the constitution needed wider discussion following Alfred Harris' initiative. An Emergency General Meeting was suggested for early 2006.

The financial records for the year show that the Group spent £7,533.72 on the Bankside exhibition, a very large sum considering income from members' subscriptions was only £3,655.25. This expenditure resulted in a huge £8,333.45 deficit but one the Group was happy to shoulder bearing in mind the facilities offered and the Banksides' location next to Tate Modern. The General Fund now stood at £70,930.16 whilst last year it had been £79,263. Officers would have to look more carefully at plans for future exhibition venues as this level of spending could not be maintained.

2006

Civil war between Sunni and Shiite Muslims in Iraq, thousands die. Al-Zarqawi, the leader of Al-Qaeda in Iraq, is killed by US troops. On December 30th, Saddam Hussein is executed by hanging. In the US Mid-Term Elections the Democrats gain control of both houses as voters protest against the Iraqi war and President George W. Bush. Iran defies the UN and USA in refining Uranium "for generating electricity". Israel makes incursions into Lebanon in pursuit of Hezbollah 'terrorists', United Nations sends in a peace-keeping force. North Korea detonates a nuclear weapon, the ninth member of the "Nuclear Club". The Stern Report on the devastating economic impact of global warming is published. Tony Blair faces internal revolt as to when he will step down as Prime Minister. Twitter is launched. Richard Dawkins publishes "The God Delusion". Identity cards come a step closer.

Tate Britain "Tate Triennial 2006: New British Art", thirty-six artists including Cosey Fanni Tutti, Peter Doig, Ian Hamilton Finlay (who died this year), Liam Gillick, Douglas Gordon, John Stezaker and Cerith Wyn Evans. There seems to have been a diplomatic selection of artists from across the UK with an equal split between those who studied at 'the big three', Goldsmiths, RCA and the Slade. Also a Howard Hodgkin retrospective. Meanwhile, at **Tate Modern**, the permanent collection was refreshed and re-hung by means of four "terminals" devoted to the four main "isms" of modern art - futurism, minimalism, surrealism and abstract expressionism. Also a Kandinsky exhibition, "The Path to Abstraction".

Hayward Gallery "How to Improve the World: 60 Years of British Art", an exhibition of works from the Arts Council Collection curated by Michael Archer (guest curator) and Roger Malbert (Senior Hayward Curator). 10% of those exhibited were, at some time in their lives, members of The London Group. Of these fifteen artists, eleven were painters and four sculptors. They were mainly active and important in the 1950s and 60s. No contemporary artists were London Group members. The Arts Council Collection was started in 1946 and now comprises over 7,500 works by more than 2,000 artists. "(The Collection) is one of the UK's foremost national collections of post-war British art. It is also, importantly, the most widely circulated collection of its kind." Also an exhibition of Dan Flavin's work.

Serpentine Gallery an exhibition of works from Damien Hirst's 'murderme collection'. This would appear to give an indication of who was 'hot' at this moment in time, given Hirst's standing in the contemporary art world. The exhibition featured "over 60 works by 24 artists, representing a cross-section of the most interesting contemporary art today". Artists included were, Francis Bacon, Banksy, Don Brown, Angela Bulloch, John Currin, Tracey Emin, Angus Fairhurst, Steven Gregory, Marcus Harvey, Rachel

Howard, John Isaacs, Michael Joo, Jeff Koons, Jim Lambie, Sean Landers, Tim Lewis, Sarah Lucas, Nicholas Lumb, Tom Ormond, Laurence Owen, Richard Prince, Haim Steinbach, Gavin Turk and Andy Warhol.

Victoria & Albert Museum "Modernism", a 'blockbuster' exhibition subtitled "Designing a New World" covering the period 1914-39. A major figure from the exhibition was E. McKnight Kauffer who was elected to The London Group whilst he was still a painter (and dishwasher to make ends meet) in 1916. In 1915 he landed his first major poster design commission with London Underground Electric Railways. By 1921 he was so successful in his design business that he gave up easel painting for commercial art. The catalogue attempts to locate Modernism in an historical context, "We live in an era that still identifies itself in terms of Modernism, as post-Modernism or even post-post-Modernism".

ICA "Beck's Futures" chosen by Jake and Dinos Chapman, Martin Creed, Cornelia Parker, Yinka Shonibare and Gillian Wearing. "The Internet is a huge and tangible cultural presence" (Waldemar Januszczak, "Sunday Times", 02.04.06).

John Moores Exhibition 2006 it would appear that painting is not dead as the John Moores submission received 2,300 entries this year, the largest since 1963 (2,403). Martin Greenland was the Winner with "Before Vermeer's Clouds". Other prize-winners were Matthew Burrows, Graham Crowley, Vincent Hawkins and James White. Only one London Group member, Alex Ramsay, was accepted by the selection committee of Sir Peter Blake, Tracey Emin, Jason Brooks, Andrea Rose and Ann Bukantas.

Celeste Painting Prize one thousand, one hundred and twenty artists submitted their paintings in this first year of the new prize. The submission was in two sections, Professional Artists with a prize of £10,000 and Student Section with a prize of £5,000. One hundred and seventy Professionals were short-listed and seventy Students. From the shortlist thirty finalists from each section were chosen. These thirty finalists were then asked to vote for who they thought should receive the prize in each section. The Celeste Painting Prize described its function as, "an examination of painting practise in the UK". It further stated that "the term painting can also be interpreted in the widest possible sense". The phrase "widest possible sense" stretched the definition to its limit as the professional winner, Natasha Kidd, exhibited an installation made from central heating equipment (copper pipes, radiators, etc.) and emulsion paint. Oona Grimes was the only successful London Group member in the Professional Artist category.

British Art Show 6 an Arts Council touring exhibition starting in venues across Nottingham. The British Art Show occurs every five years and is selected by a group of worthies from the best of young artists to emerge in the last five years. Artists included Phil Collins, Siobahn Hapaska, Hew Locke, Goshka Macuga, Heather and Ivan Morison, Nils Norman, Zineb Sedira and Mark Titchner.

Turner Prize 2006 those nominated this year were Tomma Abts (painter and winner of the 2006 Turner Prize), Phil Collins (film-maker), Mark Tichner (urban sign-maker) and Rebecca Warren (plaster figurettes of women).

Pallant House Gallery, Chichester the gallery reopened with a new wing and an exhibition entitled, "Modern British Art: The First 100 Years". Of fifty-eight artists represented in the collection, thirty (52%) had been elected members of The London Group.

Mall Galleries London Group member David Gluck (1978) wins the Singer & Friedlander/Sunday Times Watercolour Exhibition 2006 first prize. James Faure Walker (2000) and David Redfern (2000) were also selected.

London Group President: Philip Crozier (2001)

At the beginning of January, the President contacted each member expressing best wishes for the New Year ahead and reminding them that the annual subscription, as voted at the last AGM, had been raised from £50 to £80, largely to cover the cost of the Group's part time administrative assistant. He also gave further details of the Annual Exhibition to be held at the Bankside Gallery, the same venue as 2005. Members liked the location of the Bankside Gallery, it being close to Tate Modern and its rich shoals of art lovers walking beside the river. More importantly, there was to be an Extraordinary General Meeting following a normal Working Committee Meeting, to discuss policy on small shows (as opposed to Annual Exhibitions were all the membership were invited to exhibit work). The EGM was held on Wednesday, 8th March at the City Pride pub but it was not quorate.

The AGM was held in the Conway Hall on Monday, 20th March. Twenty-eight members attended with apologies from a similar number. Robert Coward as Treasurer reported that the Group was in sound financial health despite running up an £8,333 deficit for the year (2005 a £2,743 deficit). The largest sum was the Bankside Gallery exhibition expenses coming in at £7,533. Current assets were £70,930.16. The Treasurer reminded the Group to change their annual subscriptions to £80 and related an amusing story about John Piper who unknowingly, having left The London Group, failed to have his annual subscription cancelled. The President's report began with an historical analogy to the present day London Group, in particular, "the story of Roger Fry priggishly objecting to the fact that Christopher Nevinson had invited the 'wrong sort of people' to a London Group exhibition. Nevinson had hoped to make some sales and rounded on Fry for being financially cushioned by 'chocolate' money (he was an heir to the Fry's chocolate fortune) and cut off from the reality of life for other artists. A classic London Group cavaliers versus roundheads dispute, except today the cushion would be an academic stipend." He continued by reanalysing the contemporary position of the Group, especially when, "exhibitions are overwhelmingly market led, most obviously among dealers and art fairs, but this extends as well into the state funded sector which reflects market-formed reputations." The good news was that there had been positive exploratory talks with the new management of the Menier Gallery (which was good value and large) and a two part Open Exhibition was planned for the autumn of 2007. The last open submission exhibition had been the "Biennale 1995 Open Exhibition" organised at the Concourse Gallery in the Barbican Centre and the Group was anxious to revive open submission for non-member artists. Crozier ends his report with what could be seen as his re-election manifesto endorsed by discussion in the Working Committee. "If I continue as President I intend to again seek devolution in the belief that anyone's initiative, once duly sanctioned by the Working Committee, which is in turn mandated by the Group as a whole, is OK." The mandatory annual elections were then facilitated by Jane Humphrey and Tony Collinge as Returning Officers. Philip Crozier was returned as President, Clive Burton stepped down as Vice President to be replaced by John Crossley, Wendy Smith continued as Deputy Vice President, Robert Coward as Honorary Treasurer and Susan Haire as Honorary Secretary. Elected to the Working Committee were Clive Burton, Tony Carter, Mark Dickens and Suzan Swale whilst Wendy Anderson, David Redfern and Tom Scase were elected to the Membership Committee. Tamara Thomas continued as the invaluable paid administrative assistant. There then followed a vigorous and robust discussion on small group exhibitions doggedly pursued by Alfred Harris and Jane Humphrey following discussion in a recent City Pride adhoc meeting chaired by Mike Philipson. The AGM decided that selection criteria for members invited to participate in these shows should be clear, fair and transparent. The President and meeting felt quite happy with this small group devolution first floated in Tony Carter's 2004 paper. The meeting closed with the President's memorable phrase echoing in members' ears, "Unfortunately you have elected an Anarchist who likes to do things correctly!"

The Sassoon Gallery, 213 Blenheim Grove, London SE15. "The Sassoon Gallery is a contemporary arts space in Peckham, South London, which emerged from Ben Sassoon's desire to create a cultural centre for film, music, poetry and the visual arts and offer its contributors the opportunity to disseminate their critical insights and creative practices to a particular inner London community. The themes of the events and exhibitions are selected by a group of artists, journalists and curators led by the artist Philippa Beale". (From a Private View information card). "To The London Group Artists from Philippa Beale, Curator at the Sassoon Gallery. As you will have already heard from the Working Party, there is to be a London Group Annual at the Bankside Gallery in April 2006. Also at this time Jane Humphrey and Clive Burton have selected two London Group shows of ten artists per show to exhibit at the new Sassoon Gallery in Peckham. The Committee of the Sassoon is now calling this 'The London Group Festival', and through one of its members, Lorna Collins, have obtained two review slots in the Southwark News and have also placed two adverts for these shows in Living South Magazine."

"Part 1" showed from 10th to 22nd April with Wendy Anderson, Oona Grimes, Susan Haire, Richard Kemp, Matthew Kolakowski, Prudence Kurrle, Ken Oliver, Eugene Palmer, Philippa Tunstill and Bill Watson.

"Part 2" showed from 25th April to 6th May with Mark Ainsworth, Slawomir Blatton, Tony Carter, John Crossley, James Faure Walker, William Henderson, Ian Parker, Michael Phillipson, Wendy Smith and Neil Weerdmeester.

"The 93rd Annual Exhibition" at the Bankside Gallery, 48 Hopton Street, London SE1, showed from 13th April to 1st May 2006. Sixty-three members exhibited one work each with a size restriction of 1 metre due to the limited space in the Bankside Gallery. The Private View on Wednesday 12th April was very well supported and the weather remained dry, the previous two openings had been virtually washed out! The great majority of exhibited works, thirty-eight out of sixty-three, were paintings. The remainder were drawings, prints, mixed media but only one plinth mounted sculpture from Clive Burton. Annie Johns' wall mounted diptych was made from walnut, spruce, aluminium, brass kapok and pencil. Prices were varied, ranging from £18,000 for Slavomir Blatton's, "Four studies for Crucifiction" (sic) to £250 for an etching by David Carr, but mainly in the £1,000 to £3,000 bracket with the gallery taking 10% commission. Four works were eventually sold from this exhibition.

The Selection Committee felt at home in the paint and plaster spattered studio environment of the City & Guilds Art School. A full committee of seventeen as well as some spares turned out to review the work of fifteen candidates for election, eight women and seven men. All four of the successful candidates gaining the magic number of nine votes or more were men, with an average age of 48. They were Clyde Hopkins (painter, who later, regretfully, declined membership), Daniel Preece (painter), Simon Read (examining the interface between culture and nature) and Tommy Seaward (three-dimensional and wall mounted). This brought total membership for 2006 to ninety-seven. The meeting was chaired by President Philip Crozier and was extremely well organised by the Honorary Secretary, Susan Haire. Images were presented to the selection committee by 35mm slides, digital files and actual work supported by written statements from each candidate. All fifteen bodies of work were run through twice with open discussion and comment, followed by a secret ballot. Following the meeting, it was the duty of the nominating member to acquaint their nominee with the Committee's decision.

In November eight London Group members were exhibited in an exhibition entitled "Arti de Salon" at Rokin 112, Amsterdam, The Netherlands, from 16th November to 10th December. This was the first time in sixty years that the Group had extended beyond UK shores, the last being an exhibition just after the war at the David Jones Art Gallery in Sydney, Australia in 1946. "Arti de Salon" was an Amsterdam equivalent of The London Group Annual Exhibition. The Salon was organised by a group called Arti et Amicitiae who had a similar function to The London Group. Arti had been formed in

1839 and had three hundred and fifty artists and five hundred 'friends' in 2006. Unlike their London counterpart, Arti had invested early in its life in a beautiful property built in 1859 along the Rokin, a major artery in Amsterdam close to Dam square. They were able to organise a programme of contemporary exhibitions in large galleries on the first floor of the building, the ground floor being occupied by an impressive bar and restaurant from which Arti gained income. London Group member Marcelle Hanselaar was also a member of Arti and she originally floated the idea of co-operation. Ex-President Peter Clossick travelled to Amsterdam to meet with Dirk Jan Jager and a reciprocal agreement was negotiated to exchange artists' works. Following the eight London Group members showing in Amsterdam, The London Group Annual Exhibition at the Menier Gallery in 2007 was to find space for Arti artists from Amsterdam. The long-term aim was for every London Group member to be given the opportunity to exhibit with Arti in Amsterdam that would incur individual shipping expenses and travel arrangements. This first European exhibition fulfilled one of the aims of Tony Carter's vision of The London Group future, "If we look into what a more directed PR effort might target, and if one of these targets was - for example - a venue, or venues outside the UK, it would, I think, be necessary to identify the existence, or not, of organisations like our own in other European cities. If they do exist, then some sort of collaboration ought to be possible which could justify British Council support (without which, all such schemes would probably be financially impossible)." Peter Clossick had tried to gain funding from the British Council, but they rejected the application. The eight London Group exhibitors were Peter Clossick, Mark Dickens, Julie Held, Ken Oliver, Ian Parker, David Redfern, James Faure Walker and Neil Weerdmeester. They represented as near as possible a cross section of the variety of work currently being produced by individuals within The London Group. They were allocated 2 square metres each and hung in a smaller gallery alongside their Dutch colleagues. "De Salon 2006" was Arti's annual member exhibition which showed sculpture, prints, drawings, photographs, paintings and other media, one hundred and eighty-two members showing one work each.

Rokin 112
Amsterdam, The Netherlands

In 2006, eight London Group members were shown at the Arti de Salon Exhibition from the 16th November to the 10th December. This was the first overseas showing since 1946 and was seen as a 'dry run' with a view to offering this opportunity to all group members in the future. Arti et Amicitiae were a similar artists' association to The London Group but based in Amsterdam. A number of their members showed in the annual exhibition at the Menier Gallery, 2007, in return.

The final Working Party of the year was held on the 5th December in Susan Haire's beautifully converted studio, an old 'cello factory close by the South Bank complex. Items on the agenda for discussion were, the Deutsche Bank exhibition which had elicited twenty-eight responses from members wishing to exhibit (a second was planned for 2007), the dates for the Menier Gallery Open 2007 booked for November at a cost of £6,700, (Vic Kuell reminded the meeting of the fact that open submission exhibitions always ran at a loss and that sponsorship was required to support both submission fees and members' subscriptions), an exhibition of London Group sculpture which Officers felt had been neglected in recent years and a report back from Peter Clossick on the Arti de Salon exhibition in Amsterdam. Clossick invited the Group to consider hiring Arti's galleries in Amsterdam for the 2008 Annual Exhibition and for The London Group to see itself as a lynchpin for international artists' groups in the future. Curiously enough, a group called "artistes4paris" had recently made contact with The London Group putting forward the prospect of exhibition collaboration. They were a small, recently formed group of mainly painters who lived or worked in Paris's 4th Arrondisement. The meeting ended with a Christmas party with nearly half the membership and partners attending.

Income from members' subscriptions increased dramatically this year. In 2005 £3,655 had been raised from subscriptions, but this year the Group benefited from £6,795.25 membership fees. Similarly the Bankside exhibition expenses had been reduced to £5,673.96, a figure comfortably within the fees total. However, £2,400 spent on secretarial and administrative assistance plus other expenditures resulted in a deficit for the year of £2,651.56. The drain on the General Fund, standing this year at £68,278.60, had also been halted. The value of the General Fund in the previous financial year had been £70,930. Interestingly other income from that same year came from the sale of the 2003 Anniversary Yearbook at £1,440 and from commission on exhibition sales at £215.

2007

President Bush introduces a "New Strategy" for dealing with the escalating civil war in Iraq, he sends in more troops. Diplomatic incident when Iran arrests 15 British service personnel in the Gulf and accuses them of violating Iranian waters. The US is overtaken by China as the biggest carbon emitter. BBC reporter Alan Johnston taken hostage in Gaza, released after 114 days. Three-year-old Madeleine McCann is taken from a hotel room in Portugal. Al Gore wins the Nobel Peace Prize fighting global warming. Middle East Peace Talks begin in Annapolis, USA after a seven year break. Benazir Bhutto assassinated whilst campaigning in Pakistani elections. The iPhone is introduced by Apple. Projected cost of the 2012 Olympics in London reaches nearly £10 billion. Power sharing established at Stormont in Northern Ireland. Tony Blair steps down as Prime Minister after ten years in office; Gordon Brown succeeds him unopposed and experiences a series of embarrassing administrative blunders. Serious floods hit large parts of England. Terrorist attacks in London - the bombs fail to explode but in Glasgow the airport is ram-raided by a blazing Jeep. Smoking ban introduced in the UK.

National Gallery Leon Kossof (1963) exhibition in the Sunley Gallery.
Tate Modern (second) Gilbert and George retrospective.
Tate Britain Hogarth, Millais.
Tate Liverpool The 2007 **Turner Prize** was held in Liverpool this year, as part of Liverpool becoming European Capital of Culture in 2008. This was the first time that the Turner Prize was held outside of London. Mark Wallinger was the winner with Zarina Bhinji, Nathan Coley and Mike Nelson short-listed.
Hayward Gallery Antony Gormley.
Royal Academy a George Baselitz major exhibition.
White Cube Gallery Damien Hirst at Masons Yard and Hoxton Square "For the Love of God" including the diamond encrusted platinum skull.
Frieze Art Fair made a big splash. (As did Zoo and Bridge).
Venice Biennale Great Britain was represented by Tracey Emin who was also elected as a Royal Academician in the same year.

London Group President: Philip Crozier (2001) followed by Susan Haire (2004)

"The London Group at Deutsche Bank", Part 1 was held at the Deutsche Bank staff restaurant exhibition space, Deutsche Bank, 24 Great Winchester Street, London EC2 between 18th January and 18th April 2007.

Deutsche Bank
24 Great Winchester Street
London EC2

Twenty-six members showed work in this exhibition, Martin Abrahams, Wendy Anderson, Victoria Bartlett, Slavomir Blatton, Bryan Benge, Robert Clark, Philip Crozier, John Crossley, Gus Cummins, Jeffery Dellow, Mark Dickens, Susan Haire, Marcelle Hanselaar, Alfred Harris, Prue Kurrle, Graham Mileson, Eric Moody, Janet Nathan, Ken Oliver, Daniel Preece, Tom Scase, Tommy Seaward, Suzan Swale, Neil Weerdmeester, Arthur Wilson and Susan Wilson.

This year's AGM was held on April 17th in The Cello Factory, Cornwall Road, Waterloo at the end of an unseasonably warm period in London where temperatures hit 26°C. The AGM quickly heated up too as the well attended meeting began to discuss issues under matters arising from last year's AGM, particularly around issues relating to selection for London Group small exhibitions, doggedly pursued by Alfred Harris, and for the appropriate nomenclature for Honorary Members and their status. Robert Coward then delivered his financial report that basically indicated that the Group was in sound financial shape and that, despite the fact that the subscription increase to £80 had caused some administrative problems; the increase had ensured a secure financial footing. However, almost thirty members still had sums outstanding and Coward appealed to these members to pay up. There were ninety-seven members in The London Group this year, ninety-three ordinary and four Honorary. Michelle Avison, Bert Irvin and Laetitia Yhap had resigned for various reasons, but all indicated a desire to step down to give younger artists an opportunity for membership. Irvin had declared, "The London Group is a difficult group to leave". Outgoing President Phil Crozier also proposed a toast to absent friends, David Gluck and David Whitaker who had died this year. The President's Report was short in that the year had been reported in the April 2007 Newsletter available at the AGM. Crozier wrote, "What have I learned as President? One thing is that Members assume one has total control of policy, whereas in reality one sometimes has to allow others to do what they want despite one's own misgivings". The meeting then moved on to elect new officers. Susan Haire was elected unopposed as the third female President of The London Group, the two previous being Dorothy Mead and Philippa Beale. John Crossley continued as Vice President for another year and Mark Dickens was elected unopposed as Deputy Vice President. Jane Humphrey stood for Honorary Secretary and was elected unopposed whilst Robert Coward continued as Honorary Treasurer. The eight elected members of the Working Committee for 2007-2008 were Tony Carter and Suzan Swale (completing their second year), Philip Crozier, Marcelle Hanselaar, Annie Johns, Ian Parker, David Redfern and Wendy Smith. Elected to the Selection Committee were Tony Collinge, Tom Scase and Neil Weerdmeester. Susan Haire then addressed the meeting laying out her vision for the Group's future and her part in it. Her first priority was reinstating open submission annual exhibitions. This initiative was already in place for the 2007 annual at the Menier Gallery but needed to be followed through and to become an annual event as enshrined in The London Group Constitution. It was absolutely vital to look for commercial sponsorship in order to cover the costs of an open exhibition. With that goal in mind the Working Committee were to meet with two people who might find sponsorship for the Group. Recent papers by Tony Carter and Mike Phillipson had given voice to new aspirations and possible directions for the future of The London Group and Haire wished to maintain this critical momentum. The London Group website was to be updated and also used as the submission portal for the 2007 open submission exhibition. Individual members were encouraged to refresh their personal pages and to send in images to form part of a new opening page showing, as a slide show, one work from each member. Mention was made of proposed future exhibitions, The London Group at Deutsche Bank Part 2 in Spring 2008, The Highgate Gallery in May 2008, BayArt Gallery in Cardiff in 2008 and London Group Sculptors at The Cello Factory, London to be curated by members Bill Watson and Clive Burton.

The Selection Committee Meeting was held on Thursday, May 24th at Chelsea School of Art and Design courtesy of the Vice President John Crossley who taught at Chelsea. The committee met in a large panelled room overlooking the river Thames, an evocative setting for a group centred on London. Nine artists had been proposed for membership this year, whilst three members had died and four had withdrawn during the past year. Each nominee had six images viewed by the committee as Robert Coward read out information and statements by the artists. Following a short discussion on the work the members of the committee then filled in secret ballot forms and the vote produced three new members for the Group, David Chalkley (three-dimensional work), Angela Eames (painter) and the re-election of Philippa Beale who had withdrawn from the Group eighteen months previously. This brought total membership to ninety-one (eighty-eight members and three Honorary). A discussion then followed on the definition of 'Honorary Member', and a unanimous vote was then taken adopting a short paper by Wendy Smith which stated: "The term 'honorary' means 'held or given only as an honour', i.e., without the normal privileges or duties of 'full membership', as in 'an honorary degree'; or (of a secretary, treasurer etc.), unpaid. Thus an Honorary Member of The London Group would, normally speaking, be a non-exhibiting member, for example, and in all probability not an artist. Or, in so far as a Member serves as secretary or treasurer unpaid, (s)he is, technically, Honorary Secretary or Honorary Treasurer."

On the 6th July Tamara Thomas stepped down as Secretary to seek full time employment after serving the group for three years. She was replaced by Mike Liggins, put forward by Suzan Swale and Robert Coward, who had retired as General Manager of Covent Garden Market Authority in 2005. If Mike's idea was to relax after his time at Covent Garden and to concentrate on his own drawing and painting, then this notion was to be sorely tested over the coming years. Mike Liggins proved to be totally invaluable to The London Group, a real administrative powerhouse supporting the officers and cheerfully working way beyond the part-time hours he was paid by the Group.

The selection from the open submission took place on Wednesday, September 12th. Four hundred and eighty-eight artists had sent in images stored on CDs for consideration by the Selection Committee who chose sixty works in total, forty-two wall hung pieces, nine floor/plinth, six video and three other. The average age of non-members selected was 40 and 45% of them were under 35. No one over the age of 65 was selected.

"Collective Response" was shown at the Guildhall Art Gallery from 8th October to 11th November 2007 and was curated by Wendy Anderson and Annie Johns. Artists taking part in this exhibition were Wendy Anderson, Bryan Benge, Clive Burton, Tony Carter, Tony Collinge, Mark Dickens, Annie Johns, Eugene Palmer, Ian Parker, David Redfern, Susan Skingle, Wendy Smith, Bill Watson and Arthur Wilson. Artists were asked to make work in response to objects, paintings or themes associated with the Guildhall Art Gallery.

Trafalgar Hotel
Trafalgar Square, London WC2

"Bridge Art Fair, London 07", in the Trafalgar Hotel, Trafalgar Square, London from 11th October to 14th October 2007. Laurie McDonald, who had taken on the job of raising sponsorship for The London Group, had secured a free room for all the members to contribute work to the Fair. Room 305 was used to rotate the work of London Group members, there being so many wanting to take part (forty-seven in total). The windows overlooking Trafalgar Square were filled with London Group members' large paintings.

"The London Group Open Exhibition 2007" at the Menier Gallery, The Menier Chocolate Factory, 51 Southwark Street, SE1 1RU. Part 1 from 7th to 16th November 2007 and Part 2 from 21st to 30th November 2007. A two-part exhibition of contemporary artists working in a range of media selected from open submission, invited artists and London Group members. This exhibition marked a landmark resumption of the open submission for non-members to exhibit with The London Group after a break of fifteen years. A total of four hundred and eighty-eight images were submitted for The London Group Selection Committee to choose from. The invited artists were members of "Arti et Amicitiae" from Amsterdam, a reciprocal invitation from The London Group's 2006 showing in Amsterdam. A number of prizes were awarded, The Chelsea Arts Club Trust (Stan Smith Travel Award) for an artist under 35 was won by Rose O'Gallivan, the David Gluck Memorial Student Prize by Julie Masterton and the Mel Gordon Memorial Prize by Yoshimi Kihara. Both exhibitions were sponsored by Bridge Art Fair. Sixty-nine out of eighty-five members exhibited work, with sixty non-members selected from the open submission, nine Arti artists from Amsterdam and five members who had unfortunately died during the year. One hundred and eighteen pieces were wall mounted, fifteen on the floor, five video/digital and five 'other'. The two Private Views were overflowing, especially the second where the prizes were awarded by the President, Susan Haire.

It is also interesting to note that either side of The London Group Open, many other artists' societies were using the Menier Gallery to mount exhibitions. In August, "Paintings in Hospitals" held a Summer Show, in September, "The Society of Graphic Fine Art" held their 86th Annual Open Exhibition and in December, the "National Society of Painters, Sculptors & Printmakers" were to show. The Menier exhibition facility at the Chocolate Factory was obviously much in demand at this time.

2008

There is a global financial crisis thought to be the worst crash since the 1920s in which Lehman Brothers goes bankrupt. Rioting in Kenya kills hundreds following a disputed election. Unrest in Pakistan following Bhutto's assassination also disrupts elections. Robert Mugabe manipulates elections in crisis-torn Zimbabwe. War between Georgia and Russia. Cyclone disaster kills 146,000 in Burma. Major earthquake in Sichuan Province, China. The Olympic Games are held in Beijing, China. Casualties continue to mount in the Afghanistan conflict. Obama wins the US Presidency over McCain. Terrorists murder hundreds of innocent victims in Mumbai shootings, India. Israel bombs the Gaza Strip. The Large Hadron Collider is switched on at CERN in an attempt to find "the god particle". In the London Mayoral elections Boris Johnson (Conservative) beats Ken Livingstone (Labour), Brian Paddick (Liberal Democrat) and others. The Olympic Torch procession through London is severely disrupted by protesters highlighting China's continuing 'occupation' of Tibet. Knife crime, especially in the younger age group, gives rise for serious concern. £400 billion is pumped into the banking system and some banks are partly nationalised.

Courtauld Institute Sickert's Camden Town nudes brought together as a group for the first time.
Royal Academy a huge exhibition "From Russia", followed by "Byzantium 330–1453".
Hayward Gallery Rodchenko photographs. Fortieth birthday celebrations.
Tate Britain "The Camden Town Group" focussing on Sickert, Gilman, Gore and Ginner.
Tate Modern Duchamp, Picabia and Man Ray. Cy Twombly.
Turner Prize 2008 nominated this year were Mark Leckey, Runa Islam, Goshka Macuga and Cathy Wilkes. The London free paper Metro headlines, "Artist whose work includes a model on a loo is nominated for prize" (Cathy Wilkes). Mark Leckey was the eventual winner.
National Portrait Gallery an exhibition of Wyndham Lewis (1913) portraits.
Notable new galleries opening this year were the **Saatchi Gallery** in the old Duke of York's in Chelsea and the **Kings Place** complex in Kings Cross (which opened with an exhibition of paintings by Bert Irvin).
"Terracotta Warriors", "Hadrian" and "Babylon" continued at the British Museum and "Tutankhamun" was installed at the 02 (The Dome).

London Group President: Susan Haire (2004)

February brought "The London Group at Deutsche Bank", Part 2, from 6th February to 15th April 2008, which opened in the bank's staff restaurant. Twenty-four members submitted work in a large variety of media with prices ranging from £160 for David Chalkley's digital photograph, "Wine Glass 2 (Full)" to £5,090 for Angela Eames' ink on canvas, "Clearing". There was a size limitation of one metre and the exhibition was beautifully presented with each work enjoying individual space on the walls of the labyrinthine but spatially coherent staff amenity area. This was a typical London Group sortie that came about by one member (Mark Dickens) cultivating a personal contact to the benefit of all Group members.

The 2008 AGM was held on Tuesday, 29th April at The Cello Factory in Cornwall Road. It was a swift and efficient AGM with uncontested elections and pretty much "steady-as-you-go". The Treasurer's Report was not received due to Robert Coward's illness and the Presidents Report was printed in the April 2008 Newsletter, beautifully produced by Jane Humphrey. The Small Group Exhibitions proposal from the Working Party was adopted unanimously by the meeting. The policy had been formulated to help allay concerns from some members, notably Alfred Harris, that clear and fair criteria were applied to all small exhibitions receiving funding from The London Group or using the name. Susan Haire was re-elected as President, Peter Clossick was elected as Vice President, Jane Humphrey as Deputy Vice President, Robert Coward as Honorary Treasurer and Tommy Seaward as Honorary Secretary. Following their two-year membership of the Working Committee, Suzan Swale and Tony Carter were re-elected. David Chalkley, Richard Kemp and Slawomir Blatton also put their names forward for election. The four seats on the Membership Committee went to Wendy Anderson, Tony Collinge, John Crossley and David Chalkley. Membership at this point in the year stood at eighty-six.

The Membership Committee Meeting was held on Tuesday, 20th May at The Cello Factory. Members had submitted twenty-two nominees (thirteen women, nine men) for the committee to consider. From the initial twenty-two, four nominees received the minimum nine votes required for membership. They were Amanda Loomes (video and digital prints), Chris Poulton (3D), Victoria Rance (3D) and Paul Tecklenberg (photographic processes). This brought the total membership for 2008 to ninety.

Mark Dickens was also involved in setting up an all members' show at Mauger Modern Art, 6 Bartlett Street, Bath from April 21st to May 24th. Thirty-nine members sent in a range of small works which were beautifully shown in this newly refurbished gallery well situated just to the north of Bath centre. The Private View on Saturday 19th April was well attended despite unseasonably cold temperatures and rain. Mauger made a big effort to market The London Group coming down to Bath, linking it to the recently opened Camden Town Group exhibition at Tate Britain. "Mauger Modern Art is very pleased to present an exciting exhibition of 40 paintings and sculptures from the members of this famous artist collective which is one of the most highly esteemed and distinguished art collectives in the UK". Prices ranged from £200 to £5,000.

Mauger Modern Art
Bartlett Street, Bath

London Group member Tom Scase, assisted by fellow member Richard Kemp, curated an exhibition of small works at the Highgate Gallery, 11 South Grove, London N6 from the 9th to the 22nd May. A sixty centimetre size limit was in operation to ensure that all members could exhibit in this small but accessible gallery. Thirty-seven members responded with works for exhibition with an incredibly diverse approach. Exhibits ranged from David Shutt's oil on canvas, "Pigsty at sunset" to Tommy Seaward's "Conspectus" fabricated from wood, polyamide, acrylic paint, acrylic gel, oil paint and polyethylene. Prices were very reasonable, the most expensive being David Tebbs' "The Cleansed", oil on canvas, at £2,000 and C. Morey de Morand's "Capturing Time", pigments and acrylic mediums on linen, at £1,950. The average price was between £500 and £750. Due to the nature of this small group exhibition no catalogue was produced but a Price List was printed and available in the gallery. On Wednesday, 14th May Peter Clossick delivered a talk entitled, "Why The London Group" as part of the Group's aim to reach out to local communities.

The Highgate Gallery
11 South Grove, London N6

The hall in which the Highgate Gallery is situated was opened by Angela Burdett-Coutts "philanthropist and benefactor" in March 1880 as a resident of Highgate and a member of the Institution. She was the first woman to receive the Freedom of the City of London. Further to the north is The Grove where Roger Fry, influential art critic and writer and member of The London Group, was born at number 6 in 1866. Could the 14 year old Fry have been at the opening?

At a Working Committee Meeting on the 16th June there was a packed agenda. The Committee met with Denise Shenton to discuss raising sponsorship for forthcoming shows including the 2008 95th Anniversary Member's Show at the Menier Gallery and an open submission annual in 2009. Also planned were a small group sculpture show at The Cello Factory, a whole group drawing exhibition at the Morley Gallery, opportunities with Arti in Amsterdam and a tour to Southampton Art Gallery. The Group was strong, enthusiastic, upbeat and very much looking forward to its centenary in 2013.

The "95th Anniversary Exhibition 2008" was held at the Menier Gallery, 51 Southwark Street, SE1, from 29th October to 7th November 2008. Sixty-two members submitted work which was hung on ground and basement floors and was curated by Tony Collinge. There was a 1.5 metre size limitation for this members only exhibition. Visitors commented on the huge variety of media and approaches used this year. Floor space was comfortably filled with three-dimensional works and the wall mounted work had ample space to 'breathe'. New members work brought a refreshing bite to the whole exhibition. Frank Bowling RA was asking top price for "Knightryder", an acrylic painting priced at £9,000, followed by Graham Mileson's acrylic "Without a Shadow of Doubt" at £8,000 and Kathleen Mullaniff's "A Pocket Full of Posies" at the same price. Jane Humphrey designed the A4, 24 page catalogue in which every exhibitor was represented with a colour image. A small amount of sponsorship enabled the Working Committee to take the decision to give away the catalogue to visitors this year instead of selling it in the belief that the catalogue 'sold' The London Group and spread the word. For critics and more professional visitors David Redfern's post war history of the Group was also given free. Croydon College (where Redfern taught) had sponsored the printing of this publication and as well as every member receiving a free copy, the history was to be used to publicise The London Group in its ninety-fifth year. The Private View on Tuesday 28th October was, not for the first time, opened by a clap of thunder and a torrential downpour! Even though global warming (and the meltdown of the global banking system) was on everyone's mind, snow had briefly settled in England for the first time since 1934.

The year ended with a Christmas Party following the last Working Committee Meeting of the year on Tuesday, 2nd December at The Cello Factory where publicity and sponsorship, future exhibitions and the 2013 Centenary arrangements were discussed. Trevor Frankland spoke to his paper on the future funding of the Group. This was followed by an introduction to Gill Cutbill who had expressed an interest in working with the Group and to look for sponsorship once financial conditions had improved. Cutbill's remark, "You haven't got a long life unless you get some money coming in", struck a cold note for the New Year. Unfortunately, the next few months were to bring an economic crisis of historic proportions where business and commerce were to plummet into a huge global recession.

2009

The global financial crisis continues as Britain enters recession and unemployment rises. Israel sends armed forces into the Gaza Strip, over 1,000 killed. Barak Obama is inaugurated as 44th President of the United States of America as America's first black president. He closes down Guantánamo Bay and introduces a billion dollar health scheme. Michael Jackson dies. In the UK some banks are nationalised and the whole banking system is bailed out to the tune of billions of pounds. The G20 Summit 2009 takes place in London to discuss the global financial crisis. There is increasing disillusionment in the UK's role in Afghanistan following heavy troop casualties. The follow-up to the Kyoto Climate Change Conference takes place in Copenhagen. The wettest day ever recorded results in catastrophic floods in Cumbria. Swine 'Flu outbreak. Carol Anne Duffy becomes the first female poet laureate.

Tate Modern "Futurism" charting the many faces of this movement in Italy, France and Russia. In the British section, virtually all the paintings and sculptures had first public exposure in London Group exhibitions. Gaudier-Brzeska's "Red Stone Dancer", Bomberg's "In the Hold" and Nevinson's "The Arrival" were all shown in the First London Group exhibition in March 1914, Wyndham Lewis' "The Crowd" and "Workshop", Nevinson's "Bursting Shell" in the Second (March 1915) and Epstein's "Torso in Metal from The Rock Drill" in the fourth (June 1916).

Tate Britain "Altermodern: Tate Triennial 2009", altermodernism was defined as "an attempt at branding art made in today's global context" (as part of a commercial backlash). Curated by Nicholas Bourriaud and exhibiting Marcus Coates, Shezad Dawood, Subodh Gupta, Nathaniel Meadows and Bob and Roberta Smith amongst others.

The **2009 Turner Prize** was won by Richard Wright. Lucy Skaer, Roger Hiorns and Enrico David were also nominated.

Royal Academy "Byzantium". "Wild Thing", Gaudier-Brzeska, Epstein and Gill. A reconstruction of Epstein's "Rock Drill" was shown as a whole for only the second time since its first showing in the Second London Group Exhibition in March 1915.

The Whitechapel Gallery (re)opens with 78% more space following a £13.5 million refit. The gallery was now able to be open all year round and launched with a number of exhibitions including Isa Genzken, Goshka Macuga, "British Council Collection: Great Early Buys" and "The Whitechapel Boys". The Whitechapel Boys were descendants of Jewish immigrants who lived in London's East End and included David Bomberg, Jacob Epstein, Mark Gertler, Jacob Kramer and Bernard Meninsky, all of whom were members of The London Group at some time.

London Group President: Susan Haire (2004)

The year began with a sculpture exhibition, "Stand Alone" at The Cello Factory, 33-34 Cornwall Road, SE1 8TJ from the 19th to the 24th January. This exhibition was one of the new style small group exhibitions that the Group had voted in at the last AGM. The show was curated by Clive Burton and Bill Watson who also showed Bryan Benge, Tony Carter, David Chalkley, Janet Patterson, Chris Poulton, Victoria Rance and Tommy Seaward. Encouragingly nearly half of these exhibitors were newly elected. Nicholas Usherwood wrote in the January issue of "Galleries" magazine, "Though its reputation over the last 90 years or so has always been as a home – a refuge – for independently minded painters, The London Group has always contained a small contingent of equally free-thinking sculptors. Currently there are nine of them and this show, appropriately entitled 'Stand Alone', gives them a chance to show for once as a group by themselves, the handsome setting in a converted piano (sic) factory doing full justice to their nicely diverse range of style and subject matter."

The Cello Factory
Cornwall Road, London SE1

The Cello Factory on the corner of Theed Street and Cornwall Road close to the National Theatre. This was President Susan Haire's studio and was also used for London Group committee meetings and AGMs. "Stand Alone" was the first London Group small exhibition to be held here.

A Working Committee Meeting was held at The Cello Factory on Tuesday, 27th January. This purposeful meeting had a full and vibrant agenda with many options for small and full group exhibitions in the future. The discussion about The London Group's identity, tirelessly championed by Tony Carter, was rekindled with a commitment to hold a special meeting this year focusing on this one issue.

On March 10th the Group held its AGM at The Cello Factory with a third of the membership in attendance (33). Robert Coward delivered the Treasurer's report in a cautionary tone. Over the last two years the Group had spent £9,000 more than its income each year, leaving only £47,225.49 in the bank. Biggest expenditure was on secretarial and administrative assistance (the irreplaceable Mike Liggins), postage, stationary & printing and website maintenance. The Menier Open Exhibition in 2007 had cost £17,385.93 recouping only £9,041 with fees etc.. The Menier Members Exhibition in 2008 had cost £8,989.06 recouping only £1,300 mainly in members' hanging fees. If expenditure continued without change at this rate the Group would run out of money at its centenary! The President's Report, delivered by Susan Haire, was much more upbeat, recalling the whole group and small group exhibitions and sketching out those planned for the future. Another important agenda item was proposals for future funding of the Group, hugely problematic bearing in mind the current global financial crisis. In the ensuing elections, Susan Haire as President, Peter Clossick as Vice President, Mark Dickens as Deputy Vice President, Robert Coward as Honorary Treasurer and Tommy Seaward as Honorary Secretary were returned unopposed. Those elected to the Working Committee for the next two years were Bryan Benge, Tony Collinge, Jane Humphrey, Annie Johns, David Redfern and Tom Scase. The four additional members elected to the Membership Committee were Wendy Anderson, Vic Kuell, Ian Parker and Neil Weerdmeester.

The London Group returned to the Morley Gallery in South London for the exhibition "Drawing: Act and Artefact". The Group had exhibited at Morley several times in the past, beginning in 1979. As the title indicates, this exhibition was based on the activity of drawing. It was curated by Wendy Smith and Suzan Swale and was open to the public from the 25th March to the 9th of April. In the catalogue introduction Wendy Smith wrote "The purpose of this exhibition was to initiate and present a serious consideration of drawing per se, rather than simply to show a miscellany of 'works on paper', for instance. Submissions were invited from all members of the Group who consider drawing to play an important part in his or her practice. Presumably, those who don't have declined the invitation. Others, who do actually draw but who would never dream of exhibiting drawings will see no reason to do so now. An important aspect of the ethos of The London Group is that it is the members themselves who determine whether and in what way(s) drawing is crucial to them and which drawings best exemplify their investment. The job of curators (themselves London Group artists) is to ensure a coherent and lively exchange of (visual) ideas, thoughts and feelings about drawing not merely to 'advance public awareness of contemporary art'. But in the interests of the artists' own creative development and, more to the point, the advancement of art." Feedback from those who attended the packed Private View and those who visited the exhibition was that the curators had done just that. Indeed sales of work were made, an encouraging sign during this time of financial turmoil. Fifty-one members had accepted the invitation to show drawings. In an attempt to inject a fresh approach to the activity (and exhibiting) of drawing, members could submit two pieces of work within a one metre width restriction firstly, under the heading 'main practice', and secondly, 'other'. Bryan Benge, in his catalogue notes, wrote, "Ever since I was a schoolboy bored beyond belief in my maths, chemistry and physics lessons (one could see where I would end up) I drew machine doodles.... I have never exhibited these drawings and I have never considered them a part of my main practice. I guess they are for me; they enable me the time and thought space to consider other works in the way that I work for exhibition."

The Morley College Gallery
showing a drawing by Matthew Kolakowski in the window

The Selection Committee met at The Cello Factory on April 21st to elect new members to the Group. Three members had resigned for various reasons during the last year and this year thirteen nominees had been proposed by existing members. The Committee felt that this year had been a particularly high quality submission of work in a wide variety of formats, especially new media. Three candidates received more than the required nine votes from the seventeen strong committee, Paul & Laura Carey (a joint grouping), Sam Jarman and Valerie Jolly. Membership then stood at eighty-four, fifty-four men, twenty-nine women and one couple.

The London Group's main activity was centred on the "Open Exhibition 2009" held in two parts at the Menier Gallery, Part 1 from the 21st to the 30th October curated by Tom Scase and Mark Dickens and Part 2 from 4th to the 13th November curated by Tony Collinge and Vic Kuell. Three hundred and ninety-nine images were submitted to the Selection Committee and after a day's deliberation seventy were finally chosen for exhibition. Of the eighty-four London Group members, sixty-six exhibited in this year's Open. A fully illustrated colour catalogue was designed by Jane Humphrey and was given away free to all exhibition visitors (The London Evening Standard newspaper was relaunched as a 'freebie' at this time). Work in both parts of the Open was as varied as it was possible to be from traditional painting on a two-dimensional surface to installation and DVD projection. Albert Irvin RA was the Guest Artist who chose the exhibition prize winners and presented them with their prizes. Paul Tecklenburg interviewed Irvin recording his thoughts and observations from his election to The London Group in 1965.

At the Part 2 Private View on November 3rd prizes were awarded. A £500 Bursary with John Jones was won by Richard Cresswell for "Sapling", London Group member Anne Cloudsley awarded £100 to Maya Ramsay for "Wailing Walls" and a London Group prize of £500 went to Philip Maltman for "Picturesque No. 9". Four £100 London Group prizes were won by Jenny Lewis for "'Tights' from 'Jenny's World'", Genetic Moo for "Mother", Colin Michael for "My Life" and Kevin Jackson for "Conditions".

Bert Irvin was also awarded a prize of 'Life Member', hastily voted in to replace the title 'Honorary Member' by the Working Committee. Encouragingly, a number of sales were made from Part 2 and visitor figures for both parts were up on previous years, possibly influenced by more active advertising.

Throughout 2009 a Small Group Exhibitions sub-committee met to discuss issues raised by Alfred Harris. Harris was concerned that an analysis of London Group small group exhibitions (SGE) in the last ten years had shown that some members were shown more than once and that other members had not been chosen at all. Harris pointed out that The London Group constitution enshrined the concepts of fairness, equality and transparency and his dogged defence of these ideals were at the centre of the SGE sub-committee meetings. The final position was that Harris maintained that no SGEs could be held until all members had at least one showing. The Working Committee felt that this was unworkable and an amendment was formulated to take to the 2010 AGM.

2010

An earthquake in Port au Prince, Haiti, kills over 200,000. A volcanic eruption in Iceland causes an ash cloud which grounds UK and North European civil air traffic for five days resulting in the loss of billions of pounds for already struggling airlines. Huge oil spill in the Gulf of Mexico costs BP billions. Pakistan suffers its worst flooding in a generation; millions are displaced by the floodwaters. Thirty-three miners rescued from the San José mine in Chile. A General Election in the UK results in a hung parliament and the formation of the first post-war Coalition Government between the Conservatives and the Liberal Democrats. David Cameron becomes the youngest Prime Minister in 200 years and Liberal Democrat Nick Clegg becomes Deputy Prime Minister. Labour's Gordon Brown resigns and Ed Milliband is elected Labour leader. The economy was the main focus of the election and how each party was going to cope with the £165 billion deficit. In Cumbria twelve people are shot dead by a lone gunman. Eighty-one billion pounds is slashed from government spending to deal with the deficit. An extended cold spell delivers snow and icy conditions to the UK, the worst for thirty years and heavy snowfalls in December disrupt many peoples' travel plans. Colin Firth and Helen Bonham Carter star in "The King's Speech".

In the Queen's Birthday Honours List, London Group member Paula Rego (1965) is made a Dame. "What is it for? I don't do anything but paint pictures."
Tate Britain Henry Moore (1930) exhibition.
Tate Modern Theo van Doesburg, Arshile Gorky, Paul Gauguin.
Royal Academy "Vincent van Gogh: His Art and Letters".
Whitechapel Gallery "British Council Collection: Thresholds", selected by London Group member Paula Rego.

London Group President: Susan Haire (2004)

The year began as the Working Committee waded through persistent deep snow to the Whitechapel Gallery. An extraordinary meeting was held to discuss The London Group's future direction, governance, financial issues, membership, developments in IT, publicity and exhibitions. The afternoon meeting, attended by approximately twenty Working Committee and ordinary members, was held in the gallery housing Goshka Macuga's installation "The Nature of the Beast". Macuga's idea was for groups to meet at a round table placed before the United Nation's tapestry copy of Picasso's "Guernica" and for their meetings to be archived into the new Whitechapel Gallery archive. Two hours of useful discussion ensued, the major outcome being the clear message that unless the Group could find sponsorship or income then, as the Treasurer

Robert Coward darkly predicted, "the Group's 2013 Anniversary could be its funeral"! Coward estimated that the current £80 annual subscription would need to rise to £200 in order to continue spending at the current rate. At the moment the £80 subscription only covered the Group's administrative costs. Other items discussed were European connections (an artists from Tel Aviv who was visiting the Macuga installation reported on his group's experiences), Small Group Exhibitions and the need to modernise the Group's image, especially its website. Alfred Harris reminded the meeting of the need for fairness and transparency in future policy decisions, especially selection for Small Group Exhibitions.

The Working Committee Meeting on Tuesday 12th January 2010 at the Whitechapel Gallery

In the background is the tapestry copy of Picasso's "Guernica", part of Goshka Macuga's installation "The Nature of the Beast".

The first exhibition of the year was "Inspiration" held in the gallery at Kensington and Chelsea College, Hortensia Road, London SW10 from 20th January to 4th February. Twenty-nine members submitted work supported by a short statement hung next to the work indicating who or what had influenced them during their journey through life. The theme of this 'ground breaking' exhibition was the inspiration given to members during their development as artists, whether by tutors, other artists, or particular works or events. 'Ground breaking', in that it was a new concept put to the Group by exhibition curator Paul Tecklenberg, linking art practice and education, a link long perpetuated by The London Group members as art students and later, perhaps, as practitioner/teachers. To that effect, on Thursday, 28th January there was a "Meet the Artists" where a selection of the artists elaborated on their inspirations and how these had influenced their art practice, attended by a fifty strong audience of students and the curious. The exhibition was first mooted by past president Matthew Kolakowski supported by Gillian Ingham, both of whom worked at KCC.

Kensington and Chelsea College

Hortensia Road, London SW10

This was the venue for the exhibition "Inspiration". The gallery was behind the thin, tall arched windows which provided a large, airy and well lit environment for members' work. The building housing Kensington and Chelsea College was built in 1908 as the Sloane School for Boys.

On February 2nd the Working Committee gathered at the Arts Club, 40 Dover Street, W1 for a scheduled meeting; a new venue and a new venture for the Group. Susan Haire and other officers had been investigating the likelihood of collaboration and exhibition opportunities with the Arts Club. The meeting heard that the club wished to update its image and provide a more varied and contemporary programme of exhibitions on its club walls. Following discussion, the committee agreed to delegate the President to accept the offer of a free exhibition slot for the members only 2010 annual. Earlier the meeting had faced the hard realism of declining finances and the need to search out "good value venues". The stark warning from the Treasurer at the Whitechapel meeting was still ringing in officers' ears, "Our anniversary could be our funeral"! Topics discussed were, should the annual membership be increased and by how much, should the Group dispense with small group exhibitions, should the Annual Exhibition exhibiting fee be raised and do the Group really want or need a centenary celebration? Other topics discussed were the prospect of exhibiting at the 2013 London Art Fair, Business Design Centre, in the "Project Space" and of continuing the "Inspiration" concept with tours to Brighton, Nottingham and Canterbury.

The economic situation was causing hurt to many institutions. There were numerous articles in the art press reporting difficulties, the ICA in particular planned to make a third of its ninety staff redundant, despite an extra one off grant from the Arts Council London of £1.2 million. The Serpentine Gallery, however, appeared to be surviving the worst of the recession. An Evening Standard article reported, "Not everyone hates bankers. The new issue of Tatler has devoted a spread to the Serpentine

Council, a group of well-connected philanthropists with City connections who support the gallery in Hyde Park. Who are these people outside this 'normal sphere'? Tatler describes it as a collision of 'the world of business, banking, media and socially significant inherited wealth'".

The Group's AGM was held on Tuesday, 27th April in The Cello Factory, Cornwall Road, SE1. Over thirty members attended and twenty-two sent apologies. On the agenda were the President's and Treasurer's Reports, a report from David Corbett who indicated that he seemed to be making progress in seeking sponsorship from business, and two motions making small changes to the Constitution in order to support small group exhibitions (SGEs). Postal and proxy votes were used in the voting system for these motions in order to increase ordinary members' representation. There then followed the election of Officers and Committee Members for 2010-11. All Officers were returned unopposed and the Working Committee was comprised of Tony Carter, Tony Collinge, Jane Humphrey, Annie Johns, Amanda Loomes, David Redfern, Suzan Swale and Paul Tecklenberg. In addition to the Officers and Working Committee, Vic Kuell, Ian Parker, Victoria Rance and Wendy Smith were elected to the Selection Committee. The final agenda item was tabled by Alfred Harris, specifically "Allegations of corruption in and of The London Group". Harris was concerned that officers and others were organising SGEs for their own benefit. He reminded the AGM of the ethos of fairness and transparency required by the Group's constitution. The thirty members present at the AGM saw no evidence of these allegations and Harris' motion was defeated unanimously.

The Membership Committee met on Tuesday, 11th May at The Cello Factory and elected four new members from sixteen candidates. The four were the painter Victoria Arney, mixed media Ece Clarke, graphic artist Aude Hérail Jäger and the sculptor Jeff Lowe.

The Cello Factory was the venue for this year's Annual Exhibition of Members' Work. Following the concern expressed by the Treasurer and others, the Working Committee was looking for a good value venue or even a free one. Initially the Arts Club in Dover Street, where the Working Committee had been holding meetings recently, had made an offer to the Group, but their renovation programme prevented a convenient date being negotiated. After other ideas had been debated, the President's offer of The Cello Factory for free was accepted and an earlier date in the year (June) adopted. Other cost cutting exercises were implemented, indeed, one member, Trevor Frankland, picked up the Private View bar tab! Vic Kuell came up with a novel idea of donating twelve works on paper to be raffled each month for a year, the proceeds of which went straight to Group finances. Tickets cost twelve pounds and were on sale to members and visitors alike. The "Members' Annual Exhibition 2010" took place from the 1st to the 11th June with a Private View on Tuesday, 1st June. There was a size restriction to ensure that all works could be fitted comfortably in the compact space on the ground floor and mezzanine of The Cello Factory. Sixty-two members exhibited showing a wide variety of work from sculpture, painting and drawing to photography, prints and animation. Two Royal Academicians were asking the top prices, Frank Bowling RA £11,000 for his painting "Round Red" and Anthony Eyton RA £9,375 for his painting, "Eden Project Construction of Biomes". This year saw another new innovation, the "Virtual Annual". Exhibiting members were invited to send five additional images of recent work which would set their exhibited work in context. Visitors were able to sit and watch digitally projected images on a screen in a small upstairs room off the mezzanine. Group Secretary Mike Liggins put the whole package together receiving supportive feedback from both members and exhibition visitors.

A second helping of members' influences and enthusiasms, "Inspiration 2", opened at Kensington and Chelsea College on the 22nd September until 7th October with an opening Private View on Thursday, 23rd September. The formula had proved extremely popular with both exhibiting members of the Group and with staff and students of Kensington and Chelsea College. Twenty-one members showed their work in this round, some having previously exhibited in the first Inspiration exhibition held earlier in the year. A seminar with participating artists under the title "What makes an inspirational tutor/inspired student?" took place on Thursday 30th September where a vibrant and informative discussion ensued.

2011

A powerful earthquake and resultant tsunami devastate NE Japan causing a nuclear crisis at the Fukushima complex. The 'Arab Spring' emerges in Arab countries in the Near East. The 'Purple Revolution' replaces a regime in Tunisia, followed by the 'Lotus Revolution' replacing President Mubarak in Egypt. President Gadaffi is shot dead in Libya following a popular uprising. "The News of the World" is closed by Murdoch's News International following a phone hacking scandal. A right wing extremist kills 77 in Norway in a bomb and shooting attack. In the summer, spontaneous rioting and looting spread across the country from London, organised by use of social media. National debt problems in Greece, Ireland and Portugal destabilise the Euro currency forcing European rescue packages. England retain the Ashes. In London, statistics from the 2011 Census record a city population of 8.2 million, 850,000 more than 2001. 45% were white British, the most ethnically diverse area in England and Wales.

Tate Modern Miró, Gerhard Richter, Tacita Dean.
Tate Britain Susan Hiller, "Watercolour", "The Vorticists", John Martin.
Royal Academy Modern British Sculpture, Watteau's Drawings, Degas.
Whitechapel Gallery The Government Art Collection, John Stezaker, Mike Nelson.
Victoria and Albert Museum British Design from 1942 to 2012, "Postmodernism".
British Museum Grayson Perry.
Touring British Art Show 7.
Serpentine Gallery Nancy Spero.
Turner Prize at the BALTIC Centre for Contemporary Art, Gateshead. Karla Black (sculptor), Hilary Lloyd (moving images) and George Shaw (painter) were nominated; Sculptor Martin Boyle was the winner.

London Group President: Susan Haire (2004)

The year began with a Group discussion on small group exhibition venues and themed exhibitions. The discussion, which took place at The Cello Factory on the evening of January 11th, was chaired by Tony Carter and Amanda Loomes Over thirty members contributed to a lively debate about the difficulties of mounting temporary exhibitions which would be sympathetic to the type of work produced by each individual member of the Group. Venues could range from the atypical commercial gallery space with supporting infrastructure (as typified by White Cube Gallery) to the empty, derelict building space which could overpower some kinds of work (as typified by the basement exhibition area beneath Shoreditch Town Hall). Linked to this debate was Amanda Loomes' proposal for a small group exhibition on the theme of "Self-Portrait".

Contributions to this proposed SGE could range from the conventional, traditional likeness in the mirror to more radical and unconventional presentations of "self" as would reflect the range of approaches practiced by London Group membership. Most of the Working Committee were present and absorbed the meeting's thoughts.

On Tuesday, 1st February the Working Committee ploughed through a busy but exciting agenda. The first report was on the proposed auction at Bonhams to raise money for the centenary celebrations. Four works by current and ex members of the Group (who were considered by Bonhams to be "blue chip" auctionable) had been promised and more were in the pipeline. An initiative to shadow the 1913 'dry-run' exhibition at Brighton Art Gallery in 2013 was given the thumbs down by the Brighton authorities, citing lack of financial resources and little relevance to the local Brighton community. However, there were two very exciting prospects reported by the President, one with Ben Uri Gallery and the other at Pitzhanger Manor in Ealing. Most of the more important London galleries had not responded to London Group proposals, but these venues were positive, supportive and enthusiastic about Group proposals. The next Small Group Exhibition entitled, "The Invisible Line" was scheduled for a March opening at the Piers Feetham Gallery in Fulham. The 2011 Open Exhibition moved ahead with reports from two sub-committees, Publicity and Submissions, both packed with new ideas and initiatives for this year's Open. Other discussion was focused on a new Group logo and revisiting procedure for new members, to be more extensively discussed at a future meeting. The feeling was upbeat and optimistic.

At the Piers Feetham Gallery, 475 Fulham Road, London SW6 the Group showed twelve members in a Small Group Exhibition curated by Phil Crozier entitled "The Invisible Line" from the 2nd to the 26th March. Anthony Whishaw RA's introduction to the exhibition states, "In his invitation to exhibit, Philip Crozier wrote that he was looking to painters close to the 'invisible line' dividing abstraction and figuration, particularly those for whom the act of painting was a generative process, regardless of style. He alluded to the traditional notion that British painting depended on strong drawing, but offered an alternative tradition, through artists like Turner and Bomberg, whose improvisation and continuous alertness to the development of nuances as they worked took them to unpremeditated conclusions". Those accepting Crozier's invitation to exhibit were Victoria Arney, John Crossley, Tricia Gillman, Julie Held, Bill Henderson, Pauline Little, Peter Morrell, Daniel Preece, Alex Ramsay, Tom Scase and Anthony Whishaw RA, (including Crozier himself). Thirty-four works in various wet and dry media were hung with prices ranging from £450 for Pauline Little's "Seed" to Whishaw's triptych at £10,500. Gallery owner Piers Feetham was very satisfied with the exhibition and planned to exhibit a different cohort of members of The London Group at a future date.

Amongst other agenda items at the 15th March Working Committee Meeting were reports on Bonham's auction, the 2013 Centenary exhibitions, the 2011 Open Exhibition, the new logo design competition and other exhibition proposals. Such was the enthusiasm and commitment of membership that a proposal to hold an Open in 2012 to "keep up the momentum towards the Centenary" was warmly welcomed.

Unseasonably warm weather coincided with The London Group's AGM on 19th April held at The Cello Factory. The sunny disposition continued as the thirty or so members present heard reports from the Honorary Treasurer, Robert Coward and the President, Susan Haire. The treasurer reported that the Group had turned a deficit of £8,877 last year into a surplus of £3,006 for this year. This was due to two reasons, firstly Susan Haire had given The Cello Factory free to The London Group to hold its 2010 Members Exhibition, thereby avoiding any hire fees so crippling in previous years, and Vic Kuell had donated twelve works on paper to be raffled each month for a year, raising £888. Only a small amount was owed in arrears by members whose total subscriptions had brought in £6,675.25. The theme of the President's speech was tolerance, now that difficulties in the past had been settled, the Group was moving forward with an active group of officers and an ambitious exhibition program. Central to the speech was the 100th Anniversary Exhibition programme at Pitzhanger Manor in Ealing and the collaboration with Ben Uri Gallery. However there were two clouds on this sunny horizon. Annie Johns confirmed that the Bonhams auction would not now go ahead due to lack of offers from high profile ex-member artists. The meeting was also stunned when the President informed those assembled of the death of Trevor Frankland, a good friend and active member of The London Group. Eight members stood for four posts on the Working Committee. Mark Dickens, Annie Johns, Jeff Lowe and David Redfern were elected whilst fourteen members put their names forward for four places on the Membership Committee, Peter Clossick, Sam Jarman, Victoria Rance and Wendy Smith being successful.

Two new members were elected to the group in May, Genetic Moo a media based pair of artists and Lydia Julien, a performance, installation and photography artist.

The Working Committee met on July 5th to review arrangements for the forthcoming Open and to discuss two projects curated by London Group members. The first was a small group exhibition (SGE) based on the theme of mapping, curated by Paul Tecklenberg and another based on the concept of self-portrait curated by Amanda Loomes.

"The London Group Open Exhibition 2011" took place at The Cello Factory during October and November. The exhibition was dedicated to the memory of Trevor Frankland (1931-2011) who had been elected to the Group in 1996 and had served as Treasurer for a number of years. This large and ambitious exhibition had to be split into two parts, Part 1 from October 20th to 29th and Part 2 between November 1st and the 10th. Seven hundred and thirty-five images were submitted in the open submission, reviewed and selected by Jenni Lomax from the Camden Arts Centre and writer, critic and artist William Feaver. They chose seventy-eight works to be shown alongside members' work and also invited guests' work in the two parts. William Feaver wrote, "The Open selection of London Group exhibitions isn't just a door ajar, it's an opportunity to extend and maybe surprise. From an exceptionally large number of entries (735) the minority that have made it to the two shows are distinguished for their liveliness and distinction: paintings, photographs and sculpture that make one look and look again." The Group had revived a number of initiatives practiced in previous annual exhibitions. Guest exhibitors had been invited to exhibit with the Group throughout its history. This year Gillian Ayres RA, John Carter RA, Robyn Denny, John Hoyland RA (representative), Albert Irvin RA and Richard Wilson RA had accepted invitations to exhibit. Seventy-four members out of a total membership of eighty-eight put work into the 2011 Open. Members had also been extremely active in achieving sponsorship from eleven individuals and organisations with prize money totalling in excess of £4,000. The nine prize winners were Belinda Bailey, Paul Brandford, Nicholas Gentilli, Judith Jones, Steve Johnson, Georgina McNamara, Adeline de Monseignat, Sachiyo Nishimura and Seamus Staunton. London Group members Tom Scase (Part 1) and Ian Parker (Part 2) had the difficult but pleasurable job of placing and arranging the huge variety of submitted work from conventional painting and sculpture to photography, video and an enormous inflatable "bottle organ". Both Private Views were bursting at the seams, the first, on October 20th, shared its date with the shooting of Colonel Gaddafi in Libya. Despite the world economic crisis, The London Group seemed to be bucking the trend as a number of sales from both parts raised most welcome commission revenue for the Group. This year's Open had been a model exercise in how a well organised and enthusiastic group of artists could make effective representation to a gallery going public. At the end of 2011 The London Group was in good shape and good heart.

2012

Continuing unrest in Syria and Bahrain. The Euro economic crisis continued with Greece, Ireland, Portugal and Spain requiring extensive financial support. Hurricane Sandy devastates America's East Coast causing over 50 billion dollars of damage and weeks of disruption. President Obama was re-elected for a second term, narrowly beating Mitt Romney. In China, Xi Jinping was installed as the new leader of the Chinese Communist Party. On January 3rd Gary Dobson and David Norris were convicted at the Old Bailey of murdering Stephen Lawrence in Eltham, South East London in 1993. In the London Mayoral elections Boris Johnson was returned for a second term. The Olympic Games and Paralympics take place in London with a large area of East London around Stratford redeveloped as the Olympic Park. 2012 sees the driest spring for 100 years and the wettest year on record. Daniel Craig and Judi Dench appear in Sam Mendes' Bond film "Skyfall".

Royal Academy David Hockney recent work. Hockney had been elected to The London Group in 1964, just before he left for America.

Tate Modern Damien Hirst, Edward Munch, "A Bigger Splash – Painting after Performance".

Tate Britain "Migrations" featuring the work of a number of London Group artists, Bomberg, Gertler, Kramer and Epstein. "Pre-Raphaelites: Victorian Avant-Garde".

Turner Prize 2012 those shortlisted were Spartacus Chetwynd, Luke Fowler, Paul Noble and Elizabeth Price; Price was the winner.

Whitechapel Art Gallery Open Exhibition.

National Gallery Richard Hamilton's last works.

Borough Road Gallery housed in London South Bank University opens, showing works from the Sarah Rose Collection of Bomberg and the Borough Group (see 1940s).

Scottish National Gallery "John Bellany: A Passion for Life". Bellany (1973) was at one time the Vice President of The London Group.

London Group President: Susan Haire (2004)

In February, London experienced its first snow after what had been a dry and mild winter. On a freezing 6th February the Working Committee met for the first meeting of the year at The Cello Factory. The agenda included progress reports from sub-committees and developments in two recent exhibition initiatives based on territories & mapping and self-portraiture. A new logo was finally agreed which would incorporate an image of Epstein's iconic "Rock Drill" echoing the first days of The London Group in 1913. The very next morning four London Group officers met with Ben Uri representatives to continue planning for 2013. Most of this meeting was spent on making application to the Royal West of England Academy in Bath as a venue for the first stop on a national tour for both the historical and contemporary exhibitions planned for 2013. On the agenda for the Working Committee Meeting of 26th March were reports from the Fundraising and Publicity sub-committees, last minute details for the forthcoming "Territories and Boundaries" exhibition, proposals for the self-portraiture exhibition later in the year and discussion on this year's annual and next year's centenary.

The first exhibition of the year opened to torrential April showers in what had now been officially described as a drought situation. "Territories & Boundaries" opened on the 24th April and continued until the 3rd of May at Kensington and Chelsea College, Hortensia Road, SW10. The exhibition was devised by Paul Tecklenberg and Jane Humphrey, surveying "the appropriation of maps and charts and also exploring notions of territory and boundaries through the translation of the 3D into a scaled down 2D representation". As well as the two curators, nineteen other members took part in the show hung in the new gallery on the ground floor of the newly opened college building. Jane Humphrey designed an accompanying catalogue which unfolded like a map providing a colour image of each work and a statement about the work from each artist. On Thursday, 3rd May a number of participating artists contributed to an evening seminar where exhibiting artists discussed their work and answered questions.

The new Kensington and Chelsea College

"Territories & Boundaries" was exhibited in KCC's new gallery, readily accessible from the entrance and conveniently next to the café. London Group members Gillian Ingham and Matthew Kolakowski were tutors at KCC at the time.

The Membership Committee met on the 11th June to consider nominations for eleven candidates. Three new members were ultimately elected, Charlotte C. Mortensson, a painter, David Theobald working in animation and Erica Winstone, a painter also working with video.

The Working Committee had a lot to discuss at the meeting held on the 3rd July. The most exciting report was from the fundraising group who hoped to raise over £10,000 from an event named "Draw". The idea was to ask artists, both London Group members and others, to donate a piece of work which could be chosen by drawing a ticket out of a hat. Tickets would be priced at £100 and at least one hundred donated works were anticipated. Donated works could be seen on the Group's website and the draw itself was planned for 4th October after a short 'viewing' exhibition at The Cello Factory. Initial responses had been most encouraging with one hundred and thirteen pledges of donated works. Reports were also heard from officers dealing with a proposed tour of "Territories and Boundaries", new developments in "On my behalf" (the self-portraiture initiative), dates for this year's Annual and more details about exhibitions planned for the Centenary.

"On my behalf" opened on September 17th at the Cumberland Hotel in Marble Arch, W1. Curated by Amanda Loomes and Ian Parker, every member was invited to make work around the notion of the self-portrait, but not necessarily the conventional figurative mirror likeness. In the event twenty-seven members put work into the exhibition. The Private View was on Tuesday, 18th September in the cavernous entrance foyer of this four star hotel. The foyer had a constant stream of hotel residents ensuring a large audience in this very public space. The exhibition closed on October 5th.

The Cumberland Hotel
Marble Arch, London W1

"One Hundred Plus Draw", the major fundraising initiative intended to build up the coffers for the centenary year, took place at The Cello Factory on the evening of Thursday, October 4th. Members and 'significant' non-members sympathetic to The

London Group were asked to donate a piece of work to be chosen by ticket holders as numbers were drawn out of a hat. Invited artists included Glen Baxter, Eileen Cooper, Cosey Fanni Tutti, Ian McKeever, Robyn Denny, William Feaver, Maggi Hambling and work from the estates of Trevor Frankland, Kenneth Martin and David Whitaker. "One Hundred Plus Draw" raised over £10,000 as over one hundred tickets were sold for £100 each. The draw itself was an exciting affair as people got to choose their desired piece of work. The evening ran smoothly with wine and finger-food and it appeared that despite the chance element in the draw, most people got the work of art they had set their heart on. In an ironic coincidence, the Royal Academy organised a similar exhibition. Entitled 'RA Now' every RA was asked to donate a work for a sale which was held on October 9th. Proceeds from this sale were to "raise funds for an innovative building project on the Academy site".

Vice President Gillian Ingham, the principal organiser of "One Hundred Plus Draw", loads the numbered beads into the 'magic' tin in front of an expectant audience at the start of the draw. Once a number was called out the lucky punter chose a work from the wall and was able to take it away with them, suitably wrapped, of course, by London Group volunteers.

The Annual Exhibition for members only took place between the 13th to the 24th November at The Cello Factory, 33-34 Cornwall Road, London SE1. The Private View was held on Tuesday 13th November, an evening when London was awash with private views, particularly Tate Modern's "A Bigger Splash, Painting after Performance". The London Group private view hosted a performance itself that evening by Lydia Julien. She was one of twenty-eight women exhibiting this year out of a total sixty-eight exhibitors which also included two partnerships, Genetic Moo and Paul & Laura Carey. Painting was still a favoured activity amongst London Group members, but constructions, collages, prints, photographs and video stills were much in evidence. An A3 folding pamphlet accompanied the exhibition giving a colour illustration of each work exhibited, but no titles, sizes, media or price, just the artist's name. This was a really healthy submission by members indicating strong support for the Group on its lead in to its centenary.

Both the President and the Treasurer were both upbeat at the AGM held on Tuesday, 27th November at The Cello Factory. Susan Haire outlined the past twelve months and the packed programme for the Group's centenary year. Robert Coward reflected on his long association with The London Group, over forty years, and observed that the Group had never been so financially strong. As at the 31st January, the Group had £52,592.84 in the General Fund. Members' subscriptions had brought in £7,845.25 but perhaps the most notable figure was the surplus made on the 2011 Open Exhibition. Hanging fees alone had raised £13,710, commission on sales brought in £1,110 and total income for this exhibition was £15,335.00. With expenditure at £6,758.51 this meant that the Open was in surplus to the tune of £8,576.49. The Treasurer pointed out that this surplus was entirely due to there being now hire fee for The Cello Factory and that when the Group had to pay for exhibition space in the future, the picture would be very different. The Cello Factory's owner, Susan Haire, was given a vote of thanks by the meeting.

After the reports elections were held. Susan Haire was re-elected as President unopposed. Similarly, Gillian Ingham remained as Vice President, Mark Dickens as Deputy Vice President, Robert Coward as Treasurer and Tommy Seaward as Honorary Secretary. Five officers were elected to the Working Committee, John Crossley, Amanda Loomes, new member Tim Pickup, Suzan Swale and Paul Tecklenberg. A further four members made up the Membership Committee, Moich Abrahams, Marcelle Hanselaar, and new members Lydia Julien and Erica Winstone.

The AGM was short and business like. Twenty-eight members were in attendance and twenty sent apologies indicating that well over half of the membership was involved in some way with the Group's affairs. There had been discussion about voting methods and transparency during elections, but apart from this a.o.b. item members were wending their way home, or to the pub, in no time.

The Group's financial position was even stronger than Robert Coward had reported. His accounting date 'snapshot' was at midnight on 31st January, but since that date the Group had raised over £10,000 in the "One Hundred Plus Draw" and had a bequest of £25,000 bestowed by John Cloudsley-Thompson in memory of his wife, Anne Cloudsley who had died in January. This sum of money was ringfenced for publishing future exhibition catalogues and other publications to promote The London Group. This history of The London Group was made possible by Anne Cloudsley's bequest and is dedicated to her memory. The Group was in a position to spend and to make itself better known during the forthcoming centenary year. In December members were informed that Artsinform had been hired to organise publicity for the Group throughout 2013 for a fee of £11,000.

2013

Civil War in Syria. Spontaneous civil protests in Egypt, Turkey and Brazil. Pope Benedict XVI resigns, the first Pope in over 700 years to do so, Francis I from South America is elected in his place. The remains of King Richard III are found under a Leicester car park. Justin Welby replaces Rowan Williams as the Archbishop of Canterbury. Jimmy Savile is revealed as a serial sexual predator. Lady Thatcher dies and is honoured with a service in St. Paul's Cathedral. The Boston Marathon is bombed, killing three and injuring scores of onlookers. A serving soldier is murdered by two terrorists in Woolwich, South East London. In Egypt the military remove democratically elected President Morsi of the Muslim Brotherhood.

Tate Modern "A Bigger Splash: Painting after Performance Art", and a Roy Lichtenstein retrospective.
Tate Britain "Schwitters in Britain", Gary Hume and Patrick Caulfield, "L.S. Lowry (1948): the Painting of Modern Life".
Turner Prize 2013 Laure Prouvost, Tino Seghal, David Shrigley and Lynette Yiadom-Boakye were shortlisted this year.
Tate St Ives William Scott (1949) Centenary.
Royal Academy "Manet: Portraying Life".
Victoria & Albert Museum a David Bowie exhibition becomes the fastest selling event in its history.
Borough Road Gallery an important exhibition of Dorothy Mead's work as a member of the Borough Group and the first female president of The London Group in 1971.
Venice Biennale Jeremy Dellow represented Great Britain. Marc Quinn and Sir Anthony Caro RA held exhibitions in Venice at the same time.

London Group President: Susan Haire (2004)

The London Group began its Centenary Year in excellent health with eighty-eight members including five Honorary Members.

Pitzhanger Manor, Walpole Park, Mattock Lane, London W5 was the venue for the first centenary exhibition of many for The London Group in 2013. A Private View as held on 22nd January and the exhibition opened on 23rd January and ran until 9th March. Pitzhanger Manor had been Sir John Soane's summer residence and had previously housed Hogarth's "The Rakes Progress". London Group members were asked by Pitzhanger to produce work in response to the physical environment of the house itself and to the Sir John Soane Museum collection. Nineteen members responded to the challenge of creating 'interventions' as these works were placed throughout the

House. Other members exhibited 'non-interventional' work in Pitzhanger Manor's capacious and beautifully lit galleries. Out of a total exhibiting membership of eighty-seven, seventy-eight members showed a total of one hundred works in this centenary exhibition. This large exhibition more than any other exhibitions in recent times showed the huge range of approaches practiced by The London Group membership, from painting and sculpture through mixed media, photography and moving images to performance.

Pitzhanger Manor
London W5

Some of the media reported The London Group reaching its hundredth birthday. Mark Brown in "The Guardian" (22.01.13) wrote a short piece, "Artists celebrate the London Group's centenary with 100 new works". Brown interviewed the President, Susan Haire, "The group has managed to stage shows through both world wars and hopes to continue for the next 100 years. We are really strong at the moment." said Haire. "It is a very lively group and really a lot hasn't changed since the beginning, when it was very argumentative and very eclectic. Also, it was apolitical then and it's apolitical now, and we're not subject to fashion." The article had a photograph a Frank Bowling RA in front of his canvas, "Bowling recalled that when he was a student, the London Group was the one he desperately aspired to join. 'I admired the people who were involved with it, such as Claude Rogers, and I wanted to be part of their company. It is a very important group and the only one left: lots have came and went, but the London Group still goes on, and I think it is because of its openness – it is amazing that it is still going.'" On its Entertainments & Arts website page for 23rd January, the BBC News, under the heading "In pictures: 100 years of The London Group", showed ten images from the exhibition and the magazine "Artists & Illustrators" printed an article on the history of The London Group written by ex-President Peter Clossick. The February 1st edition of the Pulitzer Prize winning web newspaper "The Huffington Post" carried an article on The London Group and the Pitzhanger exhibition written by Susan Straughan.

The National Trust's Mottisfont Abbey in Hampshire provided the gallery for the next London Group exhibition. "The London Group at 100: Mottisfont" opened on the 9th February and closed on 21st April with a Private View on Friday 8th February. In the 1930s socialite Maud Russell had entertained many artistic characters at the Abbey and a permanent collection of artworks, many from previous members of The London Group, had been passed on to the National Trust. Forty-four current members of The London Group, about half of the total membership, submitted work for this exhibition. National Trust curators selected sixteen previous members of The London Group from Mottisfont's Derek Hill Collection to hang in an introductory room. They were Michael Andrews, Vanessa Bell, John Bratby, Anthony Fry, Roger Fry, Henri Gaudier-Brzeska, Harold Gilman, Duncan Grant, Augustus John, L.S. Lowry, Robert Medley, Victor Pasmore, John Piper, Mary Potter, Walter Sickert and Graham Sutherland. Works by current London Group members had explanatory labels next to them to help visitors understand what the artists' intentions were. The visitors' book recorded some impressions: "Pretentious, over worked. No wonder arts grants are reducing! Surely the NT don't need to show this to pretend to be 'up' with modernity" boomed one visitor. "What an interesting exhibition. Good for the NT. A splendid venture by Mottisfont. So good to see contemporary art at an NT property. Long may it continue in these beautiful galleries" countered another. The majority of vistors had a positive outlook on the NT's initiative; "Wonderful exhibition, thrills the soul", "Wonderfully refreshing. Challenging – lots to think about" and "Cold damp day, warm sunny art with a hint of storm". Total attendance for the exhibition was 19,224, one of the largest attendances in London Group history. As an additional bonus, Janet Patterson and Anthony Whishaw RA sold work.

In May "The London Group Centenary Open 2013" opened at The Cello Factory. Because of the large number of works from both members and non-members the exhibition was shown in two parts, Part 1 from 14th to the 24th May and Part 2 from 28th May to the 7th June. There were a record number of submissions for the Centenary Open. Seven hundred and sixty-six individual works were submitted by four hundred and fifty-six artists, 20% of these were under 35, six hundred and ninety works were described as wall hung, fifty-seven as floor/suspended, fifteen video and four installation with twenty-one artists from outside the UK submitting work. Judging with the London Group's Selection Committee were Jane England, gallery director/curator of England & Co., international artist Bruce McLean and curator, critic and writer Nicholas Usherwood. Usherwood observed, "Open exhibition selection committees can prove a somewhat dispiriting business – fudges, compromises and a dull consensus often taking the spirit out of things. The London Group's approach to this problem – to mix outside judges with a dozen or so Group members – worked well with enough nicely differing points of view emerging to ensure an eclectic selection came through, reflecting the excellent send in!". McLean highlighted the thinking behind The London Group's policy of organising open exhibitions, "I was delighted to be asked to be a judge as it gives an insight into what is going on in other parts of the Art world."

There were a large number of prizes awarded at the Private View to Part 2 on Tuesday, 28th May. A solo show at The Cello Factory was won by Maya Ramsay, Chelsea Art Club Trust Stan Smith Award for an artist under 35 by Caroline Jane Harris, John Jones services prize by Louise Whittles, Winsor and Newton materials prize for painting and drawing by Steph Goodger and the Patrick Gorman photographic services by Eliza Bennett. Two London Group members offered prizes, Jeff Lowe donated a sculpture prize won by Stephanie Conway and Moich Abrahams awarded three sums of money for the most innovative works in the two parts, Jane Webb winning £1,000, Anna Lewis £250 and Christopher Appleby £100.

Sixty-one members and seventy-six non-members exhibited at The Cello Factory. The range of work was enormous and difficult to categorise. There were one hundred and six works described as wall hung, twenty floor or suspended, ten videos and one installation. London Group members Genetic Moo declared, "We see a mission for The London Group in the 21st century: to do what it did 100 years ago and support artists working with the latest technologies against the grain of contemporary art practice."

Five new members were elected to the Group at the Membership Selection Committee meeting on July 2nd at The Cello Factory. They were Eric Fong and Marenka Gabeler, both working in multi-disciplinary media, Vaughan Grylls working with photography and two painters, Susan Sluglett and David Wiseman. Seventeen members of The London Group made up the committee and nominees had to gain nine votes in order to be elected. Sixteen nominees had been put forward this year exhibiting a high degree of professionalism and quality, consequently the committee's task was much more demanding.

A members only exhibition was proposed at City Hall. Arts Officers from The London Assembly had found information about the Group's 100th anniversary and had offered an exhibition in October. There had been a great deal of debate within the Group as to whether the Group should exhibit at City Hall because of the restrictions imposed by the London Assembly Officers. Artists were asked not to exhibit work which could give offence and be suitable for children. Many members voiced their opinion about the unaccustommed cencorship and declined to show; others thought that this high profile opportunity for the Group should not be turned down.

It is planned to publish this book in relation to two forthcoming exhibitions. "Uproar: The First Fifty Years" at Ben Uri, the London Jewish Museum, October

30th, 2013 to March 2nd, 2014, looks at the storm of controversy surrounding the start of The London Group and its first half-century and also celebrates the centenary of the first group meeting, held on 25th October 1913. London Group members will be creating works in response to this show in "+100 The London Group Today", November 16th to December 13th at The Cello Factory, marking the centenary of the naming of 'The London Group' by Jacob Epstein on 15th November 1913.

The London Group also plans to tour work to Southampton City Art Gallery and to show alongside paintings from previous London Group members, from their rich and extensive permanent collection. The exhibition is pencilled in for July 2014 with a current member exhibition curated by Sam Jarman and an historical selection curated by Victoria Rance and David Redfern. Initial discussions with Tim Craven, the Southampton Director, were extremely positive and enabling.

At this point The London Group history must come to a halt. The current members of The London Group would like to pass on their greetings to all future members of the Group, to those yet to be successful in future London Group open submissions and to all curious and adventurous artists working in the next one hundred years.

The London Group Presidents

1914–1919	Harold Gilman (1876-1919)
1919–1919	No President elected; Robert Bevan (1865–1925) had overall responsibility
1914–1919	Bernard Adeney (1878-1966)
1924–1926	Frank Dobson (1888-1963)
1926–1936	Rupert Lee (1887-1959)
1936–1937	R.P. Bedford (1883-1967) [Chairman]
1937–1943	H. S. Williamson (1892-1978) [Chairman]
1943–1948	Elliott Seabrooke (1886-1950) Assumed Presidency during Second World War
1948–1950	Ruskin Spear (1911-1990)
1950–1952	John Dodgson (1890-1969)
1952–1965	Claude Rogers (1907-1979)
1965–1971	Andrew Forge (1923-2002)
1971–1973	Dorothy Mead (1928-1975)
1973–1977	Neville Boden (1929-1996)
1977–1979	Peter Donnelly (?)
1979–1993	Stan Smith (1929-2001)
1983	Dennis Creffield (1931-) [for 24 hours]
1993–1995	Adrian Bartlett (1939–)
1995–1998	Philippa Beale (1946–)
1998–2001	Matthew Kolakowski (1956–)
2000–2005	Peter Clossick (1948–)
2005–2007	Philip Crozier (1947–)
2007–present	Susan Haire (1952–)

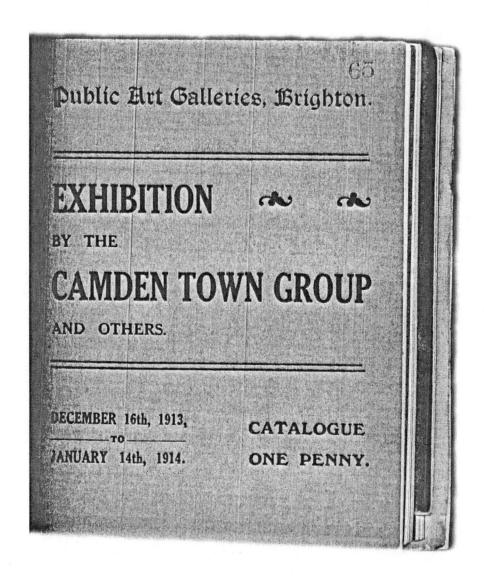

1913 Exhibition catalogue, Camden Town Group, Brighton Art Gallery
Images courtesy of Brighton and Hove Museums

INDEX TO ARTISTS.

THE LONDON GROUP RETROSPECTIVE EXHIBITION

April — May 1928

Officers

President : Rupert Lee

Vice-President : Frederick J. Porter

Honorary Treasurer : J. S. Woodger *Secretary :* Diana Brinton

Executive Committee

A. P. Allinson	Randolph Schwabe
Keith Baynes	Alfred Thornton
Roger Fry	Allan Walton
Bernard Meninsky	Edward Wolfe

Members

Bernard Adeney	Mark Gertler	Frederick J. Porter
A. P. Allinson	Charles Ginner	J. W. Power
Elizabeth Andrews	Mary Godwin	W. Ratcliffe
John Banting	Duncan Grant	William Roberts
George Barne	Cicely Hey	Ethel Sands
Keith Baynes	A. H. Hudson	Randolph Schwabe
Vanessa Bell	S. de Karlowska	Elliott Seabrooke
Horace Brodzky	Rupert Lee	Richard Sickert
Richard Carline	Thérèse Lessore	Matthew Smith
Sidney Carline	Guy Maynard	Cicely Stock
Vera Cuningham	Bernard Meninsky	Walter Taylor
E. M. O'R. Dickey	Cedric Morris	Alfred Thornton
Jessica Dismorr	K. M. Morrison	Allan Walton
Frank Dobson	Elizabeth Muntz	Ethelbert White
Ruth Doggett	John Nash	Paule Vézelay (Marjorie
Malcolm Drummond	Paul Nash	Watson Williams)
Alan Durst	René Paresce	Edward Wolfe
John Farleigh	Lydia Pearson	
Roger Fry	S. Popovitch	

Past Members

Boris Anrep
Mario Bacchelli
Phyllis Barron
Walter Bayes
Robert Bevan
David Bomberg
Gaudier Brzeska
Benjamin Coria
Jacob Epstein
Frederick Etchells
Jessie Etchells
Renée Finch
Douglas Fox-Pitt
Harold Gilman
Spencer F. Gore
Sylvia Gosse

C. F. Hamilton
James Hamilton Hay
Nina Hamnett
E. McKnight Kauffer
Jacob Kramer
Wyndham Lewis
J. B. Manson
C. R. W. Nevinson
R. O'Connor
Lucien Pissarro
Chantal Quenneville
Harold Squire
Harald Sund
Wyndham Tryon
Edward Wadsworth

THE LONDON GROUP

MEMBERS

President : Ruskin Spear

Vice-President : Elliott Seabrooke

Robert Adams
Noel Gilford Adeney
Bernard Adeney
Eileen Agar
Elizabeth Andrews
E. Ardizzone
Edward Le Bas
Keith Baynes
Richard Bedford
Vanessa Bell
David Bomberg
Phyllis Bray
J. Buckland Wright
Robert Buhler
Richard Carline
William Coldstream
Raymond Coxon
Vera Cunningham
Norman Dawson
Frank Dobson
John Dodgson
R. O. Dunlop
Alan Durst
Jacob Epstein
Elsie Farleigh
John Farleigh
Hans Feibusch
Elsie Few
James Fitton
Edna Ginesi
Charles Ginner
Mary Godwin
Henryk Gotlib
Lawrence Gowing
Duncan Grant
Anthony Gross
Nina Hamnett
Gertrude Herntes
Cicely Hey
Ivon Hitchens
A. H. Hudson
Blair Hughes-Stanton
Augustus John, O.M.
Karin Jonzen

S. de Karlowska
Maurice Kestelman
Oscar Kokoschka
Lynton Lamb
Rupert Lee
Kit Lewis
David Low
L. S. Lowry
F. E. McWilliam
Edna Manley
Kenneth Martin
Robert Medley
Bernard Meninsky
John Minton
Henry Moore
Rodrigo Moynihan
Elizabeth Muntz
Hyam Myer
John Nash
Victor Pasmore
Maresco Pearce
John Piper
K. V. Pitchforth
H. E. du Plessis
Mary Potter
Tadeusz Potworowski
Ceri Richards
William Roberts
Claude Rogers
Ethel Sands
William Scott
Matthew Smith
Cicely Stock
Graham Sutherland
Geoffrey Tibble
Julian Trevelyan
John Tunnard
Manfred Uhlman
Keith Vaughan
Ethel Walker, O.B.E.
Carel Weight
H. S. Williamson
Edward Wolfe
Jack B. Yeats

1949 Exhibition catalogue, New Burlington Galleries

THE LONDON GROUP

President: Claude Rogers   Vice-President: John Dodgson

MEMBERS

Robert Adams
Bernard Adeney
Noel Adeney
Eileen Agar
Elizabeth Andrews
Edward Ardizzone
Kenneth Armitage
Keith Baynes
Vanessa Bell
Elinor Bellingham-Smith
David Bomberg
Phyllis Bray
Richard Carline
*Lynn Chadwick
William Coldstream, C.B.E.
Raymond Coxon
Vera Cunningham
P. N. Dawson, D.Sc., A.R.C.A.
†Frank Dobson, C.B.E., R.A.
John Dodgson
R. O. Dunlop, R.A.
†Jacob Epstein, K.B.E.
John Farleigh
Hans Feibusch
Elsie Few
James Fitton, R.A.
Martin Froy
William Gear
Edna Ginesi

Mary Godwin
Henryk Gotlib
Laurence Gowing, C.B.E.
Duncan Grant
Anthony Gross
Nina Hamnett
Stanley Hayter
Josef Herman
*Gertrude Hermes
Patrick Heron
Ciceley Hey
Ivon Hitchens
A. H. Hudson
Blair Hughes-Stanton
†Augustus John, O.M., R.A.
Karin Jonzen
Morris Kestelman
*Lynton Lamb
Edward LeBas, R.A.
Rupert Lee
Kit Lewis
†David Low
*L. S. Lowry
F. E. McWilliam
Roy L. de Maistre
Kenneth Martin
*Bernard Meadows
Robert Medley

John Minton
Rodrigo Moynihan, C.B.E., R.A.
Elizabeth Muntz
Hyam Myer
Anne Neville
Victor Pasmore
Maresco Pearce
John Piper
H. E. DuPlessis
R. V. Pitchforth, R.A.
Mary Potter
Peter Potworowski
Ceri Richards
Brian Robb
William Roberts
Claude Rogers
Ethel Sands
William Scott
†*Matthew Smith, K.B., C.B.E.
Ruskin Spear, R.A.
*William Townsend
Julian Trevelyan
John Tunnard
Fred Uhlman
Carel Weight
*H. S. Williamson
*Edward Wolfe
†Jack Yeats, R.H.A.

* Present Committee Members   † Honorary Members

Hon. Secretary: E. A. Farrell   Hon. Treasurer: F. T. Nash   Hon. Asst. Secretary: Eric Lewis

1954 Exhibition catalogue, Southampton Art Gallery

1931
Raymond Coxon
R. O. Dunlop
Elsie Farleigh
Ivon Hitchens

1932
R. P. Bedford
Morland Lewis
David Low (Hon. Mem.)

1933
Eileen Agar
Phyllis Bray
William Coldstream
P. N. Dawson
Edna Ginesi
Blair Hughes-Stanton
Rodrigo Moynihan
John Piper
H. S. Williamson

1934
Hans Feibusch
James Fitton
Victor Pasmore
John Tunnard

1935
Gertrude Hermes

1936
Ethel Walker

1937
Robert Medley
Graham Sutherland

1938
Ceri Richards
Claude Rogers

1940–43
Edward le Bas
J. Buckland Wright
Kathleen Faussett-Osborne
Elsie Few
Henryk Gotlib
Laurence Gowing
Frances Hodgkins
Augustus John (Hon. Mem.)
Oscar Kokoschka (Hon. Mem.)
Lynton Lamb
Mary Potter
Ruskin Spear
Fred Uhlman
Jack B. Yeats (Hon. Mem.)

1944
Geoffrey Tibble

1947
John Dodgson

1948
Anthony Gross
Karin Jonzen
Kit Lewis
L. S. Lowry

1949
Robert Adams
Edward Ardizzone
Robert Buhler
Edward Burra
Morris Kestelman
Kenneth Martin
John Minton
F. E. McWilliam
Peter Potworowski
William Scott
Julian Trevelyan
Keith Vaughan
Carel Weight

1951
Bernard Meadows
Anne Neville
Brian Robb
William Townsend

1952
Eleanor Bellingham-Smith
Lynn Chadwick
Patrick Heron

1953
Kenneth Armitage
Merlyn Evans
William Gear
Stanley Hayter
Josef Herman

1954
Roy de Maistre
Martin Froy

1955
Louis le Brocquy
Anthony Fry
William Turnbull
Bryan Wynter

1956
Robert Clatworthy
Elizabeth Frink
Philip Sutton

1957
Norman Adams
John Bratby
Alan Davie
Terry Frost
Patrick George
Leonard Rosoman
Jack Smith

1958
Wendy Pasmore
Euan Uglow

1959
Mary Fedden
Anthony Hatwell
Mary Martin

1960
Frank Auerbach
Andrew Forge
Dorothy Mead

1961
André Bicat
Jeffery Camp
Anthony Eyton
Cliff Holden
Leslie Marr

1962
Craigie Aitchison
Michael Andrews
Dennis Creffield
Paul De Monchaux
Adrian Heath
Brian Wall

1963
Frank Bowling
Michael Elliott
David Hockney
Leon Kossoff
Evert Lundquist

1964
Anthony Green
Kenneth Turner

Past and present members of the London Group

Dates are the year of election

Present members' names are in italics

*Douglas Fox-Pitt, Duncan Grant, Henry Lamb and Lucien Pissarro were also listed among the founder members, but did not exhibit

1913   Founder Members*
Bernard Adeney
Walter Bayes
Robert Bevan
David Bomberg
Henri Gaudier Brzeska
Malcolm Drummond
Jacob Epstein
Frederick Etchells
Jessie Etchells
Renée Finch
Harold Gilman
Charles Ginner
Spencer F. Gore
Sylvia Gosse
C. F. Hamilton
A. H. Hudson
Therese Lessore
Wyndham Lewis
J. B. Manson
John Nash
C. R. W. Nevinson
W. Ratcliffe
Ethel Sands
Harold Squire
Harald Sund
Walter Taylor
Edward Wadsworth

1914
Adrian Allinson
Horace Brodzky
Benjamin Coria
Mary Godwin
James Hamilton Hay
S. de Karlowska
Jacob Kramer
Paul Nash
William Roberts

1915
Mark Gertler
Randolph Schwabe

1916
Phyllis Barron
E. McKnight Kauffer
Richard Sickert
Ethelbert White

1917
Roger Fry
Nina Hamnett

1919
Boris Anrep
Keith Baynes
Vanessa Bell
Duncan Grant
Bernard Meninsky

1920
E. M. O'R. Dickey
Ruth Doggett
Frederick J. Porter
Elliott Seabrooke
Matthew Smith
Cicely Stock

1921
Richard Carline

1922
George Barne
Sidney Carline
Frank Dobson
Rupert Lee
Lydia Pearson-Righetti
S. Popovitch
Paule Vézelay (Marjorie Watson Williams)

1923
Mario Bacchelli
R. O'Connor
Guy Maynard

J. W. Power
Edward Wolfe

1924
K. M. Morrison
Alfred Thornton

1925
René Paresce
Wyndham Tryon
Allan Walton

1926
Jessica Dismorr
Chantal Quenneville

1927
Elizabeth Andrews
John Banting
Vera Cuningham
Alan Durst
John Farleigh
Cicely Hey
Cedric Morris
Elizabeth Muntz

1929
H. E. Du Plessis
R. V. Pitchforth
Maresco Pearce
Arthur Pollen

1930
Noel Adeney
John Cooper
Barbara Hepworth
Maurice Lambert
Edna Manley
Henry Moore
Hyam Myer
John Skeaping

1964 Jubilee Exhibition catalogue, Tate Gallery

397

London Group 1970

President: Andrew Forge
Vice-President: Dorothy Mead
Treasurer: Valentine Ellis
Secretary: Margaret Courtney

Aitchison, Craigie
22 St. Mary's Gardens
SE11

Adeney, Noel (Mrs)
(Honorary Member)
34 Crooms Hill
SE3

Agar, Eileen
West House
1 Melbury Road
W14

Beattie, Basil
57 Kew Bridge Court
Chiswick W4

Bicat, Andre
Cray's Pond House
Nr. Pangbourne
Berkshire

Boden, Neville
5 Cumberland Road
Leeds

Bray, Phyllis
46 Platts Lane
Hampstead NW3

Camp, Jeffery
78 Forthbridge Road
SW11

Carline, Richard
17 Pond Street
Hampstead NW3

Coxon, Raymond
10 Hammersmith Terrace
W6

Creffield, Dennis
14 Lewes Crescent
Brighton
Sussex

de Monchaux, Paul
56 Manor Avenue
Brockley SE4

Eyton, Anthony
166 Brixton Road
SW9

Few Elsie
36 Southwood Lane
Highgate N6

* Forge, Andrew
105 Lee Road
SE3

* Fielding, Brian
22 Longstone Road
SW17

Gear, William
46 George Road
Birmingham 15

George, Patrick
33 Moreton Terrace
SW1

Ginesi, Edna
10 Hammersmith Terrace
W6

Green, Anthony
17 Liffenden Mansions
Highgate Road NW5

Grant, Duncan
(Honorary Member)
Charleston
Firle
Sussex

Green, Alan
291 Kent House Road
Beckenham Kent

Harris, Geoffrey
5 Queens Road
Faversham
Kent

Herman, Josef
Holly Lodge
Little Connard
Nr. Sudbury
Suffolk

Hermes, Gertrude
31 Danvers Street
SW3

Hey, Cicely
Tawelfryn
Tan y Craig Road
Llysfaen
Denbighshire

Holden, Cliff
Marstrand
Sweden

Hughes-Stanton, Blair
North House
Manningtree
Essex

Irvin, Albert
19 corst Road
SW11

Jonzen, Karin
92 Fordwych Road
NW2

Kestelman, Morris
74b, Belsize Park Gardens
NW3

Kossoff, Leon
147 Chatsworth Road
NW2

Kenny, Michael
93 St. Mark's Road
W10

1970 Exhibition catalogue, Royal Academy

Lundquist, Prof. Evert
Kanton Drottningholm
Sweden

* Lobb, Stephen
78 Kinreachy Gardens
SE7

* Martin, Barry
Flat 4, 3 Warwick Square
SW1

Martin, Kenneth
9 Eton Avenue
NW3

* Mead, Dorothy (D)
52 St. Marks Road
Ladbroke Grove
W10

Nash, F. T.
(Honorary Member)
Stamford House,
Stamford Street SE1

Neville, Anne
36 Belsize Grove
NW3

Perryman, Margot
29 St. Albans Avenue
W4

Paraskos, Stass
13 Lucas Street
Leeds 6

Partridge, David
26 Hesper Mews
SW5

Pasmore, Wendy
12 St. Germans Place
SE3

Rego, Paula
87 Albert Street
NW1

* Robb, Brian
10 Hampstead Grove
NW3

* Rogers, Prof. Claude, OBE
36 Southwood Lane
Highgate
N6

Schottlander, Bernard
35 Frognal
NW3

Uglow, Euan
11 Turnchapel Mews
Cedars Road
SW4

Wilson, Arthur
22 Wingate Road
Hammersmith W6

Weight, Carel
33 Spencer Road
SW18

Wolfe, Edward
Studio 1a
77 Bedford Gardens
W8

* Denotes committee member.

All enquiries concerning the
London Group to the Secretary,
10 Excelsior Gardens, SE13, and
concerning the Exhibition, to
c/o Nicholas Usherwood, The
Royal Academy of Art,
Burlington House, W1.

Typographic Design by James
Miles
Graphics by Brian Fielding

Strand Press Service Limited,
London.

The recent history of the London Group has in some ways centred around the search for suitable exhibition space. Our membership remains constant and our exhibitions always attract a large number of entries, but the group is severely handicapped by never being sure when and where the next exhibition will be held. Some will remember when it was an annual event at the R.B.A. Galleries, as an established part of the exhibition calendar. Continuity existed and a great deal of the necessary organization and administration could simply be imitated from one year to the next. This has not been the case for some time. Each exhibition has to be started afresh with the first priority being to find a suitable space capable of showing between 200 and 300 works. Certain galleries once used by the group no longer exist, some demand rents way beyond our resources, and other public galleries are now concerned with prestige shows to the exclusion of open exhibitions.

Alan Bowness and Dennis Farr in the historical note contained in the catalogue for the Jubilee Exhibition held at the Tate Gallery in 1964 referred to a past association between the London Group and the Royal Academy and regretted that the association did not persist. Although successful exhibitions were held afterwards at the Royal Academy it has not been possible to turn them into a regular occasion. The problem remains. When a permanent gallery is found for The London Group we will be able, once again, to plan ahead on an annual basis. A group of diverse established artists will be able to exhibit together and provide the almost unique opportunity for some younger artists to exhibit in their company.

This year's venue is particular apt, our exhibitions always attract a large entry from the Royal College of Art and man of our members, past and pres are its ex-students. Possibly th is an association that should be encouraged to persist.

The London Group wishes to thank the Arts Council for its continued financial support, a the staff of the Royal College Art especially the bursar, Mr. Russell Brown and Mr. St Smith. I should like to thank secretary, Mrs. Sheila Watkins whose rewards must surely be in heaven.

P.L. DONNELLY
President

It is with deep regret that we announce the death of Lyntor Lamb, a member for many ye

Moich Abrahams
70 Lots Road
Chelsea,
London, SW10

Craigie Aitchinson
32 St Mary's Gardens
London SE11

Peter Archer
40 Farrer House,
Church Street
Depford London SE8

Philippa Beale
38 Grove Park
London, SE5

Basil Beattie
57 Kew Bridge Court
Chiswick London W4

John Bellany
52 Upcerne Road
Lurline Gardens
Chelsea London SW10

Andre Bicat
Cray's Pond House
Nr Pangbourne
Berks

Neville Boden
48A Leconfield Road
London N5 2SN

Phyllis Bray
46 Platts Lane
London NW3

Anne Buchanan
10 Rutland Grove
Hammersmith
London W6

Jeffery Camp
78 Forthbridge Road
London SW11

Richard Carline
17 Pond Street
London NW3

Julian Cooper
Hart Head Cottage
Rydal Nr Ambleside
Cumbria

Raymond Coxon
10 Hammersmith Terrace
London W6

Dennis Creffield
Flat 3
45 Marine Parade
Brighton Sussex

Peter Cresswell
122 Queen's Park Road
Brighton Sussex

Peter de Francia
44 Surrey Square
London SE17

Paul de Monchaux
56 Manor Avenue
Brockley
London SE4

Peter Donnelly
130 Kennington Road
London SE11

Anthony Eyton
34 Hanbury Street
London E1

Elsie Few
36 Southwood Lane
Highgate
London N6

Brian Fielding
22 Longstone Road
London SW17

1978 Exhibition catalogue, Royal College of Art

John Fox
East Eglinton
Pittville Circus
Cheltenham
Glos

Stanislaw Frenkiel
6 Clement Road
London SW19

William Gear
46 George Road
Birmingham 15

Patrick George
33 Moreton Terrace
London SW1

Edna Ginesi
10 Hammersmith Terrace
London W6

Duncan Grant
Charleston
Firle
Sussex

Anthony Green
17 Lissenden Mansions
Highgate Road
London NW5

Geoffrey Harris
5 Queen's Road
Faversham
Kent

David Haughton
29 St James's Gardens
London W11

Adrian Heath
28 Charlotte Street
London W1

Josef Herman
120 Edith Road
London W14

Cliff Holden
Marstrand
Sweden

John Hoskin
Upper Siddington House
Cirencester
Glos

Blair Hughes-Stanton
North House
Manningtree
Essex

Albert Irvin
19 Gorst Road
London SW11

Karin Jozen
6A Gunter Grove
London SW10 0UJ

Michael Kenny
52 Bronsart Road
London SW6

Morris Kestelman
74B Belsize Park Garden
London NW3

Leon Kossoff
147 Chatsworth Road
London NW2

Evert Lundquist
Kanton
Drottningholm
Sweden

Barry Martin
30 Chapel Street
London SW1

Robert Mason
Ravenscroft Studios
49 Columbia Road
London E2

Robert Medley
Flat C
10 Gledhow Gardens
London SW5

F. T. Nash
Stamford House
Stamford Street
London SE1

Colin Nicholas
4 Approach Road
London E2

Stass Paraskos
The School House
Waltham
Nr Canterbury
Kent

Wendy Pasmore
12 St German's Place
London SE3

Keith Reeves
7 Spanby Road
London E3

Paula Rego
87 Albert Street
London NW1

Brian Robb
10 Hampstead Grove
London NW3

Claude Rogers
36 Southwood Lane
Highgate
London N6

Livia Rolandini
6 Ladbroke Crescent
London W11

Matt Rugg
Flat 5
31 Putney Hill
London SW15

Bernard Schottlander
35 Frognal
London NW3

Stanley Smith
60 York Street
Twickenham
Middlesex

Euan Uglow
71 Roxburgh Road
West Norwood
London SE27

Jesse Watkins
35 Richmond Road
New Barnet
Herts

John Watson
75 Walton Road
Wavendon
Bucks

Mary Webb
Watson's Farm
Fressingfield
Suffolk

Carel Weight
33 Spencer Road
London SW18

Arthur Wilson
22 Wingate Road
Hammersmith
London W6

Edward Wolfe
92 Narrow Street
Limehouse
London E14

Laetitia Yhap
78 Forthbridge Road
London SW11

Index of Artists

represented in this publication

Officers, Committee Members and Membership 2013

Officers

President

Susan Haire

Vice-President

Gillian Ingham

Deputy Vice- President

Mark Dickens

Treasurer

Robert Coward (Hon)

Honorary Secretary

Tommy Seaward

Working Committee

The above 5 Officers, plus:

John Crossley

Annie Johns

Lydia Julien

Amanda Loomes

Tim Pickup

David Redfern

Suzan Swale

Paul Tecklenberg

Membership Committee

The full Working Committee, plus:

Moich Abrahams

Marcelle Hanselaar

Neil Weerdmeester

Erika Winstone

Members website addresses can be found on the individual artists pages
www.thelondongroup.com

16

Mark Ainsworth

Wendy Anderson

Victoria Arney

Victoria Bartlett

Bryan Benge

Slawomir Blatton

Frank Bowling RA

Clive Burton

Paul & Laura Carey

Tony Carter

David Chalkley

Ece Clarke

Robert Clarke

Peter Clossick

Tony Collinge

Philip Crozier

Gus Cummins RA

Harvey Daniels

Mark Dunford

Angela Eames

Anthony Eyton RA

James Faure Walker

Genetic Moo

Tricia Gillman

Anthony Green RA

Julie Held

Bill Henderson

Aude Hérail Jäger

Cliff Holden

John Holden

Jane Humphrey (Hon)

Albert Irvin RA (Hon)

Sam Jarman

Richard Kemp

Matthew Kolakowski

Victor Kuell (Hon)

Mike Liggins (Hon)

Pauline Little

Jeff Lowe

Peter Lowe

Graham Mileson

Eric Moody

C. Morey de Morand

Peter Morrell

Charlotte C. Mortensson

Kathleen Mullaniff

Janet Nathan

Ken Oliver

Eugene Palmer

Ian Parker

Janet Patterson

Michael Phillipson

Chris Poulton

Daniel Preece

Alex Ramsay

Victoria Rance

Simon Read

Dame Paula Rego

Tom Scase

David Shutt

Susan Skingle

Philippa Stjernsward

David Tebbs

David Theobald

Mike Thorpe

Philippa Tunstill

Bill Watson

Anthony Whishaw RA

Arthur Wilson

Susan Wilson

Gary Wragg

2013 Centenary Open Exhibition catalogue, The Cello Factory

Exhibitions held during Presidency

Exhibitions held under the Presidency of Harold Gilman 1914–1919
First Exhibition of the London Group, Goupil Gallery, March 1914
Second Exhibition of the London Group, Goupil Gallery, March 1915
Third Exhibition of the London Group, Goupil Gallery, Nov–Dec 1915
Fourth Exhibition of the London Group, Goupil Gallery, June 1916
Fifth Exhibition of the London Group, Goupil Gallery, 23.11–14.12.1916
Sixth Exhibition of the London Group, Mansard Gallery, 26.4–26.5.1917
Seventh Exhibition of the London Group, Mansard Gallery, 2–29.11.1917
Eighth Exhibition of the London Group, Mansard Gallery, 2.5–1.6.1918
Ninth Exhibition of the London Group, Mansard Gallery, 1–29.11.1918

Exhibitions held under Robert Bevan 1919–1921 (Treasurer acting as President)
Tenth Exhibition of the London Group, Mansard Gallery, 12.4–17.5.1919
Eleventh Exhibition of the London Group, Mansard Gallery, 1–29.11.1919
Twelfth Exhibition of the London Group, Mansard Gallery, 10.5–5.6.1920
Thirteenth Exhibition of the London Group, Mansard Gallery, 18.10–13.11.1920

Exhibitions held under the Presidency of Bernard Adeney 1921–24
Fourteenth Exhibition of the London Group, Mansard Gallery, 9.5–4.6.1921
Fifteenth Exhibition of the London Group, Mansard Gallery, 24.10–16.11.1921
Sixteenth Exhibition of the London Group, Mansard Gallery, 8.5–3.6.1922
Seventeenth Exhibition of the London Group, Mansard Gallery, 16.10–11.11.1922
Eighteenth Exhibition of the London Group, Mansard Gallery, 21.4–19.5.1923
Nineteenth Exhibition of the London Group, Mansard Gallery, 8.10–3.11.1923

Exhibitions held under the Presidency of Frank Dobson 1924–1926
Twentieth Exhibition of the London Group, Mansard Gallery, 14.4–14.5.1924
Twenty-first Exhibition of the London Group, Mansard gallery, 13.10–8.11.1924
Twenty-second Exhibition of the London Group, RWS Galleries, 6–26.6.1925
(RWS= Royal Society of Painters in Watercolour)
Twenty-third Exhibition of the London Group, RWS Galleries, 9–30.1.1926
Twenty-fourth Exhibition of the London Group, RWS Galleries, 5–25.6.1926

Exhibitions held under the Presidency of Rupert Lee 1926–1936
Twenty-fifth Exhibition of the London Group, RWS Galleries, 4–25.6.1927
London Group Retrospective Exhibition 1914–28, New Burlington Galleries, April–May 1928
Twenty-sixth Exhibition of the London Group, New Burlington Galleries, 5–26.1.1929
Twenty-seventh Exhibition of the London Group, New Burlington Galleries, 14.10–1.11.1929

London Group Exhibition of Open-air Sculpture, the Roof Gardens, Selfridges, 2.6–30.8.1930

Twenty-eighth Exhibition of the London Group, New Burlington Galleries, 13–31.10.1930

Twenty-ninth Exhibition of the London Group, New Burlington Galleries, 12–30.10.1931

Thirtieth Exhibition of the London Group, New Burlington Galleries, 10–28.10.1932

Thirty-first Exhibition of the London Group, New Burlington Galleries, 13.11–1.12.1933

Thirty-second Exhibition of the London Group, New Burlington Galleries, 12–30.11.1934

Thirty-third Exhibition of the London Group, New Burlington Galleries, 11–29.11.1935

Exhibitions held under R.P. Bedford acting as Chairman 1936–37

Thirty-fourth Exhibition of the London Group, New Burlington Galleries, 12.–28.11.1936

Exhibition of Works by Members of the London Group, The Leicester Galleries, March 1937

Exhibitions held under the Chairmanship of H. S. Williamson 1937–1943

Thirty-sixth Exhibition of the London Group, New Burlington Galleries, 30.10–20.11.1937

Thirty-seventh Exhibition of the London Group, New Burlington Galleries, 14.11–2.12.1938

Thirty-eighth Exhibition of the London Group, Special Wartime Show, NBG (?), 2–25.11.1939

London Group Second Wartime Show, Cooling Galleries, London, 31.10–29.11.1940

London Group Third Wartime Exhibition, Leger Galleries (?), 22.10–19.11.1941

London Group Fourth Wartime Exhibition, Leger Galleries, 7.10–07.11.1942

Exhibitions held under the Presidency of Elliott Seabrooke 1943–1948

London Group Fifth Wartime Exhibition, Royal Academy, 26.10–25.11.1943

London Group Sixth Wartime Exhibition, Royal Academy, 12.10–9.11.1944

An Exhibition of Paintings by the London Group, Tour of Scotland organised by CEMA (Council for the Encouragement of English and the Arts), 1945

London Group, 1945 Exhibition, Royal Academy, 12.12.1945–16.1.1946

London Group, Exhibition of Paintings, David Jones Art Gallery, Sydney, Australia, 19.3–2.4.1946

London Group 1947 Exhibition, RBA Galleries, 20.5–7.6.1947

London Group 1948 Exhibition, Academy Hall, London, 21.5–6.6.1948

Exhibitions held under the Presidency of Ruskin Spear ARA 1948–1950

Exhibition of New Works by Members of the London Group, The Leicester Galleries, January 1949

London Group Exhibition of Contemporary Drawing, Painting and Sculpture, New Burlington Galleries, 20.12.1949–17.1.1950

Exhibitions held under the Presidency of John Dodgson 1950–1952

London Group Exhibition of Contemporary Painting, Drawing and Sculpture, New Burlington Galleries, Feb–3. 3.1951

London Group Exhibition of Contemporary Painting, Drawing and Sculpture, New Burlington Galleries, (?)–24.11.1951

London Group, New Burlington Galleries, November 1951

Exhibitions held under the Presidency of Claude Rogers 1952–1965

London Group Annual Exhibition, New Burlington Galleries, 25.10–22.11.1952

London Group Annual Exhibition, New Burlington Galleries, 3–28.11.1953

London Group Annual Exhibition, New Burlington Galleries, 6.11–4.12.1954

A Selection from the London Group Exhibition 1954, Cumberland House, Southsea, 1.1–6.2.1955

A Selection from the London Group Exhibition 1954, Southampton Art Gallery, 12.2–13.3.1955

London Group Prints, Zwemmer Gallery, 9.3–2.4.1955

London Group Member's Exhibition, Whitechapel Art Gallery, 10.11–9.12.1955

London Group Annual Exhibition, RBA Galleries, 14.4–4.5.1956

London Group Annual Exhibition, RBA Galleries, 18.1–7.2.1958

London Group Annual Exhibition, RBA Galleries, 18.4–8.5.1959

London Group Annual Exhibition, RBA Galleries, 15.1–5.2.1960

London Group 1961, RBA Galleries, 9–29.3.1961

London Group 62, Art Federation Galleries, 8–30.3.1962

London Group 1963, Art Federation Galleries, 7–29.3.1963

London Group 1964, Art Federation Galleries, 19.3–10.4.1964

London Group 1914 - 64, Jubilee Exhibition, Fifty Years of British Art, Tate Gallery, 5.7–16.8.1964

London Group, Art Federation Galleries, 18.3–9.4.1965

Exhibitions held under the Presidency of Andrew Forge 1965–1971

London Group '67, Royal Institute Galleries, 9.2–3.3.1967

London Group '68, Royal Institute Galleries, 12–28.11.1968

London Group Member's Choice Exhibition, Royal Academy Diploma Galleries, 1.4–1.5.1970

Exhibitions held under the Presidency of Dorothy Mead 1971–1973

London Group 1971 Member's Choice Exhibition, Royal Academy Diploma Galleries, 18.3–18.4.1971

Exhibitions held under the Presidency of Neville Boden 1973–1977

The London Group at the Whitechapel, Whitechapel Art Gallery, 4–23.12.1973

The London Group, Camden Arts Centre, 31.7–24.8.1975

The London Group, Camden Arts Centre, 8–27.2.1977

410

Exhibitions held under the Presidency of Peter Donnelly 1977–1979
London Group at the RCA, Gulbenkian Galleries, Royal College of Art, 31.3 - 15.4.1978

Exhibitions held under the Presidency of Stanley Smith 1979–1993
The London Group at Morley Gallery, 20.9–12.10.1979
London Group in Southwark Exhibition, Morley Gallery and South London Gallery, 9–29.1.1981
London Group Members Show, Morley Gallery, 20.9–8.10.1982
The London Group '82, Camden Arts Centre, 17.10–7.11.1982
    Toured to Penwith Galleries, St. Ives, 16.11–7.12.1982
    Toured to Gardner Centre, Brighton, 19.1–12.2.1983
London Group 84, Open Exhibition, Royal College of Art, 6–23.11.1984
The London Group 1987 Open Show, Royal College of Art, 24.3–22.5.1987
London Group 75th Anniversary Exhibition, Royal College of Art, 6–28.8.1988
The London Group Open Exhibition 1989, Royal College of Art, 8–24.8.1989
Open Exhibition 1990, Royal College of Art, 17.9–4.10.1990
Works on Paper, The Economist, 4–26.10.1991
The London Group and Guests, Morley Gallery, 30.1–20.2.1992

Exhibitions held under the Presidency of Adrian Bartlett 1993–1995
Paintings and Sculpture by the London Group Members and Guests, Morley Gallery, 25.3–15.4.1993
Private View Card (Whishaw image), The LG at the London Institute Gallery, 6.7–10.9.1993
The London Group 1913–1993, Michael Parkin Gallery, 20.10–12.11.1993
The London Group's 80th Anniversary Open Exhibition, Concourse Gallery, Barbican Centre,
9.12.1993–7.1.1994
A Collection of Work by Members of The London Group, The London Institute Gallery, (?)–22.9.1994
Works on Paper, Morley Gallery, 6–27.10.1994

Exhibitions held under the Presidency of Philippa Beale 1995–1998
Biennial 1995 Open Exhibition, Concourse Gallery, Barbican Centre, 8.12.1995–7.1.1996
The London Group 1996 at the London Institute, Lethaby Gallery, Central St. Martins, 4–13.7.1996
The London Group 1997, Alan Baxter & Associates, Cowcross Street, London EC1, 7–30.10.1997

Exhibitions held under the Presidency of Matthew Kolakowski 1998–2001
Selected Members Show, Lawrence Graham, The Strand, London W1, 26.5.1998
The Object and the Concept, Daniel Arnaud Gallery, Kennington Road, London SE11, 26.6–17.7.1998
Transient, Brighton University, Grand Parade, Brighton, 8–26.9.1998
The London Group, Cranleigh Arts Centre, Horsham Road, Cranleigh, Surrey, 10.5–26.9.1999
The London Group, The Farnham Maltings, Bridge Square, Farnham, Surrey, 10–29.5.1999
London 2000, Lethaby Gallery, Central St Martins, 28.7–15.8.2000

Exhibitions held under the Presidency of Peter Clossick 2001–2005

The London Group at the Woodlands Art Gallery, Mycenae Road, London SE3, 26.5–24.6.2001

The London Group at the Stark Gallery, Lee High Road, London SE12, 26.5–22.6.2001

The London Group at the Walk Gallery, King Edward Walk, London SE1,
Groups of four members, 2002–2005

The London Group, Trinity Theatre and Arts Centre, Tunbridge Wells, 16–31.8.2002

Artists of the London Group, Hatton Gallery, Newcastle, 18.1–01.3.2003

The London Group at the Woodlands Art Gallery, 16.2–15.3.2003

The London Group Ninetieth Anniversary Exhibition, The Gallery in Cork Street and Gallery 27, Cork Street, London W1, 2–7.6.2003

London Group, Works on Paper, Café Gallery, Southwark Park, London SE16, 9.7–2.8.2003

91st London Group Annual Exhibition at the Menier Chocolate Factory, Southwark Street, London SE1, 26.4–14.5.2004

Small Works, The Highgate Gallery, South Grove, Highgate, London N6, 14–27.5.2004

Exhibitions held under the Presidency of Philip Crozier 2005–2007

"Systems of Creativity", (4 members), The Green Space Gallery, East Dulwich Road, London SE22, 15.3–17.5.2005

London Group Annual Exhibition, Bankside Gallery, Hopton Street, London SE1, 8–17.4.2005

"To the Limit", SoCo Gallery, Pelham Place, Hastings, 1–30.10.2005

"The 93rd Annual Exhibition", Bankside Gallery, London, 13.4–1.5.2006

Sassoon Gallery, Blenheim Grove, London SE15, Part 1: 10–22.4.06, Part 2: 25.4–6.5.2006

"Arti de Salon", Rokin 112, Amsterdam, 16.11–10.12.2006

"The London Group at Deutsche Bank" Part 1, Deutsche Bank, Great Winchester Street, London EC2, 18.1–18.3.2007

Exhibitions held under the Presidency of Susan Haire 2007–

"Collective Response", curated by Annie Johns and Wendy Anderson,
Guildhall Art Gallery, London, 8.10–11.11.2007

Bridge Art Fair, Trafalgar Hotel, Trafalgar Square, London, 11–14.10.2007

The London Group Open 2007 at The Menier Gallery, Part 1: 7–16.11.2007,
Part 2: 21–30.11.2007

The London Group at Deutsche Bank, Part 2, 6.2–15.4.2008

The London Group at Mauger Modern Art, Bath, 6 Bartlett St, Bath, 19.4–24.5.2008

"Small Works", curated by Tom Scase, The Highgate Gallery, 9–22.5.2008

The London Group Members' 95th Anniversary Exhibition, curated by Tony Collinge, The Menier Gallery, 29.10–7.11.2008

"Stand Alone", curated by Clive Burton and Bill Watson, The Cello Factory, 33-34 Cornwall Road, Waterloo, SE1, 19–24.1.2009

"Drawing - Act and Artefact", curated by Wendy Smith and Suzan Swale, Morley Gallery, Westminster Bridge Rd, London, SE1, 25.3–9.4.2009

The London Group Open 2009 at the Menier Gallery,

Part 1: curated by Tom Scase and Mark Dickens, 21–30.10.2009

Part 2: curated by Tony Collinge and Vic Kuell, 4–13.11.2009

"Inspiration", curated by Paul Tecklenberg, Kensington and Chelsea College, Hortensia Road, SW10, 20.01–04.02.2010

Members' Annual Exhibition 2010, The Cello Factory, London SE1, 1–11.6.2010

"Inspiration", Part 2, Kensington and Chelsea College, Hortensia Rd, SW10, 27.9–7.10.2010

"The Invisible Line", Small Group Exhibition, curated by Philip Crozier, at Piers Feetham Gallery, 475 Fulham Road, London SW6, 2–26.3.2011

Open Exhibition 2011, The Cello Factory, London SE1, 20.10–10.11.2011

"Territories and Boundaries", Kensington and Chelsea College, 24.4–3.5.2012

"On My Behalf – self-portraits from The London Group", Cumberland Hotel, Marble Arch, London, 17.9–5.10.2012

Members' 2012 Annual Exhibition, The Cello Factory, 13–24.11.2012

"The London Group Centenary Exhibition", Pitzhanger Gallery and House, Walpole Park, Mattock Lane, Ealing E5, 1–9.3.2013

"The London Group at 100: Mottisfont", Mottisfont (NT), Romsey, Hampshire, 9.2–21.4.2013

"The Centenary Open 2013", The Cello Factory, London SE1, Part 1: 14–24.5.13,

Part 2: 28.5–7.7.2013

"Uproar: The First Fifty Years", Ben Uri Gallery, Boundary Road, London NW8, 30.10.2013–2.3.2014

"+100: The London Group Today", The Cello Factory, London SE1, 16.11–13.12.2013

Photographic credits

Colour section facing Page 160
Plates 1 and 2 © Tate Archive, London 2013
Plate 4 © The London Group Archive, London 2013

Page 245
Photo: Cliff Holden

Page 303
Photo: Adrian Bartlett

Pages 390, 391
Images c ourtesy of Brighton & Hove Museums

All other photographs: © David Redfern, London 2013

First published in Great Britain in 2013 by The London Group
PO Box 61045, London SE1 8RN
www.thelondongroup.com

ISBN 978–1–0–0001585–0

Designed by David Mann

Printed and bound in Italy by Lego SpA